Expert Judgment and Expert Systems

NATO ASI Series

Advanced Science Institutes Series

A series presenting the results of activities sponsored by the NATO Science Committee, which aims at the dissemination of advanced scientific and technological knowledge, with a view to strengthening links between scientific communities.

The Series is published by an international board of publishers in conjunction with the NATO Scientific Affairs Division

A Life Sciences B Physics	Plenum Publishing Corporation London and New York
C Mathematical and Physical Sciences	D. Reidel Publishing Company Dordrecht, Boston, Lancaster and Tokyo
D Behavioural and Social Sciences E Applied Sciences	Martinus Nijhoff Publishers Boston, The Hague, Dordrecht and Lancaster
F Computer and Systems Sciences G Ecological Sciences H Cell Biology	Springer-Verlag Berlin Heidelberg New York London Paris Tokyo

Series F: Computer and Systems Sciences Vol. 35

Expert Judgment and Expert Systems

Edited by

Jeryl L. Mumpower

Associate Professor
Department of Public Administration
Rockefeller College
State University of New York
Albany, NY 12222, USA

Ortwin Renn

Associate Professor of Environment
Technology, and Society
Clark University
Worcester, MA 01610, USA

Lawrence D. Phillips

Director, Decision Analysis Unit
London School of Economics and
Political Science
Houghton St.
London WC2A 2AE, UK

V. R. R. Uppuluri

Director, Mathematics and Statistics
Research Department
Oak Ridge National Laboratory
Oak Ridge, TN 37830, USA

Springer-Verlag
Berlin Heidelberg New York London Paris Tokyo
Published in cooperation with NATO Scientific Affairs Divison

Proceedings of the NATO Advanced Research Workshop on Expert Judgment and Expert Systems held in Porto, Portugal, August 25–29, 1986

ISBN 3-540-17986-0 Springer-Verlag Berlin Heidelberg New York
ISBN 0-387-17986-0 Springer-Verlag New York Berlin Heidelberg

Library of Congress Cataloging-in-Publication Data. NATO Advanced Research Workshop on Expert Judgment and Expert Systems (1986 : Porto, Portugal) Expert judgment and expert systems. (NATO ASI series. Series F, computer and systems sciences ; vol. 35) 1. Expert systems (Computer science)–Congresses. 2. Judgment–Congresses. I. Mumpower, Jeryl, 1949-. II. Title. III. Series: NATO ASI series. Series F, computer and systems sciences ; vol. 35. QA76.76.E95N37 1986 006.3'3 87-16708
ISBN 0-387-17986-0 (U.S.)

Printed in Germany

Printing: Druckhaus Beltz, Hemsbach; Bookbinding: J. Schäffer GmbH & Co. KG, Grünstadt
2145/3140-543210

PREFACE

This volume is an outgrowth of a NATO Advanced Research Workshop on "Expert Judgment and Expert Systems," held in Porto, Portugal, August 1986. Support for the Workshop was provided by the NATO Division of Scientific Affairs, the U.S. Army Research Institute, and the U.S. National Science Foundation.

The Workshop brought together researchers from the fields of psychology, decision analysis, and artificial intelligence. The purposes were to assess similarities, differences, and complementarities among the three approaches to the study of expert judgment; to evaluate their relative strengths and weaknesses; and to propose profitable linkages between them. Each of the papers in the present volume is directed toward one or more of those goals.

We wish to express our appreciation and thanks to the following persons for their support and assistance: John Adams, Vincent T. Covello, Luis da Cunha, Claire Jeseo, B. Michael Kantrowitz, Margaret Lally, Judith Orasanu, R. M. Rodrigues, and Sandor P. Schuman.

ARW Directors:

Jeryl L. Mumpower
Lawrence D. Phillips
Ortwin Renn
V. R. R. Uppuluri

CONTENTS

TOWARD A UNIFIED APPROACH TO THE STUDY OF EXPERT JUDGMENT

Kenneth R. Hammond
Center for Research on Judgment and Policy
University of Colorado, Boulder
Boulder, Colorado USA

INTRODUCTION

One of the marks of the 20th century must surely be the rise of the importance of the expert. As the operating functions of even ordinary household appliances become increasingly less and less understandable to the person who uses them, the expert who does understand them increases in importance. The same is true in the corporate and government workplace as well as in military settings. Anyone might have repaired, or at least understood, a broken harness strap; but who dares now to repair or even claims to understand a TV set, radio, VCR, washing machine, fuel injection system, or the electronic mysteries of a missile guidance system--other than the expert?

Nevertheless, the rise in importance of the expert's skills has created uncertainties and many doubts. Increased dependence on the expert has been accompanied by a growing ambivalence, if not outright mistrust, of expertise. On the one hand, there is increasing admiration of skill; on the other, growing scepticism; the catastrophic mistakes, however infrequent, have not gone unnoticed. Moreover, as laypersons lose more and more understanding of the artifacts around them, they also lose control of them. If the toaster fails, nothing can be done but buy a new one: but in the mean time, no toast. Nor will doubt, uncertainty and scepticism be reduced when the (nonrepairable) TV set brings stark pictures of the catastrophic failure of expertise demonstrated so clearly by the Challenger explosion, the Three Mile Island scare, the Chernobyl disaster, the Bhopal disaster, and (as I write) pictures of a nuclear submarine on fire and adrift in the Atlantic.

Nor will confidence in the expert be enhanced by the widespread reports of disagreements between experts: Is the

NATO ASI Series, Vol. F35
Expert Judgment and Expert Systems
Edited by J. Mumpower et al.

protective ozone layer really disappearing, and will millions die of skin cancer? Some experts say yes, others say no. Should one take those calcium supplements, or will they cause gallstones and thus do more harm than good? Experts disagree on virtually everything of importance, or so it seems. Our confidence in expertise is also diminished by the obvious and all too willing exploitation of experts by government and large corporations, as well as their opponents, circumstances in which experts often appear to be no more than hired guns. Too often each side of a legal dispute explains away disagreement between experts simply by pointing out that "they have their expert and we have ours." Nevertheless, more and more decisions rest on the judgments of experts, not only scientific and technical experts, but also experts in politics (see Mumpower, this volume), and experts in ethics ("Can you justify double-blind placebo trials for terminally ill patients?"). Thus, despite, or perhaps because of, our ambivalence toward the value of expert judgment, the topic we are to consider at this conference is of great importance to the societies that sent us here and that hope to benefit from our deliberations.

Curiously, there are two completely different, completely isolated approaches to this topic, and moreover, these approaches have produced a contradictory set of findings. Moreover workers within each approach steadfastly ignore the work produced by the other. These two different approaches are the J/DM approach and the AI approach. Our meeting, therefore, is of considerable importance. The research funder as well as the research consumer has a keen and understandable interest in knowing: "Which is correct? Why can't they agree?"

Because researchers from both groups are in the audience, and because researchers in one group are often ignorant of developments in the other, let me present a minimal chronology of the study of experts, or expert systems, within each approach.

The J/DM Development of Research on Expert Judgment

Within the J/DM approach, Thorndike (1918) studied the selection of officer candidates by military experts; Wallace (1923) studied expert corn judges; Sarbin (1942) compared actuarial predictions of behavior with clinicians' predictions; Frenkel-Brunswik (1943) modelled clinicians' judgments with the multiple regression equation; Kelly and Fiske (1951) did the same; Hammond (1955) did much the same; and so did Hoffman (1960). Since 1960 there have been numerous studies of experts within the J/DM approach; for recent examples see Gaeth and Shanteau (1984) and Hammond, Anderson, Sutherland, and Marvin (1984). Decision analysts such as Edwards, Raiffa, and others are not listed in this minimal history because experts were seldom studied within the decision analytic framework prior to 1960. All of the work mentioned above, with possibly one exception (Phelps & Shanteau, 1978), indicates that expert judgment (a) is seldom better than that of novices and (b) is easily improved upon when replaced with simple equations. These results have led J/DM researchers to develop considerable scepticism regarding the value of expert judgment.

The Development of Research on Expert Systems

In the 1960s the computer simulation of cognitive activity led to attempts to model expert judgment within the framework of the problem-solving approach introduced largely by Newell and Simon (1972). Coombs (1984) states: "Since the building of the first system 15 years ago, several exemplar projects have demonstrated that computer programs are capable of expert performance in diagnostic, interpretative, control and planning tasks within a wide range of domains." If Coombs is correct regarding this date, and other authors seem to agree (Feigenbaum, 1977) then we can assume that the building of expert systems began in 1970. Some of the expert systems listed by Coombs are DENDRAL (1970); MYCIN (bacterial infections, 1976); PROSPECTOR (geological prospects, 1978); CASNET (glaucoma, 1977); R1 (configuring VAX computers, 1980); MOLGEN (molecular genetics, 1980); and INTERNIST-1 (general internal medicine, 1982). All of this activity is based on a high regard for expert judgment and the utility of simulating it in specific cases.

Thus, if it is correct to say that the modern study of experts began in, say, 1950, then there have been at least 30 years of study of experts for J/DM researchers, and there have been roughly 15 years for AI/expert systems. But AI/expert systems now dominate the field in terms of research dollars, visibility and, I suspect, young researchers. Why did this happen?

There are many reasons for this unexpected event; I offer

six: (a) the concept of "artificial intelligence" has clearly captured the interest and imagination of scientists and the lay public alike; (b) AI is closely linked to the high-tech glamour of computers in a way that studies of judgment and decision making never have been; (c) the method employed by AI researchers appeals to the expert; (you let experts work on the problems, then simulate their efforts). There are no hard-to-believe equations involved in the AI approach, thus no leap of faith that simple equations can represent expert judgment is required; (d) successes in AI are well publicized, whereas J/DM successes have never been well publicized; and (e) AI is closely associated with major universities, a Nobel Laureate, and the robotization of industry; it smacks of the future. Moreover, (f) many believe that AI is a threat to society, not only to jobs but to human control of its own affairs. The idea of machines controlling man is something we worry about--and the media always runs stories on the things we worry about: jobs, the bomb, hazardous waste. Thus, AI has a dark side; it is sinister as well as glamorous, and this gets our attention for both reasons.

Be that as it may, J/DM techniques are undoubtedly _used_ far more often than AI expert systems; there are more decision analysts working with various experts in Washington, London, Paris and Rome than knowledge engineers in Palo Alto, Pittsburgh, or Boston. Nevertheless, there is little doubt that the tension between these two approaches is asymmetrical. The AI approach is dominant, at least in the minds of scientists, engineers, industry, and the public, if not in the opinions of those J/DM researchers who have studied experts for 30 years.

ISOLATION AND CONTRADICTION

Virtually no relationships, intellectual or otherwise, exist between these parallel endeavors. AI and J/DM offer the user two sets of researchers, two independent approaches, two independent literatures. They have often been funded by the very same agencies, which never seemed to wonder about the resulting isolation of effort and contradiction of results that have been produced. Not only are there few cross-references in the AI and J/DM literature, there are no joint meetings or other forms of communication between investigators of expertise from the two approaches (but see Kidd & Cooper, 1985; Zimmer, 1984).

A startling example of this gulf can be found in the brilliant achievement of Hans Berliner, who constructed the computer program for backgammon that defeated the world champion backgammon player in 1979, a result widely acclaimed by the AI community and wholly ignored by the JD/M community. Berliner (1980) described the event as "the first time that a world champion of a recognized intellectual activity had been defeated by a man-created entity in a head-to-head test of skill" (p. 205). Berliner then asked: "How was this achieved?" (p. 205). Curiously it turns out that Berliner achieved this result by the application of precisely the methodology (not method) that has been employed by the JD/M researchers, not by AI methodology, although he cited not one reference in the thousands of JD/M articles in the literature. Thus, what apparently was a triumph for AI, was in fact a triumph for JD/M. For when he described what he called "a new approach," he compared two methods of representing knowledge in this way:

> The usual way that knowledge is represented in a so-called "expert system" in the field of "Artificial Intelligence" in which this work was done is by a set of rules. A rule is of the form A-->B: "If A is true, then do (or deduce) B." From rules such as this it is possible to go from a set of antecedent condtions to produce very complicated conditions or actions.
>
> Another method of representing knowledge is in the form of mathematical functions. The function A = 2B says that, everywhere, A has twice the value B has. A = C/B (where C is a constant) says that A varies inversely as B. Many other basic types of functions are possible, and for certain kinds of knowledge these serve better to represent the basic domain, that knowledge in the form of rules. For instance, the rule "The warmer the weather, the lighter the clothing you should wear" is much better represented in the form of a function than by a set of rules dealing with various possible temperatures and various items of clothing. (Berliner, 1981, p. 8.)

In short, Berliner's landmark achievement and its misplacement in the field of AI expert systems research rather than JD/M research illustrates the regrettable isolation of these two fields.

The most important consequence of this independence is that the results and conclusions are startlingly different. J/DM researchers have almost without exception found expert judgment to be poor; yet AI researchers invariably demonstrate the breadth of expert knowledge, or take expertise for granted, and demonstrate their expertise in the context of simulating other experts (Coombs, 1984; Larkin, McDermott, Simon, & Simon, 1980). Despite this gulf in communication there is considerable evidence that these two approaches have a great deal in common.

Delineating similarities and differences would, I believe, be a valuable undertaking, for the reason that although these approaches are now assumed to be antithetical, closer analysis may show them to be complementary.

Similarities in Goals

There are many similarities in the goals of AI and J/DM. For example, (a) both attempt to capture, that is, describe, reproduce and preserve, the cognitive activity of the expert, (b) both wish to evaluate it, so that it can be improved, if necessary, (c) both wish to aid novices, (d) both attempt to create computerized systems that will apply expertise to new problems, (e) both want to study the expert making judgments under uncertainty, and (f) both assert that they wish to advance the scientific study of cognition through the study of experts. This is an impressive list of similarities, and even if the list is only approximately correct, these approaches clearly have many common areas. It now remains to be seen whether the differences outnumber and outweigh the similarities.

Differences

In what follows, I list what I believe are the essential differences between the two approaches:

1. What is intended to be captured/preserved/reproduced?

    a. AI: sets of mini-rules with high fidelity (plus confidence ratings)
    b. J/DM: a set of parameters of a judgment system that are of doubtful fidelity ("paramorphic")

2. What form does externalization take?

    a. AI: the expert's verbal expressions of mini-rules (plus confidence rating)
    b. J/DM: the researcher's mathematical representation (parameters) of the structure of the expert's judgment

3. What is computerized?

    a. AI: knowledge base, i.e., rules, are stored, retrieved; answers to questions, e.g., "why?"
    b. J/DM: task parameters are stored, judgment parameters are stored, retrieved, manipulated

4. Where is the uncertainty?

    a. AI: in the expert's subjective probability (expressed as a confidence rating) in the truth of rule; but this probability not examined ("unfolded," "decomposed") further
    b. J/DM: in the expert's achievement of the correct answer, the structure of the expert's judgment process; expert's judgments always "unfolded"; e.g., consistency/predictability of expert's judgments measured; heuristics and biases of probabilities ascertained; cues upon which judgments are based; uncertainty in expert's judgments separated from expert's confidence in uncertainty in rule.

5. What is the region of reference?

    a. AI: the rule inside the expert's cognitive system.
    b. J/DM: the relation between the expert's judgment and the distal variable (i.e., the right answer, the criterion)

6. How much time for the expert to think, judge?

    a. AI: much
    b. J/DM: little

7. Major form of cognitive activity induced:

   a. AI: analysis, reflection
   b. J/DM: intuition

8. Domain-specificity vs. domain-independence:

   a. AI: domain-specific
   b. J/DM: domain-independence; generality over tasks

9. Emulation of experts vs. improvement of expert ability:

   a. AI: Researchers try to produce a simulation that will be as good as the expert
   b. J/DM: Researchers try to produce a simulation that will be better than the expert

10. Method of evaluation/validation of researcher product (the expert system or "model" of the expert):

    a. AI: experts judge the product of the other experts
    b. J/DM: each model of expert's judgments tested empirically against an objective criterion (other criteria)

11. Differences in conceptions of limitations:

    a. AI: not "over 10,000 rules" (Basden, 1984, p. 69)
    b. J/DM: not more than 10 cues

12. Methodology:

    a. Coherence (AI) vs. correspondence theory of truth (J/DM)
    b. Reducible uncertainty (AI) vs. irreducible uncertainty (J/DM)
    c. Confirmation (AI) vs. disconfirmation (J/DM) strategies
    d. Subjectivist (AI) vs. frequentist (J/DM) theory of probability (almost)

13. Areas of expertise studied:

    a. AI: high degree of hard science (e.g., physicists,

chemists, expert physicians)

b. J/DM: high degree of soft science (e.g., clinical psychologists, psychiatrists, soil engineers, highway engineers)

14. Type of judgment process studied

a. AI: information search is key process
b. J/DM: information integration is key process

15. Conclusions about expert judgment:

a. AI: very good
b. J/DM: not very good

Conclusions Regarding Similarities and Differences

Thus, these two research groups share highly similar goals, but there are wide disparities between them in premises, working hypotheses, assumptions, methods, procedures, types of experts studied, and conclusions reached.

IS RECONCILIATION DESIRABLE?

Can these approaches be reconciled? Perhaps. But first we should consider whether they should be.

Advantages and Disadvantages of Independence

There are two obvious and important advantages to maintaining independence: (a) life would be simpler for the researchers. There is more information available within each approach than can be easily digested now. Being required to read a whole new literature could be considered an unbearable burden; (b) the simple life might actually produce better expert systems faster. I have little doubt that all AI researchers believe that to be the case now. And it may well be true for a large number of J/DM researchers as well. But if life would be simpler for the researcher, it certainly would be more complicated for the research funder and consumer if the two approaches persisted in developing independently. Would not funding agencies puzzle over the need to fund two separate groups of researchers working on the same problem, each in self-imposed ignorance of results in the other? A similar puzzle would confront the research consumer who would have to decide "which approach should I use?" Could consumers make the choice on rational grounds? How could they? And would not the research funder and the research consumer wonder whether ignorance of related work is part of the scientific tradition?

Advantages and Disadvantages of Convergence

Note first that convergence might be either competitive or noncompetitive.

The competitive form would be advantageous in that it would help to sharpen the issue. Thus real progress might be made in discovering where the truth lies. But there are disadvantages to competition; it often leads to pejorative remarks, disdainful attitudes, and to minimizing the successes of the "other guys" while overstating one's own successes. Such consequences are far from unheard of; they tend to discredit science and scientists. Thus, sharp competition has its dangers.

The cooperative form of convergence also has its advantages and disadvantages. The primary advantage of cooperation is that the availability of the two methods for studying experts provides an opportunity for examining the convergent and discriminant validity of the simulation (see Hammond, Hamm, & Grassia, 1986, for an example). This opportunity to pit two methods against each other rarely presents itself, but it is the most powerful research method we have for determining whether the results of experimental studies of experts are valid and can be generalized. The major disadvantage of cooperation is that it takes time; it takes time to understand new ideas and new ways of doing things, and, as noted above, these activities may well carry a higher price than a large number of researchers already committed to one approach may wish to pay.

CONCLUSION

I see no simple answer. But I take it as given that researchers with more than 10 (or maybe even 5) years' investment in one approach are not prepared to spend six months steeping themselves in a new literature, especially if some 5 or 10 years ago the other approach was judged to be uninteresting, wrong or somehow bound to fail. And if that is true, then the best if not the only alternative is to prepare circumstances in which young researchers, not more than three years from the Ph.D., can be encouraged through research funding to pursue the problem of determining the value of convergence. Open-mindedness and a willingness to pursue new directions are what is needed, but these are not likely to be provided by well-established investigators.

On the assumption that deeds speak louder than words, I briefly describe my own effort to develop a unified approach.

Toward a Unified Approach

The opportunity to develop a unified approach came when our research group began to study the cognitive activity of medical students and their teachers during their efforts to understand a patient's illness.

Our goals and methods included at least some common to both approaches. For example, our aims were to (a) describe and evaluate the cognitive activity of students and their teachers making judgments under uncertainty and thus to (b) advance our scientifically-based knowledge of cognition. And our methods included (a) presenting the student with written case materials (AI), not data profiles (J/DM), (b) asking the students to "think aloud" as they worked their way through the case material (AI), in contrast to the usual silence of subjects in J/DM studies, and (c) observing each subject's cognitive activity over time (AI), rather than in judgment trials as is customary in J/DM studies. On the other hand, (a) subjects were not queried (J/DM) in contrast to many AI studies, (b) the analysis of the verbal protocol (AI) was made in terms of a cue-judgment (J/DM) segment, rather than a production rule or similar as in AI studies, and (c) each segment was coded within the framework of Cognitive Continuum Theory (CCT). Because CCT represents an attempt to develop a unifying theory, a brief explanation of its central principles follows.

1. Tasks, or problem domains, can be located on a continuum according to their potential for inducing specific forms of cognition that range from intuition to analysis.

2. Cognitive activity can be located on a continuum that ranges from intuition to analysis; most cognitive activity involves elements of both and may thus be labeled "quasirational" (J/DM) or as "bounded rationality" (AI).

3. Cognitive activity alternates between intuition and analysis during sequences of judgments under uncertainty (J/DM), or problem-solving activity (AI).

   (Further detail and a worked out example of research on expert judgment carried out in the spirit of a unified approach can be found in Hammond, Hamm, Grassia, & Pearson, 1985).

In the present case, the coding of the protocol segments produced a number that enabled each segment to be located on the cognitive continuum described in CCT. Figure 1 illustrates the alternation in location on the cognitive continuum of several sequential protocol segments for one medical student for part of one case. As predicted from the theory, alternation occurs over time as the student tries to solve the problem.

Compare the fact of the observed alternation in Figure 1 with the philosopher Pepper's theory of alternation between common sense and refined knowledge.

> This tension between common sense and expert knowledge, between cognitive security without responsibility and cognitive responsibility without full security, is the interior dynamics of the knowledge situation. The indefiniteness of much detail in common sense, its contradictions, its lack of established grounds, drive thought to seek definiteness, consistency, and reasons. Thought finds these in the criticized and refined knowledge of mathematics, science, and philosophy, only to discover that these tend to thin out into arbitrary definitions, pointer readings, and tentative hypotheses. Astounded at the thinness and hollowness of these culminating achievements of conscientiously responsible cognition, thought seeks matter for its definitions, significance for its pointer readings, and support for its wobbling hypotheses. Responsible cognition finds itself insecure as

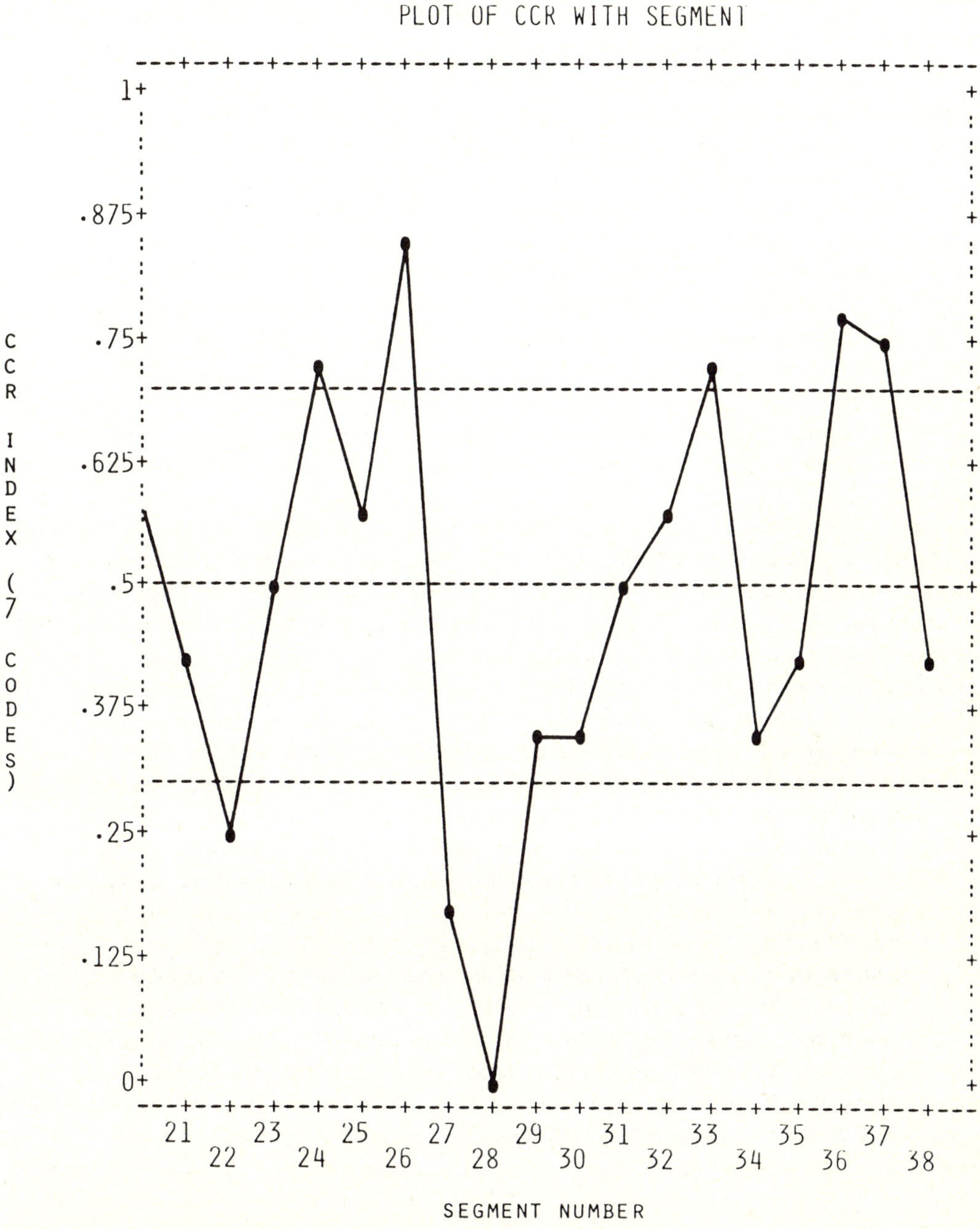

Figure 1. The index of cognitive activity is indicated on the ordinate; higher values indicate analytical cognition, lower values indicate intuitive cognition. The number of a verbal segment is indicated in the abscissa in sequence of utterance. The points plotted thus show how cognitive activity alternates in regular fashion between intuition and analysis.

> a result of the very earnestness of its virtues. But where shall it turn? It does, in fact, turn back to common sense, that indefinite and irresponsible source which it so lately scorned. But it does so, generally, with a bad grace. After filling its empty definitions and pointer readings and hypotheses with meanings out of the rich confusion of common sense, it generally turns its head away, shuts its eyes to what it has been doing, and affirms dogmatically the self-evidence and certainty of the common-sense significance it has drawn into its concepts. Then it pretends to be securely based on self-evident principles or indubitable facts.... Thus the circle is completed. Common sense continually demands the responsible criticism of refined knowledge, and refined knowledge sooner or later requires the security of common-sense support. (Pepper, 1948, pp. 22-23)

The cognitive activity of the medical student presented in Figure 1 provides a clear picture of the alternation Pepper predicted. Its significance for the integration of the AI expert systems approach with the J/DM approach lies in the fact that cognitive activity is not fully describable by any one method presently available. Since cognitive activity changes its properties over time as the subject attempts to solve the problem, each approach used separately would provide only partial knowledge of the cognitive process. But the unified approach described above will enable us to denote the different properties of that process as it alternates between intuitive and analytical cognition.

I make no hard claim regarding the value of a unified approach on the basis of the miniscule example provided here. I do claim that the example demonstrates that a unified approach is possible. My boldest claim is that unification might well provide new and important information about cognitive activity that would not have been produced by either approach alone.

REFERENCES

Basden, A. (1984). On the application of expert systems. In M. J. Coombs (Ed.), Developments in expert systems (pp. 59-75). London: Academic Press.

Berliner, H. J. (1980). Backgammon computer program beats world champion. _Artificial Intelligence_, _14_, 205-220.

Berliner, H. J. (1981). Computer games: The computation of judgment. _Computers and People_, _30_, 7-9, 31.

Coombs, M. J. (Ed.). (1984). _Developments in expert systems_. London: Academic Press.

Feigenbaum, E. A. (1977). The art of artificial intelligence: I. Themes and case studies of knowledge engineering. In L. Erman (Ed.), _Proceedings of the International Joint Conference on Artificial Intelligence_ (Vol. 2, pp. 1014-1029). Pittsburgh, PA: International Joint Conference on Artificial Intelligence.

Frenkel-Brunswik, E. (1943). Motivation and behavior. _Genetic Psychology Monographs_, _26_, 121-265.

Gaeth, G. J., & Shanteau, J. (1984). Reducing the influence of irrelevant information on experienced decision makers. _Organizational Behavior and Human Performance_, _33_, 263-282.

Hammond, K. R. (1955). Probabilistic functioning and the clinical method. _Psychological Review_, _62_, 255-262.

Hammond, K. R., Anderson, B. F., Sutherland, J., & Marvin, B. (1984). Improving scientists' judgments of risk. _Risk Analysis_, _4_, 69-78.

Hammond, K. R., Hamm, R. M., & Grassia, J. (1986). Generalizing over conditions by combining the multitrait-multimethod matrix and the representative design of experiments. _Psychological Bulletin_, _100_, 257-269.

Hammond, K. R., Hamm, R. M., Grassia, J., & Pearson, T. (1985, July). _The relative efficacy of intuition and analytical cognition: A second direct comparison_ (Report No. 252). Boulder: University of Colorado, Center for Research on Judgment and Policy.

Hoffman, P. J. (1960). The paramorphic representation of clinical judgment. _Psychological Bulletin_, _57_, 116-131.

Kelly, E. L., & Fiske, D. W. (1951). _The prediction of performance in clinical psychology_. Ann Arbor: University of Michigan Press.

Kidd, A. L., & Cooper, M. B. (1985). Man-machine interface issues in the construction and use of an expert system. _International Journal of Man-Machine Studies_ _22_, 91-102.

Larkin, J., McDermott, J., Simon, D. P., & Simon, H. A. (1980). Expert and novice performance in solving physics problems. _Science_, _208_, 1335-1342.

Mumpower, J. (1987) this volume.

Newell, A., & Simon, H. A. (1972). Human problem solving. Englewood Cliffs, NJ: Prentice-Hall.

Pepper, S. (1948). World hypothesis. Berkeley: University of California Press.

Phelps, R. H., & Shanteau, J. (1978). Livestock judges: How much information can an expert use? Organizational Behavior and Human Performance, 21, 209-219.

Sarbin, T. R. (1942). A contribution to the study of actuarial and individual methods of prediction. American Journal of Sociology, 48, 593-602.

Thorndike, E. L. (1918). Fundamental theorems in judging men. Journal of Applied Psychology, 2, 67-76.

Wallace, H. A. (1923). What is in the corn judge's mind? Journal of the American Society of Agronomy, 15, 300-304.

Zimmer, A. C. (1984). A model for the interpretation of verbal predictions. In M. J. Coombs (Ed.), Developments in expert systems (pp. 235-248). London: Academic Press.

SOME ABSTRACT PROBLEMS IN KNOWLEDGE REPRESENTATION

Michael M. Richter
University of Kaiserslautern
Kaiserslautern
Federal Republic of Germany

WHAT IS THE DIFFERENCE BETWEEN EXPERT SYSTEMS AND TRADITIONAL PROGRAMS

The term "Expert Systems" is very popular today. It is fashionable not just to produce "programs" but something which can be counted under "Artificial Intelligence". In this context it is natural to give at least an informal definition of what an Expert System really is. In fact, there are various attempts to supply us with such a definition.

One possibility is to explain the term by enumerating the areas of possible applications: systems for diagnosis, prognosis, configuration, instruction, etc. It is, however, immediately clear that a classification by areas of applications cannot provide a definition of the term itself.

An alternative way of defining Expert Systems is given by describing the capabilities such a system may have. Among these we find activities like recognition, heuristic search or various kinds of learning. But this approach also does not quite hit the kernel of the problem. The point is that in this way we cannot distinguish Expert Systems from traditional programs. Various decision support systems and other Operation Research systems have very similar properties.

In order to arrive at an useful explanation we will first describe the situations in which Expert Systems make sense. Such situations have two characteristic properties.

On the one hand they incorporate a high degree of indeterminateness. This means, there are always many possible directions in which one might proceed. It is usually far too

NATO ASI Series, Vol. F35
Expert Judgment and Expert Systems
Edited by J. Mumpower et al.

complex to test all possibilities and one looks for methods to reduce the combinatorial complexity. On the other hand one does not deal with clearly defined mathematical structures but with everyday life problems. The available information may be incomplete, vague, false or even inconsistent.

The interest focusses on cases where nevertheless a meaningful solution is possible. Such solutions may be provided by traditional programs or by Expert Systems. The reason that the problem may be solved at all is because both methods are the same: there is additional information available about the problem which makes it less complex or less imprecise than it seems to be at first glance. Such knowledge has to be incorporated in the program. The only difference between a classical program and an Expert System is the way in which this knowledge is incorporated. It should be emphasized that Artificial Intelligence does not provide a new way of "thinking" or particularly clever solutions for certain difficult problems. It only gives us formalisms for expressing ideas and making them useable.

The Classical or Static Approach

Here one tries to get a complete overview of all possible situations which might occur. For all such cases the relevant knowledge has to be encoded in the program. If one produces in this way, a fast algorithm, then the problem is solved and there is no need for an Expert System. There are wide areas of applications where indeed one has obtained a satisfying solution in this way. Examples are database operations, decision support systems or other algorithms of Operations Research.

Today, however, one faces a growing number of situations where a classical approach fails. These are complex problem areas where no a priori strategy for finding the solution can be formulated.

The Dynamic Approach of Artificial Intelligence

Human problem solvers approach a problem by changing algorithms, strategies, heuristics or control structures. This is done in such a way that the methods are optimally adapted to the situation which is under consideration. In order to select the right algorithm or strategy the human problem solver uses his information about the problem. In an Expert System one tries to mimic the human solver.

In order to formulate a system for such a task one has first to represent the knowledge in such a way that it can be used properly in arbitrary, unpredictable situations. Here one distinguishes knowledge about elementary facts, knowledge about general laws, knowledge about procedures, knowledge about more or less recommendable methods, knowledge about this knowledge, knowledge about the knowledge about the knowledge . . . etc.

On the basis of such a knowledge representation Artificial Intelligence tries to formalize analogues of human behaviour. These analogues are very often simple but nevertheless often successful. In the next section we will discuss some principles of knowledge representation.

THREE CONDITIONS ON AN ADEQUATE KNOWLEDGE REPRESENTATION

Sufficient Expressive Power

Algorithms usually contain much encoded information which cannot be expressed explicitly. A database system may, for instance, contain information about patients. One piece of such an information system can be the date of birth. If it is required that for each patient the date of birth has to be stored then usually certain integrity constraints will enforce this. An explicit representation of this constraint is, however, of a different character. It could be given by storing the sentence

> "For all patients x there is a date y which is the date of birth of x".

The truth of this sentence would then guarantee the constraint. Besides the fact that a certain property cannot be expressed explicitly it very often happens that it cannot be expressed at all. Take e.g. a decision support system which gives us advice about buying a boat. Assume that one of the parameters involved is price and another is the number of persons it can carry. A typical response of the system would be to ask the user:

1) To give a maximum and a minimum for the price you are willing to accept.

2) For the number of persons you want to take on the boat. Give the maximum number and the most likely one.

3) To correlate the price and the number of passengers by naming the percentage with which each magnitude influences your decision; e.g. "30% price" and "70% passenger number".

In this way more complicated requirements cannot be formulated. An example of such a demand is:

"I have inherited a certain amount of money. If the price of the boat is considerably less than this amount I really do not care about the price, it does not play a role at all. If the price, however, approximates this amount closely then I am becoming very thrifty and price plays an enormous role. I hate to name an exact upper bound for the price, but 90% of my total amount available is something which I will only exceed if the boat has some other additional nice properties I am not yet aware of."

The expressive power of a system is a function of the underlying language the system uses. For most O.R.-systems the expressive power is equivalent to propositional calculus. One can express disjunctions, conjunctions and negations. Any higher order features have to be encoded into the system.

Uniform Readability

Uniform readability means that an expression can be read independently of where it occurs in the program and independently even of the program itself. The meaning of a statement should only depend on the language itself and not on any ad hoc agreements. The meaning of expressions in classical programs usually depend on certain special situations. If e.g. register number 7 contains a 0, then this could mean:

1) in a first program: there exists a certain object x which has a property p,

2) in a second program: we have now proved that all objects x have a certain property p,

3) in a third program: we have now to undertake a certain manipulation.

In an adequate representation we would have one expression for existential statements, one expression for universal statements and a third expression for commands. Adequate knowledge representation means that one can distinguish independently of the situation questions from commands and these again from statements. Depending on how comfortable the representation is, one would be able to distinguish different types of statements, e.g. elementary facts, statements about procedures, temporal or causal relations. The motivation for uniform readability is that this enables the system to act dynamically in unforeseen situations. The requirement of uniform readability amounts of course to a demand on uniform representation, and this is ultimately a requirement on the underlying language used.

The representation has an impact on the problem solving capabilities of the system. One consequence of the uniformity criterion is a certain continuity property of the inference engine. That means, that the system tries to solve similar problems in a similar way. It does not mean, however, that similar problems always have similar solutions. Counter examples are the so-called catastrophic cases which show the existence of discontinuous phenomena.

Preservation of Structures

Usually there are many interconnections between different pieces of knowledge and the representation should preserve as many of them as possible. The reason for this requirement is that these interconnections support the problem solving process. The most important of these correlations are the horizontal and the vertical ones. Horizontal relations just group the objects into certain packages which have something to do with each other. In software technology this has led to the module concept and is very well developed in traditional programming languages. Among the vertical correlations we will put emphasis on hierarchies of abstractions.

1) The object-oriented hierarchy: One specifies top down the properties of an object by going down the

levels of abstraction. An example is moving object/motorcar/car of company x/model yz of company x. The different levels of abstractions are partially ordered; not all levels are necessarily comparable. This opens the possibility of representing different views, in particular views of different experts. This is important because in most complex situations just one expert would clearly be insufficient.

2) Another vertical structure is given by introducing a type hierarchy. This idea has been introduced at the beginning of the century by Whitehead and Russel in their "Principia Mathematica". If an object P is of higher type than an object Q, then P "talks about" Q. This is usually realized by allowing Q to be an argument of (the function or relation) P. As an example, P may be the predicate "is useful" and Q may be a "strategy". Then P(Q) would express a certain heuristics.

Object-oriented and type-oriented rules have been developed for Artificial Intelligence Programming Languages. In traditional systems of Operations Research they do not have a counterpart.

The above criteria, A., B. and C., are clearly not independent. An important research topic in knowledge representation is to structure them further and add other possible aspects.

SOME PROBLEMS IN MEDICAL AND TECHNICAL APPLICATIONS

The most universal way of representing knowledge is certainly given by the natural languages. Despite the fact that human beings are able to speak and to understand natural language there is nevertheless little known about the structure of natural languages. Today one has only succeeded in formalizing very small fragments of natural languages. A consequence is that we are far away from designing universal knowledge representation systems and building universal Expert Systems. Hence research has concentrated on selecting small areas of applications for Expert Systems. We do not regard this as an argument against Artificial Intelligence in general. Other sciences have been developed in the same slow way.

Among the major applications of Expert Systems one finds diagnostic systems for biological (in particular medical) and technical devices. Diagnostic problems are usually easier than configuration problems. In most cases a diagnosis amounts to a selection of an element of some a priori given set of elements. There is nothing which has to be "invented", the difficulty of the problem depends only on the size of alternatives. There are of course a number of general methods which are common to all selection processes. In order to find a solution efficiently one has on the other hand to use specific properties of the application area.

The two main aspects in which medical and technical systems differ are the following:

1) In a medical diagnosis typical human abilities often play a major role: optical and acoustical information, knowledge about everyday situations and the so-called common sense logic.

2) In a technical context one uses a poorer language, and the discussion is restricted on more well-defined and well-structured situations. On the other hand the output of the system has to satisfy a very high degree of preciseness. In order to obtain such an accurateness one uses knowledge which is extensive and of a kind that humans find difficult to store in their memories.

Besides such principal differences there is a huge number of aspects which play a role in systems of one type but not in systems of the other type. We will mention a few.

Symmetry

Symmetry plays a role in both areas. In technical systems it makes sense, however, to talk about only the general aspects of symmetry. So one might formalize the notions of "symmetry with respect to some axis" or "symmetry with respect to the origin", and one might formalize certain properties of symmetry of which one can take advantage. In medicine the general notion of symmetry is not very useful. There is only one kind of symmetry which is important, namely the left-right-symmetry.

Here it makes sense to formalize the properties of this kind of symmetry in much detail, because one very often refers to the notions of "left" and "right".

States

A technical system has in most cases a very well defined state. In particular one can distinguish between an active and an inoperative position of a machine. For the human body a totally inactive position does not exist. Other states like "having fever" are less well defined than for machines and reflect only certain specific aspects.

Time Dependencies

For technical systems time intervals, time points and their relations are important. In medicine we have in addition quite a different kind of time dependency. A human being reacts differently in the morning, during the day, in the evening, at night. An actual diagnosis may also very well depend on the time of the year, because at certain times influenza may be very likely and at others not.

Verification

In technical systems a diagnosis can usually be verified, e.g. by exchanging a part and applying a certain test. This is usually impossible in the medical situation. Here one has to work in principle with a higher degree of insecurity.

Values

The values in a technical system are in most cases easy to measure: price, performance or energy consumption. This is different in the medical context. There is no immediate measurement of "health" or "feeling comfortable". On the other hand, there is also no need for a numerical measure of these values.

CONCLUSIONS

From the viewpoint of applications the present situation is characterized by the duality of Expert Systems on the one side and traditional programs and models on the other side. Mathematical models and methods have been developed extensively over the centuries. Knowledge Representation has a much shorter history, but also sophisticated formalisms are available. What is missing is the combination of these two types of tools. It is not clear, however, that these two aspects are automatically compatible. Incorporation of one type of method may very well weaken the other tools. The problem is that most problems do not automatically split into two parts where one is adapted to AI-methods and the other can be handled by classical methods. A related question is that representation has two aspects:

1) One representation of a situation can be the natural one from the point of view of the problem itself.

2) Another representation may be suitable for an efficient solution of the problem.

Artificial Intelligence applications have mostly dealt with representations of the first kind. There is very little knowledge of how to transform it into a representation of the second kind. For this purpose special knowledge is necessary which is very little understood.

REFERENCES

K.-D. Althoff. What are Expert Systems?, to appear in: Expert Systems in Production Engineering, Springer-Verlag.

I. Doyle. Expert Systems without computers or theory and trust in AI, Dept. of Computer Science, CMU (Pittsburgh), CMU-CS-84-116, 1984.

M. M. Richter. Architecture and applications of Expert Systems, to appear in: Expert Systems in statistics, ed. R. Haux, Fischer-Verlag, 1986.

M. M. Richter. Expertensysteme und konventionelle Programme - Unterschiede und Kopplungsprobleme, to appear in: Festschrift fur L. Spath, ed. R. Henn, Springer-Verlag.

H. Voss. Representing and analyzing causal, temporal, and hierarchical relations of devices. Dissertation, Kaiserslautern, 1986.

PRINCIPLES OF THE ANALYTIC HIERARCHY PROCESS

Thomas L. Saaty
University of Pittsburgh
Pittsburgh, Pennsylvania USA

INTRODUCTION

Cognitive psychologists have classified thinking into two types. This division has gone by many names. Aristotle referred to it as active versus passive reason [35]; Freud [10] as secondary versus primary process thinking; and Hobbes [14] as thought with or without "designe." More recently the division has been referred to as directed versus autistic thinking [4] and operant versus respondent thought [16]. The terms Varendinck [33] uses for the division may be most familiar to the layman. He noted the classification as one between conscious and foreconscious or affective thought. Adopting this familiar terminology, conscious thought appears to differ from affective thought in that it is directed, checked against feedback, evaluated in terms of its effectiveness in advancing specific goals, and protected from drift by deliberately controlled attention by the thinker [16].

In contrast with the neocortex where conscious activity takes place, the visceral brain, which consists of the hindbrain, midbrain, and the limbic brain, regulates the following six affective behaviors: fight, flight, freeze, feed, feel and flirt [28].

While investigations of decision making have tended to focus on conscious thought, it is increasingly recognized that affective thinking plays a strategic role in decisions (Zajonc [36]; Klinger [16]). In particular, affective thinking may be important in the formation of generalizations about heterogeneous multiple events [9]. Hence from the flow of conscious thought, affective thought takes a special kind of generalized understanding. In a sense, these generalized understandings which go by the name of gut feelings, impressions etc. are some of the most important facets of how managers make decisions. The

NATO ASI Series, Vol. F35
Expert Judgment and Expert Systems
Edited by J. Mumpower et al.

formation of these gut feelings rely on a cooperation between conscious and affective thought, where the conscious is used as a probe to structure and clarify relationships.

Many decision theorists have talked about "biases" in judgment that result from the affective components of thought, but increasingly researchers have come to recognize that these generalized schemata serve a crucial role in the survival of the organism operating in a complex, uncertain world [8]; [11]). Our aim is to develop a model based on the "cooperation" between conscious and affective thought, emphasizing the way in which our conscious apprehension of experience can be brought into harmony with both the workings and the needs of affective thought, providing a crucial bridge between these two ways of seeing.

Our first concern is to discover how conscious thought structures the environment and its interactions in a way that is in harmony with our affective thinking.

To do this we need to address four questions:

1. How to structure a complex decision problem as a hierarchy or as a system with feedback.

2. How to make multicriterion decisions by using judgment intensities in pairwise comparisons to set priorities.

3. How priorities before and after arithmetic weighting define a ratio scale.

4. How judgments and priorities lead to the question of consistency and how consistency relates to transitivity.

The process described here has been developed in detail with applications in books and articles. It has also been compared with other people's work in many of these.

In general form, the process can be used to analyze complexity in the form of a network with feedback. It requires that not only elements in each level of a hierarchy or node in a network be relatively homogeneous, but that adjacent levels or nodes should not differ by more than one order of magnitude. Such discrimination is both a matter of expert judgment and more importantly, a result of initial comparisons of elements or clusters which yield priorities that remain within the same magnitude order. Thus the analysis of complexity is carried out stepwise, descending from the large to the small an order of magnitude at a time.

Two other features of the process are that it elicits relative intensity of preferences through pairwise comparisons and converts these to ratio scale priorities. By means of a ratio scale one can compare relative values by forming the ratios of weights. This has made it possible to deal with intangible factors on the same footing as tangible ones and hard objective data with subjective judgments, thus making it possible to include all sorts of factors in the analysis of complexity without holding back on any factor perceived to have bearing on the problem. The normalization and weighting process maintains uniformity of ratio scales so that the final set of priorities presents the weights of the alternatives with which one is concerned. There are at least three ways to justify the credibility of the resulting numbers.

1. Mathematically. The homogeneous way with which ratio scales with unit multipliers are compounded into a ratio scale also with unit multiplier avoids the possibility of fudging ratio scales to obtain a nondescript scale.

2. Physically. When the process of comparison and priority setting is applied to a hierarchy of physical objects of known weights, volumes, etc., decomposed in any reasonable fashion one can imagine, and related logically within the structure, the composition of priorities gives back the actual weights or volumes or any other measurable attribute of these objects.

3. Experience - Popperian Validation. When used by experienced people over the years the process has never produced unjustifiable results because somehow its mathematics was found not to work. In fact in hundreds of applications given in books and articles, many carried out by people or in situations initially unknown to the author, there never was a question that the final outcome was not representative of what people could accept, given their own inputs.

Finally the process allows for inconsistency in judgments. Everyone would like to have a theory that tolerates a modicum of inconsistency without rejecting the final results. In addition, a group of people working together (or against each other) use the process to test the effect of incompatibility in perceptions and judgments on the final outcome.

A final comment about foundations and axioms underlying the process: Because the process deals with ratio scales rather than interval scales, with consistency rather than transitivity, and because it is concerned with making choices by preserving the rank order of alternatives despite inconsistency and, hence, does not prejudge what is a relevant alternative, a different set of axioms than those customarily used in utility theory has been necessary. In addition, expressing preferences according to intensity requires an interpretation and a statement of how the human mind operates that is compatible with the state of the art in both the biological and the behavioral sciences. Space limitation prevents us from giving the axioms underlying the process, but they appear in Management Science, July 1986.

The confidence which one can place in the results of an AHP solution of a problem has been studied. The stability of the outcome of a set of pairwise comparisons can be tested as follows. First we note that the priorities of the elements in a comparison all fall in the interval [0,1]. It is known that consistency is the variance of the spread in the judgments. Also, all the judgments are nonnegative and the rule for majority decision must eventually satisfy the reciprocal property for each judgment. This rule has been shown to necessarily be the geometric mean. The resulting statistical distribution for each judgment is either a unimodal distribution or can be partitioned into several such distributions. Analytically only one distribution satisfies all these conditions. It is the gamma distribution which leads to a Dirichlet distribution for the solution vector and a fortiori to a Beta distribution for each component. This enables one to develop a confidence interval of the variation (or stability) of each component. The sensitivity of the entire hierarchy can be obtained from those of the components by composition. There is a closed form expression for this purpose [34].

An individual not familiar with the AHP may ask:

o Is there a systematic way to structure a hierarchy?

o Why should one use the eigenvector approach instead of

the logarithmic least squares and the least squares methods or any of the infinite number of ways to approximate a set of judgments by ratios?

o How does one deal with group judgments? There is a definite logical way for combining the judgments of many people.

o Why use a linear weighting scheme instead of the many being proposed?

o Are the results obtained from the AHP invariant to people and to change in circumstances? The answer to this question is definitely no because as the world changes and as people change the basic information changes. It stabilizes only after repetition and interaction which usually produce saturation.

STRUCTURE AND DECOMPOSITION OF COMPLEXITY

Knowledge involves identification of a concept as a problem and probing for detail about the problem. The problem is both embedded in a larger setting of factors and analyzed into smaller factors. Both of these involve decomposition from the larger setting (the environment) to the problem, to the details of the problem. Thus decomposition is a result of both induction by generalizing on the problem and deduction by breaking the problem down.

The most general method for decomposition is a network each of whose nodes is a cluster of several factors. These nodes are interconnected in a way to indicate interaction among the clusters as it may be that only a few or all clusters affect a given one.

The simplest structure for decomposing complexity is a hierarchy which is a linear network in which each cluster affects only one other. There is one cluster called the last cluster which has no further decomposition. The next simple kind of structure which has the form of a cycle (called a holarchy) is a hierarchy whose first and last clusters are directly connected to indicate an impact of the last (the alternatives) on the first (the general criteria).

The mathematical definitions of both a hierarchy and a network with feedback will be given.

Formal Description

A formal definition of a hierarchy is the following:

In a partially ordered set, we define $x < y$ to mean that $x < y$ and $x \neq y$. y is said to cover (dominate) x. If $x < y$ then $x < t < y$ is possible for no t. We used the notation $x^- = \{y|x$ covers $y\}$ and $x^+ = \{y|y$ covers $x\}$, for any element x in an ordered set.

Let H be a finite partially ordered set. H is a hierarchy if it satisfies the conditions:

a) There is a partition of H into sets L_k, $k = 1, \ldots h$ for some h where $L_1 = \{b\}$, b a single element.

b) $x \in L_k$ implies $x^- \in L_{k+1}$ $\qquad k = 1,\ldots,h-1$.

c) $x \in L_k$ implies $x^+ \in L_{k-1}$ $\qquad k = 2,\ldots,h$.

For each $x \in H$, there is a suitable weighting function (whose nature depends on the phenomenon being hierarchically structured):

$$w_x : x^- \rightarrow [0,1] \text{ such that } \sum_{y \in x^-} w_x(y) = 1.$$

Note that h=1 is the last level for which x^- is not empty.

The sets L_i are the levels of the hierarchy, and the function w_x is the priority function of the elements in one level with respect to the objective x. We observe that even if $x^- \neq L_k$ (for some level L_k), w_x may be defined for all of L_k by setting it equal to zero for all elements in L_k not in x.

The weighting function, we feel, is a significant contribution towards the application of hierarchy theory.

Definition: A hierarchy is complete if, for all $x \subset L_k$, $x^+ \subset L_{k-1}$.

We can state the central question:

Basic Problem: Given any element $x \in L_\alpha$, and subset $S \subset L_\beta$, $(\alpha < \beta)$, how do we define a function $w_{x,S} : S \rightarrow [0,1]$ which reflects the properties of the priority functions on the levels L_k, $k = \alpha, \ldots, \beta - 1$. Specifically, what is the function w_{b,L_h} : $L_h \to [0,1]$?

In less technical terms, this can be paraphrased thus: Given a social (or economic) system with a major objective b, and the set L_h of basic activities, such that the system can be modeled as a hierarchy with largest element b and lowest level L_h. What are the priorities of the elements of any level and in particular those of L_h with respect to b?

From the standpoint of optimization, to allocate a resource to the elements any interdependence may take the form of input-output relations such as, for example, the interflow of products between industries. A high priority industry may depend on flow of material from a low priority industry. In an optimization framework, the priority of the elements enables one to define the objective function to be maximized, and other hierarchies supply information regarding constraints, e.g., input-output relations.

We shall now present our method to solve the Basic Problem. Assume that $Y = \{y_1, \ldots, y_{m_k}\} \subset L_k$ and that $X = \{x_1, \ldots, x_{m_{k+1}}\} \subset L_{k+1}$. Without loss of generality we may assume that $X = L_{k+1}$, and that there is an element $z \in L_k$ such that $y_i \in z^-$. We then consider the priority functions

$$w_z : Y \to [0,1] \text{ and } w_{y_j} : X \to [0,1] \quad j = 1, \ldots, m_k.$$

We construct the priority function of the elements in X with respect to z, denoted w, w: $X \to [0,1]$, by

$$w(x_i) = \sum_{j=1}^{m_k} w_{y_j}(x_i) w_z(y_j), \quad i = 1, \ldots, m_{k+1}$$

It is obvious that this is no more than the process of weighting the influence of the element y_j on the priority of x_i by multiplying it with the importance of x_i with respect to z.

The algorithms involved will be simplified if one combines the $w_{y_j}(x_i)$ into a matrix B by setting $b_{ij} = w_{y_j}(x_i)$. If we further set $w_i = w(x_i)$ and $w_j' = w_z(y_j)$, then the above formula becomes

$$w_i = \sum_{j=1}^{m_k} b_{ij} w_j' \qquad i = 1, \ldots, n_{k+1}$$

Thus, we may speak of the priority vector w and, indeed, of the priority matrix B of the (k+1)st level; this gives the final formulation

$$w = Bw'$$

The following is easy to prove:

<u>Theorem</u>. Let H be a complete hierarchy with largest element b and h levels. Let B_k be the priority matrix of the kth level, $k = 1, \ldots, h$. If w' is the priority vector of the pth level with respect to some element z in the (p-1)st level, then the priority vector w of the qth level ($p<q$) with respect to z is given by:

$$w = B_q B_{q-1} \cdots B_{p+1} w'$$

Thus, the priority vector of the lowest level with respect to the element b is given by:

$$w = B_h B_{h-1} \cdots B_2 b_1$$

if L_1 has a single element, $b_1 = 1$. Otherwise, b_1 is a prescribed vector. We note that the pairwise comparison process takes into consideration nonlinearities. Such nonlinearities are captured by composition which is a weighting process.

<u>Network Systems</u>

A network system is a set of nodes (each of which consists of a set of elements) and a set of arcs which indicate the order of interaction among the components. The priorities of the elements in each node are components of the principal eigenvector of the matrix of pairwise comparisons of the relative impact of these elements with respect to an element or node with which they interact. The interaction is indicated by an arc of the network.

system, the supermatrix is transformed into a stochastic matrix. The limiting impact priorities are obtained by computing large powers of this matrix. Formally we have:

Definition: A partially ordered set S is a system if

a) There is a partition of S into sets C_k, k = 1, ..., s

b) There is an ordering on C_k, k = 1, ..., s such that $x \subseteq C_k$ implies either x^- or x^+ is in C_{k_j} for some k_j or both $x^- \subseteq C_{k_j}$, $x^+ \subseteq C_{k_j}$ for one or more k_j.

c) For each $x \in S$, there is a suitable weighting function

$$w_x: x^- \to [0,1] \text{ such that } \sum_{y \in x^-} w_x(y) = 1$$

and for $C_k \subseteq S$, k = 1, ..., s there is a weighting function

$$w_{(k)}: C^-_k \to [0,1]$$

where $C^-_k = \{C_h | C_k \text{ covers } C_h\}$.

We note in these definitions the presence of weighting functions. They are the result of the judgmental process described in the next section.

There are two abstract forms for a hierarchy. One is the forward process hierarchy which can be used to determine the outcome or alternative that is a logical (most likely) consequence of the present circumstances: criteria, actors, objectives, policies and contrast scenarios. The other is the backward process which help one to choose among several alternatives evaluated in terms of a set of criteria, the most desired one. Planning and conflict analysis use both hierarchies in an iterative fashion to bring the logical outcome closer to the desired one.

The number and kind of clusters associated with a given problem must derive from knowledge about the problem. A number of things can be learned about how to structure a problem by being exposed to the process described here. However, the diversity of decompositions of problems encountered in practice over the years when put together offer an enrichment to people's understanding of decomposition and may accelerate the process for a new problem. A book is being prepared by two authors for the simple purpose of providing a variety of hierarchies.

We need to emphasize that hierarchic thinking is only an approximation to the real situation because alternatives depend on criteria and criteria on alternatives. Thus, there should be a cycle connecting the two which is easily studied with the network feedback approach. However, generally people like to simplify and arrange their thinking in terms of a linear hierarchy even if the answers are only approximate.

Aids in Structuring a Hierarchy

1. Do a simple problem.

2. Look at many examples.

3. Define the overall objective - what question are you trying to answer?

4. Examine your problem as part of several problems in an overall goal.

5. Force a framework.

6. Brainstorm the problem by listing every conceivable factor. Then organize all the criteria listed as a hierarchy by grouping the factors in comparable classes appropriately aligned in positive or negative direction.

7. Make certain that you can answer questions about the importance of the elements in a level with respect to the elements in the upper level.

8. Formulate written questions you are going to answer for each level.

9. Work from the top down. When it appears difficult to go further, work from the bottom up.

A hierarchy of the Analytic Hierarchy Process must be finely graded between levels. As one descends from one level to the next, they must be carefully designed to differ by no more than one order of magnitude according to importance. For physical problems this may be easy to do. For intellectual or functional problems one needs to analyze the problem carefully in order to arrive at a well graded descending hierarchy. Examine the book Decision Making for Leaders for a large number of examples of hierarchies.

JUDGMENTS

According to cognitive psychology [5] there are two kinds of judgments. Both are relative because they are based on a framework of reference. Absolute judgments are made by comparing the strength of a perceived stimulus with some memory recollection of a similar stimulus to determine the magnitude of that stimulus. This operation is limited and inefficient because every judgment requires the comparison of the perceived stimulus with short-term access and processing from memories of earlier stimuli. In contrast to this, comparative judgments are used to compare two stimuli when both are present to the observer to identify some relation between them. The problem is to determine the magnitude of the relation among the two stimuli. In addition paired comparisons may be extended to several stimuli whereby from the magnitudes of their paired comparisons it is possible to obtain a relative comparison of all their magnitudes. This is what one does with the Analytic Hierarchy Process.

From Multiple Comparisons to Pairwise Comparisons

To compare n elements simultaneously with respect to a property is to be able to say how much of that property each element has relative to the other elements. This is a scaling of the elements among themselves. But this is precisely what one obtains by first making pairwise comparisons which are the simplest kind of comparisons and then generating from these comparisons a scale of relative measurement among the n elements. Thus it is sufficient to carry out pairwise comparisons among the elements.

Note that the elements themselves may be clusters of several elements taken as a whole and the object is to compare them with other clusters or with simple elements. The result would assign a relative value to each cluster but not to its constituent elements. These would have to be compared internally to derive their relative values with respect to the given property.

<u>Pairwise Comparisons as Ratios</u>

Assume that we are given n stones, $A_1, \ldots, A_n$ whose weights $w_1, \ldots, w_n$, respectively, are known to us. Let us form the matrix of pairwise ratios whose rows give the ratios of the weights of each stone with respect to all others. Thus we have the matrix:

$$A = \begin{pmatrix} & A_1 & A_2 & \cdots & A_n \\ A_1 & w_1/w_2 & w_1/w_2 & \cdots & w_1/w_n \\ A_2 & w_2/w_1 & w_2/w_2 & \cdots & w_2/w_n \\ \vdots & & \vdots & & \vdots \\ A_n & w_n/w_1 & w_n/w_2 & \cdots & w_n/w_n \end{pmatrix} \begin{pmatrix} w_1 \\ w_2 \\ \vdots \\ w_n \end{pmatrix} = n \begin{pmatrix} w_1 \\ w_2 \\ \vdots \\ w_n \end{pmatrix}$$

We have multiplied A on the right by the vector of weights w. The result of this multiplication is nw. Thus, to recover the scale from the matrix of ratios, we must solve the problem $Aw = nw$ or $(A - nI)w = 0$. This is a system of homogeneous linear equations. It has a nontrivial solution if and only if the determinant of $A - nI$ vanishes; i.e., n is an eigenvalue of A. Now A has unit rank since every row is a constant multiple of the first row. Thus, all the eigenvalues except one are zero. The sum of the eigenvalues of a matrix is equal to its trace, and in this case the trace of A is equal to n. Thus n is an eigenvalue of A and we have a nontrivial solution. The solution consists of positive entries and is unique to within a multiplicative constant, by the Perron-Frobenius theorem since A is irreducible; i.e., is not decomposable into blocks of the form

$$A = \begin{pmatrix} C_1 & 0 \\ C_2 & C_3 \end{pmatrix}$$

In the general case we cannot give the precise values of w_i/w_j but only estimates of them.

Our considerations later will show that we plan to use the solution for $Aw = \lambda_{max} w$ as an estimate of this ratio.

Orders of Homogeneity

One of the axioms of the AHP is that the objects being compared should be homogeneous. Homogeneity means that objects which have a property in common are sufficiently close or similar with respect to that property to make possible accurate comparisons among them. If the objects are very close, it may be necessary to use an even finer mode or scale of comparisons to make distinctions among them. The way to deal with the problem of comparing "homogeneous" objects is not unlike using a sieve for separating particles of different sizes. We first take out those particles that pass through the finest mesh; the next set of particles are separated with a slightly less fine mesh and so on.

It is useful to categorize the elements or objects being compared into homogeneous sets so that a set differs from a neighboring set by one order of magnitude. If there is not a smooth order of magnitude transition from the set of smallest elements to the set of largest elements, the intervening gaps can be filled with hypothetical sets whose objects are either aggregates of elements in the preceding sets or the decomposition of elements in the succeeding sets.

The elements in each set can be compared with an appropriate scale. They may differ from each other by a small number of multiples or they may be so close that their differences are more appropriately represented by tenths, hundredths, etc., of orders of magnitude. The result is that we have a nested set of refinements, our sieve, in scales of comparisons as shown in the following diagram.

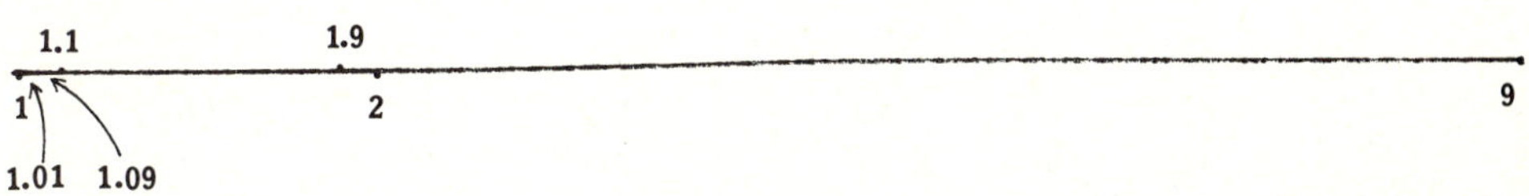

We shall refer to these orders of homogeneity as the first order scale (the scale 1-9), the refined scale (the scale 1.1-1.9), the super refined scale (1.01-1.09), and so on.

On the Measurement of Intangibles

An important area to which these ideas apply is that of finding effective measurements for intangible factors. The only meaningful way to measure an intangible factor is to compare the object exhibiting the factor or property with other objects also having it. What we mean by an intangible factor is that we have not yet derived for it through experience an objective widely used scale. Additionally, the importance of that factor can only be determined by comparing it in pairs with other factors, tangible or intangible, with respect to a higher property or goal. For example, suppose that one wishes to arrive at a relative measure of redness of a set of apples. The property of redness is the intangible factor, the apples are the objects to be compared in pairs with respect to redness. Note that to determine the importance of redness for the particular concern at hand, one must compare redness, for example, with sweetness (another intangible factor), and price (a tangible factor) and so on. It is useful to remember that no property exists uniformly in an object. The redness or sweetness of an apple varies from one position to another on the apple and one must tally up (or equivalently, average) redness or sweetness of an apple to do it justice in comparing it with another apple.

Scaling Judgments

In translating judgments to numerical intensities the scale of absolute values below has been found useful and faithful in giving back known results when compared with 28 other proposed scales.

The use of this scale is contingent on the satisfaction of the assumption that the factors being compared are of a similar order of magnitude. When a factor does not appear strictly comparable with another, clustering techniques can be applied so the comparisons are made possible at the level of the clusters.

Roughly, the scale should satisfy the following requirements:

It should be possible to represent people's differences in feelings when they make comparisons. It should also represent all distinct shades of feeling that people have.

If we denote the integer values of the scale by $x_1, x_2, \ldots, x_n$, then it would be desirable that $x_{i+1} - x_i = 1$, $i = 1, \ldots, n - 1$. The reasons are:

a) We need uniformity between difference to make sure that the scale covers all judgments. We require that the subject must be aware of all objects at the same time.

b) We agree with the psychological experiments which show that an individual cannot simultaneously compare more than seven objects (plus or minus two) without being confused. See later section for justification.

c) If a unit difference between successive scale values is all that we allow, then by requiring uniformity and using the fact that $x_1 = 1$ for the identity comparison and nine shades of judgment, it follows that the scale values will range from one to nine.

In a preliminary step towards the construction of an intensity scale of importance for activities, we use the "agreed upon" numbers in Table 1.

In using this scale the reader should recall that we assume that the individual providing the judgment has knowledge about the relative values of the elements being compared whose ratio is ≥ 1, and that the numerical ratios he forms are nearest integer approximations scales in such a way that the highest ratio corresponds to 9. We have assumed that an element with weight zero is eliminated from comparison. This of course, need not imply that zero may not be used for pairwise comparisons as we do to compare components of a system that have no impacts. Reciprocals of all scaled ratios are ≤ 1 and are entered in the transpose positions (not taken as judgments). Note that the solution of the problem remains the same if we multiply the unit entries on the main diagonal by a constant. Thus, despite scaling, each main diagonal element may continue to equal unity. In practice, one way or another, the numerical judgments will have to be approximations, but how good is the question at which our theory is aimed.

TABLE 1
THE RATIO SCALE

Intensity of Importance	Definition	Explanation
1*	Equal importance.	Two activities contribute equally to the objectives.
3	Moderate importance of one over another.	Experience and judgment strongly favor one activity over another.
5	Essential or strong.	Experience and judgment strongly favor one activity over another.
7	Very strong importance.	An activity is strongly favored and its dominance demonstrated in practice.
9	Extreme importance.	The evidence favoring one activity over another is of the highest possible order of affirmation.
2,4,6,8	Intermediate values between the two adjacent judgments.	When compromise is needed.
Reciprocals	If activity i has one of the above numbers assigned to it when compared with activity j, then j has the reciprocal value when compared with i.	
Rationals	Ratios arising from the	If consistency were to be forced by obtaining n numerical values to span the matrix.

When the elements being compared are closer together than indicated by the scale, one can use the scale 1.1, 1.2, ..., 1.9. If still finer, one can use the appropriate percentage refinement.

What Question Should One Ask?

A typical question to ask in order to fill in the entries in a matrix of comparisons is: Consider two properties i on the left side of the matrix and another j on the top; which of the two has the property under discussion more and how strongly more (using the scale values 1 to 9). This gives us a_{ij} (or a_{ji}). The reciprocal value is then automatically entered for a_{ji} (or a_{ij}).

The question asked in making the pairwise comparison can influence the judgments provided and hence also the priorities. It must be made clear from the start what the focus of the hierarchy is and how then the elements lower down either serve to fulfill that focus or are its consequence. For example, in the first case one looks down the hierarchy as a forward projection. The question may relate to importance, impact, priority or effectiveness in being a part of the higher level criteria. In the second case the question may be what is more important or likely to make it possible to attain a certain objective, policy or outcome.

Note that in making the estimates and to keep the comparisons relevant, an individual has to keep in mind all the elements being compared. It is known that an individual cannot simultaneously compare more than 7 ± 2 elements. If this is so, then how are we able to have measurement across wide classes of about seven elements each. The element with the highest weight in the class of lighter weight elements is also included in the next heavier class and serves as a pivot to uniformize the scale between the two classes. The procedure is repeated from a class to an adjacent one until we have all the elements appropriately scaled.

In passing, we note that the eigenvector approach to measurement (as one might expect) preserves ordinal preferences among alternatives; i.e., if an alternative is preferred to another, its eigenvector component is larger that that of the other.

The Analytic Hierarchy Process seeks to elicit judgments from people by asking the appropriate question that would produce the intended answer. By asking the wrong question one would obtain nonsensical results. It remains to determine whether there are right questions to ask, what they are, and how readily people can respond to them. A part of the solution lies in experience obtained using the process. The other part depends on our understanding of the types of problems for which one sets priorities. In general the situation may be normative or descriptive. In the former case the question for the pairwise comparison should be formed in terms of what is more preferred or desired in order to satisfy a certain criterion, constraint, property or scenario. In descriptive situations the question will seek judgments which identify the degree or extent that two alternatives have a certain property; e.g., of two stones, which is heavier and how much; of two roses, which is more red, and so on. More abstractly two criteria may be compared as to a higher level criterion. Which one is more likely to produce, embody, or fulfill that criterion or is closer to defining or bringing about the criterion. Generically we ask which is more "important," meaning a greater possessor of the attribute. These two categories of questions relate to two types of hierarchies discussed in the AHP literature: the forward (descriptive) and the backward (prescriptive) hierarchies that are often combined through iteration into a process of improving the likely outcome towards the desired outcome.

It should be noted here that in a hierarchy with a single top element or focus, comparison of the second level elements with respect to the focus suggests that one asks "on the average" or "on the whole" which alternative is more "preferred" or more "likely." For other levels one has specific criteria or elements for making comparisons and need not preface the question with "on the average."

Consistency

Definition: The matrix $A = (a_{ij})$ is consistent if and only if $a_{ij}a_{jk} = a_{ik}$.

Classically transitivity means that $i \geq j$, $j \geq k$ implies $i \geq k$ ($>$ preferred). Now consistency implies transitivity for $i \geq j \Rightarrow a_{ij} \geq 1$, $j \geq k \Rightarrow a_{jk} \geq 1$ and because of consistency we have $a_{ij}a_{jk} = a_{ik} \geq 1$ and hence $i \geq k$. Thus transitivity is a necessary condition for consistency. However, it is not sufficient. Thus if $i \geq j$ and $j \geq k$ then $a_{ij} = 2$, $a_{jk} = 3$ implies $a_{ik} = 6$ but we choose it to be equal to 4. Transitivity is not sufficient.

When A is consistent the entire set of entries can be constructed from a set of n judgments that form a chain across the rows and columns. Such a chain interconnecting entries is given by:

$$a_{ii_1}, a_{i_1i_2}, a_{i_2i_3}, \ldots, a_{i_{n-1}j}.$$

The AHP does not require that judgments be consistent or even transitive. The consistency (or inconsistency) of the judgments is revealed at the end. One might ask, if the judgments were totally random in nature, what kind of consistency would the AHP interpret them to have? The consistency of a matrix of such random judgments should be much worse than the consistency of a matrix of informed judgments and can be used to compare and evaluate the goodness of the consistency of informed judgments.

If a_{ij} represents importance of alternative i over alternative j and a_{jk} represents importance of alternative j over alternative k then a_{ik}, the importance of alternative i over alternative k, must equal $a_{ij}a_{jk}$ for the judgments to be consistent. If we do not have a scale at all, or do not have it conveniently as in the case of a measuring device, we cannot give the precise value of w_i/w_j but only an estimate of it.

Except for special situations in pattern recognition in which instruments are used to take measurements which are then entered directly in lieu of judgments, we assume, to preserve sanity in making pairwise comparison judgments that the matrix A is reciprocal, i.e., has the reciprocal property defined above. in the case of stones this is clear since if one stone is estimated to be k times heavier than another it does not seem unreasonable to require the other to be 1/k times the weight of the first.

For the moment let us consider an estimate of these values by an expert whom we assume makes small errors in judgment. We know that for a reciprocal matrix small perturbation of the coefficients implies small perturbation of the eigenvalues. Our problem now becomes $A'w' = {}_{max}w'$ where ${}_{max}$ is the largest or principal eigenvalue of $A' = (a'_{ij})$ the perturbed value of a_{ij} with $a'_{ji} = 1/a'_{ij}$ forced. To simplify the notation we shall continue to write $Aw = {}_{max}w$ where A is the matrix of pairwise comparisons.

The problem is now, how good is the principal eigenvector

estimate w? Note that if we obtain $w = (w_1, \ldots, w_n)$ by solving this problem, the matrix whose entries are w_i/w_j is a consistent matrix which is our consistent estimate of the matrix A. A itself need not be consistent. In fact, the entries of A need not even be transitive; i.e., A_1 may be preferred to A_2 and A_2 to A_3 but A_3 may be preferred to A_1. What we would like is a measure of the error due to inconsistency. It turns out that A is consistent if and only if $\lambda_{max} = n$ and that we always have $\lambda_{max} \geq n$. This suggests using $\lambda_{max} - n$ as an index of departure from consistency. But

$$\lambda_{max} - n = -\sum_{i=2}^{n} \lambda_i ; \quad \lambda_{max} = \lambda_1,$$

where λ_i, $i = 1, \ldots, n$ are the eigenvalues of A. We adopt the average value $(\lambda_{max}-n)/(n-1)$, which is the (negative average of λ_i, $i=2, \ldots, n$ (some of which may be complex conjugates). On calculating this value we compare the result with those of the same index obtained as an average over a large number of matrices of the same order whose entries are random. However, we force the relations $a_{ji} = 1/a_{ij}$, $a_{ii} = 1$ in these matrices. If the ratio of our index to that from random matrices is significantly small, we accept the estimates. We shall not go into the details of this procedure now.

When several people propose radically different judgments in a certain position of an otherwise acceptable matrix generated through consensus or by taking the geometric mean of multiple judgments, each judgment can be tested with the judgments on which there is wide agreement by solving the problem and measuring the consistency. That judgment yielding the highest consistency in the overall problem is retained.

It is interesting to note that $2(\lambda_{max}-n/n-1)$ is the variance of the error incurred in estimating a_{ij}. This can be shown by writing

$$a_{ij} = (w_i/w_j)\,\epsilon_{ij}, \ \epsilon_{ij} > 0 \text{ and } \epsilon_{ij} = 1 + \delta_{ij}, \ \delta_{ij} > -1.$$

It is δ_{ij} that concerns us as the error component and its value $|\delta_{ij}| < 1$ for an unbiased estimator.

To conclude this section, we note that solution of the principal eigenvalue problem when normalized yields a unique estimate of a ratio scale underlying the judgments.

Estimating the Priority Vector

There is literally an infinite number of ways to estimate the ratio w_i/w_j from the matrix (a_{ij}). But we have already shown that our formulation with particular emphasis on consistency leads to an eigenvalue formulation.

What is an easy way to get a good approximation to the priorities? Multiply the elements in each row together and take the nth root where n is the number of elements. Then normalize the column of numbers thus obtained by dividing each entry by the sum of all entries. Alternatively normalize the elements in each column of the judgment matrix and then average over each row. The exact solution is obtained by raising the matrix to arbitrarily large powers, summing over the rows and normalizing. Ordinarily the computer multiplies the matrix by itself, the result by itself and so on to obtain exponential powers and rapid convergence. It is instructed to stop when the error in the priority vector between two consecutive iterations is of a desired degree of accuracy at a certain decimal position.

We would like to caution the reader that for real applications one should only use the eigenvector derivation procedure because it can be shown that the approximation described above can lead to rank reversal in spite of its closeness to the eigenvector [22a].

How to Estimate λ_{max}

A simple way to obtain the exact value (or estimate) of λ_{max} when the exact value (or an estimate) of w is available in normalized form is to add the columns of A and multiply the resulting vector with the vector w. The resulting number is λ_{max}.

This follows from

$$\sum_{j=1}^{n} a_{ij} w_j = \lambda_{max} w_i$$

$$\sum_{i=1}^{n} \sum_{j=1}^{n} a_{ij} w_j = \sum_{j=1}^{n} (\sum_{i=1}^{n} a_{ij}) w_j = \sum_{i=1}^{n} \lambda_{max} w_i = \lambda_{max}$$

The consistency index of a matrix of comparisons is given by C.I. = λ_{max}-n/n-1. The consistency ratio (C.R.) is obtained by comparing C.I. with the appropriate one of the following set of numbers each of which is an average random consistency index derived from a sample of size 500 of randomly generated reciprocal matrix using the scale 1/9, 1/8, ..., 1, ...8, 9 to see if it is about 10% or less (20% may be tolerated but not more). If it is not less than 10% study the problem and revise the judgments.

n	1	2	3	4	5	6	7	8	9	10
Random Consistency Index (R.I.)	0	0	.58	.90	1.12	1.24	1.32	1.41	1.45	1.49

<u>DeSchutter's Conjecture</u>

John DeSchutter has conjectured the following relationship between the index R.I. and n, the size of the matrix:

$$R.I. = 1.845 \frac{n-2}{n} = 1.845(1- \frac{n-1}{n(n-1)/2})$$

where 1.845 is the average value of the ratio of each value computed so far from n = 3 to n = 15 divided by (n-2)/n for the corresponding value of n. Here (n-1) is the minimum number of judgments needed to measure consistency and n(n-1)/2 is the number elicited for redundancy. Alternatively, a plot of values of R.I. against n shows that the resulting curve approaches 1.845 as an asymptote, i.e., $\lim_{n\to\infty}$ R.I. = 1.845. An observation drawn from the conjecture is that a redundancy factor of $(n(n-1)/2)/(n-1) = n/2$ which depends on n linearly, may not be necessary and one should devise efficient ways of taking fewer than $n(n-1)/2$ judgments, i.e., that the redundancy should have a constant value.

Useful Examples for Inconsistency and Intransitivity

Near consistency is preserved despite changes in judgments:

1) $a_{12} = 2$, $a_{13} = 9$, a_{23} should be 9/2 but is 9 (twice what it should be)

$$\begin{pmatrix} 1 & 2 & 9 \\ .5 & 1 & 9 \\ 1/9 & 1/9 & 1 \end{pmatrix} \quad \begin{matrix} .582 \\ .367 \\ .051 \end{matrix}$$

$\lambda_{max} = 3.054$, C.I. = .027, C.R. = .046 (acceptable).

2) If we change just a_{12} from 2 to 3, we have $\lambda_{max} = 3.136$, C.I. = .068, C.R. = 0.117.

3) Interchange an element (a_{12}) with its reciprocal in

$$\begin{pmatrix} 1 & 2 & 4 & 8 \\ .5 & 1 & 2 & 4 \\ .25 & .5 & 1 & 2 \\ .125 & .25 & .5 & 1 \end{pmatrix} \text{ get } \begin{pmatrix} 1 & .5 & 4 & 8 \\ 2 & 1 & 2 & 4 \\ .25 & .5 & 1 & 2 \\ .125 & .25 & .5 & 1 \end{pmatrix}$$

$\lambda_{max}=4$ C.R = 0 $\lambda_{max}=4.250$ C.R. = .092

Intransitivity

Consider the matrix:

$$\begin{matrix} 1 & 2 & 1/5 \\ 1/2 & 1 & 2 \\ 5 & 1/2 & 1 \end{matrix}$$

C.R. = .933

Construct a matrix with $a_{ij}=1$ except as shown, using values from the above matrix:

$$\begin{pmatrix} 1 & 2 & 1/5 & 1 & 1 & 1 \\ 1/2 & 1 & 2 & 1 & 1 & 1 \\ 5 & 1/2 & 1 & 1 & 1 & 1 \\ 1 & 1 & 1 & 1 & 1 & 1 \\ 1 & 1 & 1 & 1 & 1 & 1 \\ 1 & 1 & 1 & 1 & 1 & 1 \end{pmatrix}$$

C.R. = .105

The inconsistency is increased.

If 1/5 is changed to 1/7 and 5 to 7, C.R. = .099.

If 1/5 is changed to 1/9 and 5 to 9, C.R. = .124.

If some of the 1s are again replaced to obtain

$$\begin{pmatrix} 1 & 2 & 1/5 & 1 & 1 & 1 \\ 1/2 & 1 & 2 & 1 & 1 & 1 \\ 5 & 1/2 & 1 & 1 & 1 & 1 \\ 1 & 1 & 1 & 1 & 2 & 1/5 \\ 1 & 1 & 1 & 1/2 & 1 & 2 \\ 1 & 1 & 1 & 5 & 1/2 & 1 \end{pmatrix}$$

then C.R. = .135.

<u>An Inconsistent Matrix and Its Corresponding Consistent Matrix</u>

$$A = \begin{pmatrix} 1 & 5 & 9 \\ 1/5 & 1 & 3 \\ 1/9 & 1/3 & 1 \end{pmatrix} \begin{pmatrix} .751 \\ .178 \\ .070 \end{pmatrix}$$

C. R. = .025

Forming the matrix of ratios from the derived scale values we have:

$$\left(\frac{w_i}{w_j}\right) = \begin{pmatrix} 1 & 4.2 & 10.7 \\ .238 & 1 & 2.5 \\ .093 & .4 & 1 \end{pmatrix}$$

If instead of the above we use a consistent matrix then we get:

$$\begin{pmatrix} 1 & 5 & 15 \\ 1/5 & 1 & 3 \\ 1/15 & 1/3 & 1 \end{pmatrix}\begin{pmatrix} .789 \\ .158 \\ .052 \end{pmatrix}$$

and we have:

$$\left(\frac{w_i}{w_j}\right) = \begin{pmatrix} 1 & 5 & 15 \\ 1/5 & 1 & 3 \\ 1/9 & 1/3 & 1 \end{pmatrix}$$

The scale 2^x reverses ranks:

x = n: 1-9 Scale

$$\begin{pmatrix} 1 & 2 & 3 & 1 \\ 1/2 & 1 & 6 & 1 \\ 1/3 & 1/6 & 1 & 1/3 \\ 1 & 1 & 3 & 1 \end{pmatrix}\begin{pmatrix} .3477 \\ .2939 \\ .0808 \\ .2775 \end{pmatrix}$$

C. R. = .062

$2^{(n-1)/2}$

$$\begin{pmatrix} 1 & 2^{1/2} & 2^{1} & 1 \\ .707 & 1 & 2^{2.5} & 1 \\ 1/2 & .176 & 1 & 1/2 \\ 1 & 1 & 2 & 1 \end{pmatrix}\begin{pmatrix} .2966 \\ .3334 \\ .1064 \\ .2636 \end{pmatrix}$$

C. R. = .065

and some ranks are reversed.

The Consistency of a Hierarchy

The consistency of a hierarchy is obtained by taking the ratio of the sums of products of each consistency index C.I., with the composite priority of its criterion to the sums of the products of the random consistency index for that order matrix with the composite priority of the corresponding criterion (as used in the numerator). In general the ratio should be in the neighborhood of 0.10 in order not to cause concern for needed improvements in the judgments.

Let n_j, $j = 1, 2, \ldots, h$, be the number of elements in the jth level of the hierarchy. Let w_{ij} be the composite weight of the ith criterion of the jth level, and let $\mu_{i,j+1}$ be the consistency index of all elements in the (j+1)st level compared with respect to the ith criterion of the jth level.

The consistency index of a hierarchy is defined by

$$C_H = \sum_{j=1}^{h} \sum_{i=1}^{n_{i_{j+1}}} w_{ij}\mu_{i,j+1}$$

where $w_{ij} = 1$ for $j = 1$, and $n_{i_{j+1}}$ is the number of elements of the (j+1)st level with respect to the ith criterion of the jth level.

The Consistency of a System

Let $|C_{\bar{k}}|$ be the number of elements of $C_{\bar{k}}$, and let $w_{(k)(h)}$ be the priority of the impact of the hth component on the kth component, i.e., $w_{(k)(h)} = w_{(k)}(C_h)$ or $w_{(k)} : C_h \quad w_{(k)(h)}$.

If we label the components of a system along lines similar to those we followed for a hierarchy, and denote by w_{jk} the limiting priority of the jth element in the kth component, we have

$$C_S = \sum_{k=1}^{s} \sum_{j=1}^{n_k} w_{jk} \sum_{h=1}^{|C_{\bar{k}}|} w_{(k)(h)}\mu_k(j,h)$$

where $\mu_k(j,h)$ is the consistency index of the pairwise comparison matrix of the elements in the kth component with respect to the jth element in the hth component.

Why Tolerate 10% Inconsistency

The priority of consistency to obtain a coherent explanation of a set of facts must differ by an order of magnitude from the priority of inconsistency which is an error in the measurement of consistency. Thus on a scale from zero to one, inconsistency should not exceed 10% by very much. Note that the requirement of 10% should not be made much smaller such as 1% or .1%. The reason is that inconsistency itself is important for without it, new knowledge which changes preference order cannot be admitted. Assuming all knowledge to be consistent contradicts experience which requires continued adjustment in understanding. Thus the objective of developing a wide ranging consistent framework depends on admitting some inconsistency.

Why the Limit of Seven Elements

There are two explanations which one can give to justify the use of not much more than seven elements in a comparison scheme.

Neural Explanation

The first has to do with the brain limit on the identification of simultaneous events. The perception or simultaneity span is the ratio of the buffer-delay time to the attentional integration time. Some psychologists have found that the more intense the stimulus the greater the perception or simultaneity span. The reason for this is that with increased intensity the time of rapid additional integration is reduced. The most common duration time estimate for the short term memory (buffer-delay) is 750 milliseconds and that for item-integration time is 100 milliseconds. Their ratio is about seven.

Consistency Explanation

In making pairwise comparisons, errors in judgment and errors arising out of inconsistency in judgments affect the final answer. If the number of items is large, then their relative priorities would be small and error can distort these priorities considerably. If the number of items is small and the priorities are comparable a small error does not affect the order of magnitude of the answers and hence the relative priorities would be about the same. For this to happen, the items must be less than ten so their values on the whole would be over 10% each and hence remain relatively unaffected by 1% error for example.

RATIO SCALES

The AHP is used to arrange the objects in comparable magnitudes from the very large to the very small in levels of the hierarchy. After performing comparisons of the stimuli (or elements) in each level, it synthesizes the relative magnitudes in the entire hierarchy to make it possible to compare and rank all the stimuli in all levels.

The top element or goal of the hierarchy, whatever its absolute magnitude g, when compared with itself yields a ratio of g/g=1. From then on the comparison process decomposes this derived unit among the elements in each succeeding level. Let us examine the kind of numbers obtained in this operation.

At each level of the hierarchy, the total priorities derived must reflect an appropriate distribution of the unit value of the goal among the elements of that level. For example, all the elements of the second level must be compared according to how much of the goal each accounts for. Their resulting priorities, $w_1, w_2, \ldots, w_n$ must sum to unity. To determine what portion of the goal each has, we perform a complete set of pairwise comparisons. We have a method for obtaining the priorities $w_1, w_2, \ldots, w_n$. It can be shown that these weights belong to a ratio scale. It is known that the priorities are unique to within a positive multiplicative constant and hence belong to an underlying ratio scale. They become unique by normalizing. The resulting derived vector reflects the portion of the decomposition of unity which each element receives. For the third level elements let us assume that the priorities with respect to the n criteria of the second level are given in the following columns:

$$\begin{pmatrix} w_{11} & w_{12} & w_{1n} \\ w_{21} & w_{22} & w_{2n} \\ \cdot & \cdot & \cdot \\ \cdot & \cdot & \cdot \\ \cdot & \cdot & \cdot \\ w_{m1} & w_{m2} & w_{mn} \end{pmatrix}$$

Each column belongs to a different ratio scale, i.e., each scale has a different constant multiplier that is positive. Thus we may write $w_{ij} = a_j x_{ij}$, $j = 1, \ldots, n$ for all i. For each scale a_j transforms the x_{ij} reading on that scale derived with respect to the jth criterion in the second level to w_{ij}.

Hierarchic composition with the w_{ij} scales yields

$$\sum_{j=1}^{n} w_j w_{ij}, \; i = 1, \ldots, m \qquad (1)$$

On the other hand, hierarchic composition with the x_{ij} scales yields

$$\sum_{j=1}^{n} w_j x_{ij}, \quad i = 1, \ldots, m \tag{2}$$

First the problem is to show that (1) and (2) belong to the <u>same</u> ratio scale. We need the following theorem. Before stating the theorem let us define the standard form of a vector x, from a ratio scale, to be its normalized form which is

$$x_i / \sum_{j=1}^{n} x_j, \quad i = 1, \ldots, n.$$

<u>Theorem</u>: Two vectors derived from the same set of comparisons belong to the same ratio scale if, and only if, they are identical in standard form.

<u>Proof</u>: Two vectors $x = (x_1, \ldots, x_n)$, $y = (y_1, \ldots, y_n)$ belong to the same ratio scale if they differ by a multiplicative constant. Thus $x = ay$, and

$$\frac{x_i}{\sum_{i=1}^{n} x_i} = \frac{ay_i}{\sum_{i=1}^{n} ay_i} = \frac{y_i}{\sum_{i=1}^{n} y_i}$$

and they have the same standard form.

Conversely, if the normalized values of two scales coincide then they must belong to the same ratio scale since

$$\frac{x_i}{\sum_{i=1}^{n} x_i} = \frac{y_i}{\sum_{i=1}^{n} y_i}.$$

implies

$$x_i = \left(\sum_{i=1}^{n} x_i / \sum_{i=1}^{n} y_i\right) y_i \text{ or } x_i = ay_i \text{ for all } i.$$

Thus we may take the normalized form of a ratio scale as its standard representation. Since x_{ij} belong to a ratio scale, we assume it is already in standard form and hence $\sum_{i=1}^{m} x_{ij} = 1$

We now show that hierarchical composition yields a ratio scale if all ratio scales used are expressed in their standard form.

<u>Theorem</u>: $\sum_{j=1}^{n} w_j w_{ij} = C \sum_{j=1}^{n} w_j x_{ij}$ for all i for some $C > 0$ if a_j = constant

<u>Proof</u>: (1) can be written as $\sum_{j=1}^{n} w_j w_{ij} = \sum_{j=1}^{n} a_j w_j x_{ij}$. To prove that a_j $j = 1, \ldots m$ is a positive constant we show that the normalized values of (1) coincide with the normalized values of (2). Thus we must show that the following equality holds:

$$\frac{\sum_{j=1}^{n} a_j x_{ij} w_j}{\sum_{i,j=1}^{m,n} a_j x_{ij} w_j} = \frac{\sum_{j=1}^{n} x_{ij} w_j}{\sum_{i,j=1}^{m,n} x_{ij} w_j} \text{ for all } i.$$

This equality can be written as follows. (Recall that $\sum_{j=1}^{n} w_j = 1$ and $\sum_{j=1}^{m} x_{ij} = 1$)

$$\sum_{j=1}^{n} \frac{a_j w_j}{\sum_{h=1}^{n} a_h w_h} x_{ij} = \sum_{j=1}^{n} w_j x_{ij}$$

A sufficient condition for this equality to hold is

$$\frac{a_j w_j}{\sum_{h=1}^{n} a_h w_h} = w_j \text{ or } a_j = \sum_{h=1}^{n} a_h w_h = C, \; j = 1, \ldots, n$$

i.e., a_j is constant C for all j. In general, this is not a necessary condition since $\sum_{i=1}^{3} \alpha_i x_i = \sum_{i=1}^{3} \beta_i x_i$, $\sum_{i=1}^{3} \alpha_i = 1 = \sum_{i=1}^{3} \beta_i$, $0 \le x_i \le 1$ does not imply $\alpha_i = \beta_i$. Take $\alpha_1 = .4$, $\alpha_2 = .2$, $\alpha_3 = .4$; $\beta_1 = .2$, $\beta_2 = .5$, $\beta_3 = .3$; $x_1 = .4$, $x_2 = .5$,

$x_3 = .7$. However, it can be shown by substituting $\alpha_1 = 1 - \alpha_2$, $\beta_1 = 1 - \beta_2$ that the condition is necessary for $n = 2$.

The foregoing sufficiency condition can be ensured if and only if all vectors in the hierarchy whatever their underlying ratio scale are taken in their standard form, i.e., instead of $w_{ij} = a_j x_{ij}$ we write

$$\frac{w_{ij}}{\sum_{i=1}^{m} w_{ij}} = \frac{a_j x_{ij}}{\sum_{i=1}^{m} a_j x_{ij}} = \frac{a_j x_{ij}}{a_j \sum_{i=1}^{m} x_{ij}} = \frac{x_{ij}}{\sum_{i=1}^{m} x_{ij}}$$

and hence $C = 1$ and $a_j = 1$.

LINEARITY AND NONLINEARITY - THE COMPOSITION PRINCIPLE

Cognitive psychology points out that we learn by making comparisons of which pairwise comparisons are the simplest. At least in theory one can speak of comparisons of any number of objects. Comparisons lead to ratios which generate ratio scales linking judgments to measurement.

It is desirable to preserve the ratio scale property when we conduct comparisons on alternatives with respect to diverse criteria. Multiplying the weights of the alternatives by the weights of the criteria and adding is one way of doing this. In addition this approach can be generalized to feedback systems in a way that is consistent with the theory of Markov Chains. Thus the weighting procedure of alternatives and criteria is a special case of a more general approach dealing with systems with feedback.

Still it has been suggested that alternative methods of normalization and composition be used. It is worth examining these. At the end we give a conjecture that is relevant to all these procedures.

Several proposals have been made to change the method of normalization and composition in the AHP. One proposal has been to normalize each eigenvector by the value of its maximum component which implies that the constant multiplier for each ratio scale is different and the composition no longer yields a ratio scale. The reason for this proposal was to make sure that if an additional alternative is introduced into the comparison, the ranking of the original alternatives would be preserved.

It has also been suggested that the linear composition principle of the AHP should be replaced by other procedures, e.g., by a quasi-concave function

$$f\left(\sum_{i=1}^{n} m_i x_i\right) \geq \min_i f(x_i)$$

Another suggestion is: instead of multiplying an eigenvector by the weight of its corresponding criterion, each of its components should be raised to the power of that criterion, perhaps relating the two by approximating $(1 + x)^p$ by $1 + px$ (or px by $(1 + x)^p - 1$).

Division by Maximum Component Value

As already mentioned it has been proposed by V. Belton and her colleague T. Gear to divide each eigenvector component by the value of its largest component. It was believed that this would preserve rank order among the old alternatives when a new one is introduced. The weights of the criteria are kept the same. The usual process of normalizing the eigenvector to unity can reverse rank (as it might when new information is introduced) and the authors felt that people's customary intuition calls for it to remain the same - particularly when the weights of the criteria do not change. We offer a counter example to show that the proposed procedure does not always preserve rank. Consider three criteria a, b, and c and three alternatives A, B and C. Let us first compare alternatives B and C with respect to each criterion. We have:

a	B	C
B	1	1/2
C	2	1

b	B	C
B	1	35/30
C	30/35	1

c	B	C
B	1	3
C	1/3	1

The normalized eigenvectors are given by

a	b	c
.33	.5385	.75
.67	.4615	.25

If we assume that the criteria have weights (1/3, 1/3, 1/3) the composite weights of B and C are .540 and .460 and B is preferred to C. If we divide each eigenvector by the value of the largest component in the eigenvector we have

1/2	1	1
1	.8571	1/3

and the composite weights show that B is again preferred to C. Now let us introduce A and maintain the above comparison values for B and C. We have

a	A	B	C
A	1	2	1
B	1/2	1	1/2
C	1	2	1

b	A	B	C
A	1	1	35/30
B	1	1	35/30
C	30/35	30/35	1

c	A	B	C
A	1	2	6
B	1/2	1	3
C	1/6	1/3	1

The normalized eigenvectors are

.4	.35	.6
.2	.35	.3
.4	.30	.1

The composite values are A = .450, B = 283, C = .267 and A is preferred to B which is preferred to C (the last two preserve their rank order). However, the proposed procedure yields:

$$\begin{pmatrix} 1 & 1 & 1 \\ 1/2 & 1 & 1/2 \\ 1 & .8571 & 1/6 \end{pmatrix}$$

from which A = 3, B = 2 and C = 2.024 and here C is preferred to B.

With different normalization, one would lose the ratio scale property in composition. Contrary to a long held belief that the rank of old alternatives should remain the same when new ones appear this may not always be the case as new knowledge can alter our appreciation of the old-essential to allow for growth. The supermatrix approach is an abstract procedure for dealing with complex systems. It assumes that there could be interdependence between criteria and alternatives and that the weights of both could change when new alternatives and that the weights of both could change when new alternatives are added. Thus one cannot simply assume that in general the weights of the criteria would remain the same. (See Appendix for discussion of rank.)

New Rules of Composition

Now let us examine the general concern that one should adopt other methods for composing priorities to deal with different structural criteria such as preserving some kind of constraint on rank order. For example, it may be desired to advance an undominated alternative as the most desired one. This may be a reasonable expectation as we now show by an example due to Pekka Korhonen of Helsinki.

Consider the problem of two criteria (English and typing) and three alternatives (secretaries who apply for a job). Assume that the two criteria are equally weighted and that the weighting of the alternatives with respect to the two criteria when normalized to unity is as follows:

Secretary	Criterion 1(.5)	Criterion 2(.5)
A	.111	.615
B	.278	.231
C	.611	.154

Alternative B cannot come out as the best alternative using linear weighting although it is not fully dominated by either A or C, and is thought to show greater balance with respect to both criteria taken together. Thus it is easy to prove that for no choice of α & β is $.287\,\alpha + .231\beta$ for $\alpha \geq 0$, $\alpha + \beta = 1$ greater than $.111\alpha + .615\beta$ or $.611\alpha + .154\beta$.

Take another case without normalization. Suppose in fact B is a winner as shown below.

	α =.5	β =.5	Composite
A	1	10	5.5
B	6	6	6
C	10	1	5.5

Let us now change the judgments as follows

	α =.5	β =.5	Composite
A	1	10	5.5
B	5	5	5
C	10	1	5.5

so that B is now a loser on a slight change of the values in the second row. Because B shows greater balance, it may be desired to keep it the winner which cannot be done by linear weighting. However it can by using a quasi concave function although in practice it is not easy to find a unique form for such a function. What should be done? Can one continue to use linear weighting or should one now change to the new function?

Assume that we are dealing with a situation where in addition to balance we also require a balancing of the weighting for the alternatives judged according to some criterion but not others. Some of the important criteria may have many descendants which then each receives a smaller overall value than others, not a desirable outcome. What should the new weighting function be? Or alternatively consider a situation when taken as a group a subset of alternatives is undominated although single ones among them may actually be dominated, how do we satisfy such a situation? The subset may be policies which must be applied together and not singly?

Again consider a hierarchy of several levels when the above properties hold among the different levels, now the composition rule may have to be varied among the levels.

Finally, one can think of a number of other "structural" requirements in addition to the two just cited, how do we develop a composition scheme that is so general that it can cope with all contingencies? An adaptive and hence a modifiable scheme that appears to be general enough to respond to such needs is to choose one rule of composition, but increase the number of criteria to include the desired structural criteria. Then the judgment process should favor those alternatives that are desired as an outcome under these criteria. In this manner one can deal with a situation in which the desired mathematical structure becomes a part of the overall evaluation.

Finally it is useful to note that the feedback systems approach does in fact lead to a linear composition and to a ratio scale scheme. It would be interesting to see how one would handle such a general situation under alternative considerations and what meaning one would attach to the numbers obtained that way.

Conjecture: Given a desired property for the alternatives and given a composition scheme which captures this property, there is always some other desired property which is not satisfied by the composition and requires a new composition scheme that now must satisfy both properties together.

Solution: A solution of the problem stated in the conjecture is to include among the functional criteria for evaluating the alternatives other criteria, which we call structural criteria. They are simply another kind of functional criteria which relate to abstract relations desired for the alternatives. The above conjecture indicates that, like functional criteria, there is always the possibility of new structural criteria and there is no reason to hope that there would be closure on what they can ever be. They are properties of the mind seeking order and these properties and their importance can change with experience.

Thus one should preserve the ratio scale property and introduce criteria in order to derive the desired weights for the alternatives to meet certain structural requirements.

Recapitulation

From cognitive psychology we know that perception is acquired through pairwise comparisons. Pairwise comparisons give rise to ratio scales provided they use positive numbers. These numbers would become useful if the numbers used in the comparisons can be shown to express the intensity of perception reflected in the comparisons. Hierarchical composition is a way of generating scales by comparing homogeneous objects from level to level, with one order magnitude difference. If it is possible to compare alternatives directly with respect to the goal we would also obtain a ratio scale. Then what property must scales satisfy so that their composition gives rise to a ratio scale? Composition requires that all ratio scales be in standard form. This is necessary and sufficient.

It is sufficient because from

$$\Sigma a_j w_j b_j w_{ij} = \Sigma a_j w_j w_{ij} = k\Sigma w_j w_{ij}$$

we can put $a_j = k$ and in particular because the goal has unit weight $k = 1$.

It is necessary because if $a_j \neq k$ then the result cannot yield a ratio scale and would not be equivalent to the ratio scale obtained by comparing the goal.

When dealing with group judgments we had proved sometime ago (which has been generalized in a recent paper with J. Aczel [1]) that the geometric mean is the unique way to combine group judgments to maintain consistency for that group.

COMPARISONS WITH OTHER WORK

For a long time people have been concerned with the measurement of both physical and psychological events. The physical is concerned with things outside the person doing the measuring. It is objective. The psychological is concerned with how we perceive and interpret internally what we experience and how we feel. It is subjective. Scientists have used a diversity of mathematical approaches to structure the problems they encounter and to perform measurement within this structure. Many have worked on measurement and on judgment solicitation. The AHP falls into this broad category of mathematical and behavioral science interests. In the AHP dominance matrices play a central role. Special effort has been made to characterize them.

Shepard [25] has noted a more extensive research on proximity, profile and conjoint measurement than on measurement associated with dominance matrices.

The AHP uses pairwise comparisons in its dominance matrices. Thurstone's model [30] of comparative judgment also uses pairwise comparison of the objects, but only to the extent that one is more preferred to or greater than another but does not get into how strongly greater. He then recovers information over the stimuli by imposing assumptions of normality on the judgmental process. Under additional assumptions on the parameters, he recovers various "metric" information on the stimuli. A number of restrictions are associated with Thurstone's approach. For example, Guildord [12] recommends limiting the range of probabilities that one stimulus is judged to be more than another.

Torgerson [31] has systematized and extended Thurstone's method for scaling; in particular, concentrating on the case in which covariance terms are constant, correlation terms equal, and distributions homoscedastic, i.e., they have equal variances.

Luce and Suppes [19] and Suppes and Zinnes [29] have proposed what Coombs [7] calls the Bradley-Terry-Luce (BTL) model using the logistic curve which is a log transform of the probability distribution. Although this is different from assuming normality, in practice it is difficult to distinguish between the BTL model and the case in Thurstone's work where he assumes normal distributions and equal variances. The BTL model is more rigorously grounded in a theory of choice behavior. Coombs discusses the essential distinction between the two models.

We can contrast the assumptions used in the AHP with those used in the psychometric tradition above. We do not begin with the supposition that ratio judgments are independent probabilistic processes. Instead, we investigate the consequence of changes in the judgments through perturbations on the entire set of judgments. This type of approach leads to the criterion of consistency. Thus, obtaining solutions in our method is not a statistical procedure.

Briefly, many psychometric methods perform aggregation of judgments in the course of solving for a scale. We assume that if there is aggregation of judgments, it occurs prior to the ratio estimate between two stimuli. Therefore, our solution procedure is not concerned with assumptions of distributions of judgments. However, if we want to compare any solution with the criterion of consistency, we appeal to statistical reasoning and perturbations over the entire matrix of judgments.

Our use of metric information in the matrix of subjects' judgments generates strong parallels with principal component analysis, except that the data give dominance rather than similarity or covariance information. In principal component analysis λ_{max} is emphasized, but one also solves for all the λ's. However, the results must be interpreted differently [15].

In our analysis the nature of the stimuli and the task presented to subjects are also similar to "psychophysical" scaling, as typified by Stevens and Galanter [27] and recently used widely in many attempts to construct composite measures of political variables including "national power." Stevens' technique imposes consistency by asking the subjects to compare simultaneously each stimulus with all others, producing only one row of our matrix. This means that the hypothesis of unidimensionality cannot be tested directly. If Stevens' method is used, one should take care that the judgments over stimuli are known to be consistent or nearly so. In addition, there is no way of relating one scale to another as we do in the AHP.

Krantz [17] has axiomatized alternative processes relating stimuli to judgments and has derived existence theorems for ratio scales. Comparable axiomation has not been extended to hierarchies of ratio scales.

Some people have approached problems of scaling as if the cognitive space of stimuli were inherently multidimensional, but we choose instead to decompose this multidimensional structure hierarchically in order to establish a quantitative as well as qualitative relation among dimensions. The individual dimensions in multidimensional scaling solutions functionally resemble individual eigenvectors on any one level of our hierarchy.

The formal problem of constructing a scale as the normalized eigenvector w in the equation $Aw = \lambda w$, for λ a maximum, is similar to extracting the first principal component. When subjects are asked to fill the cells of only one row or one column and the other cells are computed from these (to insure "perfect consistency") the first eigenvalue, n, represents 100% of the variance in the matrix. If, however, "perfect consistency" applies to the data except that a normally distributed random component is added to each cell of the matrix, then one's theory of data would lead to principal factor analysis, and a "single-factor" solution would result. Thus, the imposition of perfect consistency by the experimenter produces an uninteresting result of exact scalability, which was assured by the experimental design of single comparisons. In fact, one can see that if the subjects fill only one row or column of the matrix and if the subjects' task is to generate ratios between pairs of stimuli, then the procedure is formally equivalent to having the subjects locate each stimulus along a continuum with a natural zero at one end: this is the "direct-intensity" technique of psychophysical scaling.

We have often used the logarithmic least squares approach as a quick way to estimate the eigenvector by normalizing the geometric mean of the columns. In a recent work with L. Vargas we have studied the eigenvalue approach with the least squares and logarithmic least squares methods to develop conditions for rank preservation.

Tucker [32] presents a method for the "determination of parameters of a functional relation by factor analysis." He states, however, that "the rotation of axes problem remains unsolved ...," that is, the factor analysis determines the parameters only within a linear transformation. Cliff [6] suggests methods for the determination of such transformations where a prior theoretical analysis or observable quantities provide a criterion toward which to rotate the arbitrary factor solution.

The hierarchical composition is an inductive generalization of the following idea. We are given weights of elements in one level. We generate a matrix of column eigenvectors of the elements in the level immediately below this level with respect to each element in this level. Then we use the vector of (weights of) elements in this level to weight the corresponding column eigenvectors. Multiplying the matrix of eigenvectors with the column vector of weights gives the composite vector of weights of the lower-level elements.

Because the matrix of eigenvectors is not an orthogonal transformation, in general the result cannot be interpreted as a rotation. In fact, we are multiplying a vector in the unit m-simplex by a stochastic matrix. The result is another vector in the unit simplex. Algebraists have often pointed to a distinction between problems whose algebra has a structural geometric interpretation and those in which algebra serves as a convenient method for doing calculations. Statistical methods have a convenient geometric interpretation. Perturbation methods frequently may not.

In the works of Hammond and Summers [13] concern is expressed regarding the performance of subjects in situations involving both linear and nonlinear relations among stimuli before concluding that the process of inductive inference is primarily linear. In our model, subjects' responses to linear and nonlinear cues seem to be adequately captured by the pairwise scaling method described here, by using the hierarchical decomposition approach in order to aggregate elements which fall into comparability classes according to the possible range of the scale used for the comparison.

Note that our solution of the information integration problem discussed by Anderson [3] is approached through an eigenvalue formulation which has a linear structure. However, the scale defined by the eigenvector itself is a highly nonlinear function of the data. The process by means of which the eigenvector is generated involves complex addition, multiplication, and averaging. To perceive this complexity one may examine the eigenvector as a limiting solution of the normalized row sums of powers of the matrix.

Anderson [3] also makes a strong point that validation of a response scale ought to satisfy a criterion imposed by the algebraic judgment model. Such a criterion in our case turns out to be consistency.

Multicriterion decision analysis offers a number of alternative approaches. These have been recently reviewed by B. Roy and P. Vincke [20]. They include Multiattribute Utility Theory (MAU) which has been compared with the AHP on several occasions. From a theoretical standpoint MAU seeks to generate utilities on (an interval scale) whereas priorities in the AHP belong to a ratio scale. From a practical standpoint the AHP elicits judgments directly and uses them to synthesize priorities. MAU first derives a utility function by asking questions and then uses it to complete the analysis of a particular decision problem. Two other general approaches to multicriterion decision making are outranking methods and interactive methods. These often involve well defined decision rules in the form of indicators or objective functions sometimes leading to a linear program which is maximized or minimized as the case may be. There is no such optimization in the AHP unless of course one is allocating resources to maximize overall benefits. Finally, differing from most of these procedures the AHP allows for inconsistency as an integral part of the theory. Recognizing that people's ideas are in continuous change and growth, one should not insist on 100% consistency because that could change immediately after the problem is solved. Still one cannot make reliable decisions without an acceptable level of consistency. These concepts are dealt with through the formalization of the AHP.

REFERENCES

[1] J. Aczel and T.L. Saaty, "Procedures for Synthesizing Ratio Judgments," Journal of Math Psychology, Vol. 27, No. 1, 1983.

[2] J.M. Alexander and T.L. Saaty, "The Forward and Backward Processes of Conflict Analysis," Behavioral Science, March 1977.

[3] N.H. Anderson, "Information Integration Theory: A Brief Survey," in D.H. Krantz, R.C. Atkinson, R.D. Luce, and P. Suppes (eds.) Contemporary Developments in Mathematical Psychology, Vol. 2, San Francisco: Freeman, 1974.

[4] D.E. Berlyne, Structure and Direction in Thinking, New York: John Wiley and Sons, 1965.

[5] A.L. Blumenthal, The Process of Cognition, Prentice Hall, 1977.

[6] N. Cliff, "Complete Orders from Incomplete Data: Interactive Ordering and Tailored Testing," Psychology Bulletin, Vol. 82, No. 2, 1975.

[7] C.H. Coombs, A Theory of Data, New York/London/Sydney: Wiley, 1964.

[8] H.J. Einhorn and R.M. Hogarth, "Behavioral Decision Theory: Processes of Judgment and Choice," Annual Review of Psychology, Vol. 32, 1981, pp. 53-88.

[9] D.W. Fiske, Observables and Judgments: Their Utilities in Personality and Behavioral Science, San Francisco: Tossey-Bass, 1979.

[10] S. Freud, The Interpretation of Dreams, (J. Strachey, ed. and trans.) New York: Wiley, 1961.

[11] A.G. Greenwald, "The Totalitarian Ego: Fabrication and Revision of Personal History," American Psychologist, Vol. 35, 603-618, 1980.

[12] J.P. Guilford, "The Method of Paired Comparisons as a Psychometric Method," Psychological Review, Vol. 35, pp. 494-506, 1928.

[13] K.R. Hammond and D.A. Summers, "Cognitive Dependence on Linear and Nonlinear Cues," Psychological Review, Vol. 72, No. 3, pp. 215-224, 1965.

[14] T. Hobbes, _Leviathan_, Indianapolis: Bobbs-Merrill, 1958.

[15] H. Hotelling, "Analysis of a Complex Statistical Variables Into Principal Components," _Journal of Educational Psychology_, Vol. 24, 498-520, 1933.

[16] E. Klinger, "Modes of Normal Conscious Thought," in _The Stream of Consciousness: Scientific Investigations into the Flow of Human Experience_ (K.S. Pope and J.L. Serger, eds.) New York: Plenum Press, 1978.

[17] D.H. Krantz, "A Theory of Magnitude Estimation and Cross Modality Matchings," _Journal of Mathematical Psychology_, Vol. 9, pp. 168-199, 1972.

[18] H. Lebesgue, "Measure Theory," in _Measure and the Intergral_, Holden-Day, 1966; in French Gauthier-Villars, Paris, 1928.

[19] R.D. Luce and P. Suppes, "Preference, Utility and Subjective Probability," in _Handbook of Mathematical Psychology_, Vol. III, 1964.

[20] B. Roy and P. Vincke, "Multicriterion Analysis: Survey and Directions," _European Journal of Operational Research_, Vol. 8, pp. 207-218, 1981.

[21] T.L. Saaty, _The Analytic Hierarchy Process_, New York: McGraw-Hill, 1980.

[22] T.L. Saaty and L.G. Vargas, _The Logic of Priorities_, Boston: Kluwer-Nijhoff Publishing, 1981.

[22a] T.L. Saaty and L.G. Vargas, "Comparison of Eigenvalue, Logarithmic Least Squares and Least Squares Methods in Estimating Ratios," _Mathematical Modelling_, Vol. 5, No. 5, pp. 309-324, 1984.

[23] T.L. Saaty, "A Scaling Method for Priorities in Hierarchical Structures," _Journal of Mathematical Psychology_, Vol. 15, pp. 234-281, 1977.

[24] T.L. Saaty, _Decision Making for Leaders_, Belmont, California: Lifetime Learning Publications, a division of Wadsworth Publishing, 1982.

[25] R.N. Shepard, "A Taxonomy of Some Principal Types of Data and of Multidimensional Methods for their Analysis," in R.N. Shepard, A.K. Romney, and S.B. Nerlove (eds.), _Multidimensional Scaling: Theory and Applications in the Behavioral Sciences_, Vol. I, New York: Seminar Press, pp. 21-47, 1972.

[26] S. Stevens, "Measurement, Psychophysics, and Unity," in C.W. Churchman and P. Ratoosh (eds.) _Measurement, Definitions and Theories_, New York: Wiley, 1959.

[27] S. Stevens and E. Galanter, "Ratio Scales and Category Scales for a Dozen Perceptual Continua," _Journal of Experimental Psychology_, Vol. 54, pp. 377-411, 1964.

[28] W. Suojanen and D.R. Hudson, "Coping with Stress and Addictive Work Behavior," Management and the Brain, (R.C. Bessinger, W. Suojanen, eds.), Georgia State University, 1983.

[29] P. Suppes and J.L. Zinnes, "Basic Measurement Theory," in R.D. Luce, R.R. Bush, E. Galanter (eds.) Handbook of Mathematical Psychology, Vol. 1, 1963.

[30] L.L. Thurstone, "A Law of Comparative Judgment," Psychological Review, Vol. 34, 273-286, 1927.

[31] W.S. Torgerson, Theory and Methods of Scaling, New York: Wiley, 1958.

[32] L.R. Tucker, "Determination of Parameters of a Functional Relation by Factor Analysis," Psychometrika, Vol. 23, No. 1, March 1958.

[33] J. Varendinck, The Psychology of Daydreams, New York: MacMillan, 1921.

[34] L.G. Vargas, "Reciprocal Matrices with Random Coefficients," Mathematical Modelling, Vol. 3, pp. 69-81, 1982.

[35] W. Windelband, A History of Philosophy, (J.H. Tufts, trans.), New York: Harper & Row, 1958.

[36] R.B. Zajonc, "Feeling and Thinking: Preferences Need No Inferences," American Psychologist, pp. 151-175, 1980.

APPENDIX

Rank Preservation and Reversal: Absolute and Relative Measurement in the Analytic Hierarchy Process (References below)

The Analytic Hierarchy Process uses two types of measurement, absolute and relative. Absolute and relative comparisons have been known to cognitive psychologists for some time as the two important ways in which the mind acquires understanding [1]. Absolute comparisons are useful when there is a standard to serve as a frame of reference. Relative comparisons are useful when dealing with intangibles and abstractions and when there are no standards, particularly in new problems where learning takes place.

Traditionally when alternatives are compared with respect to a single attribute it is known that the ranking of the alternatives should not change when a new alternative is introduced, or an old one deleted. If two apples are compared according to redness, the redder one can in no way become less red than the other if a third apple is introduced. This is true no matter how red the third apple is.

If there are several criteria and relative measurement is used, then the introduction of a third apple can lead to rank reversal for the following reason. Each alternative is evaluated in terms of each criterion and a weighting process is applied to these values using the weights of the criteria to obtain a final measurement and ranking for the alternatives. When a new alternative is introduced, it has been traditionally thought that unless it brings new information, there should be no rank reversal. New information was identified with a new criterion because traditionally people used absolute measurement and could see no other way in which there can be new information. However, with relative measurement, new information can take the form of the number of alternatives itself, which changes with the coming and going of alternatives, and the actual measurement values under the different criteria of added or deleted alternatives. Were one to always include in the traditional approach a criterion to represent the number of alternatives being compared, that criterion would change values, and the ranking of alternatives would be seen to change under existing interpretation. In relative measurement, representing such information is in harmony with the mathematics used which requires that all information be considered: the usual familiar kind which we call functional information, having to do with the criteria and the alternatives and their connection to each other, and a new kind which we call structural, having to do with the number of criteria and alternatives and the actual numerical values derived for them. Instead of explicitly writing down criteria for this structural information, it can be interpreted as a set of transformations on the functional criteria which modifies the usual weights they receive. In other words, in relative measurements the weights of functional criteria are modified or rescaled if new alternatives are added or deleted. Thus the criteria can depend on the alternatives in a new way so far not recognized by insisting that one always use absolute measurement. As we said before, rank reversal can only happen under more than a single criterion.

Let us now look at absolute measurement. There are situations in which alternatives may be compared with standards, or ratings, established for each criterion [3], and assigned a position on a relative scale of values. In such cases structural criteria do not affect the calculations, although the information they contain is there, and there can be no rank reversal of alternatives. It may be unrealistic to always keep that information out as has been the case in the traditional approach. There are also situations where it may be desired to include new information from some added alternatives and ignore it for others. In this case the first set may be pairwise compared and the second absolutely measured, and the two pooled together by absolutely measuring a pivot alternative from those that are relatively compared.

Finally, the effect of copies and near copies of alternatives may be of mathematical interest. In some, though not all, decision problems it is desired to keep copies aside so that they have no effect on the final ranking. In the end the copy is assigned the same weight as the original. When an alternative, due to uncertainty of certain tolerable magnitude is regarded as a near copy, it can be absolutely measured and compared with the absolute measurement of the original. If it differs in this absolute comparison on any of the standards, it can be assumed to be a different alternative, otherwise it is treated as a copy. Here a computer program [2] used in relative comparisons is instructed when two alternatives fall within a narrow range for all the criteria (see [4] for further detail) and there is concern that they may actually be copies, to set up an absolute ranking scheme for these alternatives. Such a scheme would involve a quick qualitative check on the ratings of the two alternatives. In this manner, concern about the effect on rank of slight numerical changes in the measurement of alternatives is removed. In reality the problem of copies and near copies is not a mathematical exercise of perturbing numbers, but depends on the perception of the intensity of the attributes in each of these alternatives. When no distinction can be made on all the attributes, the two alternatives would have to be considered identical. The numerical approach to measurement is never a substitute for people's ability to make distinctions, unless it is desired to abdicate control in which case one is at the mercy of the scheme of manipulations being used.

Our expectations regarding what should or might happen to rank has not come from multicriteria methods because the subject is new. It has not come from real life problems, because there is no clear and justifiable theory about rank behavior in practice. Structural information described above cannot be simply swept under the rug even when sometimes people have habitually used absolute instead of relative measurement. In fact, systems theory tells us that things are interdependent and so far we have had little idea of how to deal with dependence with our simple ways of modeling and thinking. Thus it must have come from single criterion behavior which is only a small part of the complexity of multicriteria situations. It may be that our expanded framework will enable us to perceive many new situations where it is legitimate and expected that rank should change because of new alternatives and structural information. Generalization of the AHP to situations with functional dependence enables us to deal with a wider complexity than we have been able to handle so far. In such situations our framework is generalized from hierarchies to network systems with feedback.

[1] Blumenthal, Arthur L., The Process of Cognition, Prentice-Hall, 1977.

[2] Expert Choice (1986). Software Package for the AHP for the IBM PC. Decision Support Software, McLean, VA.

[3] Saaty, Thomas L., "Absolute and Relative Measurement with the AHP," The Most Livable Cities in the United States, Journal of Socio-Economic Planning Sciences, December,1986.

[4] Saaty, Thomas L., "Rank Generation, Preservation and Reversal in the Analytic Hierarchy Decision Process, Decision Sciences, April 1986.

POLICY ANALYSIS AND DECISION AIDS

Stephen Watson
Emmanuel College
Cambridge, UK

PROBLEM DEFINITION

In this paper we shall explore the use of decision aids in policy analysis; but our title is probably too broad since we will be giving an incomplete and partial account of the subject, based on some experiences of constructing decision aids.

First, however, let us define our terms. We take policy analysis to be the activity of analysing, for a particular issue, what policy options are available, evaluating these options, and making recommendations on which option the institution concerned should adopt as its policy. Governmental institutions are the ones that we shall be particularly discussing here, although policy analysis, and the consequent potential for aiding it, takes place in almost all bureaucracies. Policy analysis is, therefore, principally done by civil servants, and what we shall examine in this paper is how decision aids can be of use to civil servants, in that role.

What is a decision aid? The term is used widely, and freely, and, like the term 'expert system,' needs some definition before we can use it in a careful discussion. We shall use a fairly narrow meaning here: we think of a decision aid as a procedure which not only presents information to the policy analyst but also provides a facility for helping him or her to think through the implications of that information. What is more, we shall be particularly interested in aids which the policy analyst can easily use, seated at a desk, and operating a personal computer.

In the next section we shall describe three examples of situations in which attempts have been made to construct such aids, and in the discussion section we place our experience in the context of some of the literature, drawing some tentative conclusions and making some suggestions for research.

NATO ASI Series, Vol. F35
Expert Judgment and Expert Systems
Edited by J. Mumpower et al.

SOME EXAMPLES

An R & D Problem

The first example we shall discuss must necessarily be disguised, but the essence of what we discover will come through the disguise. We were approached by part of a governmental bureaucracy whose task is to fund research and development projects in a particular technological area. They received proposals from a very large number of different sources to support R & D of many different types, and the task of allocating a possibly variable budget devolved onto a committee of representatives of different interests. One member of the committee, an enthusiast for the methods of systems analysis, and frustrated by the decision processes of the committee, suggested that what was needed was a decision aid to help the committee with their work. Members of the secretariat of the committee, some of them keen on the idea of a decision aid, asked us to put forward a proposal. Our suggestion was straightforward; we would establish a scheme for estimating the value, or benefit of each proposal, based on assessments of chance of success, and the potential range of benefits if successful. This evaluation scheme would recognise the value judgments necessary to determine the relative importance of one benefit against another by using an additive value function, the weights for which would be at the disposal of the user. Graphical display methods would rank projects by cost and benefits, and would allow the effect of changing weights to be quickly seen on a screen. We claimed that representation of the problem in this way would distinguish fact from value, would clarify the issues involved, and would lead to greater fairness and consistency in the allocation of funds.

The bureaucrats who approached us liked our proposal, and put it forward for approval by their director. The director, a very able and highly political man, was not at all enthusiastic about our ideas. He was clearly doubtful that any quantitative, computer-based method would be of value in helping him to guide the complicated and subtle decision-making process which he was clearly very good at handling intuitively. To make his point he told us that he had recommended the decision-making committee to approve a project which would almost certainly not have been approved if the clarity which our decision-aid promised had been available. Yet it was important for some overarching political reason that the project was approved, and this reason could not have been disclosed to the committee; if it had, they would have used their power to block the project. So our proposal was not accepted.

What can we learn from this experience? The following points are worth making:

- The clarity of representation afforded by a computer based decision may hinder, rather than enhance, organisational decision making processes. If everybody in an organisation had a clear understanding of everything that was going on, it is likely that nothing could be done.

- Enthusiasm for decision aiding as a concept does not inevitably lead to the construction of a useful decision aid. People who wish to see greater consistency and objectivity in decision making may understate the value of obscurity.

- Care must be taken, in the construction of a decision aid, to ensure that (a) the aid addresses a real decision problem, (b) the potential users of the aid are likely to find the representation of their problem valid, and (c) there are not extraneous factors which will render the aid useless, or worse, dangerous.

Radioactive Waste Management

We can be more open about this second example, since the results have appeared in a British government publication [1]. An enquiry into the use of sea dumping for radioactive waste [2] recommended that the UK Department of the Environment should make a comparative assessment of all options for the disposal of radioactive waste. In particular, the Department was asked to determine the 'Best Practicable Environmental Option' (BPEO) for a number of different types of waste. This concept had been introduced by the Royal Commission on Environmental Pollution. While attractive, in that it sought for an option that was not too expensive and did not produce too many negative effects, it remained an ill-defined concept.

The Department sought our advice, and we suggested a decision aid which we felt would help them in their representation of the situation. We pointed out that while it might be possible, in a reasonably non-controversial way, to identify possible management options, and even to measure the likely performance of these different options with respect to a number of criteria (such as cost, radiological exposure to workers, to the public, etc.), there was likely to be considerable difference of opinion in the community about how to weigh these criteria against each other. We stressed that there was, therefore, no unique scientific answer to the question of what the best option was; it all depended on trade-offs, such as how much money ought to be spent to reduce the exposure of workers to radiation by one unit. It was important for the Department to present a method that could be defended, was easy to understand, and yet recognised the essentially political nature of the choice of disposal option. We constructed a simple additive value function as an index of goodness; moreover it was linear in the quantities measured, which were mostly monetary (in millions of pounds), or concerning exposure to radiation (in millisieverts). Consultants were engaged to determine how each option scored with respect to each criterion, but the weights by which these scores were multiplied, representing as they did judgments on the relative importance of the different criteria, could not be objectively determined.

We argued for representing the analysis on a simple spreadsheet program so that senior advisors and decision makers could see how differences in the weights affected the ranking of the options. This was not acceptable, however, since it was felt that the senior people concerned would be unlikely to have either the time or the interest to use a computer rather than the executive summary of a report. Therefore, we could not do what we felt to be proper, that is, to leave the choice of weights to the decision-maker; on the other hand we had no basis for suggesting weights of our own, and indeed such an intrusion of an analyst's views into the political process is one of the phenomena that quantitative decision aids are designed to overcome. We compromised by putting forward four different sets of weights, which might be interpreted as a consensus position. We chose our sets of weights to illustrate positions which different groups seem to have taken. One set put no weight on radiation doses which would be incurred more than 1000 years into the future, and limited the cost of current radiation doses to standards currently adopted in the nuclear industry; this set could well represent views of managers in the nuclear industry. Another set put a far higher price on a unit of radiation exposure, and valued future doses as an order of magnitude more significant than current doses; people in the environmental movement could well subscribe to such views.

The report of the study [1] ranked the management options for each set of weights (using the weighted score to determine the rank). The report then used the resulting information to argue that while for some kinds of wastes there seemed to be agreement as to what to do (and it was not sea dumping!), this was not generally so. The analysis showed that the Best Practicable Environmental Option depended on such important questions as how much we should pay to prevent a member of the public from being exposed to radiation, and how significant are the spatial and temporal distribution of doses. While, stated coldly, these conclusions are obvious, the analysis showed that there is no objective answer to what to do with nuclear waste, despite politicans' desires that this might be so!

The analysis has been well received in general, although some aspects of its reception have demonstrated some of the subtleties involved in getting this sort of decision aid used. Some points we have noticed include:

- Senior decision-makers in government seem to be suspicious of computer-based representations of problems. There is, at least in part of the British government, insufficient enthusiasm for the use of personal computers to allow a high-level decision aid, implemented on a computer, to be accepted. It is not clear if this is simply a lack of familiarity with machines, as we suspect, or a genuine appreciation that decision aids of this type can alter organisational decision-making processes for the worse.

- Decision aids have to recognise the tension between scientists and administrators. In the UK Civil Service there has long been a clear cut distinction between the scientists, who determine the facts, and the administrators, who determine policy. Our decision aid bridged that gap, since, although it was sponsored by the scientists, who had been asked to determine the facts about radioactive waste, the aid discussed policy options, and even showed how differences in value judgments led to different policies. There was some opposition to this approach from senior administrators who felt that the scientists had overstepped the traditional dividing line between them.

- The simplicity of the aid was a definite advantage. There are clearly many ways that a more sophisticated and complex evaluation procedure for management options could have been constructed. We could have taken explicit account of uncertainty and risk preference using a multi-attribute utility function; we could have investigated whether non-linear or non-additive representations were more faithful to people's value structures; we could have constructed more detailed economic models of the costs of different systems. None of these, in our view, would have assisted the representation of the problem, since they would have made the aid more difficult to understand, without being significantly more faithful to the realities.

- We only included a subset of the possible criteria in our model. We represented cost and radiological damage, but did not give explicit representation to non-radiological environmental damage, or to the many social and political factors which the management of radioactive waste is likely to engender. They were omitted because the time and money was not available to measure these effects well, and also because considerable judgment was needed to obtain measures. Our sponsors did not want subjectivity to enter into the measurement of the effect of options, as well as into the weights. There was an understandable unwillingness of the scientists to present figures which did not have the apparent 'hardness' of pounds or sieverts.

Acid Deposition

Our third example concerns work which was again performed for the UK Department of the Environment, this time to provide a decision aid to help policy makers think through the acid rain problem. We have documented the first stage of its development elsewhere [3], and the second stage is currently under way; we shall give only a very brief summary here. We have constructed a simple representation of the relationship between actions open to a government (legislation to limit the emission of sulphur and nitrogen oxides), and the likely costs and benefits to be derived from such action. The representation is realised as a program on a personal computer. The user of the program specifies particular emission levels for the UK, and probability distributions for action taken by other governments, the movement of pollutants across frontiers, the relationship between the deposition of pollutants and damage and the stock of sensitive material at risk. As in the previous example, the trade-offs between costs and benefits, being a subjective matter, must be considered by the decision-maker; the computer program allows the user to specify what these weights will be.

So far this aid has had only potential success, rather than actual success, since it is yet to be used in earnest by policy analysts. It is worthwhile, however, mentioning some points we have encountered in its development.

- A problem in the way of this aid is the organisational context in which it has been sponsored. Economic advisers have perceived the need for an analysis of this kind, but support among scientists and administrators has been mixed. Scientists are concerned about the roughness and inexactness of the model, while administrators do not see the relevance of the analysis for their particular problems. In this organisational context the analyst has to be open to what is really needed, and the virtues of the aid must be carefully explained to those who formulate policy.

- A feature of this decision aid is the graphical input and output provided. A map of the UK, divided up into grid squares, can show pollutant emissions and depositions, and estimated costs and benefits, on a disaggregated or aggregated basis. Dose-response relationships between pollutant levels and damage are also displayed graphically, and there are bar chart representations of the benefits available. It appears that this use of computer graphics is a valuable part of this aid, and that several potential users find this aspect appealing.

DISCUSSION

There is a growing body of literature on the construction and use of decision aids for policy analysis. In this last section we shall discuss some of the key ideas from some of this literature, in the light of the three cases discussed above.

Accounts of the use of models (as distinct from decision aids) in policy analysis have been available for some time (see, for example, [4]), and some of the difficulties that the formality of such models entail are well-documented [5]. The problems of using a Decision Support System (as opposed simply to models) in policy analysis has not been so well discussed, although P. G. W. Keen, in his now standard 1978 book [6] has some very valuable things to say about the need to work very closely with potential users when constructing a DSS.

A more recent paper by Keen [7] makes some important observations to which our examples may be related. He talks about the frequent presence of 'social inertia' and 'counterimplementation' when Decision Support Systems are introduced to an organisation. The first of these phenomena is the tendency of organisations to resist change in the way decision-making is done, and the second is the appearance of positive initiatives to ensure that the changes don't come about, or are ineffective. While some of this resistance may be for negative reasons, such as avoidance of work, protection of spheres of influence, or fear of change, there are some important positive reasons why social inertia and counterimplementation may come about. As Keen points out: formal analysis of quantitative information is often only a minor aspect of the situation; data are not merely an intellectual commodity, but also a political resource, whose redistribution affects the interests of particular groups; managers prefer concrete and verbal data to formal analysis. Lenz and Lyles [8] support the view that there can be too great a stress on rationality in decision aids. We have definitely encountered opposition to our ideas for the introduction of decision aids into the policy process. In all three cases discussed above, some members of the bureaucracies involved displayed social inertia, by not being interested, or by not seeing the relevance of the aid; and in the first case we see a very strong example of counterimplementation, where the counterimplementer, the director, refused to allow development of the aid in the first place!

More detailed considerations of how decision aids might fit into policy analysis have been given by Vari and Vecsenyi [9] and Humphreys and Berkeley [10]. They point out how important it is to identify the level in an organisation at which a decision aid is to operate, if it is to be effective. Humphreys and Berkeley use Jacques' [11] characterisation of roles within an organisation into a number of different levels to argue that the kind of decision aid which is useful for people at one level in an organisation may not have any value for people operating at another level. Vari and Vecsenyi [9] stress the importance of determining the roles and the motives of the participants in the decision-making process, if the aid is to be successful.

Our examples provide evidence of the truth of the latter hypothesis. What stands in the way of our acid rain model is that we are not close to the decision-makers. Responding as we are to the needs of one group of civil servants, as perceived by another group of civil servants, we are not in a very good position to ensure that our aid fits in with the roles and motivations of the decision-makers. In the first example, we are currently trying to ensure that we gain access to the committee which makes the R & D decisions, although this is proving difficult for political reasons.

On the other hand, there does not appear to be any easy way that the concept of levels in a hierarchy, stressed by Humphreys and Berkeley, is relevant to our examples. It may be that government departments do not fit into the Jacquesian framework, since so many civil servants are 'staff' rather than 'line' to use a military analogy. Our difficulty in each of these examples is not so much the different levels within the organisation, but rather the diffuse nature of decision-making, distributed as it is between officials, expert committees and ministers.

Our experiences of trying to construct decision aids for policy analysis have shown that it is not an easy matter. What one official wants, another finds unacceptable or, at best, irrelevant. Sometimes for good reasons, such as the preservation of flexibility, and sometimes for bad, such as the fear of novelty, we have encountered opposition to our ideas. But we do not conclude that government cannot be improved by decision aids; what we must do is to learn, through doing, what kind of aid, and in what kind of bureaucratic conditions, can lead to better government.

REFERENCES

[1] Assessment of Best Practicable Environmental Options For Management of Low- and Intermediate-Level Solid Radioactive Wastes, HMSO, London, March 1986.

[2] Report of the Independent Review of Disposal of Radioactive Waste in the North-East Atlantic, HMSO, London, 1984.

[3] Watson, S. R., 'Modelling Acid Deposition for Policy Analysis', Journal of the Operational Research Society, 37, 1986.

[4] Greenberger, M., Crenson, M. A., and Crissey, B. L., 'Models in the Policy Process', Russell Sage Foundation, New York, 1976.

[5] Hoos, I. R., 'Systems Analysis in Public Policy: a Critique', University of California Press, 1972.

[6] Keen, P. G. W. and Scott Morton, M.S., 'Decision Support Systems: An Organisational Perspective', Addison-Wesley: Reading, Mass., 1978.

[7] Keen, P. G. W., 'Information Systems and Organisational Change', Communications of the ACM, 24, 24-33, 1981.

[8] Lenz, R. T. and Lyles, M. A., 'Paralysis by Analysis: Is Your Planning System Becoming Too Rational?', Long Range Planning, 18, 64-72, 1985.

[9] Vari, A. and Vecsenyi, J., 'Designing Decision Support Methods in Organizations', Acta Psychologica, 56, 141-151, 1984.

[10] Humphries, P. and Berkeley, D., 'Problem Structuring Calculi and Levels of Knowledge Representation in Decision Making', in R. W. Scholz (ed), 'Individual Decision Making Under Uncertainty', North-Holland, 1984.

[11] Jacques, E., 'A General Theory of Bureaucracy', Heinemann, 1976.

KNOWLEDGE SYSTEMS, EXPERT SYSTEMS, AND RISK COMMUNICATION

Joseph Fiksel
Teknowledge, Inc.
Palo Alto, California USA

Vincent T. Covello
National Science Foundation
Washington, D.C. USA

NOTE: Portions of this paper are based upon Reference [1].

INTRODUCTION

Efforts by government agencies and industrial organizations to communicate risk information are frequently hampered by social, behavioral, and institutional difficulties. Government officials, industry executives, and scientific experts often complain that laypeople do not understand technical risk information. Individual citizens and representatives of public groups are often equally frustrated, perceiving government and industry officials to be uninterested in their concerns and reluctant or unwilling to allow them to participate in decisions that intimately affect their lives. In this context, the media often play the role of transmitter and translator of information about health and environmental risks, but have been criticized for exaggerating risks and emphasizing drama over scientific facts.

Knowledge systems technology (KST) is an emerging field in information science that may be useful in resolving many of these risk communication difficulties. KST is a branch of artificial intelligence that attempts to represent and simulate human reasoning. Historically, the dominant application area for KST has been the development of expert systems. Expert systems are designed to provide advice to decision makers and are based on heuristic rules extracted from human experts [2]. In recent years, a number of such systems have been developed. For example, analysts in the risk management field have designed expert systems to support decision making related to emergencies caused by chemical spills [3]. The inherent capabilities of KST,

NATO ASI Series, Vol. F35
Expert Judgment and Expert Systems
Edited by J. Mumpower et al.

however, are applicable to a much broader range of knowledge processing tasks, including risk communication.

The purpose of this paper is to explore several potential applications of KST to risk communication. Specifically, it is suggested that KST can:

o represent the complex knowledge involved in risk communications;

o provide a clear, common language for the all actors involved in the risk communication process;

o enhance the consistency and objectivity of risk communications.

While it is recognized that no single approach can overcome the many barriers to effective risk communication, recent developments in information science suggest that KST can be used to (1) extend the depth, clarity, and adaptability of the risk communication process and (2) allow fuller use of research findings and conclusions from the literature on the challenges of risk communication.

CHALLENGES OF RISK COMMUNICATION

A Risk Communication Model

A recent review [1] of the literature on efforts to communicate information about health and environmental risks--such as the controversies over the risks of saccharin, the pesticide EDB, dioxin, AIDS, toxic wastes, smoking, driving without seat belts, and nuclear power plant accidents--suggests that communication problems arise from:

(1) message problems (e.g., limitations of scientific risk assessments);

(2) source problems (e.g., limitations of risk communicators and risk assessment experts);

(3) <u>channel</u> problems (e.g., limitations of the print and electronic media); and

(4) <u>receiver</u> problems (e.g., characteristics of the intended recipients of the communication).

Provided below is a summary of some major problems organized according to these four components of the communication model -- message, source, channel, receiver:

Message problems:

- deficiencies in scientific understanding, data, models, and methods resulting in large uncertainties in risk estimates;
- highly technical analyses that are often unintelligible to the non-scientist

Source problems:

- disagreements among scientific experts;
- lack of resources and legal constraints;
- failures to disclose limitations of risk assessments and resulting uncertainties;
- limited understanding of the interests, concerns, fears, values, priorities, and preferences of individual citizens and public groups;
- use of bureaucratic, legalistic, and technical language;
- lack of trust and credibility.

Channel problems:

- o selective and biased media reporting that emphasizes drama, wrongdoing, disagreements, and conflict;
- o premature disclosures of scientific information;
- o oversimplifications, distortions, and inaccuracies in interpreting technical risk information.

Receiver problems:

- o inaccurate perceptions of levels of risk;
- o lack of interest in risk problems;
- o overconfidence in one's ability to avoid harm;
- o strong beliefs and opinions that are resistant to change;
- o exaggerated expectations about the effectiveness of regulatory actions;
- o desire and demands for scientific certainty;
- o a reluctance to make trade-offs between different types of risks or between risks, costs, and benefits;
- o difficulties in understanding probabilistic information.

Each of these problems is often complicated further by the variety of interest parties, or stakeholders, involved in the risk communication process. These stakeholders include:

- Corporation managers
- Corporation employees, stockholders, or suppliers
- Population groups exposed to the technological risk
- Owners of property or resources exposed to the technological risk

- Agency officials responsible for regulating the technological risk

- Associations representing corporations or exposed populations

- Third parties with economic and other interests (e.g. competitors)

- Scientists and risk assessors

The variety of interactions that may occur among these different stakeholders makes clear the difficulties of risk communication, particularly in cases involving technological risks.

To address risk communication problems, it is helpful to organize risk communication tasks into four general types according to the primary objective or intended effect of the communication [1]:

- o information and education;
- o behavior change and protective action;
- o disaster warnings and emergency information;
- o joint problem solving and conflict resolution.

In the real world, these four types of risk communication tasks overlap substantially, but they still can be conceptually differentiated. The task of informing and educating the public can be considered primarily a non-directive, although purposeful, activity aimed at providing the lay public with useful and enlightening information. In contrast, both the task of encouraging behavior change and personal protective action and that of providing disaster warnings and emergency information can be considered primarily directive activities aimed at motivating people to take specific types of action. These three tasks, in turn, differ from the task of involving individuals and groups in joint problem solving and conflict resolution, in which officials and citizens exchange information and work together to solve to health and environmental problems.

A Risk Analysis and Management Framework

To support the risk communication tasks described above, it is useful to view risk communication in the broader context of risk assessment and risk management. Recent efforts to describe the state of the art of risk assessment have led to the development of a conceptual framework for risk analysis and management [4]. This framework, depicted in Figure 1, helps to identify how KST can support risk communication.

As defined here,

> Risk communication is an effort to convey to interested parties the outputs of various stages of the risk analysis and risk management process, including:
>
> - the nature of the risk (risk identification)
> - the magnitude of the risk (risk assessment)
> - the urgency of the risk (priority-setting)
> - the acceptability of the risk (risk evaluation)
> - strategies for mitigating the risk (option generation)
> - the relative merits of different options (option evaluation)
> - the justification for the decision (option selection)

This definition permits the knowledge content of risk communication to be formally linked to existing principles of risk analysis and risk management. For example, the model suggests that there are several different modes of risk communication at different stages in the risk analysis and management process:

Descriptive	--	risk identification and assessment, option generation
Interpretive	--	priority-setting, risk evaluation, option evaluation
Prescriptive	--	option selection
Reactive	--	emergency response

Figure 1. A Framework for Risk Analysis and Risk Management

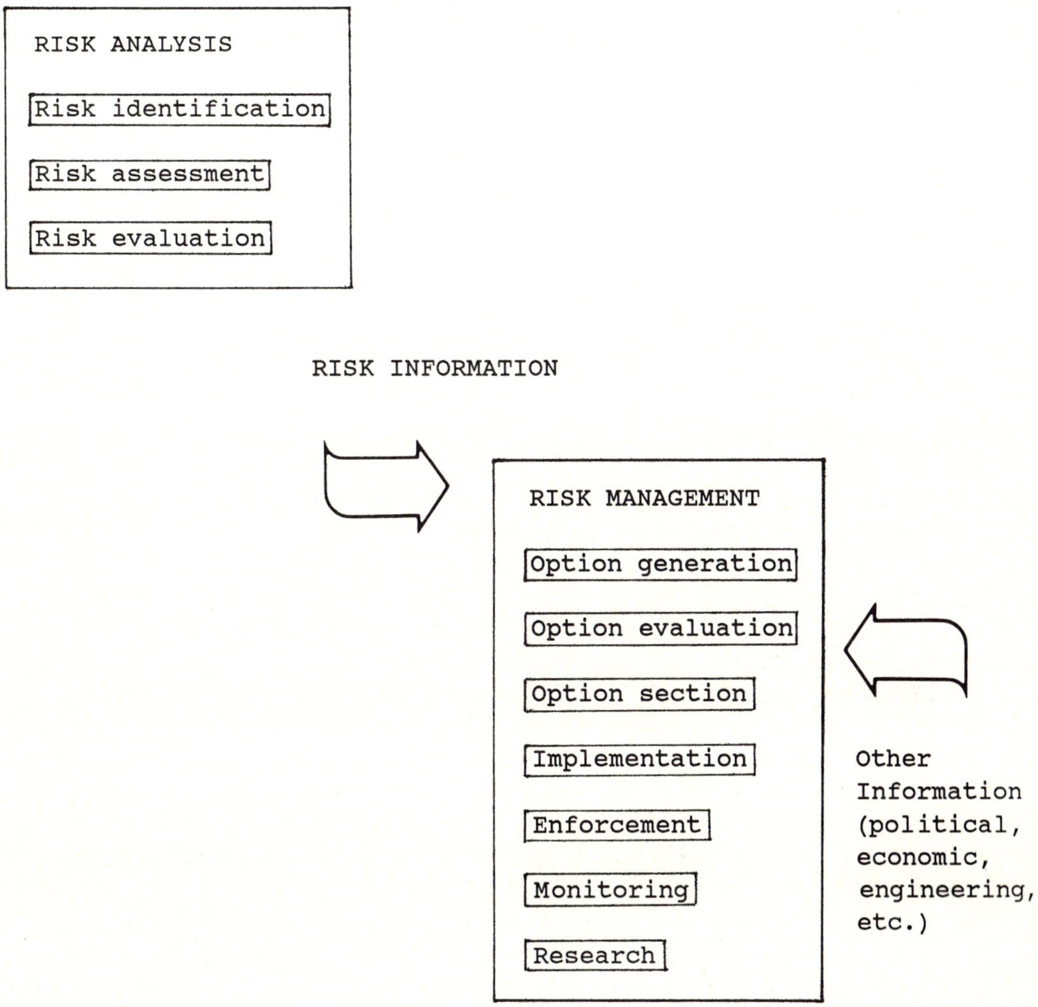

Descriptive communication is ideally free of values, and corresponds to information and education activities. Interpretive communication requires the introduction of values for particular stakeholders, and corresponds to joint problem-solving and conflict resolution activities. Prescriptive communication incorporates both values and tradeoffs, and corresponds to behavior change and protective action. Finally, reactive communication is initiated by the occurrence of specific events or situations, and corresponds to disaster warnings and emergency response. As mentioned earlier, the latter category of activity has already been recognized as an area where knowledge systems such as emergency response advisory systems can make an important contribution. The next section therefore focuses on the other three areas.

CONTRIBUTIONS OF KST TO RISK COMMUNICATION

Characteristics of Knowledge Systems

Knowledge systems are usually defined as computer programs that give advice, solve problems, or perform other "intelligent" tasks. More generally, knowledge systems automate the application of knowledge, just as calculators automate the application of arithmetic or data base management programs automate the indexing and retrieval of records [5]. Thus, knowledge systems technology involves the computer-aided representation of human knowledge and reasoning in symbolic form. The design and development of knowledge systems requires a specific form of expertise called *knowledge engineering*.

Although many knowledge systems use specialized artificial intelligence languages and workstations, knowledge systems have been developed and implemented using a variety of commonly-available hardware and software. The distinguishing features of knowledge systems are primarily functional in nature. There are several ways in which knowledge systems can be contrasted with conventional computer programs:

- While conventional computer programs operate mainly on numeric data, knowledge systems operate mainly on symbolic information.

- While conventional computer programs tend to use a procedural approach, knowledge systems tend to use a declarative approach, in which knowledge is explicitly represented as declarations of facts and relationships.

- Unlike conventional programs, knowledge systems can utilize "soft", qualitative, inexact, or incomplete information, and can seek additional information from the user if appropriate.

- Unlike most conventional programs, the symbolic representations used to encode and manipulate knowledge are generally English or English-like phrases.

The major components of a typical computer-based knowledge system are:

- a user interface, usually with an interactive display (accepting input via keyboard or mouse)

- a knowledge base of facts and inference rules (in particular, expert systems contain expert knowledge)

- an inference engine, which performs logical reasoning (combining facts and rules to achieve goals)

The potential uses of knowledge systems are only beginning to be explored. Early applications tended to view the knowledge system as an independent agent that offered expertise in response to user requests. However, in recent years this perspective has changed and knowledge systems are now viewed as a class of support tools that extend the scope and power of human knowledge processing, including information access, reasoning, and explanation.

Advantages of Knowledge Systems

There are a number of distinct ways in which KST can contribute to enhanced risk communication:

1. Generic Knowledge Representation

Knowledge about risk phenomena can be organized into well-defined categories of attributes, impacts, and other important factors. For example, there is a considerable literature on the various characteristics of risk that are important to public perception. Recent work on risk taxonomies suggests that classification of risks according to their key characteristics can form a basis for computer-aided risk analysis and risk management [6]. A few of the important characteristics that can be represented in a qualitative classification scheme include:

- occupational vs. nonoccupational risks
- delayed vs. immediate consequences
- routine vs. catastrophic events
- acute vs. chronic risk mechanisms
- statistical vs. identifiable victims
- necessary vs. replaceable risk sources

While these types of characteristics are known to influence both risk perception and decision-making, information about these characteristics is currently contained in available computer models that support risk analysis. Knowledge systems will make it possible to explicitly account for these considerations and to acknowledge their importance in the risk communication process. Thus, systematic use of generic knowledge representation will encourage both consistency and completeness in risk communication.

2. Repository for Consensus Knowledge

KST permits the electronic capture, maintenance, and distribution of a large body of knowledge regarding technical, economic, or scientific aspects of various risks. In the risk communication field, KST will permit the creation of a consensus body of knowledge which can be examined and critiqued by the scientific community. This capability will help clarify the nature of scientific controveries and disagreements about facts and assumptions. Moreover, new knowledge regarding specific areas of risk can be accumulated over time, providing a basis for continual improvement of the data base.

3. Control Over Reasoning Logic

KST will permit the reasoning, logic, and assumptions used in the process of constructing statements about risk to be carefully controlled and examined. For example, knowledge systems can be used to explore the sensitivity of statements to particular assumptions about risk mechanisms or pathways. Statements can also be critiqued to see if they are consistent with approved reasoning guidelines and assumptions.

4. Transparent Explanation Capability

KST makes it possible to delve as deeply as needed into the knowledge base to explore particular questions about assumptions, facts, models, or theories. For example, different users may require different levels of justification for claims made about levels of risk. Whereas a non-scientist might be willing to accept at face value a communication that "the predicted cancer incidence associated with a specific carcinogen is one in ten million," a more technically-oriented receiver of this same communication might wish to examine the underlying assumptions about toxicity and exposure pathways. Such differences in communication requirements can be accommodated by a knowledge system that can address the "deep structure" of risk assessment statements.

5. Handling of Qualitative Information

KST can simultaneously accommodate both qualitative and quantitative information for a specific risk problem. For example, if data are sufficient for quantification of a specific risk, such as health risks of low-level contaminants in drinking water, KST can provide verbal descriptions of the risk in relative, comparative terms such as: "we are reasonably certain that the risks are negligible compared to the background incidence level." If data are available, however, the system also provides a precise computational model.

6. English-Like Presentation

KST can overcome the use of technical jargon through transformation of conceptual information into programmed English phrases. These phrases, can, in turn, be adapted for different audiences. For example, a scientific communication which discusses the results of a "linear quadratic dose-response model" can be automatically transformed for communication purposes to the following surrogate statement: "a model that assumes human disease occurrence is roughly proportional to the average daily intake at low dose levels."

7. Handling of Uncertainty

KST can treat uncertainty through the use of certainty factors (degrees of belief) that are propagated through the inference process. Certainty factors are less restrictive than probabilistic measures of uncertainty, although there is still debate about their theoretical interpretation [7]. For example, consider a rule which might appear in the knowledge base of a system that addresses off-site impacts of hazardous waste disposal:

if the substance is soluble
and the aquifer is used for drinking water
then a possible exposure route is ingestion (cf 80).

The expression (cf 80) indicates that the conclusion is "believed" with a certainty factor of 80 (on a scale from 0 to 100). Moreover, if the degree of belief in one of the premises of the rule (e.g. "the substance is soluble") were less than definite (e.g. cf 70), then the certainty factor associated with the conclusion would decrease in proportion.

8. Interactive Dialogue

Knowledge systems are capable of engaging in an interactive dialogue with a receiver. For example, KST can be used to probe for factors that increase or decrease levels of public concern about health or environmental risks, such as those shown in Table 1.

9. Graphic Visual Aids

The use of knowledge systems with active graphic interfaces can help users understand complex subjects. For example, the visual representation of risk categories as a hierarchy or tree can be helpful in communicating the different types of risks. By the same token, visual comparison of risk magnitudes in the form of computer-generated bar charts or histograms can help to communicate quantitative data more effectively than actual numbers.

10. Rapid Information Retrieval

The use of knowledge systems enables specific types of information about risks and risk management strategies to be

Table 1. Factors Involved in Public Risk Perception

FACTOR	CONDITIONS ASSOCIATED WITH INCREASED PUBLIC CONCERN	CONDITIONS ASSOCIATED WITH DECREASED PUBLIC CONCERN
CATASTROPHIC POTENTIAL	FATALITIES AND INJURIES GROUPED IN TIME AND SPACE	FATALITIES AND INJURIES SCATTERED OR RANDOM IN TIME AND SPACE
FAMILIARITY	UNFAMILIAR	FAMILIAR
UNDERSTANDING	MECHANISMS OR PROCESS NOT UNDERSTOOD	MECHANISMS OR PROCESS UNDERSTOOD
UNCERTAINTY	RISKS SCIENTIFICALLY UNKNOWN OR UNCERTAIN	RISKS KNOWN TO SCIENCE
CONTROLLABILITY (PERSONAL)	UNCONTROLLABLE	CONTROLLABLE
VOLUNTARINESS OF EXPOSURE	INVOLUNTARY	VOLUNTARY
EFFECTS ON CHILDREN	CHILDREN SPECIFICALLY AT RISK	CHILDREN NOT SPECIFICALLY AT RISK
EFFECTS ON FUTURE GENERATIONS	RISK TO FUTURE GENERATIONS	NO RISK TO FUTURE GENERATIONS
VICTIM IDENTITY	IDENTIFIABLE VICTIMS	STATISTICAL VICTIMS
DREAD	EFFECTS DREADED	EFFECTS NOT DREADED
TRUST IN INSTITUTIONS	LACK OF TRUST IN RESPONSIBLE INSTITUTIONS	TRUST IN RESPONSIBLE INSTITUTIONS
MEDIA ATTENTION	MUCH MEDIA ATTENTION	LITTLE MEDIA ATTENTION
ACCIDENT HISTORY	MAJOR AND SOMETIMES MINOR ACCIDENT	NO MAJOR OR MINOR ACCIDENT
EQUITY	INEQUITABLE DISTRIBUTION OF RISKS AND BENEFITS	EQUITABLE DISTRIBUTION OF RISKS AND BENEFITS
BENEFITS	UNCLEAR BENEFITS	CLEAR BENEFITS
REVERSIBILITY	EFFECTS IRREVERSIBLE	EFFECTS REVERSIBLE
PERSONAL	INDIVIDUAL PERSONALLY AT RISK	INDIVIDUAL NOT PERSONALLY AT RISK

rapidly accessed and displayed. Information searches can be focused and structured based on the user's current concern. For example, in emergencies and disasters, it is often critical that large amounts of data be accessed immediately for transfer to officials, the media, and the public.

The RISK-AID Prototype

An early example of how knowledge systems can communicate with non-technical users is RISK-AID, a demonstration knowledge system recently developed by Teknowledge, Inc. The system was designed under the auspices of Teknowledge's Program in Risk and Decision Systems to explore the potential applications of knowledge system technology to risk assessment and risk management. RISK-AID is not yet available, since it contains an incomplete, illustrative knowledge base. However, it does serve as a prototype for development of knowledge systems that can support health or environmental decision-making.

A consultation with RISK-AID consists of the following steps:

- Risk identification -- RISK-AID prompts the user to select a specific hypothetical risk, and identifies a number of key characteristics, such as the possible risk causes, pathways, and effects.

- Risk assessment -- RISK-AID assists the user in performing some elementary risk calculation procedures; if the quantitative data are insufficient it suggests a qualitative approach.

- Risk control -- RISK-AID advises the user on a number of possible options for reducing either the likelihood or the magnitude of the risk.

There are two types of knowledge represented in the RISK-AID system: analytic knowledge and heuristic knowledge. The analytic knowledge includes a formal understanding of risk taxonomy and risk analysis procedures, which are applicable to broad classes of risk (e.g. acute vs. chronic hazard categories). The heuristic knowledge includes expertise regarding the salient characteristics, mechanisms, and control options for various types of risk (e.g. possible human exposure routes following a liquid spill). This design approach gives RISK-AID the capability to treat almost any conceivable risk situation, from forest fires to food additives, with less than two hundred rules.

RISK-AID is a "broad and shallow" system, in the sense that it has superficial knowledge about a large number of different classes of risk. In practice, knowledge systems like RISK-AID should be developed with a narrower focus and a deeper knowledge base; for example the EPA is currently developing advisory systems that recommend risk control technologies for hazardous waste disposal sites. Indeed, RISK-AID illustrates a number of possible uses of knowledge systems, including:

- Risk identification, screening, and priority-setting
- Risk analysis methodology selection and implementation
- Risk control option definition, evaluation, and selection
- Risk communication in the regulatory decision process

The following section discusses how knowledge systems designed along the lines of RISK-AID might help with some of the communication problems identified in Section 2.

APPLICATIONS TO COMMUNICATION PROBLEMS

Information and Education

As noted above, a variety of problems complicate the task of informing and educating people about risk assessment and management. The following examples illustrate how knowledge systems technology (KST) might address some of these problems.

- Handling of uncertainty and qualitative information

  Risk information is often highly technical, complex, and uncertain. Because of uncertainties deriving from a lack of scientific data and from deficiencies in available methods and models, it is not uncommon to find substantial variations in risk estimates. KST provides a means for addressing this issue by offering a language for communicating uncertain or incomplete information in ways that are intelligible to a broad audience.

o Repository for consensus knowledge

Experts often disagree on the assumptions underlying a risk assessment and, as a result, often provide widely different risk estimates. One result of these disagreements is public confusion about the validity of risk estimates. KST offers a means for addressing this issue by permitting the development of explicit consensus knowledge in electronic form.

o Transparent explanation and English-like presentation

Government officials often use technical, legalistic, or bureaucratic language. Besides being difficult to comprehend, such language gives the impression that officials are being unresponsive or evasive. Government officials may argue that technical language is unavoidable, given the constraints placed on them by the nature of the data, by agency regulations, and by the law. KST provides a means for addressing this issue by permitting the translation of technical language and reasoning into terms that are accessible and meaningful to non-specialists.

In general, knowledge systems offer several advantages for informing and educating people about risk. They allow risk communicators to:

- use simple, graphic, and concrete material, avoiding technical or specialized language wherever possible;
- compare risks within a carefully defined context that is relevant to the target audience;
- avoid comparisons of risks that may appear to the audience to be non-comparable because of different qualitative characteristics, for example, the risk of smoking compared to that of living near a nuclear power plant;
- understand and recognize people's qualitative concerns, such as concerns about catastrophic potential, dread, equity, and controllability;
- identify and explain the strengths and limitations of

different risk measures;

- identify, acknowledge, and explain uncertainties in risk estimates.

Behavior Change and Protective Action

In addition to problems already noted in relation to information and education, a variety of problems complicate the task of encouraging behavior change and protective action. KST can help risk communicators to:

- identify a specific target audience and tailor the communication to that audience;

- attract the attention of the target audience through the use of an innovative communication technology;

- present recommendations in the context of a balanced argument that accurately describes the strengths and weaknesses of both sides, especially if the target audience is likely to be exposed to strong counter-arguments and recommendations;

- build on expertise, trust, and credibility; people are more willing to accept a communication if the communicator is believed to be knowledgeable, unbiased, and representative of a consensus body of knowledge;

- draw explicit conclusions and actively involve the audience in the argument through interactive dialogue.

Joint Problem Solving and Conflict Resolution

Knowledge systems can help risk communicators (1) design structured dialogues that recognize the concerns of all interested parties and (2) design options (such as safeguards or compensation schemes) that specifically address these concerns. In particular, KST can help to:

- involve the public early in decision making, that is, before assumptions have been set, alternatives have been narrowed, key decisions have been made, and decision makers have become committed to a particular course of action;

- leave room for option invention and exploration (e.g. "what-if" scenarios) by those directly involved or affected by the decision;
- establish elaborate procedural safeguards to ensure that all voices with an interest or stake in the decision can be heard;
- carefully analyze the nature of the conflict and distinguish between different types of conflict, for example, distinguish factual disagreements from deeply rooted ideological conflicts;
- adopt different communication strategies for different types of conflict and disagreement.

CONCLUSIONS

This paper has argued that knowledge systems technology can make a significant contribution to the risk communication process by providing a structured, interactive environment in which qualitative knowledge about specific risk situations can be examined and interpreted. Knowledge systems can help decision makers (1) focus their attention on the specific concerns of different stakeholders, (2) systematically review alternative courses of action, (3) explain the reasoning or factual basis for risk assessments or control decisions, and (4) show the effects of assumptions and uncertainties. Knowledge systems can also help promote consistency and continuity in the development of a scientific knowledge base for risk assessment and risk management.

REFERENCES

[1] Covello, V., D. von Winterfeldt, and P. Slovic "Communicating Scientific Information about Health and Environmental Risks: Problems and Opportunities from a Social and Behavioral Perspective," in V. Covello, A. Moghissi, and V.R.R. Uppuluri, Uncertainties in Risk Assessment and Risk Management, Plenum, New York (in press, 1986).

[2] Hayes-Roth, F., D.A. Waterman, and D.B. Lenat, Building Expert Systems, Addison-Wesley, Reading, MA (1983).

[3] Ichniowski, T., "Computers Aid Emergency Response," Chemical Week, April 30, 1986, p.28.

[4] Merkhofer, M. and V. Covello, Risk Assessment and Risk Assessment Methods: The State of the Art, New York: Plenum (in press, 1986).

[5] King, D. and R. Morgan, "An Overview of Knowledge-Based Systems," Data Processing Management, Auerbach, 1986.

[6] Fiksel, J., "Trans-cultural Framework for Risk Classification, Analysis, and Management," presented at the Conference on Risk Analysis in Developing Countries, Hyderabad, India, October, 1985.

UNCERTAINTY IN ARTIFICIAL INTELLIGENCE: IS PROBABILITY EPISTEMOLOGICALLY AND HEURISTICALLY ADEQUATE?

Max Henrion
Carnegie Mellon University
Pittsburgh, Pennsylvania USA

INTRODUCTION

Historically, probability has been by far the most widely used formalism for representing uncertainty. However, the majority of AI researchers have not, hitherto, found standard probabilistic techniques very appealing for use in rule-based, expert systems. Among the many alternative numerical schemes for quantifying uncertainty that have been developed are the Certainty Factors used in Mycin (Shortliffe & Buchanan, 1975) and its descendants, Fuzzy Set Theory (Zadeh, 1984), the quasi-probabilistic scheme of Prospector (Duda et al., 1976), and the Belief functions of Dempster-Shafer theory (Shafer, 1976). There have also been attempts to develop non-numerical schemes, including Paul Cohen's theory of endorsements (Cohen, 1985), Doyle's theory of reasoned assumptions (Doyle, 1983), and various linguistic representations of uncertainty (Fox, 1986). We shall refer to both probabilistic and alternative methods, generically, as uncertain inference schemes, or UISs.

Each of these techniques has its partisans and its detractors, and the debate about their various merits and drawbacks seems to be heating up of late (e.g., see Kanal & Lemmer, 1986; Gale, 1986; Cohen et al., 1984). The purpose of this paper is to provide an introduction and give some personal views on several basic issues in evaluating and comparing UISs, with particular emphasis on probabilistic representations. In evaluating any representation it is useful to bear in mind the distinction between epistemological adequacy -- how well can each UIS represent the different aspects of reasoning with uncertainty? -- and heuristic adequacy -- how easy is it to use and what are its computational demands (McArthy & Hayes, 1969)? In their influential paper, McArthy and Hayes dismissed probability as "epistemologically inadequate" for properly representing uncertainty. However I shall argue that, to the contrary, there are several important kinds of reasoning under uncertainty, which are performed naturally by coherent probabilistic schemes, but which are hard or impossible for currently proposed alternatives. The question of the heuristic adequacy of general probabilistic representations may still be open, although there are several promising developments, which I shall discuss briefly.

The first part of this article will provide a brief overview of the key issues in the debate about probabilistic schemes, starting with the traditional arguments for the appeal of the personalist or Bayesian view of probability, and a summary of various approaches to implementing probabilistic UISs. This is followed by a list of the most common objections to probabilistic schemes and attempts to rebut them that have appeared in the literature. The second part of the article will focus on four particular issues that have hitherto attracted less attention. The first issue concerns the treatment of correlated sources of evidence, and assumptions about dependence and independence. The second is the issue of combining diagnostic and predictive reasoning, and the related issue of separating inference rules from domain knowledge. The third is the question of whether or not UISs for expert systems should try to approximate human reasoning. The last is the question of whether it matters much which approach you use, and I shall argue the importance of systematic comparisons of alternative UISs to find out. The issue is not simply what can each UIS do or not do, but how much practical difference to the conclusions can it make which you use?

There has been considerable controversy on several of these topics. Researchers are operating under different paradigms with different programmatic goals: Some have been primarily concerned with epistemological criteria, where others emphasize heuristic criteria. It would be naive to expect a speedy resolution. My hope for this paper is that it may be a contribution towards creating a more focussed debate, as a prerequisite for more cumulative science.

THE APPEAL OF PROBABILITY

The probability of a proposition or an event, according to the Bayesian or personalist view, is a measure of a person's degree of belief in it, given the information currently known to that person. The notion of probability may be derived from a set of simple axioms of rational decision-making under uncertainty, which form the basis of decision theory (Savage, 1954). The force of these axioms, and hence of the laws of probability derived from them, arises from the fact that a people who violate them and are willing to act on incoherent probabilities (for example, which do not satisfy Bayes' rule) are liable to demonstrable loss. Notably, an opponent could always design a "Dutch book", that is a combination of bets that they would be willing to accept, according to their professed beliefs, but which, in sum, would result in a guaranteed loss (de Finetti, 1974).

Unlike any of the alternative proposals for representing uncertainty, personal probability is embedded in a theory of rational decision-making. One advantage of this is that it provides an operational definition for the probability of an event, in terms of the person's behavior, that is willingness to take bets based on the outcome of the event. It also provides a theory for how to use the uncertainties computed by some artificial system in making decisions. Thirdly, probabilistic schemes provide well-known ways of incorporating empirical data. And fourthly, there are well developed methods for evaluating judged or computed probabilities by comparison with empirical frequencies, in terms of accuracy, resolution and calibration (Lichtenstein, Fischhoff & Phillips, 1982). No non-probabilistic measure of uncertainty offers these advantages. It has also been shown that for any reasonable scoring rule (which rewards a decision maker based on his or her probability assessments and the actual outcomes or truth of the propositions), any scalar measure of uncertainty is either worse than probability (produces an expected lower score) or is equivalent to it (Lindley, 1982).

PROBABILISTIC UISs

A set of m propositions, $\{A_1, A_2 \ldots A_m\}$, each of which may be true or false, gives rise to 2^m different possible elementary events, each being a particular combination of proposition values. e.g., $(A_1 \& \sim A_2 \& \ldots A_m)$. A complete joint probability distribution over these propositions specifies a probability for each event, and so requires specification of 2^m-1 parameters. (The last parameter is specified by the constraint that the probabilities sum to 1.) The exponential complexity of this complete representation rules it out as a viable approach for practical systems and so simplifying assumptions are essential.

In most practical UISs, the evidential relationships are modelled as an inference network, in which each proposition (or variable) is directly related to only a few others. Each such link is represented by a rule, which provides evidence about a consequent proposition, C, based on the degree of belief in some logical combination of its antecedents, A_i, for example, $(A_1 \& \sim A_2)$ ---> C_3. The "strength" of the rule is specified by one or more numbers, whose probabilistic interpretation varies according to the scheme. Each such UIS needs to provide functions for propagating the uncertainty measures through logical conjunction, disjunction, negation, and generalized modus ponens, as well as a function for combining the evidence from multiple rules that bear on one consequent. The best known schemes are Certainty Factors (CFs) developed for Mycin (Shortliffe & Buchanan, 1975) and the scheme used in Prospector (Duda et al., 1976), from which many variants have been derived. Both of these were originally intended as approximations to Bayesian inference.

Neither system is completely consistent with a complete probabilistic scheme, and the implied probability distributions are incoherent. Pearl has devised a coherent probabilistic representation, known as the Bayes' Network (or Causal Network), (Pearl, 1986). These are similar in spirit to the influence diagram developed for decision analysis (Shachter, 1985). A Bayes' Network is a directed, acyclic graph, in which each arc represents an uncertain causal dependence of a child variable on its parents (predecessors in the network). Each dependence is quantified as the conditional probability distribution of the variable given the states of its parents. Kim and Pearl have devised an ingenious scheme for propagating uncertain evidence through a Bayes' network, which preserves global coherence over the network, using only efficient local updating mechanism (Kim & Pearl, 1983). This requires that the network is a Chow tree, that is, singly connected.

An approach to dealing with a partially specified probability distribution is to estimate the full distribution using the Maximum Entropy Principle. This minimizes the additional information assumed in filling out the distribution, consistent with the specified constraints (usually marginal and conditional probabilities). While this approach has several desirable properties (Shore and Johnson, 1980), computation of maximum entropy distributions is, in general, prohibitively expensive with more than a few propositions, despite attempts to improve algorithms (Cheeseman, 1983). However, many popular probabilistic updating schemes, including, conditional independence assumption, Jeffrey's rule, and odds-ratio updating, and Pearl's scheme for Bayes' Networks are actually special cases of Maximum Entropy, and the related Minimum Cross Entropy update (Wise, 1986).

OBJECTIONS TO PROBABILITY

Despite its attractions, probability has been under sustained attack as a viable scheme for representing uncertainty in AI. Among the criticisms have been the following:

1. Probability requires vast amounts of data or unreasonable numbers of expert judgments.

2. It can't express ignorance, vagueness or "second-order uncertainty."

3. It doesn't distinguish reasons for and against, or identify sources of uncertainty.

4. The inference process is hard to explain.

5. It can't express linguistic imprecision.

6. It requires unrealistic independence assumptions.

7. It is computationally intractable.

8. It is not how humans reason.

9. It doesn't make much difference what method you use anyway.

Several recent articles have addressed various subsets of the first six objections listed above, and have provided eloquent rebuttals (Spiegelhalter, 1986; Pearl, 1985; Cheeseman, 1985). Below is an extremely brief summary of their conclusions, without attempt at explanation. The interested reader is referred to the original articles. The focus of the rest of this article will be objections 6 to 9 and some related issues of the heuristic adequacy of probabilistic schemes, which have been less discussed in the literature.

SUMMARY OF REBUTTALS

In evaluating the criticisms and rebuttals, it is important to distinguish claims about probabilistic inference in general from claims about specific quasi-probabilistic UISs incorporating various heuristic assumptions, such as the schemes of Emycin or Prospector. These rebuttals have been primarily in defense of the theoretical possibilities of probability rather than particular UISs. Failure to keep in mind this distinction has sometimes resulted in misunderstanding and fruitless argument.

The belief that probabilistic representations require vast amounts of data seems to derive from frequentist interpretations of probability, and does not apply to Personalist or Bayesian interpretations. Neither should inordinate numbers of probabilistic judgments be needed to express expert knowledge, provided the inference structure created is a reasonable reflection of the way the expert thinks about the domain. An understanding of causal relationships between variables allows judgments of conditional independence between variables that are not directly related, and may be directly represented by Bayes' Networks. The construction of a Bayes' Network allows the expert to express his or her qualitative understanding of the probabilistic relationships and independences in a simple graphical form. Since these networks are typically fairly sparse, relatively few quantitative judgments are needed to encode the conditional probability distributions (Pearl, 1985). The acyclic structure of the Bayes' network guarantees that the resulting assessments will be coherent (Pearl, 1986).

Ignorance, vagueness or second order uncertainty may be represented by a range of probabilities, or by a predictive distribution over a probability, expressing how the prior probability might change after consulting a specified information source (Cheeseman, 1985; Spiegelhalter, 1986). But it is often sufficient to represent each probability by its mean value, unless decisions about gathering new information are being contemplated.

It is true that a single probability by itself doesn't distinguish the sources, type and effect of the pieces of evidence on which it is based, but it is certainly possible to retrieve and

clearly express this information in probabilistic schemes (Pearl, 1985). For example, the evidence weight (log likelihood ratio) provides a convenient additive measure of the relative importance of each piece of evidence for a conclusion. The weights of supporting evidence can be added to the prior weight, and weights of disconfirming evidence subtracted in a sort of "ledger sheet" to arrive at the total final weight (Spiegelhalter, 1986). Evidence weights are also useful in explaining probabilistic reasoning. As long as the underlying inference network is sparse, as Pearl argues it will be, the inference process should be explainable in simple, intuitively meaningful steps (Pearl, 1985).

The advantage often claimed for Fuzzy Set Theory over probability is that the former can model linguistic imprecision, whereas probabilities are only defined for unambiguously specified ("crisp") events or propositions (Bonissone, 1982). Indeed, until recently, probabilists have generally not addressed the issue of linguistic imprecision, aside from studies of the correspondence between probability phrases and numbers (Beyth-Marom, 1982). However there seems to be little theoretical difficulty in so doing, and arbitrary assumptions can be avoided (Wise, 1986; Cheeseman, 1986). There is plenty of experimental evidence that probabilistic inference is not a very good model for human linguistic reasoning (Kahneman, Slovic & Tversky, 1982). But there has been little experimental investigation of claims that alternative UISs offer better models. One study comparing human judgment to Fuzzy Set Theory found that subjects' judgment of the "plausibility" of the intersection of two fuzzy sets was better modelled by the multiplication of "plausibilities", analogous to the probabilistic rule for the intersection of two independent events, rather than by the minimum plausibility rule of Fuzzy Set Theory (Oden, 1977). A serious problem in such studies of non-probabilistic schemes is setting up a convincing comparison when the measure of uncertainty has no operational definition.

ASSUMPTIONS ABOUT DEPENDENCE

While probability can in theory cope perfectly with non-independent sources of evidence, most actual UISs cannot. Consider the following:

Chernobyl example: The first radio news bulletin you hear on the accident at the Chernobyl nuclear power plant reports

that the release of radioactive materials may have already killed several thousand people. Initially you place small credence in this, but as you start to hear similar reports from other radio and TV stations, and in the newspapers, you believe it more strongly. A couple of days later, you discover that the news reports were all based on the same wire-service report based on a single unconfirmed telephone interview from Moscow. Consequently, you greatly reduce your degree of belief again.

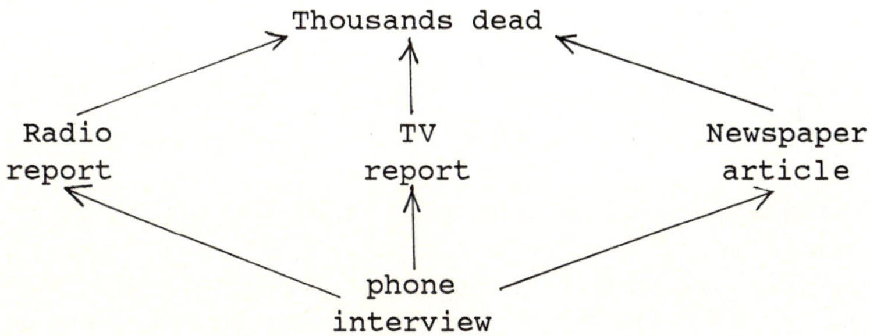

Figure 1: Inference network for Chernobyl example

This illustrates how multiple, independent supporting sources of evidence increase the confirmation of a hypothesis, but the degree of confirmation is reduced if they are correlated. Most of us seem quite capable of handling this kind of intuitive reasoning, at least qualitatively, even if we don't have the terminology to describe it. However none of the better known UISs are actually capable of distinguishing between independent and correlated sources of evidence. Instead they each make various arbitrary fixed assumptions about the presence or absence of dependence. So they are inherently incapable of performing this <u>commonsense</u> reasoning.

For example, the Fuzzy Set operators for <u>and</u> and <u>or</u>, are equivalent in effect to probabilistic rules assuming <u>subsumption</u> among antecedents, i.e. where the least likely proposition logically implies the more likely one(s). This is equivalent to assuming the <u>maximum possible</u> correlation between input propositions. Prospector and Mycin CFs use similar rules for

"and" and "or". On the other hand, Prospector, and singly connected Bayes' networks assume conditional independence when combining evidence from different rules, as in the Chernobyl example. Figure 2 shows Pr(A&B) as a function of Pr(A) given Pr(B)=0.6, assuming minimum overlap between A and B (Minc), independence (Ind), or maximum overlap (MaxC). The latter is the Fuzzy Set assumption. It illustrates the range of results possible from alternative assumptions about correlation.

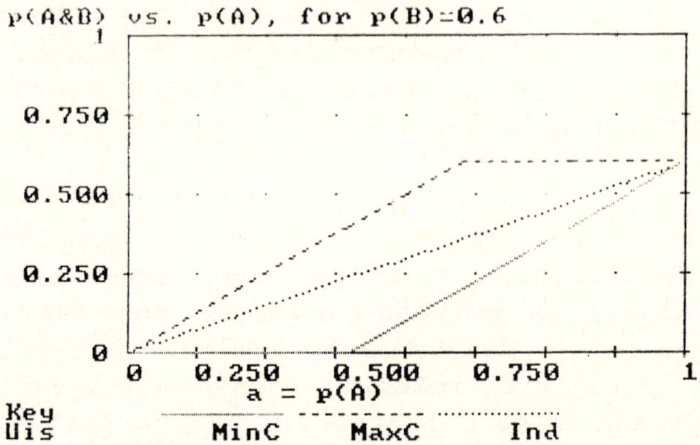

Figure 2: The effect of assumptions about correlation (Wise & Henrion, 1986)

It has sometimes been claimed as an advantage of some non-probabilistic UISs, including Fuzzy Set Theory (Bonissone, 1986), that they avoid having to make any assumptions about dependencies. But in fact, as we have seen, the Fuzzy Set combination functions are equivalent in effect to specific probabilistic assumptions. It is true that non-probabilistic languages for uncertainty do not provide a general framework for modelling dependent evidence, since they do not provide a well-defined language for expressing the ideas. But to claim that they can therefore avoid making unsupported assumptions about correlations is akin to claiming that a new settler in Alaska can cope effectively with the winter precipitation by adopting the language of an equatorial tribe with no word for snow.

Although probability in principle provides a general framework for modelling and combining dependent evidence, the better known probabilistic UISs, including Prospector and Bayes' networks, actually make independence assumptions and do not deal

with it. In fact, any system using only one or two numbers to represent uncertainty in propositions is inherently incapable of representing these kinds of dependencies, and so cannot avoid such problems. On the other hand any system in which all dependencies are explicitly represented, for example representing the probabilities for each proposition conditional on all propositions on which it depends, is liable to exponential complexity. An alternative approach is to represent uncertainty by a range of two probabilities and to compute both the largest and smallest probabilities compatible with the ranges of the antecedents and extreme positive or negative correlations. This does avoid making any specific, unsupported assumptions, although there is a danger of ending up with vacuous results (i.e. probability limits of 0 and 1).

The original Bayes' Network scheme of Kim and Pearl is restricted to Chow Trees, i.e. singly connected graphs, so that conditional independence between convergent sources of evidence can be preserved (Kim & Pearl, 1983). Pearl has discussed several approaches for coping with multiply connected graphs (Pearl, 1986). One approach is to collapse all the variables in a cycle into a single compound variable, with as many states as all possible combinations of its components. Another is to condition on a variable in the cycle, so that it can in effect be removed. Both approaches are liable to exponential complexity. A third approach is to try to remove the cycles, by adding extra nodes (hidden variables). This approach allows restructuring the probabilistic dependencies to avoid cycles, although it is unclear how often this is feasible (Pearl, 1986). Cooper has presented an approach which uses a causal network and partial information on probability distributions, and employs linear programming to compute bounds on probabilities (Cooper, 1986).

Another approach is the use of stochastic simulation, representing uncertain propositions by a random sample of truth values. The probability of each proposition is approximated by the fraction of the sample that is true. This appears capable of avoiding the exponential complexity of exact techniques, but can estimate derived probabilities to arbitrary accuracy, depending on the sample size. One such technique is the incidence calculus, which supports estimation of the probabilities of arbitrary Boolean expressions, given the probabilities and correlations of their components (Bundy, 1986). I have developed a related approach, termed logic sampling, designed to propagate evidence

through a multiply connected Bayes' Network (Henrion, 1986). The probabilistic world specified by the conditional distributions for each variable conditional on its parents is represented by a random sample of possible deterministic cases. In each deterministic case the dependence of each variable on its parents is specified by a simple truth table, randomly generated from the underlying conditional distribution. Similarly, each source variable (without parents) is assigned a truth value generated according to its prior probability. In each deterministic case, the implications of the source values can easily be propagating through the network using the usual mechanisms of deterministic logic. Correlations due to multiple paths in the inference network or dependencies specified between inputs are handled correctly without special mechanisms. Conditional probabilities may be similarly estimated from the fraction of cases which are true of those cases where the condition applies, e.g., where the outcome accords with the observations. This approach can be reasonably efficient (it is linear in the network size) and seems promising, but its full potential remains to be explored.

DIAGNOSTIC AND PREDICTIVE INFERENCE

Diagnostic inference involves reasoning from observable manifestations to hypotheses about what may be causing them, for example reasoning from symptoms to diseases. Predictive or causal inference involves reasoning from causes (or causal influences, such as genetic or environmental factors that might increase susceptibility to a disease) to possible manifestations (Tversky & Kahneman, 1982). Consider the following:

> The sneeze example: Suppose you find yourself sneezing unexpectedly in the house of an acquaintance. It might either be due to an incipient cold or your allergy to cats. You then observe animal paw marks, which increases your judged probability of a cat in the vicinity (diagnostic inference), which, in turn, increases the probability that you are having an allergic reaction (predictive inference). This also explains away the sneezing, and so decreases the probability you are getting a cold.

Notice that this reasoning involves a mixture of both diagnostic and predictive inference. Having rules that allow reasoning backwards and forwards like this creates a danger of vicious circles, where, say, the probability of a cat would increase the probability of the allergic reaction, and vice versa. To avoid this, it seems necessary to keep a record of the sources of different uncertain evidence for each variable, so that you can avoid possible double counting. Pearl's scheme for Bayes' Networks keeps the flows of diagnostic and predictive evidence separate to avoid such cycling, and only combines them to calculate the aggregate degree of belief in each node (Pearl, 1986). Figure 3 shows a Bayes Network representation of propositions mentioned.

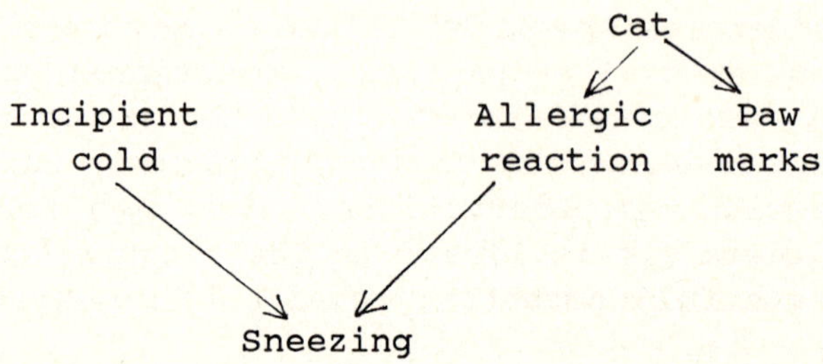

Figure 3: Bayes' network for sneeze example

Independent evidence for the allergy helps to explain the sneezing and so reduces the probability of a cold. Alternatively, the observation of a mild fever might increase the probability that it was a cold and so decrease the probability of the allergy. Thus the presence of sneezing induces a negative correlation between the cold and the allergy, which would otherwise be independent. This kind of reasoning, which we may term intercausal, is a natural consequence of the simple logical relation that sneezing can be caused either by a cold or an allergy. Pearl's propagation scheme for Bayes' Networks models this correctly, but other rule-based schemes have a very hard time with it.

Consider the following rule for medical diagnostic inference which performs intercausal reasoning (Clancey, 1983):

> If the patient has a petechial rash and does not have leukemia, then neisseria may be present.

This reflects the medical fact that a petechial rash can be caused either by neisseria or by leukemia, and so the rash is evidence for neisseria (and hence meningitis) unless it has been explained by leukemia.

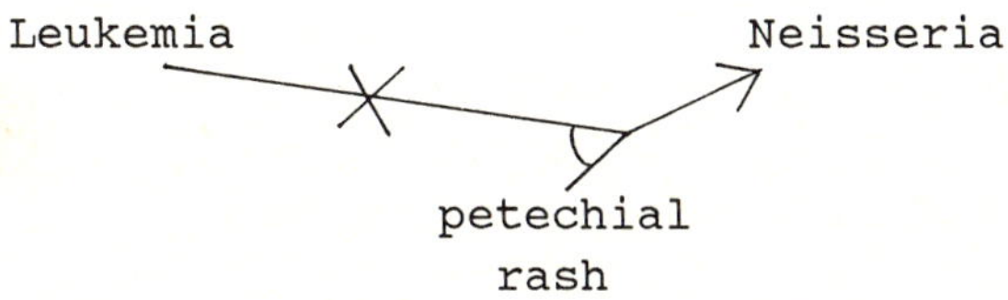

Figure 4: Bayes' network for rash example

If the system was also intended to help diagnose leukemia, it would need an additional rule:

If the patient has a petechial rash and does not have neisseria, then leukemia may be present.

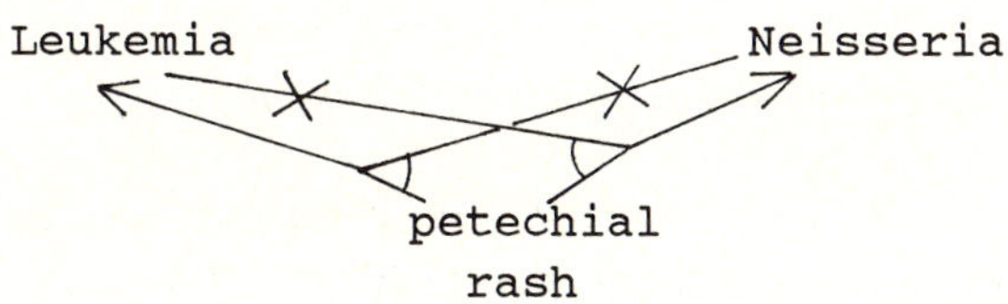

Figure 5: Inference network with both rules

Figure 5 shows the Inference network with both these rules. It now contains a cycle (from leukemia to neisseria and back again), which is liable to cause looping during updates, or at least sensitivity to the sequence in which evidence arrives.

The underlying problem is that, in addition to specific medical knowledge, these rules also embody a general heuristic for intercausal reasoning, namely:

A symptom is evidence for a disease only in the absence of an alternative disease that could explain it.

Ideally, domain knowledge should be represented quite independently from such general knowledge about inference under uncertainty, which should be applicable to all domains. This can be achieved much more easily in a probabilistic UIS in which the essential medical knowledge is expressed in causal form, by two independent relationships:

A petechial rash can be caused by neisseria.

A petechial rash can be caused by leukemia.

The conditional probability of the symptom, given each disease may be estimated from data or by a medical expert. These causal relationships are diagrammed in the Bayes' Network in Figure 6:

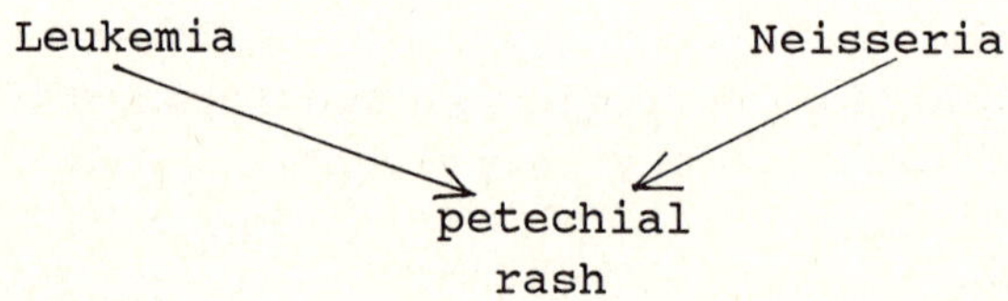

Figure 6: Bayes' network for rash example

This approach is more modular in that the rule relating to neisseria is separate from the rule about leukemia. Additional rules could be added for other diseases that may cause a petechial rash without requiring any modifications of the existing ones. The UIS should then be able use this information to make the uncertain diagnostic inferences implied by either rule, or even reason predictively from a changed probability of a disease to an updated probability of a symptom, according to the demands of the situation. Coherent probabilistic schemes, such as Pearl's inference scheme or logic sampling, can do this effectively and consistently, while maintaining a clear separation between the inference methods and domain knowledge. Clancey, in a critique of Mycin, has emphasized the desirability of separating the representation of inference strategy from domain knowledge (Clancey, 1983). But it does not appear that schemes, like Mycin, or Prospector, which represent knowledge primarily in the form of diagnostic rules rather than probabilistic causal relations, are entirely capable of this.

SHOULD UISs EMULATE HUMANS?

The objection that probabilistic inference is not a good model of human inference under uncertainty has been forcefully stated by Paul Cohen:

> [it is] puzzling that AI retains models of reasoning under uncertainty that are derived from normative theories..., because the assumptions of the normative approaches are frequently violated, and because the probabilistic interpretation -- and numerical representation -- of uncertainty summarizes and fails to discriminate among reasons for believing and disbelieving. ... models of humans as perfect processors of information are not only inaccurate, but also unlikely to lead to efficient and intelligent reasoning (Cohen, 1985, p.9).

Cohen here advocates the strategy, which appears to have been successful elsewhere in AI research, of adopting heuristic approaches based on human intuitive reasoning, rather than theoretically optimal, but computationally intractable schemes. Cognitive psychologists have indeed provided us with ample evidence that human inference under uncertainty is not accurately modelled by Bayesian decision theory (Kahneman, Slovic & Tversky, 1982). Typically the discrepancies have been quantitative but not qualitative, although psychologists have been ingenious in concocting cases in which human judgment under uncertainty is not even qualitatively correct according to Bayesian models. However, they have had less success in devising descriptive models of how we do reason under uncertainty. Despite claims for the "naturalness" of Certainty Factors or Fuzzy Set theory for representing human inference under uncertainty, so far there is little experimental evidence that such non-probabilistic UISs are better descriptive models. Very likely there is considerable variation between tasks and between individuals.

It is an important and challenging task for cognitive psychologists to build better models of judgment under uncertainty, but it seems quixotic for those primarily interested in developing better expert systems to seriously attempt to emulate human judgment. That is not to say that evidence about human reasoning, including evidence from introspection, may not give us excellent ideas for devising new and better UISs. But the criterion for judging their usefulness should be the quality of their performance, rather than how well they simulate human thought processes.

One feature of human judgment observed by psychologists has been termed the representativeness heuristic: When asked the probability that object A belongs to class B, people typically evaluate it by the degree to which A is representative of B, that is by the degree to which A resembles B (Kahneman, Slovic & Tversky, 1982). This leads to judgments which are insensitive to the prior probability of A, and contrary to Bayes' rule. Cohen and his colleagues explicitly adopt the representativeness heuristic for representing uncertainty in the classification system, GRANT, (Cohen et al., 1985), which deliberately ignores prior information.

> we suggest that representations of uncertainty for classification systems should be interpreted in terms of the similarity of fit between data and solution, not in terms of the relative frequency of their co-occurrence (Cohen et al., 1985, p.137).

Other UISs also explicitly exclude prior probabilities, including Mycin (Buchanan & Shortliffe, 1984). Since Certainty Factors represent changes to priors, Mycin-like systems could in principle incorporate priors, but typically applications of CFs have not. The rationale has been that prior probabilities are too hard to estimate, and it is better to avoid them. However, for both GRANT and Mycin (and its derivatives), ignoring priors is functionally equivalent to assuming equal priors (e.g., equal probabilities that each agency might fund a proposal, or equal prevalence rates of disease organisms). Occasionally such uniform priors may be appropriate, but more often it means ignoring important information about differing frequencies.

The following example points up the dangers of ignoring base-rate information:

> Blood test example: James is engaged to be married, and takes the routine pre-marital blood test required by the state. To his horror, the test comes back positive for syphilis. His physician tells him that the test is very reliable, having a false positive rate of 1%, and explains that the chance he has the disease is therefore 99%. Aghast, James wonders what to tell his fiancee.

Most physicians will give the same advice as James' one does. Like other people, they are poor intuitive Bayesians (Kahneman, Slovic & Tversky, 1982) and tend to ignore prior or base-rate information. Using the representativeness heuristic, the chance that James has VD is judged by the degree to which he (having a positive blood test) is representative of people with VD. In this, and many similar cases, the heuristic leads to a conclusion that is badly wrong:

> Fortunately, James' fiancee, Alice, is not only understanding, but also a Bayesian statistician. She finds out from the physician that the prevalence of syphilis among men from James' background is about 1 in 10,000. Based on this, she concludes that the actual probability he has the disease given the test result is about 1%. So she decides to go ahead with the wedding.

Suppose we (or our physician) are consulting a medical expert system, would we rather that it employed inference strategies modelled on typical human judgment which ignores base-rate information, or would we prefer that it used normative Bayesian principles?

DOES IT MATTER WHICH YOU USE?

Even if one accepts the arguments sketched above that probability is epistemologically adequate to represent uncertainty, some simplifying approximations may be necessary to construct a UIS which is computationally tractable for real problem domains. Despite the theoretical differences between systems, does it really make much difference to the conclusions of a rule-based expert system which scheme you use? There has been a common perception in the AI community that the performance of systems is relatively insensitive to the choice of UIS; that the important differences are to do with qualitative knowledge rather than quantitative uncertain inference. This may be true, at least for some domains, although the Blood Test Example illustrates an important class of diagnostic problems in which a common heuristic can lead to serious errors. But so far, belief in this insensitivity seems to have been based primarily on informal impressions. Until very recently, there has been little systematic analysis or experimental evidence published, and what there has been should not have been comforting.

One early piece of evidence was a comparison of Mycin's method for combining evidence from different rules with a probabilistic model (Shortliffe & Buchanan, 1975). Subsequent analysis of the data originally presented by Shortliffe and Buchanan reveals some interesting behavior. The system shows a pronounced tendency to under-respond, that is information tends to be interpreted as less diagnostic, either for or against the conclusion, than it actually is. On average, strong aggregate evidence for or against a conclusion was computed to be about half as strong as it should be (49% of the CF) (Wise, 1986). In itself, this may not have mattered much, since Mycin used the relative sizes of CFs for making decisions. But in 25% of the cases the system actually responded in the wrong direction, that is, confirming evidence actually reduced the CF or vice versa.

Another study by the Mycin team examined the sensitivity of Mycin to the granularity of CFs (Buchanan & Shortliffe, 1984). CFs, which can be any number between -1 and 1, were rounded to coarser scales, for example with 5 points at equal intervals (-1, -.5, 0, .5, 1). In experiments with 10 cases of meningitis, change from the continuous scale to an 11 point scale caused different identification of disease organisms in 3 cases. Change to a 7 point scale, caused different identification of 5 organisms. And change to a 5 point scale caused misidentification of 9 out of 10. The recommended therapy was less affected by the coarsening of the scale, since a single drug can cover many organisms, and so misidentification of the organism did not always lead to incorrect therapy. Of course, this study of the sensitivity to the precision of the numbers used says little about sensitivity to the assumptions of the inference rules for combining them, relative to alternative UISs.

The rules for conjunction and disjunction with Mycin Certainty Factors seem at first sight to be the same as those for Fuzzy Sets (also used in Prospector):

$$CF(A \& B) = Min(CF(A), CF(B))$$
$$CF(A \text{ OR } B) = Max(CF(A), CF(B))$$

However, a Certainty Factor actually represents a change in degree of belief (an update) rather than <u>absolute</u> degree of belief.

Consequently, these combination rules behave quite differently from Fuzzy Sets. In effect they ignore all but one source of information combined in a conjunction or disjunction. This leads to under-response if all sources agree (all are confirming or all are disconfirming), and over-response if sources conflict (some are confirming and some disconfirming) (Wise, 1986). Since conjunctions pay attention only to the most disconfirming (or least confirming) evidence, and the CF modus ponens rule ignores disconfirming evidence entirely, in combination they lead to zero response in rules based on a conjunction of conflicting information. Taken altogether, these effects help to explain the observed tendency to under-respond.

On the basis of comparison of Mycin with human experts, the developers of Mycin suggested that Certainty Factors are satisfactory for the initial application domain (selecting antibiotic therapy), but cautioned that:

> We would need to perform additional experiments to determine the breadth of the model's applicability (Buchanan & Shortliffe, 1984, p. 700).

However, few expert system developers seem to have taken notice of this, and CFs and related UISs are now being widely applied to other problem domains, apparently without the benefit of such experiments.

Recently there have been a few studies comparing the behavior of different UISs. Tong and colleagues have compared 12 variants of the Fuzzy Set Rules for <u>and</u>, <u>or</u>, and <u>modus ponens</u> combinations in terms of their performance in a fixed rule base (Tong, 1985). They found that the performance of all rules with smooth response (i.e., not discontinuous) did reasonably well in their specific example. Vaughan and colleagues have done a comparison of the Prospector scheme with odds-ratio updating for a random sample of single rules (Yadrick et al., 1986). They found that Prospector did well in many cases, but that there are some situations in which it performs poorly. Wise has argued that the appropriate standard for comparison of any UIS with partially specified probabilities is a system using Maximum Entropy to fit a complete prior to specified input probabilities and rule strengths, and Minimum Cross Entropy for updating it (Wise & Henrion, 1986; Wise, 1986). This ME/MXE approach is actually a generalization of the odds-ratio approach used by Vaughan et al. Wise has performed comparisons of six UISs, including CFs, Fuzzy Set Theory, and a probabilistic scheme with Conditional Independence, against the ME/MXE scheme, for individual rules, and small assemblies of 2 to 12 rules, 30 cases in all, each with all input probabilities systematically varied (Wise, 1986). For purposes of comparison, the degree of membership of a Fuzzy Set was equated to probability. The performance of the UISs varied considerably over the different situations. All worked well in at least some cases, and none worked well in all cases. There were some situations in which some UISs were worse than random guessing. The conditional independence scheme seemed overall most robust for the set of cases examined.

It is not hard to construct examples in which CFs and other widely-used UISs produce results that disagree significantly with a complete probabilistic analysis, even having the wrong qualitative sensitivities. Experienced knowledge engineers may be aware of at least some of the problems inherent in the UIS they use, and may know how to modify rule-sets to mitigate the undesirable behavior, at least for some anticipated situations. However, some of the problems are quite subtle, even though their effects can be severe. In any case it seems dangerous to rely on the ability of the knowledge engineer to "program around" such problems, particularly given our sketchy understanding of what all the problems are. It would be valuable to have a more systematic exposition of the classes of situation in which each UIS is reliable, where errors are likely, and which directions the biases are likely to be.

Of course, if it doesn't make much difference which method we use, then we may continue to use the simpler methods, such as Certainty Factors, without having to worry about the complexities of some of the other UISs. But if, as preliminary examination suggests, there are situations in which commonly used UISs produce clearly biased or incorrect results, then, at the very least, we should be aware of these so we can avoid them. If these situations are common then perhaps we should use a different UIS, or maybe there is a need to develop new methods which combine theoretical validity with greater pragmatic ease-of-use.

CONCLUSIONS

Probability has often been criticized as epistemologically inadequate for representing uncertainty in AI, but many of these criticisms seem to have stemmed from an incomplete understanding of probabilistic inference. In this paper, I have focussed on a number of important advantages that probabilistic representations have over other proposed measures of uncertainty, which have not loomed so large in the debate hitherto. Personal probability has an unambiguous operational definition, and it is embedded in a rational theory of decision-making under uncertainty -- we know what it means, and we know how to make decisions using it. Coherent probabilistic inference is epistemologically adequate to perform three important kinds of qualitative reasoning that humans are capable of, but which competing non-probabilistic schemes, in general, are not:

1. taking into account non-independence between sources of evidence,

2. engaging in mixed diagnostic and predictive inference, and

3. inter-causal inference, between alternative causes of an event, as in "explaining away".

These types of inference are important, and we can learn a great deal from studying human reasoning. But it is not necessarily desirable that a UIS should duplicate <u>all</u> features of human judgment under uncertainty, including such strategies as the representativeness heuristic that can lead to severe biases, as in the blood test example. Where cognitive limitations cause human judgments to diverge from the results of normative theory, surely it is better to use the latter when expert systems are advising on important decisions, as in medical applications.

Even if one accepts the arguments for the epistemological adequacy, or superiority, of probability, serious questions may still be raised about its heuristic adequacy -- can practical, computationally efficient implementations be built? The maximum entropy/minimum cross entropy approaches seems to be computationally intractable for systems of realistic size, unless more powerful decomposition techniques can be devised. The Bayes' Network approach seems very promising, but work still remains to be done to deal conveniently and generally with multiply connected networks (i.e. dependent sources of evidence). Logic sampling and stochastic simulation seems to offer possibilities here, both as a practical implementation and as an intellectual link to deterministic logic.

Although probabilistic methods have been suggested for dealing with second-order uncertainty, distinguishing the effect of different sources of evidence, and explaining probabilistic reasoning, there remains considerable work to be done to demonstrate and evaluate applications to large, real-world domains. Whatever the theoretical merits of probabilistic representations, the AI community has a venerable tradition of pragmatism, and many will understandably remain unconvinced until these more sophisticated probabilistic schemes have demonstrated success in large scale applications. On the other hand, disturbing evidence is emerging about the performance of the most popular UISs, and complacency would be inappropriate as they are applied to new tasks with major potential consequences. There is an urgent need for more rigorous experimental evaluations of UISs for a range of realistic rule-bases to find out under what circumstances they can be relied on, and when they may be seriously wrong.

ACKNOWLEDGEMENTS

I gratefully appreciate helpful comments by several colleagues, including Ben Wise, Chris Elsaesser, and Judea Pearl. Responsibility for the opinions expressed is all my own. This work was supported by the National Science Foundation under grants IST-8603493 and by academic funds from Carnegie Mellon for the Social Impacts of Robotics and Information Technology.

REFERENCES

Beyth-Marom, R. How probable is probable? A numerical taxonomy translation of verbal probability expressions. J. of Forecasting, 1982, 1, 257-69.

Bonissone, P. P. A Fuzzy Sets based linguistic approach: Theory and applications, pages 329-39, 1982.

Bonissone, P. P. Plausible Reasoning: Coping with Uncertainty in Expert Systems, 1986.

Buchanan, B. G. & Shortliffe, E. H. Rule-based Expert Systems: The MYCIN Experiments of the Stanford Heuristic Programming Project. Addison-Wesley, Reading, Mass, 1984.

Bundy, A. Incidence Calculus: A mechanism for probabilistic reasoning, 1986.

Cheeseman, P. A method of computing generalized Bayesian probability values for expert systems, pages 198-202, Karlsruhe, W. Germany, 1983.

Cheeseman, P. In Defense of Probability, pages 1002-9, Los Angeles, Ca., 1985.

Cheeseman, P. Probabilistic vs. Fuzzy Reasoning, pages 85-102, 1986.

Clancey, W. J. The Epistemology of a Rule-Based Expert System - A Framework for Explanation. AI, 1983, 20, 215-251.

Cohen, Paul R. Heuristic Reasoning about Uncertainty: An AI Approach. Pitman: Boston, 1985.

Cohen, P., Davis, A., Day, D., Greenberg, M., Kjeldson, R., Lander, S., & Loiselle, C. Representativeness and Uncertainty in Classification Systems. The AI Magazine, Fall 1985, }, 139-149.

Cohen, M. S.; Schum, D. A.; Freeling, A. N. S.; and Chinnis, J. O. On the Art and Science of hedging a conclusion: Alternative theories of uncertainty in intelligence analysis. Technical Report 84-6, Decision Science Consortium, Inc, Falls Church, VA, August 1984.

Cooper, G. F. A diagnostic method that uses causal knowledge and linear programming in the application of Bayes' formula. Computer Methods and Programs in Biomedicine, 1986, (22), 223-237.

de Finetti, Bruno. Theory of probability. New York: Wiley, 1974.

Doyle, J. The Ins and Outs of Reason Maintenance. Technical Report CMU-CS-83-126, Carnegie Mellon University, 1983.

Duda, R. O., Hart, P. E., and Nilsson, N. J. Subjective Bayesian Methods for Rule-Based Inference Systems. Technical Report SRI Technical Note 124, SRI International, 1976. Fox, J. Knowledge, decision making and uncertainty, 1986.

Gale, W. (ed.). AI and Statistics. Addison-Wesley: Reading, MA., 1986.

Henrion, M. Propagation of Uncertainty by Logic Sampling in Bayes' Networks. Technical Report, Department of Engineering and Public Policy, Carnegie Mellon University, June 1986.

Kahneman, D. Slovic, P. & Tversky, A. Judgment under Uncertainty: Heuristics and Biases. Cambridge: Cambridge University Press, 1982.

Kanal, L. N. & Lemmer, J. (eds.). Uncertainty in AI. North-Holland: Amsterdam, 1986.

Kim, J. & Pearl, J. A Computational Model for Combined Causal and Diagnostic Reasoning in Inference Systems, pages 190-193, 1983.

Lichtenstein, S., Fischhoff, B. & Phillips, L. D. Calibration of probabilities: The state of the art to 1980, Cambridge, 1982.

Lindley, D. V. Scoring rules and the inevitability of probability. International Statistical Review, 1982, (50), 1-16. (with commentary).

Some philosophical problems from the standpoint of Artificial Intelligence, pages 463-504, 1969.

Oden, G. C. Integration of Fuzzy Logical Information. J. Experimental Psychology: Human Perception and Performance, 1977, 3(4), 565-75.

Pearl, J. How to do with probabilities what people say you can't. Technical Report CSD-850031, Cognitive Systems Laboratory, Computer Science Department, University of California, Los Angeles, CA, 1985.

Pearl, J. Fusion, Propagation, and Structuring in Bayesian Networks. Artificial Intelligence, September 1986, 29(3), 241-288.

Savage, L. J. The Foundations of Statistics. New York: John Wiley & Sons, 1954.

Shachter, R. D. Intelligent Probabilistic Inference, 1985.

Shafer, G. A Mathematical Theory of Evidence. Princeton University Press, 1976.

Shore, J. E., and Johnson, R. W. An Axiomatic Derivation of the the Maximum Entropy Principle. IEEE Transactions on Information Theory, January 1980, pp.

Shortliffe, E. H. & Buchanan, B. G. A model of Inexact Reasoning in Medicine. Mathematical Biosciences, 1975, (23), 351-379.

Spiegelhalter, D. J. A statistical view of uncertainty in expert systems, 1986.

Tong, R. M., Shapiro, D. G. Experimental Investigations of Uncertainty in a Rule-based System for Information Retrieval. International Journal of Man-Machine Studies, 1985.

Tversky, A. & Kahneman, D. Causal Schemata in Judgments under Uncertainty, Cambridge, 1982.

Wise, B. P. An experimental comparison of uncertain inference systems. PhD thesis, Carnegie Mellon University, Department of Engineering and Public Policy, 1986.

Wise, B. P. & Henrion, M. A Framework for Comparing Uncertain Inference Systems to Probability, pages 69-84, 1986.

Yadrick, R. M., Vaughan, D. S., Perrin, B. M., Holden, P. D., Kempf, K. G. Evaluation of Uncertain Inference Models I: PROSPECTOR, pages 333-338, 1986.

Zadeh, L. A. Making Computers Think Like People. IEEE Spectrum, August 1984.

THE USE OF CAUSAL KNOWLEDGE FOR INFERENTIAL REASONING

Helmut Jungermann and Manfred Thüring
Institute for Psychology
Technical University of Berlin
West Germany

INTRODUCTION

Experts from industry, economics, and science are asked to predict which information and communication techniques will be available in a private household in 25 years and which of these services will be supplied by state and industry. We ask social science experts to predict the effects of such techniques and services. While most expect a growth in these techniques and services, they disagree about their effects on social contacts, creativity among the young, and feelings of state control.

One method to assess long-range technical, economic, political, and societal developments is through the construction of scenarios. Scenarios are descriptions of alternative hypothetical futures: They do not describe what the future will be, i.e., they are not prognoses, but rather which alternative futures we might expect (Jungermann 1985b).

Here is an example of a scenario describing the potential impact of specific technical conditions on some aspect of private life -- the time spent on watching television in 25 years:

> It is the year 2010. The Broadband Integrated Services Digital Network (BISDN) has been installed everywhere in West Germany. We take a look at the household of Mrs. Smith, a 65-year old pensioner living in a big city. The household is connected to the BISDN. Mrs. Smith owns a comfortable TV set; she can choose among 30 channels. She also owns a disc recorder for recording programs. Furthermore, Mrs. Smith can order programs for recording (copy on demand). Therefore all TV programs are highly available for her and it is very likely that she will spend more time watching TV than a comparable person today.

NATO ASI Series, Vol. F35
Expert Judgment and Expert Systems
Edited by J. Mumpower et al.

Such a scenario seems easy to build. However, if its content, its assumptions, and conclusion are to represent more than arbitrary assertions or science fiction, i.e., if they are to reflect expertise, then the task is not so easy: The assertions must be, for example, plausible, consistent, and scientifically justified.

How can experts generate a scenario describing the impact of future information and communication technology on private life? What information is used and how? What cognitive processes would allow experts to explore the future?

In this paper we will propose a conceptual framework for understanding and analysing the cognitive processes involved in the intuitive generation of scenarios. The core of this framework is the conceptualization of retrieval and inference processes based on mental models of causal knowledge. The approach will be illustrated with examples from a recent research project on the future impacts of new information and communication technology on private life (Jungermann, Fleischer, Hobohm, Schöppe and Thüring, 1986). A more extensive treatment of the subject is presented in Jungermann and Thüring (1987).

A Theoretical Framework

The cognitive activity of constructing a scenario is assumed to have four steps, as shown in Figure 1.

- First, knowledge relevant to the problem will be activated in the expert's memory. For example, a social scientist asked to generate a "TV-watching scenario" might activate his knowledge about studies on how families spend their time or about indicators describing the quality of private life.

- Secondly, the expert will constitute an internal model of the domain that maps its important features. For example, an expert might consider the number of channels, the amount of free time, the purchase power, the need for social contact, etc., and relate these aspects to each other.

- Thirdly, inferences will be drawn by running the mental model. For example, if an expert wanted to identify which

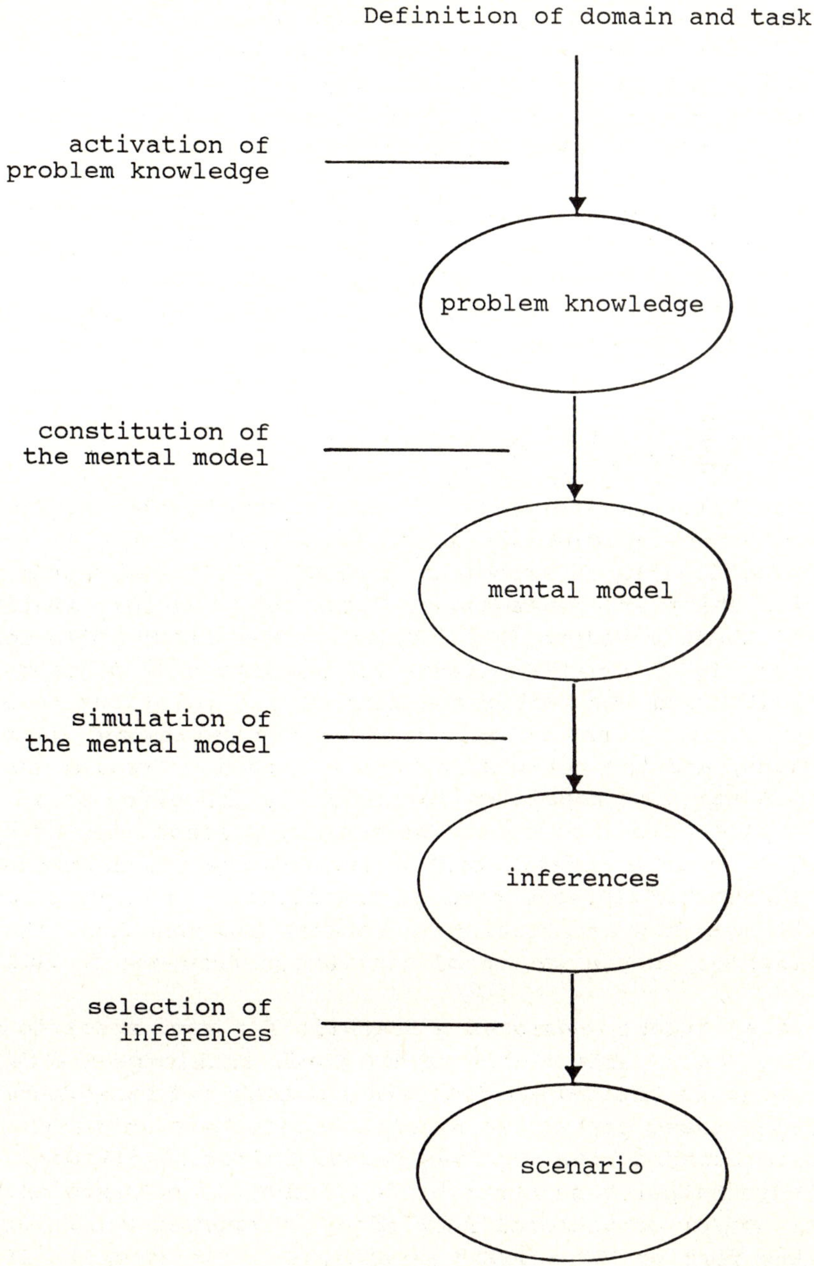

Figure 1 : The cognitive process of scenario construction

measures were required today to prevent unfavorable effects on social contacts, he might check how the number of unplanned social contacts would possibly vary as a function of the kind and cost of special services like buying food or account managing via home terminals.

- Finally, scenario knowledge is composed by selecting the inferences required by the task and / or the expert's intention. For example, to answer resistance to computers in schools, an expert might want to explore the potential effect of increased children's creativity levels.

Activation of Problem Knowledge

The relevant knowledge is part of the "world knowledge" stored in the individual's long-term memory. Memory is mostly conceptualized as an associative network of nodes representing concepts which are connected by links representing relations between these concepts (e.g., Anderson and Bower 1973, Norman and Rumelhart 1975, Anderson 1983). The meaning of a concept is defined through the number and kind of its relations to other concepts (e.g., class relations, property relations, causal relations) and the network is thus a closed, circular structure. The activation of knowledge is basically conceived as a neurophysiological process: The sensory presentation of some stimulus (e.g., a spoken word) activates the respective node and this activation spreads through the network to other concepts. The stronger the association is between two concepts, the faster and stronger is the spread of activation from one to the other.

If an expert generates a scenario for some specific area of interest, only parts of his or her world knowledge are relevant and should be activated. The person's task and background determine these parts. Two aspects should be pointed out: scenario construction requires causal and/or conditional knowledge rather than other kinds of knowledge. Based on this causal and/or conditional knowledge, inferences can be drawn that take the form of "IF - THEN" assertions; for example, if each household will have access to 30 television programs in 25 years, then people will have fewer social contacts. Secondly, different answers will usually be given by different people depending on their expertise and values. For example, an engineer asked about the significance of new information technologies, would probably give quite a different answer than an economist. Both answers would differ from the answers given by a politician and a psychologist.

The activation of the relevant problem knowledge does not take place in an entirely unstructured field, however. Our knowledge is organized in many ways. One particular kind of organization is a schema (see Alba and Hasher 1983 for an overview). A cognitive schema is a complex unit of knowledge, based on generalized experiences. (The schema concept is also used in artificial intelligence but it is still undetermined whether human schemata have the same properties as postulated in this field). One type of schema has found particular interest in cognitive psychology: the event schema, also called script (Schank and Abelson 1977). A script represents stereotypic sequences of events, such as "dining in a restaurant" or "attending a workshop." Cognitive scripts work as bundles of expectations about the order as well as the occurence of events. For instance, the restaurant script consists, on a rather molar level of analysis, of "entering, ordering, eating, paying, and leaving." Event schemata offer a very efficient organization of knowledge, facilitating storing, processing, and retrieving of information. But since the elements of a schema are mostly only probabilistically related to each other, the reliance on the "usual," i.e., the schematic course of events might also cause mistakes, e.g., incorrect assumptions about some course of events. For example, Bower, Black, and Turner (1979) found that subjects who had read a stereotypic story and were then asked to recall what they had read, tended toward false recognition of non-mentioned events. They apparently filled their memory gaps with elements that were part of their schema and thus "should" have occured in the story. The development and use of schemata is obviously a highly efficient cognitive mechanism. It distinguishes the professional from the amateur. But at the same time, it is part of the "déformation professionelle" hindering professionals to perceive or imagine the world in a non-schematic way and to understand other people who use their own particular schemata.

In short, the first step of a scenario construction process is less trivial than those authors seem to assume who advise experts simply "to define the relevant components or descriptors." The activation of problem knowledge within the world knowledge of an individual is influenced by a number of task-specific and personal factors.

Constitution of a Mental Model

The activated problem knowledge forms the basis for the constitution of an internal model. This mental model maps the essential characteristics of the domain to be described, i.e., its essential elements and their interrelations.

The mental model concept was introduced by Craik (1943) who defined its functions as follows: "If the organism carries a small-scale model of external reality and of its own possible actions within his head, it is able to try out various alternatives, conclude which is the best of them, react to future situations before they arise, utilize the knowledge of past events in dealing with the present and the future, and in every way to react in a much fuller, safer, and more competent manner to emergencies which face it."

The mental model approach has been revived in recent years (cf. Gentner and Stevens 1983, Pitz and Sachs 1984), but surprisingly little has been said about the forms of mental models. One possibility is to conceive of mental models as causal nets (Thüring and Jungermann 1986). Since the scenario task requires the operation on causal knowledge, this conceptualization might be appropriate. A simple hypothetical causal mental model is given in Figure 2, representing factors related to the descriptor "TV watching time."

If there exists a scientifically proven "true" model of the domain, e.g., for technical devices like a pocket calculator, one might compare the mental and the scientific model and analyse the differences (e.g., Norman 1983). But if the domain is an economic problem like the future of the energy market or the future impact of information technology on private life, the constitution of the mental model itself becomes a major object of analysis because there is no "true" model. It is then interesting to study the cognitive strategies experts might use to constitute a mental model. Two strategies can be distinguished, retrieval and reasoning.

Retrieval. The constitution of a mental model probably begins with retrieving elements, relations and part-structures from the activated knowledge base. This process is influenced by a number of factors. One such factor is the saliency of information in memory, i.e., the strength of preactivation of an

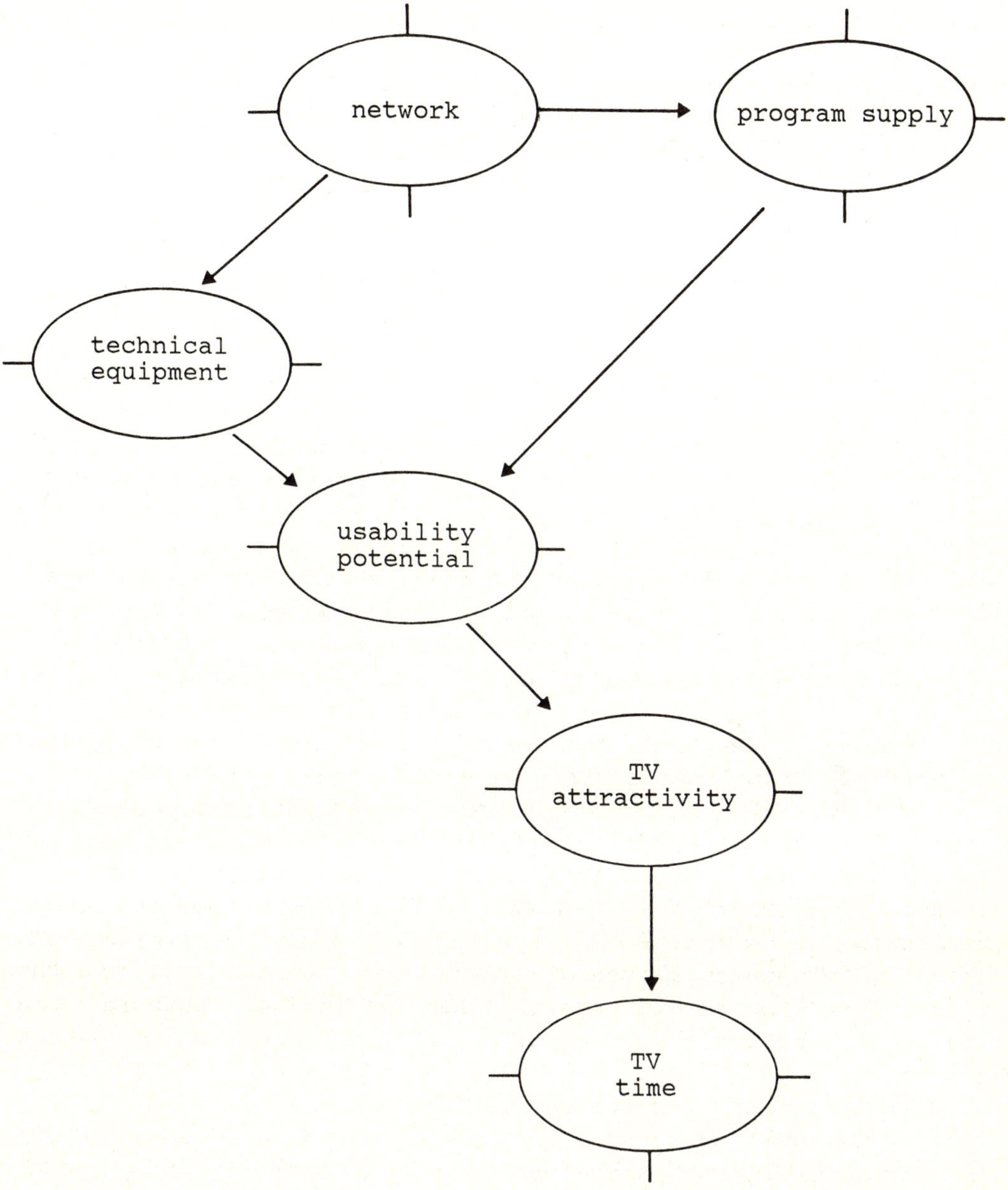

Figure 2 : Section of a simple mental model of factors influencing "TV watching time in 25 years"

element or the strength of some association between elements. The more salient some information is, the easier it is retrieved and becomes a member of the mental model, probably after some evaluation of its importance. A number of studies have revealed factors influencing the saliency of information. For example, saliency is strongly influenced by the frequency with which an event has been directly or indirectly observed. For experts, this usually means professional experience, whereas for the public it means report in the media.

Little is known about the retrieval of causal relations, but we might speculate: Assume some element X has been retrieved. This element may be causally related to Y (in memory). If the strength of the causal relation is above some level, element Y and the relation between X and Y will be retrieved automatically; otherwise, Y will not be retrieved (at least not automatically with X) and, consequently, the (subliminal) relation between X and Y will not become part of the model. Generally speaking, the retrieval of substructures might be an almost simultaneous and automatic retrieval of all those elements among which causal relations exist which exceed some associative strength.

Reasoning. Although the retrieval of information may often be sufficient for constituting a mental model, the task of exploring possible futures also requires a more constructive, reasoning activity, particularly if no models exist yet, as for the interrelations among factors in our information technology example. The expert must then go beyond the available information by forming new elements or inferring relations. One strategy is checking for potential causal relations by attending to "cues to causality" (Einhorn and Hogarth 1982, 1986). These authors distinguish four kinds of cues:

1) Covariation of two variables X and Y,
2) temporal order of X and Y,
3) spatial and temporal contiguity of X and Y, and
4) similarity of X and Y.

Whether a causal relation is cognitively established between X and Y depends on the number and strength of cues for such a relation, which may be direct (X causes Y) or indirect, i.e., with intervening variables (X causes A ... B which causes Y). The stronger the causal connection of the chain of variables is, the more probable is their integration into the mental model. This implies, for example, that the longer the chain, the weaker the causal strength of its elements, and therefore more complex combinations of variables have a lower chance of becoming part of the mental model compared to simple combinations.

An expert has also knowledge about the strength and form of causal relations, i.e., the functional relation between variables. For example, she might know that, if variable X increases, then variable Y decreases; or, more precisely, that there is a linear inverse functional relation between X and Y. Or, she might have some knowledge about whether X and Y are deterministically or probabilistically related, and, in the latter case, how strong this relation is. Such knowledge is needed for "running" the model. If there preexists knowledge about the functional relation between two variables, it will probably be activated simultaneously with the variables, and if there is no such knowledge, it must be inferred from other information. It is also possible, however, that at this stage only easily available functional knowledge is activated and that reasoning processes are postponed until the respective knowledge would be actually required in the mental simulation.

Summarizing, the second step of the scenario construction process consists of the constitution of a mental model mapping the relevant variables of the area of interest and their causal interrelations. The reproductive as well as the constructive part of the required search, retrieval, and reasoning, are prone to a number of pitfalls.

Simulation of the Mental Model

The mental model is not a scenario, but scenarios are inherent in the model. Take the model given in Figure 2. Selected variables are "television time," "network," "number of programs," and "attractivity of the programs." These variables can take various values; for example, "number of programs" can vary between 5 and 50, "program attractivity" can take the values low, mean, and high, etc. A combination of such values is a scenario; for example, a combination like "5 TV programs," "low attractivity," "BISDN network," and "low TV watching time" makes one scenario.

There are as many scenarios as combinations of values, but the causal knowledge embedded in the mental model restricts the number of combinations. For example, if some variable X ("attractivity of TV programs") causes an increase of some variable Y ("TV watching time"), then a scenario describing just the opposite effect of X on Y ("high attractvity of programs but low TV watching time") would not be consistent with the mental model. It is the function of the model to help generating "correct" scenarios, i.e., scenarios which are correctly derived from the causal knowledge. The correct use of a mental model for deriving scenarios distinguishes the scientific expert from the science fiction author who is not restricted (but, of course, also not helped) by the structure of a mental model.

The required knowledge can be expressed as a production, i.e., as an "IF - THEN" proposition like "IF network BISDN is installed, THEN 30 programs will be offered." While some of this knowledge might be available in memory, most must usually be inferred by "running" the mental model. A "run" is assumed to have four steps:

- First, an input variable is chosen from which the simulation cycle can start. For example, one might select as input variable the most important variable and use as an index of importance the number of relations a variable has to other variables.

- Next, a value is specified on the input variable. Depending on the task, this might be, for example, the most probable or the most extreme value that the variable can take. The output of the first two steps may be conceived as the first part of a production: "If variable X takes the value x(i), then ...."

- Then, a search is started from the input variable for other, causally related variables. We will distinguish two types of strategies, one concerning the direction and one concerning the specificity of the search.

  The first type has two variants, a forward and a backward directed search strategy: With a forward, causal reasoning strategy, the expert starts from the input variable, taken as a cause, and searches for potential effects. With a backward, diagnostic reasoning strategy, the input variable is taken as an effect for which potential causes or conditions are inferred. Both strategies require quite different cognitive activities and imply different pitfalls (Jungermann 1985a).

The second type has also two variants, a non-specific and a specific search strategy: In a non-specific search, the search starting with the input variable has no specific aim, i.e., no particular output variable is specified. In a specific search, on the other hand, the output variable of interest is specified and the search is limited to the path leading from the input to the output variable.

One example might be sufficient to illustrate for which kind of questions and answers each combined strategy might be appropriate: A non-specific forward search strategy would apply if the question is "What might happen if variable X takes the value x(i)?" For example, what effects can be expected if the variable "network" takes the value "BISDN?" Starting from a specific input variable, the search proceeds along all links which emanate from this variable within the mental model without any particular aim and leads to variables causally related to the input variable, e.g., "technical equipment" or "program supply."

- Finally, a value is assessed on the output variable of interest. Which value will be assessed should depend on the task as well as on the knowledge. For example, if an accident scenario is intended, the least probable value might be of interest. And knowledge about the functional relationship between input and output variable enables the expert to assess that value on some output variable Y that corresponds to, and is consistent with, the value specified on the input variable. The result of the last two steps may be conceived as the second part of a production: "IF ..., THEN variable Y takes the value y(i)."

Kahneman and Tversky (1982) have related mental simulation to probability judgments: "The ease with which the simulation of a system reaches a particular state is eventually used to judge the propensity of the (real) system to produce that state." The task seems to require a non-specific backward search: Which states on which variables could produce a particular state? If only a few variables need to be considered, the simulation is easier than when many variables are involved. And if the simulation is easy, the probability of the state is judged higher than when it is complicated. Tversky and Kahneman (1983) have suggested the "conjunction fallacy" as evidence for this assumption. Their subjects estimated the probability of a conjunction of events higher than the probability of single conjuncts if they could establish a causal relation between the events in the conjunction. This violates the rules of probability theory according to which the probability of a conjunction can never be higher than the probability of one of its conjuncts. The mental model approach allows the following interpretation: If a person has to estimate the probability of some event X, she might ask which events could produce event X; she would thus apply a non-specific backward search through which a number of potential causes could be generated. But a non-specific strategy is difficult since all links leading to the event must be taken into account. But if the probability of a conjunction of two events X and Y is to be estimated and one event (Y) can be interpreted as a cause of the other (X), then a specific backward search would be sufficient to check whether event Y could possibly cause event X. Such a strategy is easier than a non-specific strategy, and, consequently, a higher probability judgment will be given for the conjunction than for the single conjunct.

In summary, the third step is the simulation of the mental model in order to draw the required inferences. This simulation process consists of a complex pattern of search for effects or causes of some input variable and the assessment of corresponding values on output variables.

Selection of Inferences

The simulation cycles produce the inferences from which scenarios are generated. The type of scenario wanted determines primarily the selection of inferences, but aspects like expectation and desirability can also play a role. Two possibilities of selecting inferences shall be mentioned: the snapshot scenario and the chain scenario.

Snapshot scenario. The snapshot scenario is a description of a possible state of affairs at the time horizon. For example, take the situation in a private household in 25 years as affected by information technology. Which inferences are needed to construct such a scenario? The variables passed in the course of the inferential process from input to output variable and the inferences drawn about the values the passed variables might take, i.e., all the intermediate inferences, are entirely irrelevant. Only the inferred values of the output variables are of interest. In our example these might be, the number of social contacts, the time spent on watching television, the feeling of control over technical equipment, etc. This type of selection is largely determined by the task, i.e., the scenario type intended.

The basis for other selection processes are less obvious. First, a selection may be made among the output variables considered. For example, one might implicitly forget or explicitly exclude variables for which values have been generated that do not differ from the values these variables take in the present, i.e., that do not signal a significant change in the future (e.g., time spent on watching television, due to a ceiling effect). Such variables may seem uninteresting for the scenario since they do not seem to suggest actions in the present. Second, a selection may, and usually must be made among the various values that the output variable could possibly take. The expert knows that the relation between input and output variables is usually probabilistic and that therefore the output variable can take various values with certain probabilities. Furthermore, these values are not only more or less probable, they are also more or less desirable. These features might influence the selection of inferences: With respect to probability one might assume that usually the most probable value would be chosen. If, however, a peripheral rather than a trend scenario is intended, values with extreme probabilities would be selected (e.g., a strong decrease in unplanned social contacts). With respect to desirability one might argue that this aspect should not influence the scenario construction at all. But even experts' attention will often implicitly be drawn to the desirable or undesirable states of affairs the future might hold for us. And they often should indeed focus their attention on these output values in order to show us the range of potential future risks and benefits.

Chain scenario. The chain scenario is a sequence of causally or conditionally related actions and events. For example, we might want to describe how certain information and communication techniques might actually bring about certain effects on private life. For such a scenario not only the final inferences, i.e., the ones concerning the output variables are required but also the variables that mediate the relation between the input and output variable.

The required outcome of the mental simulation is then not just one value of the output variable, i.e., the final part of the chain, but a sequence of values on principally all variables that have been passed from the input to the output variable. For example, if the input variable is the technical network structure and the output variable of interest is the frequency of social contacts, intermediate variables might be the technical equipment of the household, the kind and number of available services, the income of the household, etc. Again, not all possible inferences drawn in the simulation will usually be useful for the scenario.

First, more than one path may have been inferred leading from the input to the output variable, and a selection must then be made among the various paths. Second, not all intermediate variables will necessarily be chosen for a scenario. The selection will depend on the degree of analytical fineness aimed at, on the perceived importance of links, and also sometimes on the desirability of states of intermediate variables. For example, if the value of the output variable, i.e., the final outcome, is very desirable, one might tend to implicitly forget or explicitly leave out intermediate states which are very undesirable, in order to make the whole scenario more acceptable to others. The revolutionary usually does not mention the bloodshed implied by the glorious goal.

In short, the construction of a scenario requires as a final step a selection of the inferences resulting from the simulation for the scenario. The selection depends on the task, i.e., the type of scenario wanted and other criteria like desirability and probability, and it depends on the expert performing the task, i.e., his or her knowledge and values. This step implies, as the other steps described before, many intricate patterns of information processing on the side of the expert.

CONCLUSIONS

This paper should have served two goals: On the one hand, to provide an approach for better understanding what actually goes on in experts' minds when they construct scenarios of possible futures, i.e., how their intuition might work. On the other hand, to provide a perspective for designing techniques which might help experts to exploit their knowledge optimally and to protect themselves against cognitive pitfalls, i.e., for disciplining intuition.

Although the analysis was guided by recent developments in cognitive psychology, it is evidently neither descriptively nor prescriptively on safe grounds. Theoretical, empirical, and technical work is needed to examine the usefulness of the analysis and, most importantly, to validate it in real applications of scenario construction. However, the approach proposed offers a framework in which such studies can be placed and linked to each other. It is not supposed to be a theory that could be tested as a whole but rather a heuristic framework that might stimulate future studies.

REFERENCES

Alba, J. W., and Hasher, L. (1983). Is memory schematic? Psychological Bulletin, 93, 203-231.

Anderson, J.R. (1983). The architecture of cognition. Cambridge, Massachusetts, London, England: Harvard University Press.

Anderson, J.R., and Bower, G.H. (1973). Human associative memory. Washington: Winston.

Bower, G.H., Black, J.B., and Turner, T.J. (1979). Scripts in memory for text. Cognitive Psychology, 11, 177-220.

Craik, K. (1943). The nature of explanation. Cambridge: Cambridge University Press.

Einhorn, H.J., and Hogarth, R.M. (1986). Judging probable cause. Psychological Bulletin, 1, 3-19.

Einhorn, H.J., and Hogarth, R.M. (1982). Prediction, diagnosis, and causal thinking in forecasting. Journal of Forecasting, 1, 23-36.

Gentner, D., and Stevens, A.L. (eds.) (1983). Mental Models. Hillsdale, N.J.: Lawrence Erlbaum Associates.

Jungermann, H. (1985a). Inferential processes in the construction of scenarios. Journal of Forecasting, 4, 321-327.

Jungermann, H. (1985b). Psychological aspects of scenarios. In: V.T. Covello, J.L. Mumpower, P.J.M. Stallen, and V.R.R. Uppuluri (eds.), Environmental impact assessment, technology assessment, and risk analysis. New York etc.: Springer Publishing Company.

Jungermann, H., Fleischer, F., Hobohm, K., Schöppe, A. und Thüring, M. (1986). Die Arbeit mit Szenarien bei der Technologiefolgenabschätzung. Berlin: Institut fur Psychologie, Technische Universität Berlin.

Jungermann, H. and Thüring, M. (in press). The use of mental models for generating scenarios. In: G.Wright and P.Ayton (eds.), Judgemental forecasting. New York etc.: John Wiley & Sons.

Kahneman D., and Tversky, A. (1982). The simulation heuristic. In: D. Kahneman, P. Slovic and A. Tversky (eds.), Judgment under uncertainty: Heuristics and biases. New York: Cambridge University Press.

Norman, D.A. (1983). Some observations on mental models. In D. Gentner and A.L. Stevens (eds.), Mental models. Hillsdale, N.J.: Lawrence Erlbaum Associates.

Norman, D.A., and Rumelhart, D.E. (1975). Explorations in cognition. San Francisco: Freeman.

Pitz,G.F., and Sachs, N.J. (1984). Judgement and decision: Theory and application. Annual Review of Psychology, 35, 139-163.

Schank, R.C., and Abelson, R.P. (1977). Scripts, plans, goals, and understanding. Hillsdale, N.J.: Lawrence Erlbaum Associates.

Thüring, M., and Jungermann, H. (1986). Constructing and running mental models for inferences about the future. In: B.Brehmer, H. Jungermann, P. Lourens, and G. Sevon (eds.), New directions in research on decision making. Amsterdam: North-Holland.

Tversky, A., and Kahneman, D. (1983). Extensional versus intuitive reasoning: The conjunction fallacy in probability judgment. Psychological Review, 4, 293-315.

INTERACTIVE DECISION SUPPORT SYSTEMS FOR ENHANCING EXPERT JUDGMENT

Prof. Dr. İbrahim Kavrakoğlu
Boğaziçi University
Bebek, Istanbul, Turkey

INTRODUCTION

Beginning with the first electronic version, the computer has been put to problem-solving tasks of ever greater complexity. At present, there is a considerable effort to make the computer take on the ultimate challenge: replace the human expert.

Expertise has many facets, characteristics, and traits, and each problem domain has its own demands on the combination of virtues that the expert must possess. Various authors have pointed to the difficulties in developing systems to replace or supplement experts, as have some of the speakers in this meeting.

The main thrust of my presentation is that practically all systems that have been developed so far, such as computerized OR (operations research) models, IS (information systems), DDS (decision support systems), CAD (computer aided design) tools, and expert systems (ES), are one form or another of a cooperation between man and machine to solve a given problem. It is the problem area, as well as the nature of the problem, that determines the type and extent of the cooperation. In order to utilize our resources in the most effective manner, I believe that we have to be selective in the type of problems that can be reasonably addressed with expert systems.

The domains of applicability of expert systems will surely broaden in time, and this process can possibly be expedited using tools appropriate for this purpose. The approach I shall try to describe may hopefully serve in that direction.

First, I wish to dwell a little on problem complexity, within the context of finding a solution, versus arriving at a decision or design. Subsequently I shall try to explain how interactive decision support systems (decision simulators) can contribute towards enhancing expertise and help in developing expert systems.

NATO ASI Series, Vol. F35
Expert Judgment and Expert Systems
Edited by J. Mumpower et al.

PROBLEM COMPLEXITY

We can distinguish among three inherently different types of problems. The first type is that of "finding," or discovering/identifying a unique solution. The second type is the problem of "choice," where the decision depends not only on the characteristics of the alternatives, but also on the values of the decision maker. Finally, there's the "design" problem, where a solution is actually created, and not picked from a set of alternatives.

Another dimension in appreciating the complexity of a problem is the degree to which the various factors can be quantified and measured [1].

As a rule, the less quantifiable the factors, the more difficult is the problem [2].

Combined with the previous categorization, we can construct Figure 1 to depict the situation.

	Discovery	Choice	Design
Quantitative	1	2	3
Qualitative	4	5	6

Figure 1. Problem Types

I trust we can agree that the difficulty/complexity increases as we move from box 1 to box 6. (Conceivably, the ranking from 2 to 5 would depend on the degree to which qualitative factors influence the solution.)

A number of OR techniques exist for boxes 1 through 4, employing search methods, mathematical programming, MCDM (multiple criteria decision making), fuzzy set theory, etc., including various software utilizing these techniques. Expert systems have also been designed for a small number of domain-specific problems fitting in box 1 [3]. The chances of success of OR techniques diminish, however, as we move from box 1 to box 4 [4]. I suspect that with our present capabilities, the chances of success of ES are even lower. As our understanding of expertise increases, and as we develop more powerful hardware and programming languages, we can attack problems of greater complexity. At any given time, we have to utilize our resources "optimally."

I use the concept of optimality from a production-theoretic point of view: given the two basic inputs man (expert, decision maker, etc.) and machine (hardware, programming languages, etc.), what is the optimal mix of these inputs to achieve the desired output (solution to the problem)?

Here, economic theory can provide some guidance. It tells us that, as a general rule, given the "technology":

(i) The relative shares of the inputs should be inversely proportional to their respective costs.

(ii) The expenditures on the inputs should be proportional to their productivities [5].

For the present discussion, these rules can only be taken as guidelines as to how the expertise should be shared between man and machine. Productivities and costs would refer to the relative performances of the two-factor system we have described.

The "relative complexity" schema of Figure 1, and the arguments given to support it, suggest that as we move to box 6, more of the expertise has to reside in the mind of the expert, as Figure 2 indicates. As progress is made, it is expected that the relative share may change.

Progress, of course, is needed not only in computerware, but also in our understanding of problem-solving capabilities, decision making, value systems, expertise, extracting domain-specific knowledge, etc.

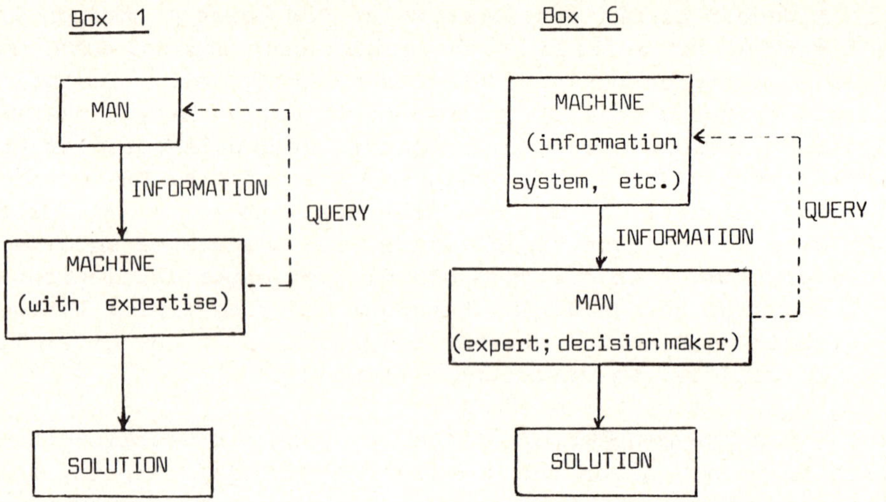

Figure 2. Man-Machine Cooperation at Different Extremes of Complexity

CONTRIBUTIONS OF DSS DEVELOPMENT

In order to achieve the stated objectives and move expert systems in the direction of box 6, considerable use can be made of the type of (interactive) decision support systems (DSS) that have been developing in the last few years. While interactive DSS have been in existence ever since the CRT was introduced, real progress in that direction came with the personal computer. The independence, user-friendliness and portability (not to mention economy!) of the PC made it possible to develop a vast number of practical DSS. The modus operandi of a typical DSS follows the interactions indicated in Figure 3.

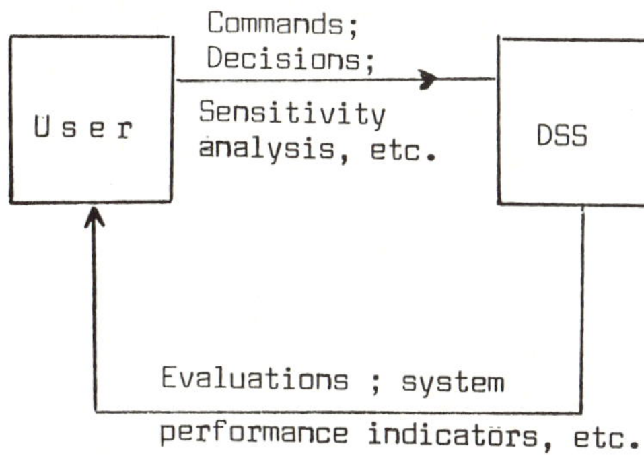

Figure 3. Using an Interactive DSS

Observing the changes in the state of the (simulated) system variables, and possibly the values of certain performance indicators, the user either converges to a particular solution, or evaluates the performance of the system he/she designed. In moderately complex system simulation, the combination of man and machine is highly effective. The machine is very suitable for carrying out the large number of computations, while the decision maker (or the expert) is capable of using his/her judgment to assess rather complex situations.

The so-called "performance indicators" may imply a number of things, such as changes in objective function(s), shadow prices, gradients of certain parameters, trade-off values, graphs of feasible domains, and possibly animated graphics of system behavior [6,7]. Other facilities that improve the interactions are voice and tablet input devices.

Interactive DSS can contribute significantly to expertise, and quite possibly to the development of expert systems. The use of simulators for training of pilots and nuclear plant operators is well-known. Over the past couple of decades, business (simulation) games have been utilized quite extensively. At Bogazici University in Istanbul, we have been employing interactive DSS for the training of professionals in the areas of production planning, quality control, facilities planning, design of distribution systems, etc., with good results.

The use of DSS for the development of expert systems would require only one further step in the same direction. Assuming that the simulator is a fair representation of the actual system (which can be checked, based on the judgment of the expert), the behavior of the (simulated) system and the decisions/controls of the expert can be recorded and analyzed to arrive at a set of rules, which may then be used to build an expert system.

CONCLUSIONS

Developing expert systems which involve "choice" or "design" is more complex than the problem where the objective is to "discover" a particular solution. Additonally, factors that can only be defined qualitatively make the problem even more difficult.

Expert systems development and modeling with OR techniques have various common elements, and both can benefit from a closer cooperation. Especially, the interactive decision support systems (or, decision simulators) can contribute to expert system development, as well as enhance expert judgment.

The latter is achieved by simply condensing a lot more experience into a shorter duration of time, while the former can be facilitated by collecting information directly from the expert who is controlling the system.

NOTES

[1] S. Eilon (1985), Structuring unstructured decisions, OMEGA, V 13, no. 5, pp 369-377.

[2] No distinction has been made here as to the nature of the system, whether it is physical or social. The latter poses yet another difficulty, in that any decision/design necessarily involves the state of the system in the future. Even the decision itself is a factor in modifying the subsequent behavior of the system. Therefore, the decision maker constructs or imagines plausible future scenarios and evaluates them before arriving at decisions. I would suspect

that such an ability is extremely difficult to define, let alone synthesize in the form of an expert system.

[3] J.K. Kastner and S.J. Hong (1984), A review of expert systems, Euro. J. Operational Res., v. 18, pp. 285-292.

[4] C.B. Tilanus (1985), Failures and successes of quantitative methods in management, Euro. J. Operational Res., v. 19, pp. 170-175.

[5] Given two factors of production, X_1 and X_2 with unit costs $C1$ and $C2$ and productivities $P1$ and $P2$, the first rule says:

$$\frac{X_1}{X_2} = k \frac{C_2}{C_1}$$

where k, the ratio of productivities, is constant.

Expressing the above equation as a function of productivities, we arrive at

$$\frac{C_1 X_1}{C2\ X_2} = \frac{P1}{P_2}$$

where $C_1 X_1$ and $C_2 X_2$ are the expenditures for the two factors.

[6] I. Kavrakoglu (1983), Judgmental programming, Bogazici University Research Report, Dept. Industrial Eng'g.

[7] R.D. Hurrion (1986), Visual interactive modelling, Euro. J. Operational Res., v. 23, pp. 281-287.

VALUE-DRIVEN EXPERT SYSTEMS FOR DECISION SUPPORT

Ralph L. Keeney
University of Southern California
Los Angeles, California, USA

This work was supported in part by the Office of Naval Research under Contract N00014-84-K-0332 titled "Value-Focused Thinking and the Study of Values." It is based on a paper originally presented at the International Conference on Multi-attribute Decision Making via O.R.-Based Expert Systems at the University of Passau, Germany, April 20-27, 1986.

INTRODUCTION

The intent of both expert systems and decision analysis is to help decision makers make better informed decisions. The manners in which these tools provide this help are quite distinct from each other. Indeed, both decision analysis and expert systems have complementary strengths. Consequently, each has significant advantages that could be usefully adapted by the other. This article focuses on how decision analysis could appropriately be used to improve the potential usefulness of expert systems designed for decision support.

This paper is outlined as follows. Section 2, "Decisions, Expert Systems, and Decision Analysis," indicates the key elements in analysis to aid decision-making and outlines the relative strengths of expert systems and decision analysis for addressing these elements. Section 3, "Inherent Values in Expert Systems," indicates that values are an inherent part of all decision processes and are, at least implicitly, a part of all expert systems. Because it is difficult to address value issues implicitly in a consistent and logical manner, it may be advantageous to use the explicit logic of decision analysis to address these issues in expert systems. The manner in which decision analysis addresses value issues in decision problems is outlined in Section 4, "Objective Functions Based on Multi-attribute Utility." Section 5, "Integrating Decision Analysis into Expert Systems," discusses the integration of

NATO ASI Series, Vol. F35
Expert Judgment and Expert Systems
Edited by J. Mumpower et al.

decision analysis into expert systems. Section 6 presents conclusions.

DECISIONS, EXPERT SYSTEMS, AND DECISION ANALYSIS

The orientation of many expert systems and of decision analysis is prescriptive. That is, the intent is to help make better decisions, rather than to describe or predict how decisions will be made. To appraise prescriptive help, it is useful to recognize that decisions should depend on three items: the alternatives available, the possible consequences and their relative likelihoods for each of the alternatives, and the relative desirability of those consequences. Items one and two concern factual issues. The third item, the one of interest in this paper, concerns values.

The fundamental premise underlying the comments in this paper is that since values are to be the driving force for making decisions, values should be prominent in any analysis designed to aid decision-making. To understand that this is the case, consider why it is worth the effort to carefully choose an alternative rather than simply let occur what will. The answer is that some concerned party (e.g., a decision maker) is interested in the possible consequences that might occur. The desire to avoid unpleasant consequences and to achieve desirable ones, especially when the differences in the relative desirability of the possible consequences are significant, is the motivation for interest in any decision problem. Hence, values should guide the allocation of time and effort spent analyzing decisions and the processes of creating and evaluating alternatives.

Given the above premise, it would seem reasonable that expert systems designed to assist decision makers should be capable of structuring the values which should and do drive the decisions. Quite simply, many expert systems treat values implicitly and heuristically (Waterman, 1986). Expert systems often do not develop an explicit objective function to provide the flexibility for decision makers to investigate the implications of their own values, as opposed to those built into the system (Lehner, Probus, and Donnell, 1985; White and Sykes, 1986; and Farquhar, 1986). Consequently, it is also not possible to investigate the implications of values representing different viewpoints. As strengths, expert systems offer remarkable abilities to process information inexpensively and efficient manners to display this information to decision makers.

Decision analysis has complementary strengths. Intuitively, decision analysis is a formalization of common sense for decision problems that are too complex for informal use of common sense. A more technical definition is a philosophy, articulated by a set of logical axioms, and a methodology and collection of systematic procedures, based upon those axioms, for responsibly analyzing the complexities inherent in decision problems. The relative strengths of decision analysis are a logical foundation to structure and analyze decision problems, provided by axioms stated in von Neumann and Morgenstern (1947), Savage (1954), and Pratt, Raiffa, and Schlaifer (1964), and sound, tested procedures to implement this logic. The implementation of these procedures is often time consuming and relatively expensive, luxuries that are often appropriate for major, one-of-a-kind decisions such as those summarized in Keeney (1982) and von Winterfeldt and Edwards (1986). By combining the logic and elicitation techniques of decision analysis and the processing abilities and relatively low expense of using an expert system, expert systems which offer users significantly more insight for better informed decision-making are possible.

INHERENT VALUES IN EXPERT SYSTEMS

Values are built into any expert system, since values are necessarily utilized in selecting the problem to be addressed, the data sources to utilize, the variables to include in the model, any rules for evaluation, and the output indices to communicate with the decision makers. The inclusion of values in an expert system is part of the responsibility of the knowledge engineer. Before being more specific, let us briefly summarize what is involved in structuring values explicitly.

The structuring of values involves identifying, organizing, and quantifying them. The process can be characterized in four steps: developing a list of objectives, organizing these objectives into an objectives hierarchy, specifying attributes useful for measuring the degree to which the objectives are met by alternatives, and developing an objective function to integrate the achievement of the various objectives into one overall measure. The first three steps rely on systematic procedures, but they are not mathematical in nature (Keeney, 1985). The fourth step does rely on a significant amount of mathematical theory, some of which is summarized in Section 4, "Objective Functions Based on Multi-attribute Utility." The rest of this section contains suggestions for knowledge engineers to explicitly structure values in expert systems.

Use Objectives, not Goals

Objectives indicate something that should be maximized or minimized, and as such always provide a clear indication of what is better. Goals, on the other hand, have an associated "standard" or "aspiration level." For instance, an objective is to maximize the return on an investment portfolio. Goals might be to obtain a twenty percent return or to maximize the probability of a ten percent return. With the former goal, it is not often clear what one should strive toward, as there are uncertainties in any investment decision and no investment would appear to guarantee a twenty percent return. The shortcoming of a goal such as maximizing the probability of a ten percent return is that it does not differentiate between a twenty percent return and an eleven percent return. Most individuals would prefer a ninety percent chance at a twenty percent return and a ten percent chance at a nine percent return to a guaranteed eleven percent return. However, the latter situation clearly maximizes the probability of a ten percent return. In summary, the use of goals as a basis for decisions is often not logically sound, and hence should not be relied upon in expert systems.

Use Fundamental Objectives Rather than Means Objectives

If the output of an expert system indicates the degree to which means objectives are met rather than the degree to which fundamental (i.e. ends) objectives are met, the decision maker must make an implicit connection between those means and the ends in order to gain insight for the decision being considered. The relationship between means and ends is one concerning facts pertaining to the expertise of a domain expert. Hence, it is often more reasonable and desirable to include the relationships between the means and fundamental objectives as part of the expert system. For instance, consider an expert system designed to guide the construction process to minimize the overall time and cost of the project. An expert system that provided only component completion times of the various tasks necessary to complete the project would not offer as much insight as one that logically integrated those into overall construction time and cost.

Consider "Degrees" Explicitly

If the intent of an expert system is to assist one in medical decision-making, the objective of "maximize the probability of survival" may not be particularly useful if there are significant degrees of survival. To be more explicit, survival after a disease so that one is capable of doing all that one was able to do prior to the onset of the disease may be much different than survival where one has a significant number of actions or activities that are not possible. Since such degrees are likely important to the decision process, it may enhance an expert system to address them explicitly.

Select Attributes with Reasonable Inherent Values

If one of the attributes (i.e. measure to indicate the degree to which an objective is achieved) is waiting time, there is the implicit assumption that any minute of waiting time is equally desirable as any other minute of waiting time. If the attribute of an investment program is the net present value of investments, there are strong implications about investment opportunities, consistency of interest rates, cost of transactions, and the relative usefulness of funds at different times automatically built into the attribute. It is often the case that these implicit value judgments are not appropriate for all uses or all users of a particular expert system.

Construct Attributes when Useful

With many of the decisions that are the concern of expert systems, there may be important objectives for which there is no easy-to-measure attribute. In such cases, it may be desirable to construct an attribute that explicitly includes value judgments deemed appropriate for the problem. In a decision system designed to assist in evaluating alternatives for the treatment of cleft lip and pallet for children, Krischer (1976) constructed an attribute for the physical visual impact of such treatment. In a different context, an attribute that may be appropriate for a general purpose expert system to assist in making financial investments is the "social desirability" of various investments to a given user.

Separate Elicitation of Factual Expertise and Values

In most complex decision problems, a decision maker with certain objectives must rely on factual expertise from one or more experts. For example, a coherent patient with cancer may have a choice of several treatment strategies that will affect his objectives concerning longevity, quality of life, pain and discomfort, and other family members. He would likely wish to rely on the medical expertise of physicians to indicate the possible consequences of each treatment strategy in terms of his four objectives. However, the appropriate value judgments for the decision problem should come from the patient. With many expert systems, both the factual expertise and the values, often only implicitly addressed, are obtained by the knowledge engineer from the domain expert. A major shortcoming of this procedure is that the domain expert may have very different values from those of the patient. Hence, the separation of facts from values can often lead both to a clarified problem structure and to an expert system capable of providing more relevant advice to users.

Complex Objective Functions Often Indicate Poorly-Selected Objectives

When the objective functions are complex, meaning that they involve more than either additive or multiplicative components of single-attribute objective functions, it is sometimes the case that the original objectives were not wisely selected. Specifically, they may involve means objectives, which may be means to several fundamental objectives; they may involve overlapping objectives and hence doublecounting; or they may involve the omission of key objectives (Keeney, 1981). A restructuring of the objectives may then be appropriate. If a complex objective function seems reasonable, both value judgments and factual judgments are interrelated, so it is worthwhile to conceptually distinguish their role and relevance.

Address Value Tradeoffs Explicitly

Value tradeoffs are often a key element of a decision problem, as they indicate how much of one objective the decision maker is willing to give up in order to achieve a specific amount of another objective. Consequently, it is often useful to explicitly address these value tradeoffs. Oversimplistic value tradeoffs, such as lexicographic orderings, are often too simplistic. One simply does not try to maximize quantity first, and only after that consider quality, nor does one try to maximize quality first, and then try to maximize quantity. Common sense requires that both be addressed simultaneously, and value tradeoffs provide a logical basis to do this.

Introduce Values Sequentially

It is usually the case that some of the values in a decision problem are not very controversial, where others may be. An expert system which allows one to introduce the relatively non-controversial values first and see how far one can get with these in terms of evaluating the relative desirability of the alternatives is useful. One can then sequentially introduce more controversial values and repeat the process. This should lead to more insight from an expert system by indicating exactly what values are crucial to a particular decision. Also, in situations where multiple decision makers or stakeholders are concerned with the same decision, it may result in agreement on a possible course of action or at least on alternatives that should be discarded.

OBJECTIVE FUNCTIONS BASED ON MULTIATTRIBUTE UTILITY

Once an objectives hierarchy has been established and an attribute has been identified for each of the lowest-level objectives in the hierarchy, an appropriate objective function for the problem can be developed.

Prior to this, let us introduce notation to concisely describe the generic problem structure. We have generated a number of alternatives $A_j, j=1,\ldots,J$, and an objectives hierarchy with n lowest-level objectives $O_i, i=1,\ldots,n$, where n may equal one. Associated with each lowest-level objective is an attribute $X_i, i=1,\ldots,n$. Furthermore, define x_i to be a specific level of

X_i, so the possible impact of selecting an alternative can be characterized by the consequence $x=(x_1,x_2,\ldots,x_n)$. An example of an objective O_i is "maximize the local economic benefit" and an associated attribute X_i may be "annual local tax paid." A level x_i could then be \$29 million.

It is probably impossible to achieve the best level with respect to each objective in a decision problem. The question is, "How much should be given up with regard to one objective to achieve a specified improvement in another?" The issue is one of value tradeoffs. For decision problems with either single or multiple objectives, it is rarely the case (except in simple problems) that one alternative is guaranteed to yield the best available consequence. There are usually circumstances that could lead to relatively undesirable consequences with any given alternative. The question is, "Are the potential benefits of having things go right worth the risks if things go wrong?" This issue is about risk attitudes. Both value tradeoffs and risk attitudes are particularly complicated because there are no right or wrong values. Basically, what is needed is an objective function which aggregates all the individual objectives and an attitude toward risk. In decision analysis, such an objective function is referred to as a utility function, symbolically written u. Then u(x), the utility of the consequence x, indicates the desirability of x relative to all other consequences. Following directly from the axioms of decision analysis, alternatives with higher expected (i.e., average) utilities should be preferred to those with lower expected utilities.

This step, unique to decision analysis, involves the creation of a model of values to evaluate the alternatives. This is done in a structured discussion between a decision analyst and the decision makers to quantify value judgments about possible consequences in the problem. As illustrated in Keeney (1980), the procedure systematically elicits relevant information about value tradeoffs and risk attitudes with provision for consistency checks. In addition to the obvious advantage of providing a theoretically sound manner to evaluate alternatives, the explicit development of a value model offers several other advantages, including indicating which information is of interest in the problem, suggesting alternatives that may have been overlooked, providing a means to calculate the value of obtaining additional information, and facilitating concise communication about objectives among interested parties. In addition, a sensitivity analysis of the value judgments can be conducted to appraise their importance for the overall decision.

The process of determining the utility function can be broken into five steps: (1) introducing terminology and ideas, (2) determining the general value structure, (3) assessing single-attribute utility functions, (4) evaluating scaling constants, and (5) checking for consistency and reiterating. For decision problems with a single objective, only Steps 1, 3, and 5 are relevant. In practice there is considerable interaction between the steps although each will be separately discussed.

Introducing Terminology and Ideas

The basic purpose of this step is to develop a rapport and an ability to communicate between the decision analyst and the decision maker or decision makers. It should be stated that the goal of the assessment process is to end up with a consistent representation of values for evaluating alternatives. The analysis should make sure that the decision makers are comfortable with the assessment procedure and understand the meaning of each attribute and the objective it is meant to measure. If the decision makers have not been closely involved in defining the attributes or describing the impact of alternatives, this phase of communication is particularly important. The decision makers should understand that there are no correct or incorrect values and that expressed values can be altered at any time.

Determining the General Value Structure

Here, one structures values with a model indicating the general functional form of the utility function $u(x_1,\dots,x_n)$. To obtain the structure for multiple objectives, one uses value independence concepts in the same way that probabilistic independence is utilized in structuring models of impacts. Most of the independence concepts concern relative values for consequences with levels of a subset of the attributes fixed. The independence concepts are used to derive a simple function f such as

$$u(x_1,\dots,x_n) = f[u_1(x_1),\dots,u_n(x_n),k_1,\dots,k_m,\dots,k_r] \quad (1)$$

where the u_i are single-attribute utility functions and the k_m are scaling constants. Specific functional forms following from various assumptions are found in Fishburn (1964, 1965, 1970), Meyer (1970), Keeney and Raiffa (1976), Bell (1977), and Farquhar and Fishburn (1981). Using (1), the overall utility function is determined by assessing the single-attribute utility functions and the scaling constants which weight various combinations of single-attribute functions.

A related approach to model values for multiple objectives involves building a value function $v(x_1,\ldots,x_n)$ which assigns higher numbers (i.e., values) to preferred consequences. This is done in a spirit akin to (1) using either single-attribute value functions or indifference curves together with scaling constants. A utility function is assessed over value providing u[v(x)] which incorporates value tradeoffs in v and an attitude toward risk in u. Models of value functions addressing multiple objectives are found in Debreu (1960), Koopmans (1960), Luce and Tukey (1964), Krantz et al. (1971) and Dyer and Sarin (1979).

Assessing Single-Attribute Utility Functions

Procedures for assessing single-attribute utility functions are well developed. In summary, one wishes to first determine the appropriate risk attitude. For instance, one is said to be risk-averse if consequence $(x_1 + x_2)/2$ is always preferred to a lottery yielding either x_1 or x_2 each with a probability of 0.5. In this case, the average of x_1 and x_2 is preferable to risking a half chance of the higher and a half chance of the lower consequence. When one is risk-averse, the corresponding single-attribute utility function is concave. As discussed in Pratt (1964), special risk attitudes restrict the functional form of single-attribute utility functions. A common utility function is the exponential utility function

$$u(x) = d - b^{-cx} \qquad (2)$$

where d,b>0,c>0 are scaling constants. This utility function is referred to as constantly risk-averse since it is the only one consistent with the following property. If x_3 is indifferent to a 0.5 chance at either x_1 or x_2, then $x_3 + E$ must be indifferent to 0.5 chance at either $x_1 + E$ or $X_2 + E$ for all possible E.

To specify the scaling constants d and b in (2), one arbitrarily sets the utility corresponding to two consequences. This is similar to defining a temperature scale by selecting a boiling and a freezing point. The utilities of all other consequences are relative to the two chosen for the scale. To specify the appropriate numerical value for the constant c in (2), one can identify both a lottery and a consequence which are equally preferred by the decision maker. For instance, suppose the decision maker is indifferent regarding the certain consequence x_3 and a lottery yielding either x_1 or x_2 with equal chances of 0.5. Then, to be consistent with the axioms of decision analysis, the utility of x_3 must be set equal to the expected utility of the lottery. Hence,

$$u(x_3) = 0.5u(x_1) + 0.5u(x_2). \tag{3}$$

Substituting (2) into (3) and solving yields parameter c.

Evaluating Scaling Constants

With multiple objectives, the same concept is utilized to determine scaling constants, which relate to the relative desirability of specified changes of different attribute levels. To illustrate this in a simple case, consider the additive utility function

$$u(x_1,\ldots,x_n) = \sum_{i=1}^{n} k_i u_i(x_i), \tag{4}$$

where k_i, $i = 1,\ldots,n$ are scaling constants. For this additive utility function, the values of the k_i indicate the relative importance of changing each attribute from its least desirable to its most desirable level. To assess these scaling constants, one generates data representing stated value judgments of the decision maker. For instance, if the decision maker is found to be indifferent between $(x_1,\ldots,x_n)$ and $(y_1,\ldots,y_n)$, the utility of these two consequences must be equal. They are set equal using (4) which yields an equation with the scaling factors as unknowns. Using such indifferences, one generates a set of n independent equations which is solved to determine numerical values for the n unknown scaling constants. The equations can be generated by sequentially considering consequences which differ in terms of the levels of only two attributes. This significantly simplifies the comparison task required of the decision makers. More details about the assessment of utility functions can be found in Fishburn (1976), Keeney and Raiffa (1976), Farquhar (1984), and von Winterfeldt and Edwards (1986).

Checking Consistency

It has been my experience that there are invariably inconsistencies in the initial assessments. In fact, this is one of the main reasons for the procedure, because once inconsistencies are identified, decision makers alter their responses to reach consistency and better reflect their basic values. Furthermore, decision makers usually feel better after having straightened out their value structure in their own mind. Thus, it is essential to ask questions in different ways and to carefully reiterate through aspects of the assessment procedure until a consistent representation of the decision maker's values is achieved.

With multiple decision makers, as discussed in Harsanyi (1955), Fishburn (1973), or Keeney and Raiffa (1976), additional value judgments are required to address the relative importance of the different decision makers and the relative intensity of the potential impact to each in order to determine an overall utility function. In addition, the decision problem can be analyzed from the viewpoints of the different decision makers by using their own utility functions. It may be that the same alternative is preferred by each decision maker, possibly for different reasons. In any case, it might be helpful to eliminate dominated alternatives, identify the basis for conflicts, and suggest mechanisms for resolution.

The value judgments made explicit in assessing u for any decision maker is an essential part of building a model of values. This process of building a model of values corresponds precisely with that used for any model. We gather some data (the decision maker's judgments), and use the data in a generic model (the utility function u) to calculate its parameters (e.g., the k_m's in (1) and c in (2)). Additional value judgments are necessary to structure values of multiple decision makers into one coherent utility function.

INTEGRATING DECISION ANALYSIS INTO EXPERT SYSTEMS

The inclusion of a value model as part of an expert system can be done in different ways. For a given expert system, one way may be better than another. At one level, in the development of an expert system, it may be useful to carefully obtain a "good" objective function to use in the expert system. Such a good objective function would have carefully thought out value judgments built implicitly into the expert system, but it would not allow the user to vary these value judgments easily.

At a second level, the expert system would include a value model that offered the user partial choice of the objective function used in his or her applications of the expert system. For instance, a value model connected to an expert system designed to aid personal financial investments may allow the user to provide value judgments about an appropriate risk attitude and appropriate value tradeoffs for income in different time periods. Other value judgments about the overall form (e.g., an additive or multiplicative utility function) would be chosen by the developers (i.e. knowledge engineers and domain experts) of the expert system and not easily changed by the user for a specific application.

The third level of a value model for an expert system would offer users a menu to select their form for the objective function and dialog to provide the value judgments necessary to imply the specific objective function with that form. It may also provide for easy sensitivity analysis with different objective functions.

The most involved and most flexible value model associated with an expert system would allow the potential user to completely assess his or her own objective function as part of the expert system. Such a flexible system would, however, have to be based on a given set of objectives and attributes, as the output information on those attributes would necessarily need to be available from the expert system. Indeed, different users may focus on a different set of fundamental objectives for their specific purposes. This option is not a great deal different from having a separate expert system to assess an individual's utility function. Along this line, Wellman (1985, 1986) has developed an expert system to identify the appropriate form of a multi-attribute utility function consistent with any set of value independence assumptions. Given the form, one would likely rely on many of the ideas in the multi-attribute utility assessment programs developed by Humphreys and Wishuda (1980) and Sicherman (1982) to identify the specific utility function.

CONCLUSIONS

The main conclusion of this paper is simple and straightforward. Namely, the use of decision analysis and multi-attribute utility theory in developing some expert systems can make a significant contribution to the quality of those systems. This conclusion is based on the following:

- Values are the basis for interest in a given decision problem.
- The values in the given decision problem are often not explicitly or consistently addressed in expert systems.
- Multi-attribute utility provides a logically sound and operationally tested method to include values in expert systems.

A very small portion of the total effort in developing an expert system is spent explicitly addressing the value judgments inherent in the problem. The shift of a small amount (e.g., 5 percent) of the total effort to focus explicitly on the values relevant to a decision problem addressed by an expert system can make substantial contributions. We would expect these contributions to enhance both the amount of usage and the usefulness of such expert systems.

ACKNOWLEDGMENT

The comments of Professors Peter H. Farquhar of Carnegie-Mellon University and Richard S. John of the University of Southern California on an early draft were very helpful in revising this manuscript.

REFERENCES

Bell, D.E. 1977. A Utility Function for Time Streams Having Interperiod Dependencies, Operations Research, 25, 448-458.

Debreu, G. 1960. Topological Methods in Cardinal Utility Theory, in Mathematical Methods in the Social Sciences, 1959, K.J. Arrow, S. Karlin and P. Suppes (eds.), Stanford University Press, Stanford, Calif.

Dyer, J.S., and R.K. Sarlin 1979. Measurable Multi-attribute Value Functions, Operations Research, 27, 810-822.

Farquhar, P.H. 1984. Utility Assessment Methods, Management Science, 300, 1283-1300.

Farquhar, P.H. 1986. Applications of Utility Theory in Artificial Intelligence Research, Technical Report 86-2, Decision Research Program, Graduate School of Industrial Administration, Carnegie-Mellon University, Pittsburgh, Pennsylvania.

Farquhar, P.H. and P.C. Fishburn 1981. Equivalence and Continuity in Multivalent Preference Structures, Operations Research, 29, 282-293.

Fishburn, P.C. 1964. Decision and Value Theory, Wiley, New York.

Fishburn, P.C. 1965. Independence in Utility Theory with Whole Product Sets, Operations Research, 13, 28-45.

Fishburn, P.C. 1967. Methods of Estimating Additive Utilities, Management Science, 13, 435-453.

Fishburn, P.C. 1970. Utility Theory for Decision Making, Wiley, New York.

Fishburn, P.C. 1973. The Theory of Social Choice, Princeton University Press, Princeton, N.J.

Harsanyi, J.C. 1955. Cardinal Welfare, Individualistic Ethics, and Interpersonal Comparisons of Utility, Journal of Political Economy, 63, 309-321.

Humphreys, P.C. and A. Wishuda 1980. Multi-attribute Utility Decomposition, Technical Report 72-2/2, Decision Analysis Unit, Brunel University, Uxbridge, Middlesex, England.

Keeney, R.L. 1980. Siting Energy Facilities, Academic Press, New York.

Keeney, R.L. 1981. Analysis of Preference Dependencies among Objectives, Operations Research, 29, 1105-1120.

Keeney, R.L. 1982. Decision Analysis: An Overview, Operations Research, 30, 803-838.

Keeney, R.L. 1985. Hierarchies of Objectives, Report 8515, Faculty of Mathematics and Computer Science, University of Passau, Germany.

Keeney, R.L., and H. Raiffa 1976. Decisions with Multiple Objectives, Wiley, New York.

Koopmans, T.C. 1960. Stationary Ordinal Utility and Impatience, Econometrica, 28, 287-309.

Krantz, D.H., R.D. Luce, P. Suppes and A. Tversky 1971. Foundations of Measurement, 1, Academic Press, New York.

Krischer, J.P. 1976. Utility Structure of a Medical Decision-Making Problem, Operations Research, 24, 951-972.

Lehner, P.E., M.A. Probus, and M.L. Donnell 1985. Building Decision Aids: Exploiting the Synergy between Decision Analysis and Artificial Intelligence, IEEE Transactions on Systems, Man, and Cybernetics, SMC-15, 469-74.

Luce, R.D., and J.W. Tukey 1964. Simultaneous Conjoint Measurement: A New Type of Fundamental Measurement, Journal of Mathematical Psychology, 1, 1-27.

Meyer, R.F. 1970. On the Relationship among the Utility of Assets, the Utility of Consumption, and Investment Strategy in an Uncertain, but Time Invariant World, in OR 69: Proceedings of the Fifth International Conference on a Operational Research, J. Lawrence (ed.), Tavistock Publishing, London.

Pratt, J.W. 1964. Risk Aversion in the Small and in the Large, Econometrica, 32, 353-375.

Pratt, J.W., H. Raiffa and R.O. Schlaifer 1964. The Foundations of Decision under Uncertainty: An Elementary Exposition, Journal of the American Statistical Association, 59, 353-375.

Savage, L.J. 1954. The Foundations of Statistics, Wiley, New York.

Sicherman, A. 1982. Decision Framework for Technology Choice, Volume 2: Decision Analysis User's Manual, EPRI Report EA-2153, Electric Power Research Institute, Palo Alto, Calif.

von Neumann, J., and O. Morgenstern 1947. Theory of Games and Economic Behavior, ED. 2., Princeton University Press, Princeton, N.J.

von Winterfeldt, D., and W. Edwards 1986. Decision Analysis and Behavioral Research, Cambridge University Press, New York, New York.

Waterman, D.A. 1986. A Guide to Expert Systems, Addison-Wesley, Reading, Massachusetts.

Wellman, M.P. 1985. Reasoning about Preference Models, Technical Report 340, Laboratory for Computer Science, Massachusetts Institute of Technology, Cambridge, Massachusetts.

Wellman, M.P. 1986. Automated Multi-attribute Utility Decomposition: Examples, Preprint, Laboratory for Computer Science, Massachusetts Institute of Technology, Cambridge, Massachusetts.

White, C.C. III, and E.A. Sykes 1986. A User Preference Guided Approach to Conflict Resolution in Rule-Based Expert Systems, IEEE Transactions on Systems, Man, and Cybernetics, SMC-16, 276-278.

EXPERT SYSTEMS AND CREATIVITY

Kenneth R. MacCrimmon and Christian Wagner
University of British Columbia
Vancouver, British Columbia
Canada

INTRODUCTION

In this paper we evaluate the requirements for an expert system designed to exhibit creativity. First we consider what it means to be an expert and what "expert system" means in an artificial intelligence context. Then we shift focus from "ordinary" intelligence to "creative" intelligence by examining the concept of creative behavior, followed by a discussion of the implications for the design of an expert system exhibiting creativity across various domains. In the final section of the paper we present a design overview of such a system.

WHAT ARE EXPERTS?

The definition of "expert" in the Oxford English Dictionary is one "who has gained skill from experience" and "whose special knowledge or skill causes him to be regarded an authority." Note the three key aspects implied in the definition: (1) a body of knowledge, (2) proficiency in applying the knowledge, and (3) the ability to learn from experience.

A body of knowledge, both facts and rules, in a particular area is a necessary condition for being an expert in that area. Whether we are talking about brain surgery, music composition, or traffic flow, an expert is expected to know more about the area than the average person. It is not sufficient to know more than a novice, the expert is also expected to know more than the non-expert working in the area.

Simply possessing a large body of facts, however, does not qualify one as an expert. Someone with only a large number of facts about one area is not an expert but an idiot savant. Someone with only a large number of rules about how to do

NATO ASI Series, Vol. F35
Expert Judgment and Expert Systems
Edited by J. Mumpower et al.

something is not an expert but a routine implementor. The expert must be able to use the facts and rules to obtain a deeper understanding about how the system works. In carrying out activities in the area, the expert must be able to use the domain knowledge to achieve better results than novices.

A classic example of trying to provide expertise through a large body of facts and rules was described by Kaufman in his book The Forest Ranger. Due to their geographical isolation, forest rangers must be prepared to deal autonomously with many contingencies. To provide this capability, and to assure uniformity of behavior, many manuals of procedures were supplied to each ranger station. When any situation arose, the rangers were expected to consult the appropriate manual. These procedures were undoubtedly successful in making novice rangers more expert-like but they were a major inhibition to the rangers who were real experts.

Aside from possessing knowledge, an expert has to know how to apply the knowledge. He must solve problems differently than non-experts. Experts, independent of their domain of specialization, seem to exhibit common characteristics in solving problems. To explore these characteristics, let us consider three important parts of the problem solving process: problem representation, alternative generation, and alternative evaluation.

The way the problem is represented in the problem solver's mind is a key determinant of the problem complexity and of the rules which will be used to attempt to solve the problem. Experts differ from novices in the depth of their problem representations. Bouwman (1982), for example, observed relatively short reasoning sequences for inexperienced financial analysts in contrast to much longer ones for expert analysts.

Experts are able to capture the "deep structure" of a problem compared to the "surface structure" by which novices typically categorize problems (Larkin et al., 1980; deGroot, 1965). Deep structure is a term which describes a system's causal relationships, surface structure refers to the system's visible characteristics. Focusing on the surface structure, novices assume problems are similar if their verbalization seems similar, if they look alike, or have the same objects (Woods, 1981). Experts generate a representation which allows them to classify problems according to more fundamental principles or processes. Humes (1983), for example, found that expert writers focus in their composition and review process on the meaning of their product, while poor writers are more concerned with the mechanics of writing and the correction of errors.

Experts are able to deal effectively with problem complexity while novices get lost in problem details, typically working in a depth first manner (Vessey, 1984). Experts tend to use breadth first search, by analyzing first all the subproblems at one level before breaking any subproblem into its constituent parts. Experts are able to focus on the central problem elements while novices attempt to work with those closest at hand or the superficially most prominent.

In the alternative generation phase, experts possess a portfolio of strategies, for example by searching for cues or triggers to solve the problem by analogy (Brooks, 1983; Vitalari and Dickson, 1982). Bouwman found that financial analysis experts not only employed a more balanced "operator mix," but also tended to use more complex operators in their search for alternative causes.

The third element of our definition of an expert is the way he learns from experience. The method by which knowledge is acquired is often of critical importance. Someone who is presented with a large body of knowledge may, through rote memory, be able to spew back facts and apply rules but we would not call such a person an expert unless he was able to deal with problems in the area of expertise better than a novice could. A fixed set of rules does not usually allow one to respond to unanticipated changes in a system. An expert must be able to develop rules to handle new situations.

We expect that increased expertise will enable an expert to respond faster to a situation. In other words, expert learning is more than an addition of facts and rules of the standard operating procedure type. In order to be both more accurate as well as faster in their performance, experts have to reorganize their thinking during the learning process. Kolodner (1983) calls the reorganization of memory "similarity-based generalization." The expert identifies similarities among single observations allowing him to group them together in a new category. Remembering the category properties, he can derive properties for single observations if they show the characteristics of the category. Learning therefore results in a more general and more efficient representation of knowledge.

As with the possession of a body of knowledge itself, the ability to learn from experience, although a necessary condition, is not sufficient to manifest expertise. One must have learned satisfactorily from experience to have built up a body of knowledge.

Experts know how to learn by asking good questions of others. Dating at least as far back as Socrates, the ability to ask the right questions rather than memorizing right answers has been a criterion of learning. Dewey (1933) and other influential educators have also emphasized that intelligence is not knowing all the facts, it is knowing how to get them. By asking questions, experts are able to understand the problem and its underlying processes. Novices do not know how to ask pertinent questions (Fogler, 1983).

It is likely that if one has learned from experience then one will have a sufficient body of knowledge in an area to be called an expert. The ability to learn from experience tends to imply the presence of a body of knowledge more than the presence of a body of knowledge implies the learning from experience.

Experts use hypothesis formulation and verification as a problem solving strategy (Stein, 1976). Through definition and stepwise refinement of a hypothesis, experts are able to reduce the size of the search space. When hypotheses are developed, the expert continually tests them against the facts. On failure, an expert backtracks systematically to related hypotheses or reshapes the current hypotheses.

By considering a variety of goals and possibilities, the expert does not have the narrow focus of the novice. Finer distinctions can be made of the potential effectiveness of a solution. An expert can simulate the effect of potential changes in his mind to ascertain if they would solve the problem. Experts can identify multiple solutions and can determine the sensitivity of a solution to changes in the premises. In diagnosis, experts do not give up the search after finding one possible problem cause, but rather try to understand the "total picture" (Bouwman).

The importance of learning as a criterion of expertise can be seen in space exploration. Astronauts are trained to identify and evaluate situations they are confronted with in space and to act according to standard operating procedures prepared for these situations. Most of the time when unforseen cicumstances arise, the astronauts consult with Mission Control where a large number of experts can generate new rules for the astronauts to carry out. At times, however, the astronauts decide themselves how to respond to new situations, with Mission Control playing a purely supporting role. The crucial test of whether the expertise resides on the ground or in the spacecraft is where the adaptation and learning takes place.

WHAT IS AN EXPERT SYSTEM?

The term "expert" in the computer science literature of expert systems tends to be used in the relatively narrow sense of a computer system incorporating a fixed body of knowledge and rules. The ability to adapt the facts and rules through experience has not been a requirement. In other words, an expert system does not represent the dynamics of expert knowledge but rather a snapshot of it. This emphasis on a large body of knowledge for a specific domain can be seen as a consequence of the way artificial intelligence has developed over the past several decades.

The early work on artificial intelligence focussed on systems with general problem solving skills. The most notable example was the General Problem Solver (GPS) of Newell, Shaw, and Simon (1958). It successfully solved logic problems, cryptarithmetic, algebra word problems, and the like. GPS consisted of a logic-based reasoning mechanism which was applied to a small knowledge base. The knowledge base included all the facts and rules necessary to describe the problem. Thus GPS was given a complete internal representation of the problem to be solved. GPS was unable to handle problems of real complexity but rather was used to reveal the structure of tasks and to compare computer problem solving to human problem solvers (Ernst and Newell, 1969).

In the mid-1960s, with the work of Feigenbaum and Lederberg, developments of artificial intelligence headed in the direction of simulating the behavior of experts in a particular domain of knowledge. Their program DENDRAL detects the molecular structure of unknown chemical compounds (Feigenbaum, Buchanan, Lederberg, 1971). This work has been followed by very successful implementations of computer systems in a variety of areas, such as medical diagnosis (e.g., MYCIN), geological exploration (e.g., PROSPECTOR), or computer system configurations (e.g., XCON).

These domain-specific systems demonstrated that a computer system could effectively perform some complex tasks typically performed by an expert. Thus the term "expert system" has taken on the meaning of a computer program with a body of facts and rules that can simulate a human expert in one specific domain.

What differentiates expert systems from conventional programs? According to Hayes-Roth, Waterman, and Lenat (1983), they differ not only with respect to the components of the system, but also on aspects of the problem and the problem solving process. The seven distinguishing characteristics of expert systems are: heuristics to reduce the search space, reasoning by symbol manipulation, the application of fundamental domain principles and weak reasoning mechanisms, the level of problem difficulty, the system's ability to transform a problem description in lay-terms to one the expert system can work on, reasoning about the system's own behavior, and the type of task (e.g., diagnosis or design). Although some of these criteria reflect problem solving characteristics of real experts (e.g., symbolic reasoning or the reasoning about one's own behavior), the question arises as to whether typical expert systems can in fact be called expert.

A computer program that simulates an expert on a narrow set of problems should not necessarily be thought of as an expert itself. If the problem structuring has to be done by humans and if humans have to ascertain whether a particular set of circumstances is still relevant, then expert seems to be too strong a term for the computer itself. It is precisely this structuring and adaptation that we expect of experts in the real world. The current computer systems are perhaps best thought of as knowledge-based information systems (or short "knowledge systems").

A knowledge system (where system can be thought of as solely a computer, solely a human, or a human-computer combination) possesses a large body of facts and rules. The larger the body of relevant facts and rules, the more the system should be characterized as a knowledge system rather than an expert system. To be a real expert system, it must behave similar to an expert in its overall problem solving behavior. It has to analyze problems based on means-ends relationships (rather than patterns of superficial symptoms), has to possess and apply general knowledge, and has to be able to learn from experience.

To the extent that computers alone do not presently have a strong learning capability and do not have a large capability for deep structure reasoning, an expert system in the strict sense must be a man-machine system. It would be more appropriate to think of the computer program as a component of such a system. Of course if the human is relegated to mundane tasks such as starting the program and inserting answers requested by the machine, the human component may be so minimal as to imply that it is inessential. In such a case, it is the machine that supplies all the expertise. However, if humans are modifying inputs, are monitoring the system to be sure that the computer outputs make sense, or are making adjustments when unanticipated conditions arise, then considerable expertise still resides in the human part of the system.

In addition to specific problem domain knowledge, real experts possess general domain knowledge (i.e., knowledge of literature, language, political and social affairs, etc.) as well as knowledge of general problem solving strategies. In expert systems on the contrary, strategies are expressed in rules within the context of the task domain. To be operational, rules in an expert system have to be very specific. Yet, the human expert can operationalize general strategies by providing them with new meaning in a new task domain. A human expert, for example, will attempt to limit problem complexity in any kind of problem encountered but might do this differently in design tasks than in diagnosis tasks. Similarly, a human will be able to use general principles such as "minimize," "focus on critical factors," etc. and adapt them to a problem at hand. Expert systems can do that only to the extent that possible uses of a principle were preconceptualized.

This argument holds despite the fact that expert systems are described as having the ability to apply their knowledge differently to new problems. The ability to apply knowledge selectively to different problems should be viewed as the result of a strict separation of conditions and actions in the system's knowledge representation. It allows the application of knowledge even to situations (condition patterns) that have not been considered in advance. Thus we might want to conceptualize an expert system as a condition-action mechanism that is not implemented in tree-form (conventual programming) but rather in decision table form. Decision tables disentangle logical conditions for different alternatives from each other. Thus the expert system seems to react in novel ways, because it executes a different subset of the predefined actions for a different set of conditions. Expert systems derive their strength from the ability to handle a large and dynamically changing decision table and to reduce its size very effectively through the posing of good questions and the use of good heuristics.

In their reasoning mechanism, expert systems differ from human experts in that they typically employ surface reasoning instead of deep structure reasoning. "Surface reasoning classifies symptoms without considering the cause and effect relationship" (Sowa, 1984). Although Sowa mentions both surface and deep structure (model-based) reasoning as employed by expert systems, most expert systems perform only the former (Waterman, 1986).

With respect to learning capability, expert systems have to be considered quite static at this stage in artificial intelligence research. Most systems are restricted to utilizing a fixed body of knowledge with no capability for learning. Those systems with a learning capability have a primitive one. Hayes-Roth, Waterman, and Lenat describe a few systems with so called automated knowledge acquisition, such as META-DENDRAL or EURISKO, but also point out the current lack of generalized learning facilities for expert systems.

In summary, existing expert systems have demonstrated that they can be effective in handling a limited set of activities of an expert in a particular domain. They certainly possess a large body of facts and rules and can apply these very efficiently. This does not necessarily imply an understanding of the causal structure of the problem and a capability for dealing with unanticipated events. At this stage of development, little real learning capability has been demonstrated. Overall, existing systems have been quite successful in dealing with well-defined problems (Riesbeck, 1984), but none has yet addressed the solution of problems that one would call creative.

WHAT IS CREATIVE INTELLIGENCE?

Problem-solving situations such as medical diagnosis require considerable information processing and elaborate inferences. Even though we wouldn't hesitate to label them as "tasks requiring intelligence," they are not tasks requiring creativity. They are problems that recur and are difficult because the search space is complex; namely, there are many facts to sort out and many rules to apply.

Creativity, however, requires "creative intelligence." Although there might be debate about whether machines have already exhibited intelligence, we are not aware of any claims of machines exhibiting true creativity. Few people can be called creative so it is not surprising that no machines have reached this level. Although Simon points out that BACON (Langley, Bradshaw, and Simon, 1981), a program that "discovers" natural laws, would have been called creative in earlier time periods, it is questionable whether this actually is the case. BACON seems to discover particular laws because it has been fed with the right data sets. However, the more creative part of the discovery process is to observe the right phenomenon or to ask the right questions.

There are two principal criteria for creativity: novelty and usefulness. Novelty (or originality) is obvious. No one is likely to describe some mundane alternative as being creative. Although novelty is necessary, it is not sufficient. The product (or process) must also be useful, where the term "useful" is meant in a broad sense. Not only is a toaster that makes better toast deemed useful, but a work of art that expands our understanding of the world is also considered useful. A nuclear powered vacuum cleaner or the scribblings of a psychotic personality may be novel but would hardly be considered useful. Sometimes it is desirable to break usefulness into its two main components: feasibility and relevance. To be useful a product must work and it must be relevant to solving some problem, defined broadly, in the area of concern.

It should be noted that we are not explicitly dealing with the outstanding creative geniuses, such as Galileo, Shakespeare and Mozart, but rather with the type of creativity that is possible for many people under the right conditions. In Arieti's terms we are dealing with "ordinary creativity" not "great creativity" (1976, p. 3). We want to consider the type of creative behavior that, with a "little help," is within the grasp of most people. The central question we address is how the average person can be provided with the "little help" to become a more creative problem solver.

What is the relationship between creativity and problem solving? The discussion in the previous sections focused around problem solving and the expert problem solver. In light of the achievements of great creativity, we might assume that creativity is a talent that does not require painstaking problem definition and analysis, but rather is characterized by sparks of imagination. Evidence of this form of creation can be found in a series of examples compiled by Ghiselin (1952) such as Mozart's description of how whole compositions occurred in his mind and he simply had to write them down. Nevertheless, not all forms of creativity are instantaneous. Goethe's greatest product of creation, the Faust, took over 60 years from its conceptualization to the final product (letter to W. v. Humboldt, March 7, 1832, in Goethe, 1982). Hence, it seems that the initial idea, the foundation of a creation, might be generated in relatively short time. Its operationalization or the composition of a number of new ideas into a complete product often requires substantial additional work.

Keeping this difference in mind, we will call the idea generation the "creative act," but the whole process of perceiving the problem, describing the problem and later implementing a creative idea, we will label "creative problem solving." In short, the creative act is the part of problem solving in which new alternative solutions are envisioned. Thus, every creator is a problem solver in the broader context. A problem solver will have to be creative, to find new solutions if current ways of problem solving fail. Nevertheless, some problems will be more creativity bound, while others will be more problem solving bound. Problems with solutions close to existing ones will require less creativity. These can be classified as "well-structured" or incremental problems. If more distant solutions are desired (on "ill-structured" problems), creativity becomes more essential.

To exemplify this point, let us consider an engine design problem. The task is to develop a combustion engine with smoother running characteristics. An incremental solution may involve increasing the number of cylinders which would alleviate the roughness of discontinuous piston movement. A more creative approach is to change the motion characteristics of the engine. This is realized in the Wankel engine, in which the rotary element rotates in a perfectly circular motion.

Creativity is exhibited by chess grand masters in both problem formulation and alternative generation. Good chess players remember a larger number of partial chess-field scenarios (chunks) as well as being able to store larger chunks. Good chess players were able to reconstruct with high accuracy a chess board with 25 figures on it if the figures formed meaningful patterns. If figures were positioned randomly, the chess playing experts could not remember significantly more figure positions than average players (DeGroot).

Thus experts can use the larger chunks directly as the basic building blocks to deeper understanding. Such large chunks appear to be different to the less creative person who does not possess the thorough understanding of the problem context. The creative person's ability to deal with ambiguity allows him to use incompletely defined building blocks and later to complete the definition. With respect to our previous classification of problem solving and creativity, one problem might be viewed either as a creativity problem or as a problem solving problem, depending on the type of problem solver. The gifted person, being able to deal with the complete problem in its full complexity, might solve the problem as an act of creativity, somehow immediately seeing a solution. The less gifted may require substantial problem structuring and decomposition to find a solution.

HOW SHOULD AN EXPERT SYSTEM FOR CREATIVITY BE DESIGNED?

Let us propose a distinction between "artificial intelligence" and "artificial creative intelligence" based on the distinction between (ordinary) intelligence and creative intelligence above. Since creativity implies intelligence but not conversely, a computer system for creative intelligence is more demanding. Can such an expert system be built and how would it be tested?

In 1950 Turing proposed a test of whether machines can think. This test can be applied to the question of whether machines can think creatively. In applying the Turing test we would provide the same set of challenges to an acknowledged creative person (or group of people) and to an expert system purporting to exhibit creative intelligence. Then we ask how an independent judge would assess the results of such an session. Could the judge tell the difference between the output (and perhaps the process also) of an acknowledged creative person and a computer expert system? Perhaps it would be most effective to consider a three-way Turing test between (1) an acknowledged creative human used as a benchmark, (2) a good computer-only system, and (3) an ordinary human augmented by a computer system designed to enhance his creativity.

At this stage of technological development, the third alternative seems more promising than the second. It appears to be necessary to design an expert system exhibiting creativity by incorporating a major human component. Having either a large amount of domain knowledge (across several domains) or a large amount of creative problem solving knowledge (applicable across various domains) is very difficult to imbed solely in a computer. Even if one could do so there would still be the question of why exclude human inputs that can enhance the performance of the system.

Two distinct approaches, then, can be identified for bringing together the relevant domain knowledge and the general problem solving skills into an expert system for (artificial) creative intelligence:

Approach 1: have a computer with domain specific knowledge, such as Mycin or Prospector, and a human to supply the general problem solving strategies.

Approach 2: have a computer with general problem solving strategies and a human to supply the domain knowledge.

In deciding which of these approaches to take, one should

make use of comparative advantage. What can computers do most effectively and what can humans do? What knowledge can we take for granted as residing in the human component? Where and how should learning take place? Where should the capability for adapting to new situations reside?

In dealing with problems in one specific domain, such as medical diagnosis, Approach 1 is the most reasonable. In a limited domain, a computer can store and evaluate more knowledge than both the average person as well as a single expert. The computer also has additional advantages such as consistent performance and unbiased judgment. In this approach, the user can make assessments on whether the system's use is appropriate for the problem at hand and whether the system has considered all important elements of the available information.

Other problems might be less amenable to Approach 1. If problem solving is required over a variety of domains, if a number of different problem types have to be dealt with (e.g., diagnosis and planning), or if the problem is too difficult, it might be inefficient or even impossible to let all domain expertise reside in the computer. Instead, the computer program should know how to elicit the relevant domain knowledge from the human. The purpose of this knowledge elicitation should not be the creation of a complete problem representation within the computer, as formerly done in systems such as GPS. Rather the aim is to manage and improve, by means of the computer's general problem solving strategies, a knowledge representation that is shared by both the human and the computer. The computer program should also combine the general problem solving capabilities of the human with its own. Thus we are talking about a highly interactive program in which each component (man and machine) is utilized sensibly.

Under Approach 2, the comparative advantage of humans and machines is used in the best possible way given the undefined character of the problems the system will have to deal with. The computer does not store as much domain information as in current expert systems, it does not perform as much knowledge base evaluation and it works less "magically" than its conventional counterparts. It trades magic, the power to find a solution almost independently of the user, for general applicability. It does this by providing general problem solving strategies that can deal with a knowledge base that partially resides in the human and partially in the machine.

THE DESIGN OF AN EXPERT SYSTEM FOR CREATIVITY

Following the rationale and directions implied by the above discussion, in this section we describe a computer program that we have developed for enhancing creativity.

We have taken the second approach by placing the general problem solving skills in the computer, while the major part of the problem domain knowledge resides with the human. Over the course of using the system, however, the human learns more general problem solving skills and the computer picks up relevant domain knowledge which can be applied later.

Our overall plan for the man-machine creativity system is based on eight major components: (1) system-context, (2) goals, (3) beliefs, (4) resources, (5) activities, (6) structure, (7) problems, and (8) alternatives.

Any creative behavior occurs within the context of a system. (We will use the awkward terminology "system-context" to distinguish the system [context] we are studying from the computer system we are developing to improve its operation. The term "context" also helps to emphasize the problem context of interest.) For an artist the system-context is the conceptualization, execution and display of a work of art. For a scientist the system-context is the scientific process of formulating hypotheses based on theory, testing these hypotheses and, if necessary, revising the theory. For a manager the system-context is the organization he is managing and its connections to the environment. For a person in everyday life, the system-context is the household and family.

Let us first consider a system-context in which people are the controlling entities. The people in the system-context are characterized by their goals, their beliefs, and their resources (MacCrimmon, 1970). Their goals provide the driving force, their beliefs direct attention to the environmental conditions with which they must contend, and their resources provide the capability to change their environment. For convenience one attaches these goals, beliefs, and resources to the system-context itself without necessarily adopting a holistic approach

(Nagel, 1961). Even if the system-context is an artifact, for example a thermostat, it can still be considered to possess goals, beliefs, and resources, namely, those engineered into it by the human designer. A thermostat's goal is to keep the temperature constant, it utilizes beliefs about the current temperature of the room, and it controls resources in the form of the fuel that can be burned.

Let us now discuss the elements of the system-context representation in more detail.

Goals underlie the system-context's behavior and direct its activities. They are crucial for the generation of creative solutions because mere originality is not creative. A product or process must be useful in some sense to be creative. To be useful means to satisfy some goal. Useful is interpreted broadly. Building a toaster to make better toast can be useful but so can expanding our sensitivity and understanding of the world, as creative art or basic science does.

Understanding goals does not necessarily imply accepting those goals. Just because goals are needed to drive the system-context does not mean that particular goals should be taken as given. A main part of a creativity system is to challenge goals.

Beliefs are necessary to connect the system-context to reality. They describe the frame of reference, such as the environmental laws and the current state of the environment. They also describe hypotheses about the system-context itself. Examples of beliefs are: "oil prices will rise by 50% within the next three years," "more states will enact legislation restricting smoking in the workplace," and "internal combustion engines will be outmoded by 1995."

Beliefs are important to define and limit the solution space for the system-context's problems. They have to be stated explicitly to create awareness for what is assumed and to make these assumptions subject to questioning. If a solution is not conceivable, given a too rigidly defined set of beliefs, then "breaking the cognitive set" by a reformulation or relaxation of beliefs is necessary.

Resources can take many forms. Personal skills and knowledge are important resources. However, resources may take inanimate forms such as a particular kind of stone for carving or metal for space ship design. Resources provide the raw material from which new solutions can be constructed.

Activities or functions are the steps taken to try to achieve goals. They are the means in a means-ends network. Activities are based on the deployment of resources, both animate and inanimate, to achieve goals.

Structure describes the system-context's units, their relationships and activities. "The organization has five divisions," "division heads report to the president," "divisions compete for investment resources" are examples of structural definitions. Structural definitions support the decomposition process by indicating potential sub-units to focus attention upon.

Few system-contexts work the way we hope and expect they will. Resources that were expected become unavailable. A key precept in dealing with the environment is that the unexpected usually happens. A problem is a gap between the desired state and the actual state. On some goal dimensions performance may be fine, while on others the gap is large. Since most endeavors have multiple goals, there are often multiple problems.

When we focus attention on problems, we search for ways to solve the problems. In the process of problem solving we develop issues relating to how the system-context works and how it can be changed. As these issues are further developed they become specific alternatives for changing the system-context to solve the problem.

The eight elements of the system-context representation are highly interrelated. In a broad sense, system-context is at the core while goals, beliefs, and resources form the basic components. These components are manifested in the activities and structure which determine the system-context. For a general focus, these six factors are sufficient. In other words, a person can fully understand the system by means of these factors. For a particular focus, however, the other two elements, problems and alternatives, become the center of attention.

Unfortunately, non-experts too often tend to restrict attention to only that part of the whole system-context which seems relevant to the problem. A creative problem solver will look at the bigger picture, and hence an effective expert system for creativity will force the problem solver to leave the narrow problem focus and will deal with the problem by considering it in light of the overall system-context.

The eight-factor description is the basis for the overall design of our man-machine system for creativity. The model is shown in Figure 1.

The eight elements are the basic components of the knowledge representation. General problem solving strategies to deal with the knowledge are implemented in the form of several techniques. Strategies may be categorized in three groups: (1) problem representation strategies which direct the process of describing the system according to the above model, (2) alternative generation strategies which guide the process of developing new alternatives via creative techniques, and (3) alternative evaluation strategies which support the assessment and selection of creative solutions to the problem. This categorization of strategies does not imply that the problem solver is actually guided through a linear process of problem definition, alternative generation, and finally evaluation. Instead, the system user is expected to move back and forth within the stages of the problem solving process, incrementally enhancing and improving the system-context description, until finally a set of solution alternatives emerges.

Problem solving strategies are operationalized in the form of techniques provided for the user. One technique for problem representation is means-ends analysis. The user is requested to specify the goals of the system. Goals are then further investigated in terms of their purpose. The final result is a network of goals. An example of an alternative generation technique is brainstorming. An example of an evaluation technique is a calculation of multiple attribute utilities.

The use of the creativity system is highly interactive. Since the system draws heavily on the user's domain knowledge, it cannot, even after the problem representation is completed, generate a solution to the problem. Instead, it provides knowledge for the process of finding a solution. By means of its techniques, the program triggers user responses. The ultimate

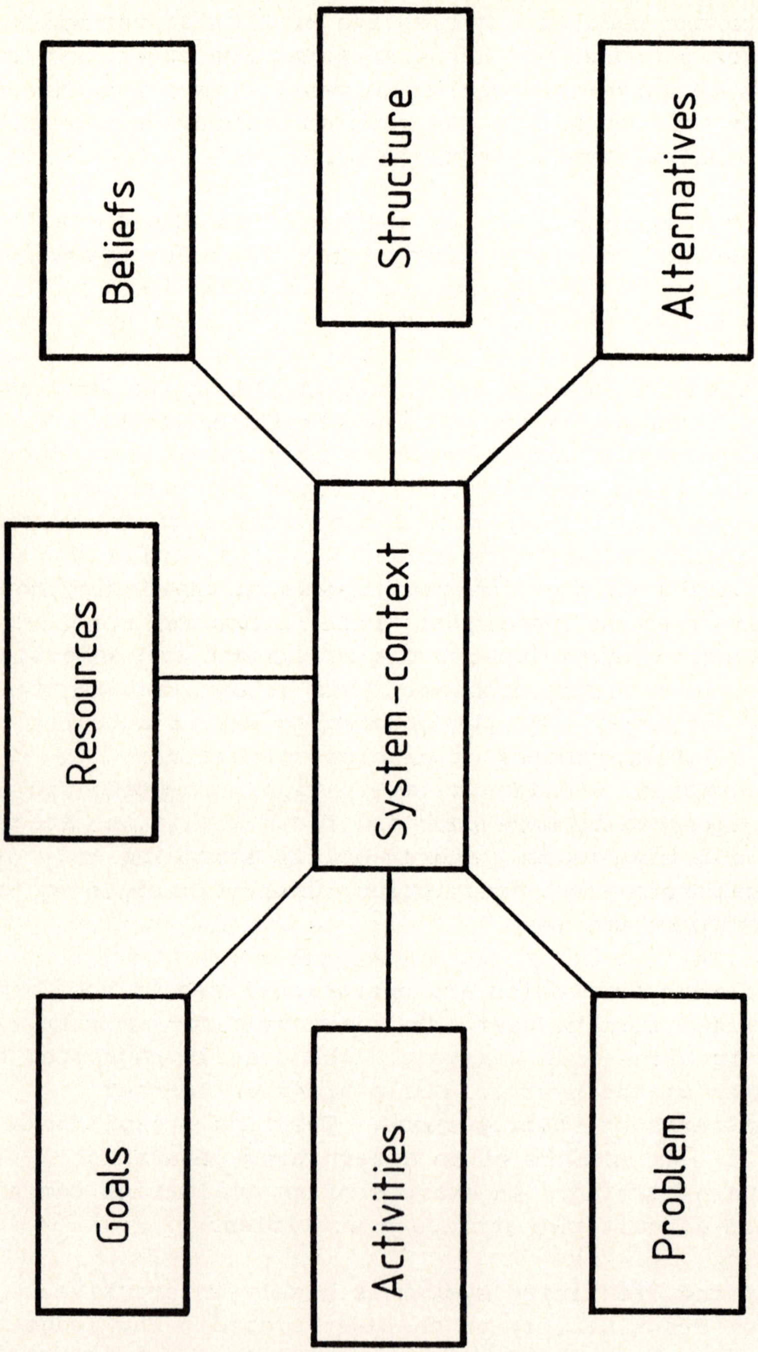

Figure 1 Eight factor system model

result is a solution the user finds "by himself." The program encourages the user to specify the system-context to a reasonable level of detail. However, a complete problem description is not required to gain support from the system. Alternative generation techniques may also be used on a fragmentary problem description.

A partial implementation of the system's model combined with general strategies was made in preparing a prototype man-machine system for creativity. The program was written in Turbo Prolog. Preliminary tests were conducted on a variety of problems. The system was demonstrated at the NATO Conference in Portugal in August 1986. Details can be found in the article by us entitled "A human-computer system for creative problem solving."

CONCLUSIONS

We have argued that for an expert system to exhibit creative behavior, the system will have to use both humans and computers according to their comparative advantages. At this time it means that substantial domain knowledge should reside in the human but that the computer should elicit relevant knowledge in the course of creative problem solving. The computer should be able to utilize considerable knowledge of general problem solving strategies to augment human deficiencies. To be creative an expert system will have to be "expert" in the sense not only of having a body of facts and rules and proficiency in applying these facts and rules but also in being able to learn from experience. At the present time, humans are more likely to provide this learning capability than are machines and so a creativity expert system needs to be highly interactive with a strong human component.

We have presented an overall design plan for a creativity expert system. Following this plan a prototype called INVENTOR was designed, programmed in Prolog. This system was demonstrated at the NATO Conference on Expert Judgment and Expert Systems held in Porto, Portugal in August 1986. The system itself is described in more detail in a separate paper (MacCrimmon and Wagner, 1987).

REFERENCES

Arieti, S., Creativity: the Magic Synthesis, New York: Basic Books, 1976.

Bouwman, M., "The use of accounting information: expert versus novice behavior", in G. Ungson and D. Braunstein (eds.), Decision Making: An Interdisciplinary Inquiry, Boston: Kent, 1982.

Brooks, R., "Towards a theory of the comprehension of computer programs", International Journal of Man-Machine Studies, 18, 1983, 543-554.

DeGroot, A.D., Thoughts and Choice in Chess, The Hague: Mouton, 1965.

Dewey, J., How We Think, New York: D.C. Heath, 1933.

Ernst, G.W., and A. Newell, GPS: A Case Study in Generality and Problem Solving, New York: Academic Press, 1969.

Feigenbaum, E., B. Buchanan, and J. Lederberg, " On generality and problem solving: a case study using the DENDRAL program", in B. Meltzer and D. Michie (eds.), Machine Intelligence, 6, 1971, Edinburgh: Edinburgh University Press.

Fogler, S., "The design of a course in problem solving", in J.T. Sears, D.R. Woods, and R.D. Noble (eds.), Problem Solving, AIChE Symposium Series, 79, 1983.

Goethe, J.W. v., Faust, by E. Trunz, (ed.), Munich: Beck, 1982.

Ghiselin, B. (ed.), The Creative Process, Berkeley, Ca: Univ. of Calif. Press, 1952.

Hayes-Roth, F., D.A. Waterman, and D.B. Lenat, Building Expert Systems, Reading, Ma.: Addison Wesley, 1983.

Humes, A., "Research on the composing process", Review of Educational Research, 53, 1983, 201-216.

Kaufman, H., The Forest Ranger, Baltimore, Md.: Johns Hopkins Press, 1960.

Kolodner, J.L., "Towards an understanding of the role of experience in the evolution from novice to expert", International Journal of Man-Machine Studies, 19, 1983, 497-518.

Langley, P., G.L. Bradshaw, and H.A. Simon, "BACON.5: the discovery of conservation laws", Proceedings of the Seventh International Joint Conference on Artificial Intelligence, Vancouver, Canada, 1981.

Larkin, J., D. McDermott, D. Simon, H. Simon, "Expert and novice performance in solving physics problems", Science, 208, 1980, 1335-1342.

MacCrimmon, K.R., "Elements of decision making", in W. Goldberg (ed.), Behavioral Approaches to Modern Management, Sweden: BAS, 1970.

MacCrimmon, K.R. and C. Wagner, "A human-computer system for creative problem solving", University of British Columbia working paper, 1987.

Nagel, E., The Structure of Science, New York: Harcourt, Brace and World, 1961.

Newell, A. C. Shaw, and H.A. Simon, "Elements of a theory of human problem solving", Psychological Review, 65, 1958, 151-166.

Riesbeck, C.K., "Knowledge reorganization and reasoning style", International Journal of Man-Machine Studies, 20, 1984, 45-61.

Sowa, J.F., Conceptual Structures: Information Processing in Mind and Machine, Reading, Ma.: Addison-Wesley, 1984.

Stein, M.I., Stimulating Creativity, New York: Academic Press, 1974.

Turing, A.M., "Computing machinery and intelligence", Mind, 59, 1950, 433-460.

Vessey, I., "An investigation of the psychological processes underlying the debugging of computer programs", Unpublished Ph.D. Thesis, Department of Commerce, University of Queensland, 1984.

Vitalari, N.P. and G.W. Dickson, "Problem solving for effective systems analysis: an experimental exploration", Communications of the ACM, 26, 1983, 948-956.

Waterman, D.A., A Guide to Expert Systems, Reading, Ma.: Addison-Wesley, 1986.

Woods, D.R. "Problem solving and chemical engineering, 1981", in J.T. Sears, D.R. Woods, and R.D. Noble (eds.), Problem Solving, AIChE Symposium Series, 79, 1983.

EXPERT SYSTEMS AND EXPERT JUDGMENT: A USER'S PERSPECTIVE

L.E. Milton
Ontario Hydro
Toronto, Ontario
Canada

INTRODUCTION

At the conference, a number of issues were raised about relationships between experts, the decision support or knowledge sciences, and users of all of these. Since Ontario Hydro's route and site selection process involves large numbers of internal and external experts from a variety of backgrounds, and has evolved into a regular process employing a variety of approaches or methods, it would seem to form a valid basis for one opinion on these issues.

Those issues that seem worthy of particular focus in this context are:

1. How do/should different types of expertise figure in decision making?

2. Conflicts between users and the decision sciences.

3. What are the relevant roles/merits of the different decision sciences viz: decision analysis, (social) judgement analysis, analytical hierarchy, and expert systems?

4. How much information (or number of cues) is required for a valid decision?

Before moving into discussion of the issues, some concepts and terms need to be defined about the nature of expertise.

Nature of Expertise

At the conference, Ken Hammond put forward the diagram in Figure 1A which was evidently meaningful to most of the participants. It can be suggested

NATO ASI Series, Vol. F35
Expert Judgment and Expert Systems
Edited by J. Mumpower et al.

Figure 1

Relationships between Knowledge and Values in Decisions or Judgements

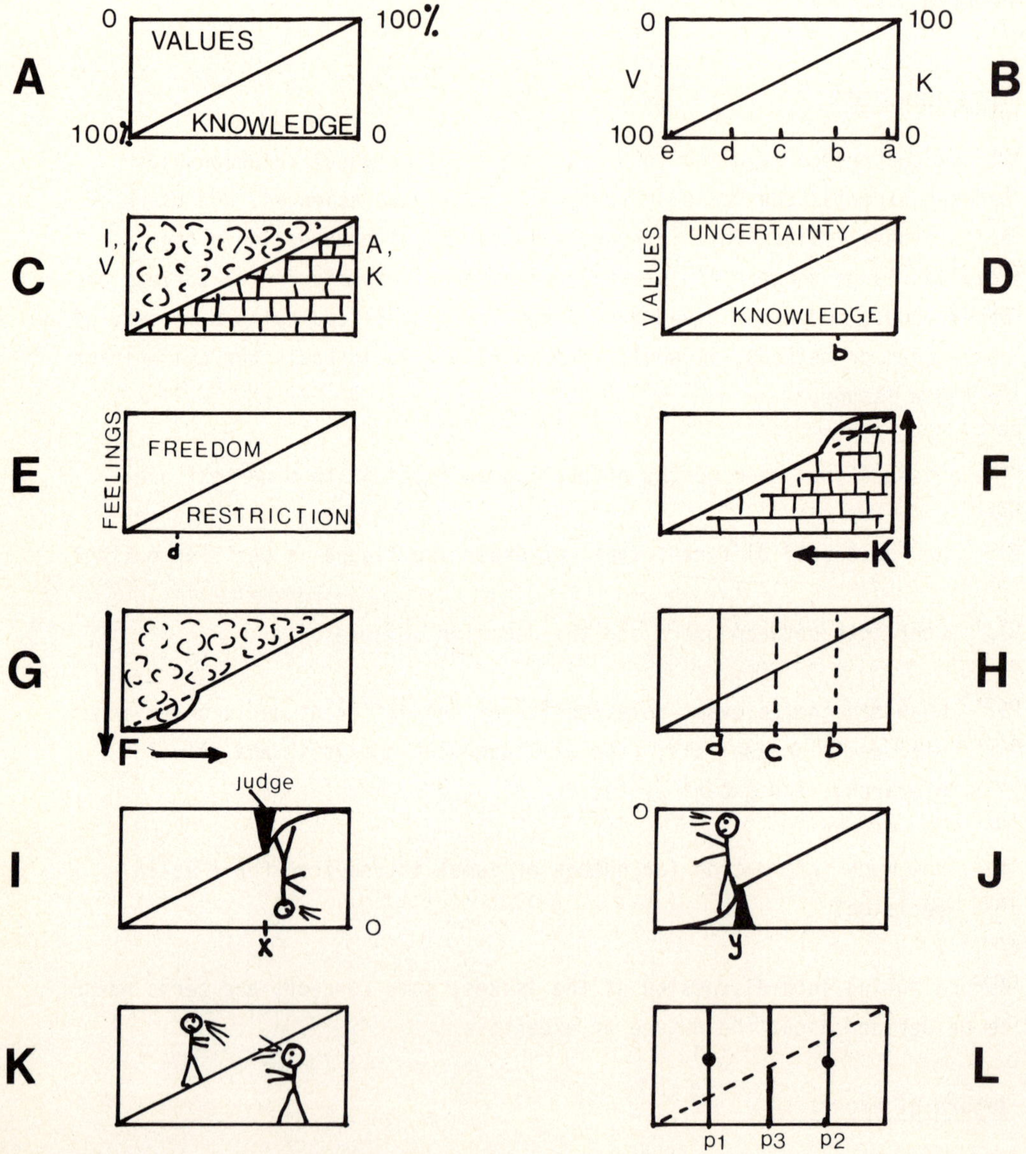

that the line joining '100% knowledge' to '100% value' represents an interface between knowledge-based decision-making and value-based judgement.

Next, there were suggestions that the horizontal axis represents a range of kinds of expertise. Thus in Figure 1B, point 'a' represents disciplines with a high degree of formal knowledge (rules) and well defined data such as an accounting procedure. Point 'b' represents the imprecise sciences involving techniques such as short range extrapolations. Point 'c' involves roughly equal inputs of knowledge and values, such as environmental assessment, and 'd' could be exemplified by a higher content of values such as general public policy making or creation of poetry. At the extreme of 'e' only values prevail, for example in creation of music and art.

There was consensus that in the general sense an expert is someone who performs or make judgements better than virtually anyone else in a particular field. A feature of such people is that they achieve their results with very little apparent effort and a great deal of confidence. Clearly some of the characteristics of an expert will vary with the field they operate in. So in Figure 1B, at point 'a' the expert fits one option of the Oxford Dictionary definition of a person who is highly informed about a special field, since the discipline is highly knowledge based. At point 'b', most experienced workers would grasp the knowledge, and the expert would appear as one who was more successful at forecasting successfully, finding new rules, or coping with uncertainty. At 'c' and 'd' the expert would produce recommendations or decisions that fit all the rules, and also have widespread acceptance of the value judgements involved. At point 'e' the other dictionary option applies viz: a person who is highly skillful in a special field. Someone such as a Mozart could create new sensations with widely popular appeal in his context of time and culture. Note that the descriptive terms used in everyday English for bringing components together and resolving them drift from right to left: 'decision-making' to 'judgement' to 'creation'.

These extremes at least partially reflect the difference between intuitive judgement, based on feelings, images, words, etc. and conscious analysis/synthesis based on systems, rules, numbers, machines (Figure 1C).

Since the conference was largely confined to engineers and scientists, most of the viewpoints expressed came from the right hand side of Figure 1C. Thus it is consistent that the term 'value', which often implies numerical expression, was used instead of 'feelings', and 'uncertainty' was used in the 'a' to 'b' range for those small intuitive judgements or arbitrary decisions required of scientists probing into these fields of operation (Figure 1D).

Being in the general public decision field ('c' - 'd') I am very much aware that there is an equally frequent and valid approach from the intuitive side. Each approach, in a pure form, has its range of comfort and discomfort, and of mild intolerance of the other. For example, expert systems specialists begin to feel uncomfortable about handling 'uncertainty' around point 'b', whilst creative people might feel unduly restricted to the right of point 'd' (Figure 1E).

Roles of Types of Expertise in Decisions

If the concepts in Figures 1A-D are acceptable, then they can be used as a basis to probe into the roles of different types of expertise in decision making. Evidently, the sloping line of Figure 1 is an interface between the two kinds of intellects, though more like a somewhat porous and flexible membrane. Knowledge engineers can be said to be working from right to left, pushing the membrane upwards as they go, by building new rule and data structures to handle some of the uncertainty (intuitive judgements), as in Figure 1F.

At the same time, energetic creators are pushing from the opposite direction by working for greater freedom and de-regulation, as in Figure 1G. Thus there is considerable intellectual competition for control of decision making, with each school thinking that the world would be a better place if only more decisions were made according to <u>their</u> approach. What that translates to is that the winning school would have the power to rule the others, since they would be in charge of the process and information used i.e. <u>how</u> the decision is made.

Evidently, the effort required to push into the other realm increases with distance from home base - for the scientist there is increasing discomfort with higher degrees of uncertainty, which require ever-increasing effort in handling greater numbers of alternatives. The creative thinker finds it increasingly difficult to 'bend the rules' as they get more numerous and rigid. An instructive caricature of these trends can be seen in the competition between two intellectual cultures in Asimov's novel 'Second Foundation'.

Analysis of Conflicts

At this point it is important to focus for a moment on which approach controls a specific decision, and where the decision lies on the horizontal axis of Figure 1B. There are three aspects to this: (a) where the decision should lie according to some ideal absolute truth, (b) where some person with a specific viewpoint (e.g. a decision analyst) feels it should lie, (c) the characteristics of the person actually in charge of the decision through some external happenstance. A number of the concerns raised by people at the conference can be analyzed from this basis (see also next section). For example, suppose an environmental decision ought to be made at point 'c' with an equal mix of approaches (Figure 1H). It might be that a scientist would wish it to be made on a highly rigorous basis 'b'. The authoritative judge 'd' might actually be a person such as a politician with a strong intuitive approach.

Now it is appropriate to look at the efforts made by the various decision sciences to expand their scope of control of decisions. Expanding on Figure 1F, I felt many of the efforts discussed at the conference could be depicted as in Figure 1I. I see the analytical school pushing into uncertainty, but with their eyes on their point of origin - the idea that decisions are problems that can be solved in terms of rules and hard data (point 'a'). Then, if at point 'x' where a specific decision is made, they come up against an intuitive judge with the power to actually make the decision, they feel they are banging their heads on the floor trying to get past him. Alternatively, if that intuitive judge is not there, and they must make the decision, the analysts feel a vacuum above the membrane and worry that they are walking on quicksand.

Next, let's look at the intuitive thinker trying to push into the realm of hard knowledge as in Figure 1J. He too is looking at his point of origin, this time up in the sky, and trying to mould decisions to his thought pattern. A critic could say he is walking backwards with his head in the clouds, trampling on the rules and facts. If at point 'y' he comes across a real judge whose knowledge and rules already master the situation, he is likely to trip over the rules or the judge's "rigid attitude". If there is no systematic authority at 'y', he may push past it but not for long because he can't get a firm grip on the clouds to push with (i.e. rules do not bend for feelings).

I apologize for using needling tactics to drive a point home. No negative connotations are meant in Figures 1I-J. The graph used in Figure 1 could just as easily have been tabled upside down and /or back to front (I've yet to really see an Australian walking around upside down in North America, except after 14 beers). But there is a point to be made from Figure 1. If the various approaches depicted in Figure 1I-J exist, what is obviously missing? Who from either end is truly looking forwards and what would their approach look like (Figure 1K)?

From the analytical approach, we seek someone who comes from an analytical background, but turns his back on the idea of transforming intuitive thinking into knowledge based systems. As he approaches a decision point 'x', he recognizes that there comes a point where machines, numbers, and systems could be better used to enhance intuitive judgement, because a major part of the decision lies in that realm and will do so for a long time to come. So instead of telling the judge at 'x' <u>how</u> the decision should be made, he offers him tools to <u>practice</u> the judgement skills beforehand.

It was very disturbing, yet a little encouraging, to find a tiny minority of people at the conference with that viewpoint. Given that intuitive judgement, if acceptably accurate, is usually very quick at handling even very complex problems compared with conscious analysis, our society could be at a disadvantage if we do not place more emphasis on this approach.

And there is a challenge for the intuitive judges to face forwards and downwards too. As they approach point 'y' in Figure 1K they must bring appropriate knowledge expertise into their decisions <u>beforehand</u> and not ask systems specialists for rationalizations afterwards. Beyond point 'y' they must accept that much of the bulk of the judgement will be based on rules and data, and their role should be limited (though still very valuable) to helping resolve tradeoffs among values or feelings about uncertainty. Overall, then, more mutual understanding and complementary co-operation between the two approaches is desirable.

And there is much more to decision making than data and processes. In the majority of the myriad decisions made in the world daily, there is obviously a mixture of the two realms of scientific problem solving and intuitive judgement. As a corollary, there must be a means of crossing the sloping line of Figure 1 to marry the two. I suggest we refer to this as the power or the authority to finalize a decision, and I think this aspect of a decision is at least as important as the types of expertise or mental approach used, and deserves a lot more attention by many conference participants. This power or authority is an external force that irons out the last unresolved differences of opinion, or differences between intuition and knowledge. Analytical judges often use authority which comes from sources such as a declared role, recognized knowledgeability, or a document such as a diploma or licence. Intuitive judges often use power, which comes from creativity, charisma, public opinion (votes), influence for examples.

Anyone working in one of the fields of decision support needs to be conscious of this aspect of decision making, because many conflicts arise from a lack of understanding of it. One point to be considered is the degree of delegation of power from the decision-maker to the contributor. Another is the principal mental approach used by the decision-maker. If the decision-maker chooses to share some of the power with the contributor, the role that is delegated and its timing must be appropriately matched to the mental approach used by the contributor, to avoid misunderstandings. For example, if an intuitive judge invites an analytical person to contribute analytical support, the contributor will likely interpret this well-meant gesture as a demand for rationalization, which is objectionable to him, whereas to an intuitive supporter it would likely be seen as an invitation to join the consensus, which it is. Although both sides should endeavour to understand one another, there is some onus on the supporter to find out what the decision-maker wants and in what form it would be useful, rather than dictate to him how to do his job better, if the judge is being successful.

The concept of 'closing the gap' by use of power can be depicted as in Figure 1L. When several different people are involved (e.g. persons 1-2) this gap is a horizontal one after individual decisions are made, and within a particular person (person 3) it is vertical. The gap that is closed may be one of practically unresolvable differences or else unknowns. However at times the gap may contain differences of opinion that could have been resolved with more time or communications but the resolution process was cut off for reasons of expediency. There must be a relationship between power required and the intensity of differences of opinion remaining, and this could be an interesting area to study further.

Roles of Various Decision Sciences

I don't know anyone who can expertly judge the roles and merits, but offer an example that seems to work in a situation around point 'c' in Figure 1.

Under Ontario's Environmental Assessment Act of 1975, Ontario Hydro has been required to conduct a very open-ended, comprehensive approach to selection of locations for new electric power facilities. A proponent under the Act must start without any pre-conceived location, and must begin by proving a need to do anything at all. Thereafter, a wide range of alternatives must be identified, and these must be logically examined and discarded until one preferred solution remains. The definition of environment is much broader than natural environment, encompassing virtually anything or anyone that could be significantly affected by the new facility in any way. Meaningful public participation by agencies, sectoral interest groups, and individuals is strongly encouraged and virtually institutionalized.

The regulations were largely silent about how approval decisions would be made and what methods and standards should be used to conduct the studies. Over some 10 years, in the course of 140+ projects, at times involving up to 20 regular staff, 100+ external participants, and 1000+ general public in each of the larger projects, a regular process evolved. This occurred under strong public scrutiny and opposition, such that virtually every aspect has been rigorously tested. The basic process is shown in Figure 2.

After listening to discussion at the conference about the various decision disciplines, it seemed that in my context, they are perfectly complementary. The basis flow charted in Figure 2 was moulded by people whose skill packages correspond with those of the decision analysts (e.g. analytical geographers and social scientists). Such people are still the ones most interested in experimenting with new techniques within the general framework. The Act requires that a visibly logical process be used, without specifying that logic. The staff with decision analysis expertise saw that as a potential point of challenge, and concentrated on putting together a documentable process that met the Act's requirements and allowed meaningful scientific and public inputs. If the process were to be seriously challenged, I would turn to those staff, or failing them, external decision analysis experts to improve the process.

It is recognized that the primary expertise or authority on public values rests with the public themselves, and in any sensitive project they are asked to determine the importance (values) of various impacts, whilst scientists estimate the degree of change that would occur. After trying a variety of techniques to obtain public values, we settled on consensus or at least majority vote, using a 'small group-like interests/large group-major tradeoffs' phased approach to achieve as much agreement as practicable. From time to time we have tried various techniques of sampling or analyzing public value judgements, mainly to determine how coherent the results are and how valid it is to use them. This area of operations corresponds closely to social judgement science, to which we turn for new ideas and techniques.

Computer tools are available to conduct every phase of the process in Figure 2. We could even write an interactive 'expert system' to guide a novice through the entire process. However, we only use computers regularly where they can equal or better our experienced humans either in terms of effectiveness (fewer mistakes, faster turn around in pressure situations) or efficiency (cheaper, lesser levels of staff etc). Early in the 1970's it was recognized that storing, weighting, overlaying, and updating maps was a 'natural' for computers, and a geographic information

Figure 2

Flow Chart of the Basic Steps of a Route Selection Project

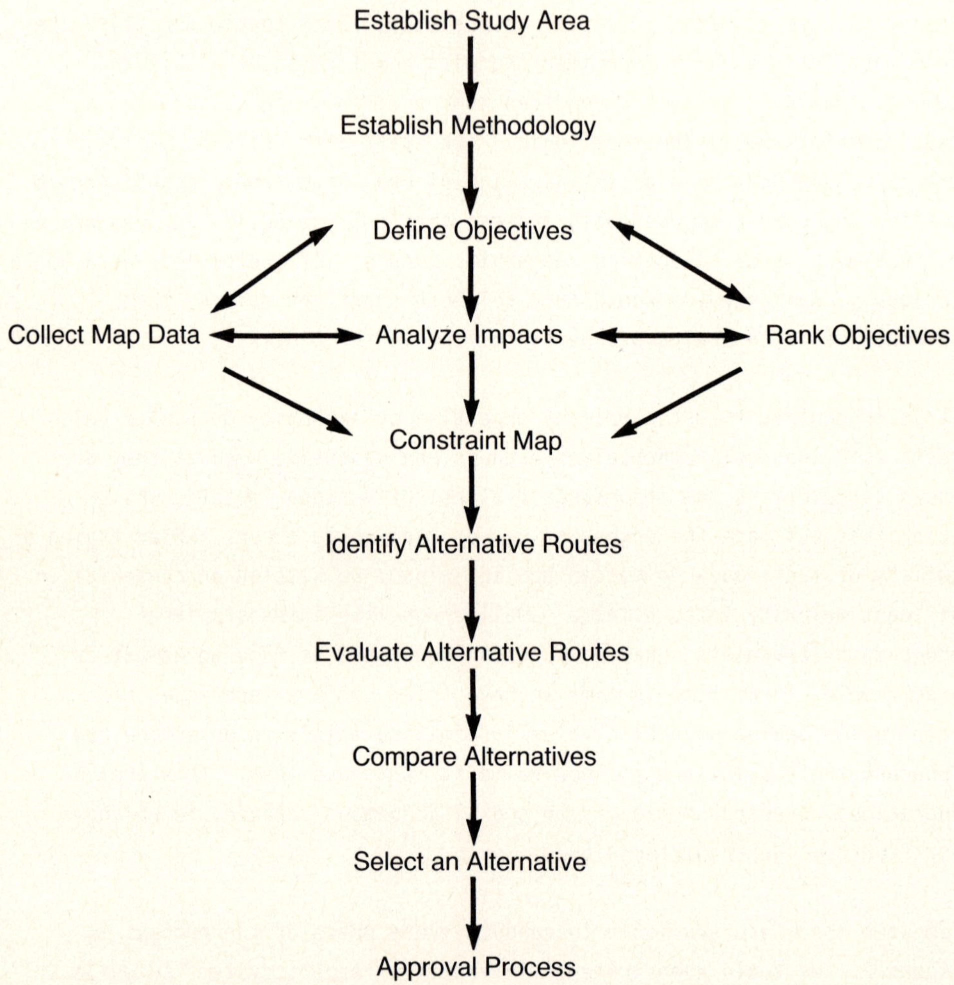

Figure 3

Study Streams in the Route/Site Selection Process

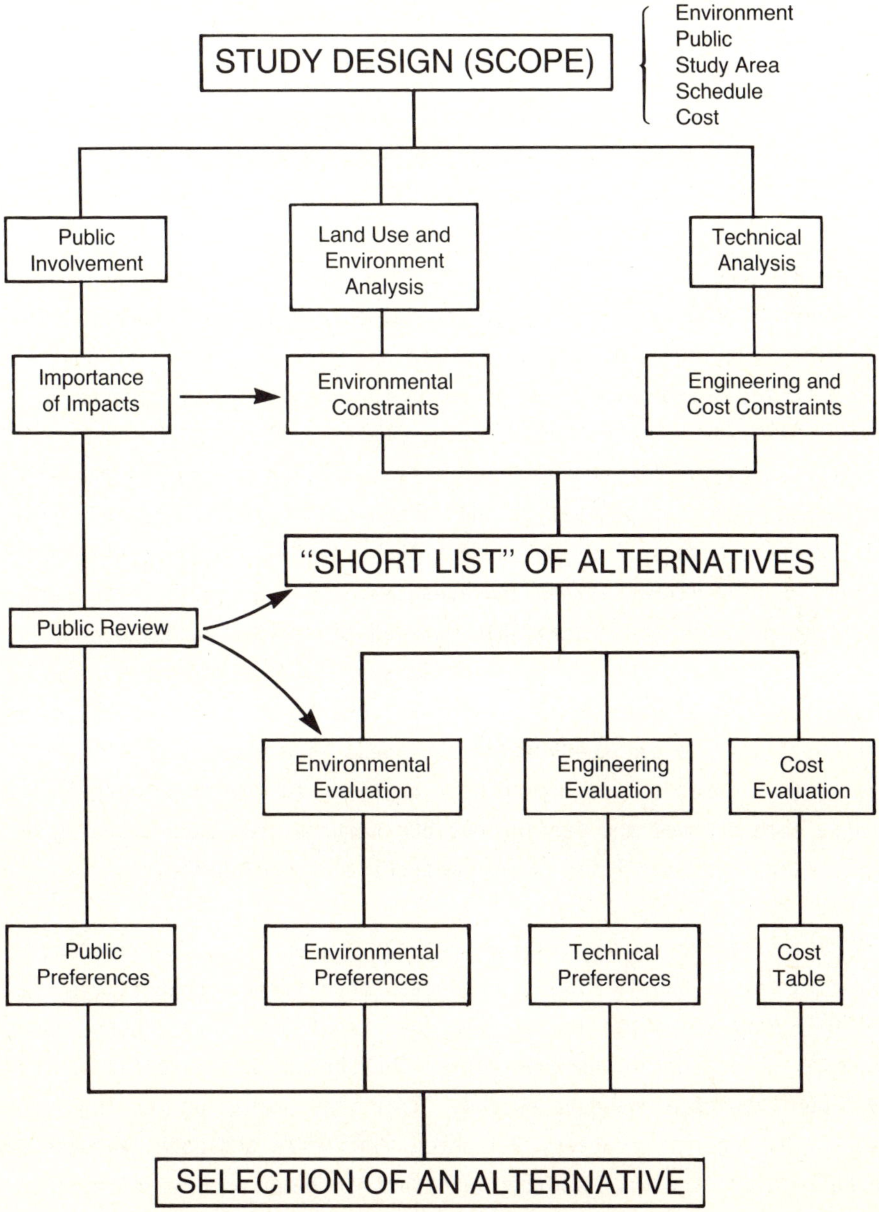

system CARSS was created. More recently we purchased an expert system for mapping natural resources from digital satellite imagery.

When the land use/environmental study depicted in Figure 2 is completed and the preferred alternatives have been selected, it is necessary to pool results with the other 3 study streams shown in Figure 3 - public preferences, technical preferences, and cost. When these preferences do not coincide, tradeoffs among very unlike criteria are required to bring about the necessary decision. We have at times used an analytical hierarchy method. It is felt that some appropriate subliminal judgements can be extracted and used with this method, although at times arbitrary sub-decisions are made. The latter should not be condemmed, since the merit of the method is that it puts the values and criteria forward clearly for scrutiny, so that some ultimate judge with the perception or power to decide a better answer can argue or amend the inputs as appropriate.

One of the strengths of the route and site selection process is the way in which various forms of perception and communication are integrated. The Act was created because the public felt they could no longer trust the judgement of major corporations and agencies. Through public information centres, we make our staff available for public scrutiny and input at several points during the process. Members of the public talk to staff individually, probe their biasses, test their data and logic, and provide new information. We can see that this happens in a variety of ways as indicated in Figure 4. Thus while we are trying to quantify their feelings, some of them are feeling out our numbers, our understanding of their concerns, and our faith in our methods and conclusions.

In the case of a few very sensitive projects, we end up at public hearings before a formal tribunal. The same process occurs, at a higher level of intensity. Here it is the lawyers who lead the feeling out process as well as scientific testing of the knowledge. They bring in scientific experts to test our knowledge and conclusions. They also probe our feelings about our work. During this process, I learned that words and body language can often be more precise than numbers, and that a tremor in the voice is a very revealing probability estimate. In addition to words, numbers, and feelings, other forms of communication depicted in Figure 4 may be used. For example, I consider it a sign of impressive maturity that a tribunal

Figure 4

Some Relationships between Aptitudes, Communication Modes and Primary Approaches to Decision Making

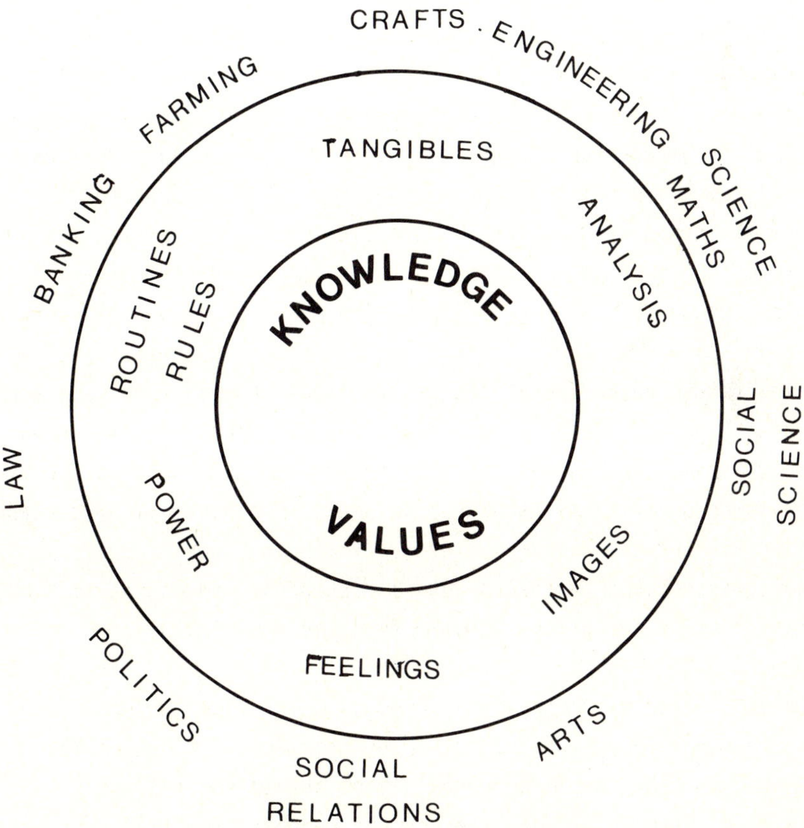

recently permitted a witness to testify in paintings, because she felt she could not express herself adequately in words or numbers. Regrettably, we could only reply with photographs, which were more accurate in terms of the degree of environmental change, but did not communicate much feeling about the importance of the change to people affected.

Following through this connection between modes of communication and approaches to decision making, it seems consistent that certain types of decision-makers would show a preference for certain types of decision support tools. At the conference, it did not seem surprising that people interested in analytical hierarchy methods tended to come from fields where decisions had to be made, using 'cheese and chalk' criteria, with elements of arbitrary judgement at times or unresolvable differences. Decision analysis techniques generally seemed to appeal to systematic thinkers, e.g. Ontario Hydro's process and managers of computer companies, but I doubt that politicians or public policy judges would have much use for them as the principal method of making their decisions.

Information Requirements for a Valid Decision

With environmental decisions, questions of level of detail or resolving power of maps are particularly important. On the one hand, sufficient detail must be available to ensure a valid decision. On the other, since often it is necessary to create large volumes of knowledge from scratch, too much detail is very wasteful. Costs of mapping, for example, are logarithmically related to scale (detail), such that to map at 1:50 000 scale (fine detail) could cost 15-20 time as much as to map at a scale of 1:250 000.

Choosing the amount and level of detail of knowledge in 'fuzzy' decisions is further complicated by the uncertainty of the components, which themselves are often judgemental to varying degrees.

Obviously, one can start determination of appropriate resolution by careful consideration of the nature of the decision being made. In the first example in Figure 5, deciding that the object is a cross requires only the first level of detail. The second level (b) is needed to discern that the cross is uneven in length and width of arms, whilst the following two

Figure 5

Relationship Between Information and Decision Resolution

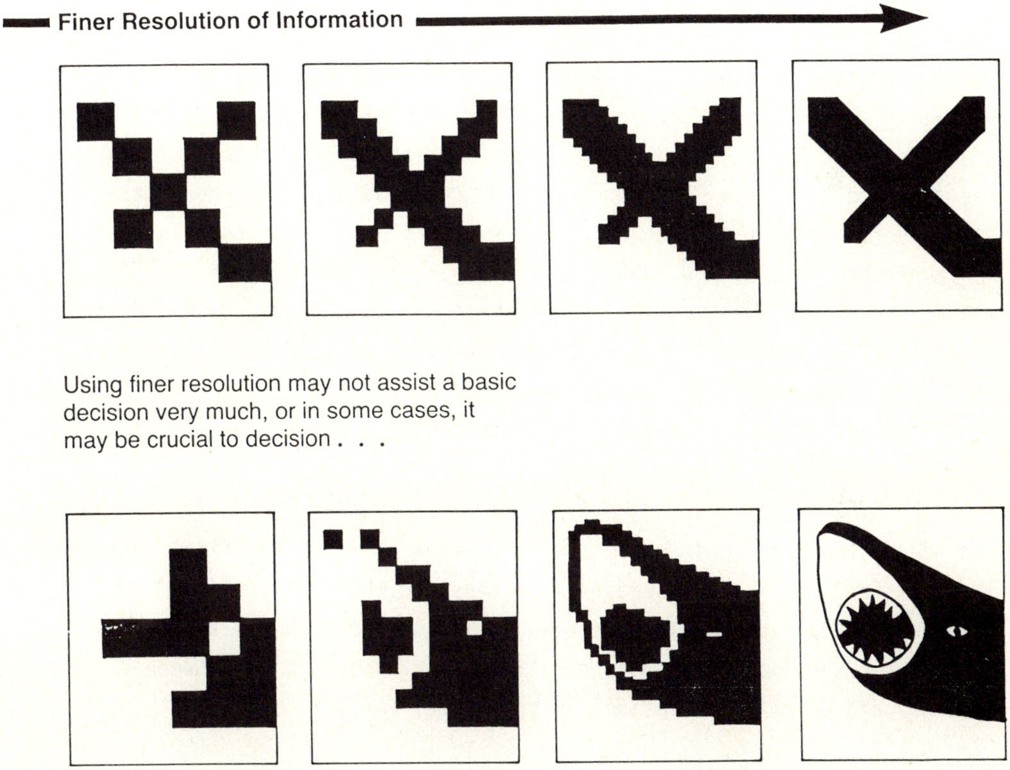

levels of detail do not add much to the understanding of the object. In the second example, a decision on whether to stay or flee would need at least level (b) resolution plus additional human inference, or more likely level (c) plus some simple inference. These examples bring out two considerations about the decision: how much additional human inference can be added to an expert system's conclusions to provide a meaningful result, and thereby substantially reduce costs; and how precise the specification of the decision needs to be.

In route/site selection studies, we can quite readily define the required detail of the decision, and have developed the term 'decision resolution' in the case of maps. This is the size of the smallest critical element of the proposed facility. In the case of a transmission line, where we want a valid decision about the location of a right of way (ROW), this is the width of the proposed ROW. If we are planning the location of the towers within the ROW this element is the width of the tower base, which is about 1/10th that of the ROW. This is consistent with empirical findings that staff are usually comfortable mapping ROW's at a scale of 1:25 000 to 1:50 000, and plan tower locations within ROW's at a scale of 1:5 000 or less.

The above considerations define the resolution at which the final decision is specified. It is then necessary to consider whether more detailed information and sub-decisions are needed if that decision is to be valid. This raises the question of the relationship or distinction between accuracy and detail (resolution) of knowledge.

Empirical and theoretical investigation show that, contrary to some initial opinions, there is not a very close relationship between accuracy and detail. In other words, greater detail will not readily compensate for errors in judgement. Figure 6 illustrates that the effect of random error in knowledge elements or sub-judgements is an obscuring effect. It is only in the case of marginal resolution (c) that moderate degrees of error might significantly increase the risk of a bad decision. Nevertheless, there is some relationship, and it can be quantified, so it is possible to work back from a given mean accuracy to determine what information resolution is required to give a valid decision at another (coarser) resolution. Conversely, if information resolution is fixed, one can estimate mean

Figure 6

Relationships Between Random Error and Resolution of Knowledge

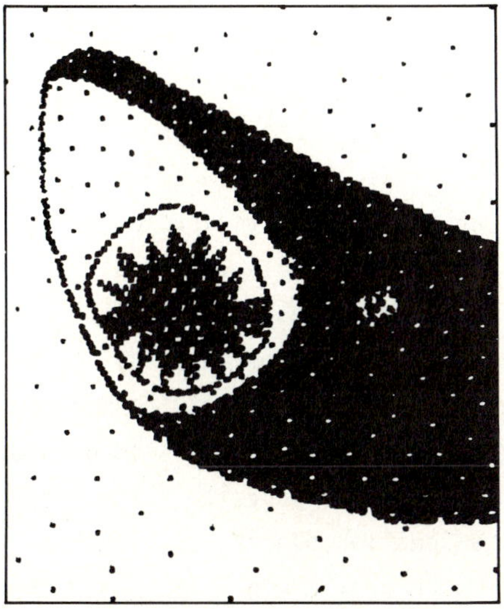

a) 10% error in classification (fine resolution)

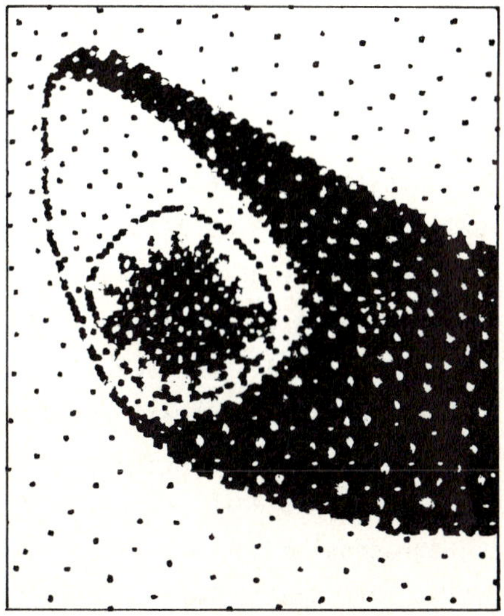

b) 20% error in classification (fine resolution)

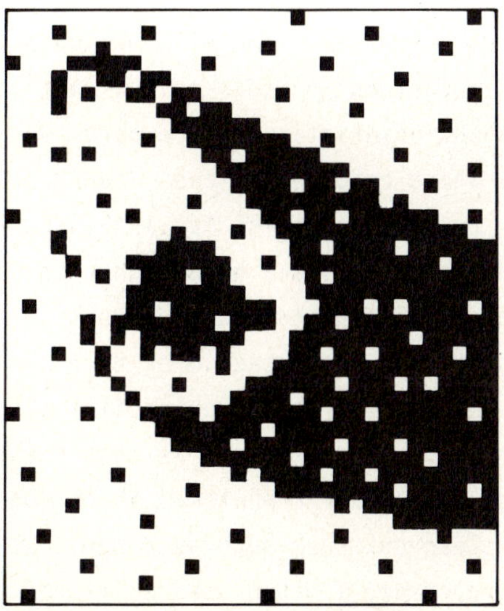

c) 20% error in classification (coarse resolution)

accuracy and define a minimum valid decision resolution, or if both resolutions are fixed, one can specify the accuracy requirements.

The resolution/accuracy relationship can be modelled by the "mean Bayes accuracy" which has been well documented by Hughes (1968). As shown in Figure 7 (modified from Hughes'), we can start with the probability that any one knowledge element (pixel or grid cell in maps) is correctly identified, and graph the probability that a group of elements indicates the right decision, against the number of elements used to make the decision (assuming they all indicate the same decision). Graphs can be drawn for various accuracies of inputs. For component accuracies in the range commonly experienced with environmental mapping (0.7 to 0.9), it is evident that the decision validity curve is rapidly asymptotic with increasing numbers of elements, and that at least 2 are required, but more than 5 would add little validity to the decision. In our environmental studies, we have adopted a requirement that input resolution should be at least 1/2 and preferably 1/4 of the decision resolution, i.e. that 2-4 sub-judgements be taken into account in a location decision. To finish the example, if a ROW is to be 100m wide, we work from a knowledge base with a resolution of 50m or preferably 25m. In mapping terms, if a ROW can be comfortably represented at a scale of 1:50 000, our working level is 1:25 000 or in the case of controversial projects, more like 1:15 000.

These conclusions from environment decision making at point 'c' in Figure 1B suggest some extrapolations to other points in that figure. The model in Figure 7 supports the observation that experts making intuitive judgements in fields where components (cues) can be recognized with a high degree of clarity or confidence (point 'a' in Figure 1B) seem to need only 2 or 3 cues, since that would give a high degree of confidence (0.9+/-) in their judgement. On the other hand, someone working in a field with very fuzzy components (point 'c') might need 6 or more cues, with a resulting final confidence of about 0.75, which would still be as good as anyone in that field could achieve. This argument is consistent with some of my own experience in mapping soils on air photos. Where there was a strong association between clear-cut cues such as a particular terrain type and a vegetation type or crop type, I often used only two cues, and tested the result with a third. Where associations were weaker with other soil types, I used more cues before making a decision, and had less confidence in the

Figure 7

Mean Bayes Accuracy of Decisions Based on Multiple Components with Various Degrees of Random Error

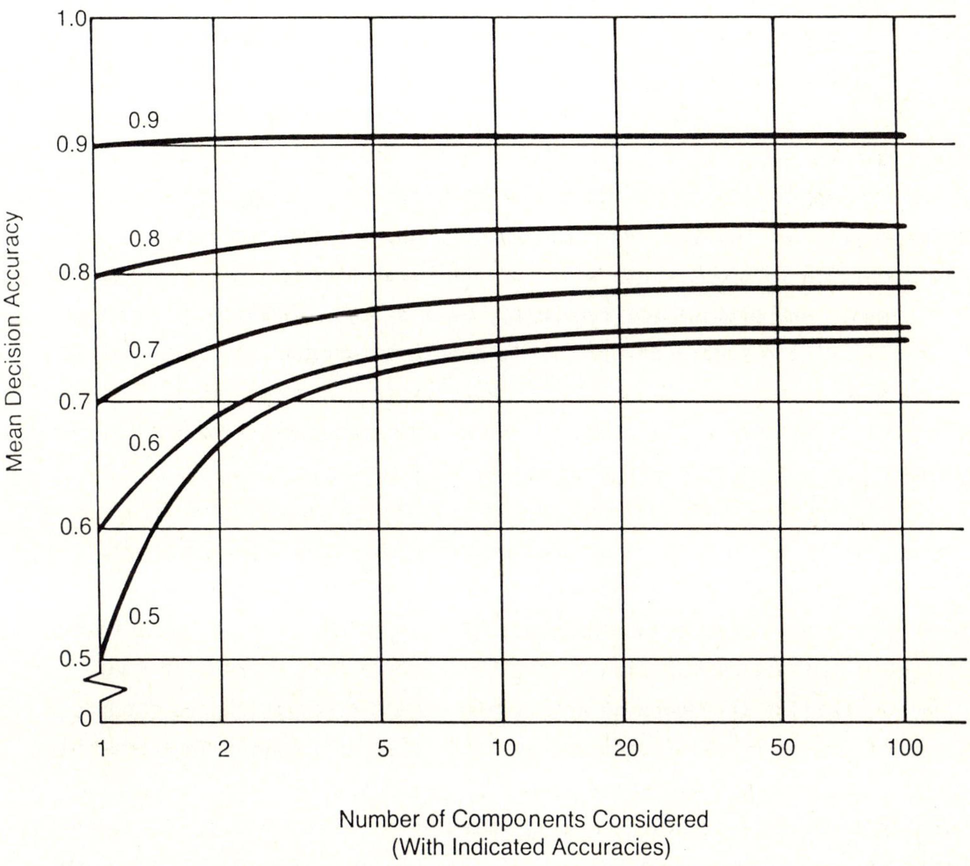

result. A common solution in the latter case is to declare the soil unit to be an uncertain one ('complex') or to define it with certain tolerances. Some judgement analysts may be interested to note that the actual cues changed with each soil type, even if the same number of cues were used, within one map.

Note that Figure 7 suggests that someone who is capable of mentally putting together a large number of extremely fuzzy cues ($p = 0.5+/-$) can attain a validity or success of 0.7 for their creations.

Conclusions

All of the approaches and concepts put forward at the conference were of interest to me as a user. By learning more about each disciplinary field, I gained better insights into who, and what literature, to turn to for improvements and problem solving in my own field of operations. In my field, all of the approaches are truly complementary, and I could not see any necessary competition. I look forward to future development of higher levels of expertise in all of them, as the requirements for overall standards to use in my field progress as they probably will.

However, to maintain proper balance in decision making, more emphasis should be placed on proper handling of intuitive judgement, and particularly more effort should be placed on turning computer tools towards enhancement of it, in addition to trying to dissect it or replace it. Likewise, outside the scope of this conference, intuitive judges need to learn the proper place of decision support sciences in their deliberations.

Everyone involved in decision making could help avoid conflicts by spending more effort in understanding where they are coming from, and who they are dealing with. I hope the scientists and engineers reading this paper can use some of the illustrations presented to analyze the situations they face from time to time and resolve conflicts, particulary by connecting Figure 4 and Figure 1H.

Having come across Bayesian Theory only 6 years ago, I am still enjoying the discovery that it can be used to express or solve numerically or graphically many of the empirical or intuitive solutions to problems about judgements based on recognition of patterns, including I suspect many more anwers to the way in which experts make judgements than the few discussed here.

Bibliography

Asimov, I. 1953 (1st edition): Second Foundation. Gnome, N.Y. 224 p. (later editions widely available in paper back - most librarys).

Hughes, G.F. 1968 On the Mean Accuracy of Statistical Pattern Recognizers. IEEE Trans. Inform. Theory IT-14 pp55-63.

VERY SIMPLE EXPERT SYSTEMS: AN APPLICATION OF JUDGMENT ANALYSIS TO POLITICAL RISK ANALYSIS

Jeryl L. Mumpower
Nelson A. Rockefeller College of Public Affairs and Policy
University at Albany, Statė University of New York USA

INTRODUCTION

A recent study of expert judgments of political riskiness (Mumpower, Livingston, & Lee, in press) contributes both to the continued development of a psychology of expert judgment, as well as to the field of expert systems. (Much of the present paper was adapted from this source.) Judgment analysis provides a yet unrecognized means for developing what are in essence very simple expert systems. Moreover, current efforts in the field of expert systems could be profitably informed by the accumulated results and experience of many years of research by students of the psychology of expert judgment.

Political risk analysis is a relatively new profession. Though some corporations have engaged in such analysis for several decades, the rapid expansion of the profession dates from the 1979 Iranian revolution and its corporate fallout (Multinational Business, 1983; Business Week, 1980). By the early 1980s, over 500 full-time political risk analysts were employed in various multinational corporations (Burstein, 1983) and numerous consulting firms specializing in political risk analysis were in operation.

The purpose of such analysis is straightforward: to protect the overseas investment of multinational corporations by anticipating potential risks emanating from the political environment of the host country. Precise, commonly accepted definitions of political risk and political risk analysis have thus far eluded both practitioners and academics. Korbin (1982) is probably correct, however, in claiming that for most analysts "political risk is usually defined in terms of events occurring in the environment (i.e. an irregular change in regime) or at the junction of environment and firm (e.g. expropriation) which are typically associated with acts of governments." In other words, the political risk of a country is deduced from the stability and policy proclivities of its government. The raw data for this

NATO ASI Series, Vol. F35
Expert Judgment and Expert Systems
Edited by J. Mumpower et al.

deduction are generally obtained from extrapolation of economic data, press reports, surveys of expert opinion, and information transmitted in-house by managers in the field.

Often this deduction is no more than a "qualitative description of the political environment [included] in an investment proposal" (Kelly, 1981), but it may also be used to create a more formalized ranking or rating of a country's political risk. It is the latter methodology that is of interest in the present study. This methodology is used by all the major political risk consulting firms, firms employed by most U.S. multinationals (Kelly, 1981), as well as many of the corporations themselves (Shreeve, 1984). It is also an approach often recommended by academics in the field (Jodice, 1985; Coplin and O'Leary, 1983).

The purpose of the present study is to critically examine numerical, judgmentally-based assessments of political riskiness by professional risk analysts. Studies of expert predictions and forecasts can be traced back at least to Wallace (1923), who found that corn judges agreed with one another fairly well, but that their ratings correlated only slightly with actual crop yields. Modern research dates back to Meehl (1954), who found that statistical methods performed better than clinical judgment in making psychological diagnoses.

Reviews of the now substantial body of literature on expert judgment (Dawes, 1976; Hogarth & Makridakis, 1981; Mumpower, 1985; Shanteau, 1985) have concluded that expert performance cannot be taken for granted. In a number of instances, recognized experts from a variety of fields have proved inaccurate, inconsistent, or overconfident. Exceptions to this general pattern of findings can also be cited, however. For instance, Wallsten and Budescu (1980) concluded that physicians are often, although not universally, quite accurate in their professional judgments. Murphy and Winkler (1974, 1975, 1977) repeatedly found professional weather forecasters to be highly accurate short-range predictors of the probability of precipitation, although not so good at longer-range predictions. Shanteau (1985) found experts, on balance, to be "careful, skilled, and knowledgeable, with little evidence of any psychological limitations."

The present study attempts to identify the determinants of professional analysts' assessments of political risk, to develop a quantitative model describing this process, and, to the extent permitted by available data, assess the quality of those judgments.

METHOD

The dependent variable for the present study was judged degree of political risk in 49 selected countries. The source of data was the Association of Political Risk Analysts (APRA) annual survey for the years 1983-1985. Respondents rated the political risk of each country on a scale of 0 (for "no risk") to 10 (for "highest risk"). They were instructed simply to use the standards that they applied in their own work. The pattern of ratings from all three years was very similar. The Pearson product moment correlation between 1983-1984 ratings was .97; for 1983-1985 the correlation was .99; for 1984-1985 it was .97. Because of the high degree of redundancy, only data from the survey with the largest number of respondents, the 1984 survey to which 51 members responded, were used in most analyses.

The independent, or predictor, variables consisted of nine variables widely thought to be related to levels of political riskiness. Four variables were related to economic indicators. Two variables were related to level of socio-economic development, as reflected by indicators of public health. Three were related to political stability.

Economic Indicators:

1. Estimated inflation rate. Projected annual rates of inflation in 1984 were calculated as unweighted averages of the Consumer Price Index and the Wholesale Price Index. Data were obtained from Business International (1984).

2. Current accounts. Current account balances are of crucial importance to a country's liquidity position. In order to achieve comparability between countries, current account balances were divided by the total value of exports of goods and services for each country. Data were obtained from Business International (1984).

3. Exchange rate differential. This variable was defined as the percentage difference between the officially approved exchange rate and the parallel market rate in units per dollar.

When a country has serious inflation, a large debt burden, a deteriorating liquidity position, or a doubtful political climate, differentials may be found between the values on official and parallel markets. Data were obtained from Business International (1984).

4. Foreign debt service. The level of foreign debt and the resources required to service it are of crucial importance to a country's economic vitality. In order to achieve comparability between countries, current account balances were divided by exports of goods and services for each country. Data were obtained from Business International (1984).

Developmental Level Indicators:

5. Life expectancy. Life expectancy provides a good general measure of level of socio-economic development. Data were obtained from World Bank (1985).

6. Infant mortality rate. Infant mortality rates provide a related, more directly observable measure of level of socio-economic development. Data were obtained from World Bank (1985).

Political Stability Indicators:

Data for the following indicators were obtained from Taylor and Jodice (1978) and updated relying on chronologies in annual volumes of the Institute for Strategic Studies' Strategic Survey and Foreign Affairs' America and the World.

7. Coup attempts. The number of attempted coups between 1948 and 1983 provided a measure of political stability.

8. Successful coups. The number of successful coups between 1948 and 1983 provided a measure of political stability.

9. Civil disturbances. The number of civil disturbances (riots, etc.) between 1948 and 1983 provided a measure of political stability.

RESULTS

Ratings of Political Risk

The average ratings of political risk for each country appear in Table 1. Switzerland was rated as the "safest" country, with an average rating of 1.05, while Iran was rated as the "riskiest," with an average rating of 9.36.

Table 1. Mean Ratings of the Level of Political Risk, 1984 Association of Political Risk Analysts Survey

Rank	Mean	Country	Rank	Mean	Country
1.	1.05	Switzerland	25.	5.06	China (PRC)
2.	1.26	United States	26.	5.18	Thailand
3.	1.44	Japan	27.	5.39	Kuwait
4.	1.83	New Zealand	28.	5.44	Indonesia
			29.	5.50	Venezuela
5.	2.04	West Germany	30.	5.53	Greece
6.	2.08	Australia	31.	5.60	Colombia
7.	2.10	Canada	32.	5.67	Turkey
8.	2.11	United Kingdom	33.	5.69	Morocco
9.	2.35	Singapore	34.	5.79	Mexico
10.	2.51	Norway	35.	5.81	India
11.	2.53	Netherlands			
12.	2.56	Sweden	36.	6.04	Egypt
13.	2.85	Denmark	37.	6.15	Kenya
14.	2.87	Belgium	38.	6.70	Pakistan
			39.	6.73	Chile
15.	3.04	Finland	40.	6.77	Brazil
16.	3.70	Taiwan			
			41.	7.04	Nigeria
17.	4.02	France	42.	7.13	Peru
18.	4.13	Malaysia	43.	7.58	Zaire
19.	4.15	South Korea	44.	7.73	Angola
20.	4.47	Italy	45.	7.81	Argentina
21.	4.64	Spain			
22.	4.83	South Africa	46.	8.08	Philippines
23.	4.90	Portugal	47.	8.60	Libya
24.	4.95	Saudi Arabia	48.	8.93	Iraq
			49.	9.36	Iran

Ratings were quite stable across the three-year period. One-way analyses of variance found significant differences (at the .01 level) over time for only 5 countries: Brazil, France, Norway, Iraq, and Turkey. In each case, the ratings of riskiness were higher in 1984 than in the preceding or following year. Given the high intercorrelations of ratings across years, the obtained differences probably reflect merely fluctuations over time in the use of response scales by a partially overlapping set of respondents.

Correlational Analysis of the Relations among Political Risk Ratings and the Predictor Variables

The intercorrelations among ratings of political risk and the nine predictor variables appear in Table 2. All predictor variables are significantly correlated at the .01 level with the political riskiness ratings. The highest first-order correlation is with infant mortality and life expectancy. Either of these variables alone can account for roughly 50 percent of the variance in ratings of political riskiness.

Different variables might be better predictors of political risk within different regions. To address this possibility, correlations between ratings of political risk and the nine predictor variables were calculated for each of the five regions defined in the APRA survey -- Europe, the Americas, Asia/Pacific, Africa, and the Middle East. The resulting statistics should be interpreted with caution, because of the small ns in each region, ranging from a low of 6 for the Middle East to a high of 14 for Europe. In a few instances, missing data further reduced the number of cases upon which the correlations were computed.

Table 2 suggests several interesting observations, nonetheless. For instance, within Europe, life expectancy is not significantly correlated with ratings of political riskiness, even though this variable accounts for 50 percent of the variance in ratings in the overall sample. From a statistical point of view, this is not wholly surprising because the range is sharply restricted. Within the overall sample, life expectancy ranged from 43 years (Kenya) to 79 years (Switzerland). Within Europe, however, life expectancy ranged only from 71 to 79 years. Given such a restricted range, lower correlations are not surprising.

Perhaps for similar reasons, life expectancy is not a good predictor of political riskiness within Africa, where it ranges from 43 to 64 years and its correlation with political riskiness is also nonsignificant. In sum, life expectancy is a good predictor for discriminating between less risky (usually more-developed countries) and more risky (usually less-developed) countries. Within the European or African regions, however, other variables are needed to discriminate between relatively risky and relatively safe countries.

Table 2. Correlations with Political Risk by Region, 1984

	Overall	Europe	Americas	Asia/ Pacific	Africa	Mideast
Inflation	.43**	.85**	.66*	.75**	-	-
Current Accounts	-.55**	-.74**	-	-	-	-
Exchange Rate Diff.	.56**	.75**	-	.62*	.74*	.97*
Foreign Debt Service	.56**	-	.73*	-	-	ISD
Life Expectancy	-.74**	-	-.71*	-.76**	-	-
Infant Mortality	.75**	.60*	.72*	.75**	-	-
Coup Attempts	.47**	.54*	-	-	-	-
Successful Coups	.53**	.67**	.70*	-	-	-
Civil Disturbances	.37**	-	-	-	-	-
n =	49	14	9	13	7	6

** - Significant at the .01 level
* - Significant at the .05 level
ISD - Insufficient data for computation
\- - Not significant

For instance, inspection of first-order correlation coefficients suggests that inflation is the variable most highly associated with ratings of political riskiness within Europe, with a correlation of .85. Within Africa, however, the correlation between inflation and political risk was not statistically significant. These regional disparities occur despite the fact that the range of inflation was greater in Africa (8% to 75%) than in Europe (3% to 23%).

To pursue this issue further, the 49 countries were divided into 24 "safe" countries (those with ratings of 5-or-less on the 0-to-10 point scale) and 25 "risky"ones (those with ratings of 5-or-more.) The average value of the nine predictor variables for these two groups appears in Table 3. As can be seen, the values for the "risky" countries are more negative for all nine variables. In comparison to safer countries, risky ones tend to have higher inflation rates, less favorable current accounts status, a larger differential between nominal and actual exchange rates, higher levels of foreign debt service, shorter life expectancies, higher infant mortality rates, and histories of more frequent coup attempts, coups, and civil disturbances.

Table 3. Mean Values of Predictor Variables, "Risky" Countries versus "Safe" Countries

	Overall	"Safe" Countries	"Risky" Countries
Inflation	26.4%	6.4%	46.3%
Current Accounts	-12.7%	-2.4%	-23.4%
Exchange Rate Diff.	14.7%	1.4%	28.6%
Foreign Debt Service	27.2%	19.0%	36.7%
Life Expectancy	66.8 yrs.	73.0 yrs.	61.0 yrs.
Infant Mortality	4.8%	1.9%	7.5%
Coup Attempts	2.3	.4	4.2
Successful Coups	1.5	.2	2.8
Civil Disturbances	1.0	.4	1.6
Political Risk Rating	4.9	3.0	6.6
n =	49	24	25

Within the two groups, however, different variables are most strongly associated with relative levels of riskiness. Correlations between ratings of political riskiness and the nine predictor variables for "safe" versus "risky" countries appear in

Table 4. Inflation, life expectancy, and infant mortality are significantly correlated with relative levels of riskiness in "safe" countries, but not in "risky" ones. Current accounts and foreign debt service are significantly correlated with relative levels of riskiness in "risky" countries, but not in "safe" ones. Exchange rate differential and number of civil disturbances are significantly correlated with riskiness in both subgroups, and the number of successful and unsuccessful coups is not significantly correlated with riskiness in either subgroup.

These results should be interpreted only tentatively, but they suggest that certain variables may be more useful when making grosser discriminations among risky and safe countries, while others may be required for making finer discriminations among relatively risky (or, relatively safe) countries.

Table 4. Correlations with Political Risk, 1984: "Risky" Countries versus "Safe" Countries

	Overall	"Safe" Countries	"Risky" Countries
Inflation	.43**	.63**	-
Current Accounts	-.55**	-	.47*
Exchange Rate Diff.	.56**	.54**	.65**
Foreign Debt Service	.56**	-	.55**
Life Expectancy	-.74**	-.66**	-
Infant Mortality	.75**	.59**	-
Coup Attempts	.47**	-	-
Successful Coups	.53**	-	-
Civil Disturbances	.37**	.47*	.45*
n =	49	24	25

** - Significant at the .01 level
* - Significant at the .05 level
ISD - Insufficient data for computation
\- - Not significant

Factor Analysis of the Predictor Variables

Because of the high level of intercorrelations among the nine predictor variables, the initial data set is difficult to analyze and interpret. Intercorrelations among variables are presented in Table 5. Of the 36 possible pair-wise correlations, 23 are significant at the .05 level. Six of the variables (foreign debt service; successful coups; current accounts; exchange rate differential; life expectancy; infant mortality) are significantly correlated with six or more of the eight other variables in the predictor set. In several instances, most notably in the case of life expectancy and infant mortality, the correlation between variables is so great that it is clearly inappropriate to include both in statistical analyses.

Table 5. Intercorrelations among Predictor Variables

	1	2	3	4	5	6	7	8	9
Inflation									
Current Accts	-								
Exch Rate Diff	-	-.64							
Debt Service	.82	-.45	.27						
Life Expect	-	.57	-.32	-.29					
Inf Mortality	-	-.48	.30	.26	-.94				
Coup Attempts	.43	-.44	.56	.47	-	-			
Coups	.54	-.51	.45	.56	-.34	.35	.71		
Civ Distrbnces	-	-	-	-	-	.28	-	-	

In order to decrease the dimensionality of the set of predictor variables, a factor analysis was performed (using the principal components extraction and varimax factor rotation techniques of the SPSSX computer package.) The analysis suggested the presence of three underlying factors which accounted for 76 percent of the variance in the data. Results are summarized in Table 6.

Table 6. Factor Analysis of the Predictor Variables, Varimax Rotated Factor Matrix

	Factor 1	Factor 2	Factor 3
Current Accounts	-.73	-.18	-.40
Exchange Rate Diff.	.88	.04	.08
Attempted Coups	.69	.49	-.07
Inflation Rate	.04	.94	.06
Foreign Debt Service	.21	.88	.17
Successful Coups	.58	.61	.11
Life Expectancy	-.37	-.07	-.85
Infant Mortality	.30	.09	.89
Civil Disturbances	-.22	.09	.59

The first factor is defined primarily by the exchange rate differential and current accounts variables. Attempted coups also loads heaviest on this factor. This factor seems to reflect primarily the strength of a country's position within the world economy.

The second factor is defined primarily by the inflation rate and foreign debt service variables. The number of successful coups also loads most heavily on this factor, but only marginally more so than on the first one. This factor seems to reflect primarily the internal health of each country's economy.

The third factor is defined primarily by the life expectancy and infant mortality variables. The civil disturbances variable also loads most heavily on this factor. This factor appears to reflect the level of socio-economic development reached by the country, as indicated by levels of public health and civil order.

Regression Analyses -- Predicting Ratings of Political Risk

The relationship between the predictor variables and judgments of political riskiness by APRA members is the central focus of this study. Least square stepwise multiple regression analysis was used to address this issue. The criterion variable was the average rating of political riskiness for each country from the 51 respondents to the APRA survey. Because of the high levels of inter-correlations among predictors, problems of interpretation and instability were anticipated if the full set of all nine predictors was used. The number of predictor variables was thus reduced to three, the variables with the highest loading on each of the three factors:

Factor 1 -- Exchange Rate Differential
Factor 2 -- Estimated Inflation Rate
Factor 3 -- Infant Mortality Rate

Selecting one variable to represent each factor contributes toward simplicity and ease of interpretation. Other more sophisticated but less straightforward techniques (e.g., use of factor scores as predictor variables) are likely to improve predictability, but in the present instance such improvements were marginal.

Results of the three-predictor analysis for the overall data set are summarized in Table 7. All three predictors entered the equation. The results indicated that ratings of political risk can be predicted with a high degree of accuracy on the basis of a linear combination of the three predictor variables. Roughly 75 percent ($\underline{R}^2 = .76$) of the variance in such ratings can be accounted for by these variables. (Including all nine variables as potential predictors would raise $\underline{R}^2$ only to .82.)

Table 7. 3-Predictor Regression Analysis: Prediction of Political Risk Ratings

Variable	Beta	r	*	R	RSQ	Adj. RSQ
			*			
Infant Mortality Rate	.60	.75	*			
Exchange Rate Diff.	.34	.56	*			
Inflation Rate	.27	.43	*	.87	.76	.74

In order to check for regional differences, three-predictor stepwise multiple regression analyses were carried out for each of the five regions. Previous cautions about interpretation of results based upon such small <u>n</u>s apply doubly here, but the results appearing in Table 8 give little reason to suspect that

Table 8. 3-Predictor Regression Analysis: Prediction of Political Risk Ratings, by Region

Variable	Beta	r	*	R	RSQ	Adj. RSQ
			*			
<u>Europe</u>			*			
Inflation Rate	.85	.85	*	.85	.73	.70
			*			
<u>Americas</u>			*			
Infant Mortality Rate	.79	.72	*			
Exchange Rate Diff.	.63	.55	*	.96	.92	.89
			*			
<u>Asia/Pacific</u>			*			
Inflation Rate	.75	.75	*			
Infant Mortality Rate	.50	.75	*	.87	.75	.70
			*			
<u>Africa</u>			*			
Exchange Rate Diff.	.74	.74	*			
Inflation Rate	.61	.50	*	.95	.91	.85
			*			
<u>Middle East</u>			*			
Exchange Rate Diff.	.97	.97	*	.97	.95	.93

the overall analysis obscures large and meaningful differences between regions. The adjusted $\underline{R}^2$ values ranged from approximately 70 to 90 percent, suggesting that the three identified factors are likely to be adequate for predicting risk across a range of regions and types of countries.

Similar analyses were carried out on the previously identified "safe" and "risky" subgroups. Results appear in Table 9. The adjusted $\underline{R}^2$ values are .62 for "safe" countries and .53 for "risky" countries, indicating that the three-predictor model provides a fair degree of predictive power even within relatively homogeneous groups of countries.

Table 9. 3-Predictor Regression Analysis: Prediction of Political Risk Ratings for "Safe" vs. "Risky" Countries

Variable	Beta	r	*	R	RSQ	Adj. RSQ
			*			
"Safe" Countries			*			
Inflation Rate	.41	.63	*			
Infant Mortality Rate	.40	.59	*			
Exchange Rate Diff.	.34	.54	*	.82	.67	.62
			*			
"Risky" Countries			*			
Exchange Rate Diff.	.66	.65	*			
Inflation Rate	.38	.37	*	.76	.57	.53

<u>Cluster Analysis -- Differences among Respondents</u>

The 51 respondents to the APRA survey come from a variety of academic backgrounds and are engaged in a variety of activities within a number of different employment settings. The preceding analyses obscured such differences by averaging together ratings to produce a single risk rating for each country. It seemed possible that there might be significant disagreement within the group concerning the level of risk of specific countries and thus differences in the types of predictors associated with such differential judgments of riskiness.

In order to examine the issue, a cluster analysis was performed (using the BMDP software package). Three statistically distinct clusters emerged, distinguished primarily by differences in the level of ratings of riskiness which they attributed to certain countries (especially the relatively "safe" ones), rather than by differences in ranking. The Spearman rho correlation coefficient value among the three clusters ranged from .95 to .98. Respondents were highly homogeneous with respect to their rankings, if not their ratings, of the political riskiness of the present sample of countries. In sum, little difference among subgroups was found.

Expert and Naive Political Risk Analysts

Fifty-nine members of an undergraduate political science class at the State University of New York at Albany were asked during Winter 1986 to rate each of the 49 focal countries on a scale of 0 (least risk) to 10 (greatest risk). These students had expressed no special interest nor had received any formal training in political risk analysis.

In the main, their ratings exhibited close resemblance to those of the APRA membership. Correlations among average student ratings, APRA ratings, and the nine predictor variables are given in Table 10. Student ratings and APRA ratings are highly correlated, ranging from .87 to .90 across the three years of APRA ratings. Correlations between student ratings and the nine predictor variables exhibit a similar pattern to that for the APRA ratings.

Table 10. Correlations between Student Ratings, APRA Survey Ratings, and the 9 Predictor Variables

	Average Student Rating
Average APRA Rating, 1983	.87
1984	.90
1985	.87
Inflation Rate, 1984	.35
Current Accounts, 1984	-.51
Exchange Rate Diff., 1984	.58
Debt Service, 1984	.50
Life Expectancy	-.64
Infant Mortality	.65
Coup Attempts	.56
Coups	.52
Civil Disturbances	.37

Using the data from the 1985 APRA survey (the one closest in time to the student ratings), student ratings and APRA ratings differed on average by .20 scale rating points (s.d.=1.1) across the 49 countries. Although differences between average APRA and average student ratings tended to be slight, students exhibited greater variability in ratings of individual countries than did APRA members. The median value of the standard deviation for students' ratings of countries was 1.98; for the APRA ratings, the median value was 1.66. (Countries which students tended to judge as riskier than the APRA membership included South Africa, Singapore, and Malaysia; APRA members judged Brazil as riskier than did the students.)

DISCUSSION AND CONCLUSION

The Expertise of Political Risk Analysts

Approximately 75% of the variance in professional analysts' judgments of the political riskiness of 49 focal countries could be accounted for on the basis of 3 predictor variables: exchange rate differential; estimated inflation rate; and infant mortality rate. A cluster analysis revealed little difference among judges. Ratings by undergraduate students closely paralleled those of professional analysts.

Political risk analysts are members of a new, but relatively well-established profession. The average salary of an analyst employed by a major corporation is in the $60,000-75,000 range (*New York Times*, Sept. 9, 1985). Several successful consulting firms sell extensive, detailed risk analyses to a number of customers. The Association for Political Risk Analysis (APRA) numbers approximately 300 members. The present study revealed a high degree of stability over time and a strong consensus among APRA members regarding the riskiness of target countries. By any conventional measure, political risk analysts possess the hallmarks of expertise.

The precise nature of their expertise is more problematic. One important element of expertise is command of and access to a factual knowledge base. Substantive knowledge seems essential for any imaginable type of expertise; content-free expertise is difficult to imagine.

Inarguably, the APRA members who responded to the survey possess command over a far larger store of facts and information than the undergraduate participants in this study, or even well-informed lay political observers. A great depth and breadth of political, financial, and economic data are routinely collected and analyzed by practitioners in the field. The claim to expertise is clearly warranted with respect to mastery of a knowledge base.

A second element of expertise is mastery of an efficacious rule system for using facts and information in order to make forecasts, predictions, or diagnoses. In this respect, the APRA claim to expertise is cloudier. Methodologically, substantial obstacles exist to evaluating the quality of APRA judgments of political riskiness. Ideally, such evaluations would be based on longitudinal data that would make it possible to determine actual outcomes in countries judged to be "safe" versus "risky." Data over time are currently being collected (now in its fourth year), but data from much longer time periods will be required before an adequate basis is created for making firm conclusions about the degree of accuracy of prior APRA ratings of riskiness.

In the meantime, the close parallel between APRA ratings and average student ratings is somewhat troublesome for APRA claims of expertise. Differential accuracy is a more appropriate and rigorous test for claims of predictive expertise than is simply degree of accuracy. Experts should not only predict well, but do better than nonexperts. Pertinent outcome data are not yet available, but given the present set of ratings, there are few possible outcomes that would lead to the conclusion that professional political risk analysts are better predictors than the average response of SUNYA political science undergraduates. APRA members undoubtedbly know more; it is not clear that they can predict better, at least on the present task. Once again (Meehl, 1954; Oskamp, 1962; Chan, 1982), novice judges rival the performance of experts.

To what extent is the present assessment of political risk analysts fair? In particular, to what extent is the profession characterized by the numerical ranking or rating of countries? Most risk analysts are probably primarily involved in providing general, subjective input into investment decisions (Kelly, 1981). But attempts to rate and rank risk are an important part of the profession. At many major corporations, risk analysts explicitly rank countries along with their other duties.

The senior political risk analyst for General Motors noted that the academic consensus is that risk ratings are of dubious value, but defended them on grounds that "any theory, system, or model for comparative analysis must ultimately be able to accomplish such a task" (Rayfield, 1983), arguing that "the narrow focus of corporate analysis ... makes it somewhat more realistic to attempt such an exercise." General Motors rates all countries on a 0-100 scale as part of its political risk analysis exercises; see Shreeve (1984) and Arrowsmith (1985) for other examples. As Shreeve (1984) noted, "for most companies, the easy way has been to quantify..." Such rankings also form the core of the activities of the consulting firms which occupy a high profile within the political risk community and which are widely employed by multinational corporations. Much of the profession thus is concerned to a significant extent with numerically ranking or rating countries.

Implications for Expert Systems

The present research points to a number of potential implications for the field of expert systems.

1. Although neither psychologists nor the developers of expert systems are accustomed to thinking of it as such, the present simple three-variable predictive model is in essence a very simple expert system.

This descriptively motivated analysis provides the basis for a prescriptive model with capabilities quite like those desired for expert systems. According to Lemmon (1986), "Expert systems are computer programs that perform at the level of human experts in some particular domain." In order to predict the political riskiness of specific countries, the present model applies a very simple set of rules -- a regression-based, weighted linear model -- to a small data set consisting of three variables. This "very simple expert system" closely replicates the expert judgments of professionals in the area. One could, of course, build a more complicated expert system to do the same thing, but why bother?

As Stewart and McMillan (1986) noted, psychologists have been developing very simple expert systems for many years, although they don't ordinarily call them that. For several decades, psychologists have studied problem solving, intelligence, and intuitive judgment; they have developed and tested models capable of approximating human behavior in situations requiring intuitive judgment. The models successfully reproduced expert judgment and led to important insights into judgment processes, but they were used only as research tools. No one thought of them as "expert systems."

These models relied extensively on what Dawes (1979) has characterized as the "robust beauty of linear models" -- the ability of simple, even demonstrably incorrect, linear models to replicate the results of human judgmental processes. The use and virtue of such models is a potentially important, but presently unrecognized, contribution of psychologists to expert systems. (The simplest expert system in the present instance might be the average ratings of SUNYA undergraduates.)

2. The present study is not terribly favorable in its overall evaluation of the judgmental performance of professional risk analysts. Such findings are not atypical. Many previous studies of expert judgment have reached similar conclusions. These studies should perhaps caution those working on expert systems. It may not be enough simply to "perform at the level of human experts in some particular domain" as Lemmon (1986) stated the goal of expert systems. Performing at the same level as experts may not always be good enough. Sometimes it may be preferable -- and possible -- to perform better than human experts, or at least more efficiently.

Psychologists who developed simple descriptive linear models found that they often performed better than the judges themselves, a phenomenon that came to be known as "bootstrapping." Several factors help account for this perhaps surprising finding (see Dawes & Corrigan, 1974), but an important one for those working with expert systems is the distinction between <u>knowledge</u> and <u>cognitive</u> <u>control</u> (Hammond & Summers, 1972). One can distinguish between knowledge -- knowing in general how to combine multiple pieces of information into a judgment -- and cognitive control -- being able to exercise this facility in a consistent manner across particular instances.

When researchers attempt to develop expert systems that replicate the performance of human experts, they should be fully cognizant that actual performance is usually suboptimal because of lack of perfect cognitive control. Good expert systems will be based on the knowledge of experts, but avoid incorporating errors arising from imperfect and inconsistent attempts to apply such knowledge.

3. Two key elements of expertise -- command of facts and mastery of an efficacious rule system -- frequently become confused. As suggested by the present study, knowledge of and access to an information base is sometimes mistaken as the signal criterion of expertise, even when the ability to predict or diagnose is more properly the critical measure. Such inappropriate overgeneralization is not surprising. Command of large numbers of facts is a necessary if not sufficient condition for expertise. Moreover, the quality of expert forecasts and predictions is often difficult for laypersons to evaluate. Einhorn and Hogarth (1978) concluded that it is often difficult for experts themselves to evaluate accurately the quality of their judgment. Under such circumstances, relying on factual command as a surrogate for expertise, even when predictive accuracy would be the more appropriate criterion, represents a perhaps understandable shortcut.

For those working on expert systems, this points to the need for heightened concern with evaluations of the validity of experts' claims to expertise. Such claims may sometimes be based more on acquaintance with a large knowledge base than on abilities to predict, diagnose, or forecast. The value of developing expert systems that reproduce with great fidelity the inferential behavior of experts who have little predictive ability is questionable.

4. Not all expert systems can be "very simple" ones, of course. Simple linear models will not prove an adequate basis for all, or even most of, the types of problems with which developers of expert systems are concerned. Nonetheless, in more complicated applications these techniques may play an important part. In particular, the tools developed by psychologists to study expert judgment may prove useful to developers facing the problem of knowledge extraction (Vandamme et al., 1985; de Waele & Theunis, 1985).

Vandamme et al. (1985) observed that "...the primary problem is to obtain relevant knowledge from the experts. The straightforward solution to this question is 'ask them.' But asking the expert proves rapidly to be inefficient. Not that we question the willingness of the expert earnestly to answer our questions. The truth is that most of the time the experts have no adequate verbal access to their expert knowledge. And even if they have, we usually find an enormous difference between their practice and their conscious verbal description."

Psychologists studying expert judgment came to similar conclusions. At least two different approaches were taken to the problem. One was to develop the type of linear models previously discussed. Such models were based on behavior, not on self-reports. Even though they did not faithfully replicate the cognitive processes of the judges under study, they were <u>paramorphic</u> (Hoffman, 1960) in that they approximated such processes sufficiently closely to be of value in studying, understanding, and facilitating human judgment.

A second approach was to rely on observations of experts as they make judgments and on the experts' verbal descriptions of their reasoning. In psychology, this approach is usually described as "process tracing" or "protocol analysis." As Stewart and McMillan (1986) observed, this is the approach most often taken by knowledge engineers in expert systems development.

In a very instructive study, Einhorn, Kleinmuntz, and Kleinmuntz (1979) compared linear regression and process-tracing models, based on the same data, in an attempt to resolve which model is better from a psychological perspective. They came to the perhaps surprising conclusion that both types of models are capturing the same underlying process, although at difference levels of generality.

For knowledge extraction activities, developers of expert systems might sometimes find it efficient or otherwise advantageous to use an approach incorporating linear regression-based models, rather than process tracing or protocol analysis. Simple linear models might then serve as inference engines (or part of inference engines) for expert systems, despite the fact that such models don't replicate precisely experts' cognitive processes. An expert system that embedded simple linear models (more like intuition) within more deductive-like processes (involving production, logic, or frame systems, or the like) would be quite consistent with psychological theories that see human cognition as a quasirational (Hammond, 1966) process: complex, characterized by the ability to get to the same place via a number of different routes, and incorporating elements of both intuitive and deductive rationality. Thus, "very simple" expert systems might constitute components of more complex ones.

5. The present model is based on only three variables. Experts normally use, or at least believe that they use, many more variables than that. Like most other experts, the professional political risk analysts collect, collate, and attempt to attend to massive amounts of information. The seductiveness of collecting ever greater amounts of information is generally attributed to the (frequently mistaken) assumption that more information will inevitably lead to better judgments (Oskamp, 1965; Gaeth & Shanteau, 1984; Phelps & Shanteau, 1978). Establishing and maintaining access to large amounts of information is probably not a bad generic policy, nonetheless, especially in probabilistic environments where many pieces of information are related to the criterion and specific desired pieces of information are not always readily available. Being able to base judgments on a large number of available, intersubstitutable cues is a very adaptive capability in probabilistic environments (Brunswik, 1965; Hammond et al., 1975).

While this may be a sensible, adaptive strategy for humans, it may not be so appropriate for expert systems. Building an expert system with the level of redundancy and capability for vicarious functioning corresponding to that of a human expert may be very inefficient. Quinlan (1982) observed, "Rather surprisingly, only a small amount of knowledge is necessary to drive an expert system at human-or-better levels of performance." Psychological research suggests that the amount of data and the complexity of rules required for good performance may frequently be even more modest than has been appreciated to date. Indeed, because of cue intersubstitutability (the intercorrelation of relevant pieces of data), successful expert systems might even use different pieces of information from those that human experts do.

In conclusion, the present study, based as it is in a tradition of the study of expert judgment that is over thirty years old, points to significant implications for the field of expert systems. In this respect, the present study is exemplary, not unique. The future of both the psychology of expert judgment and expert systems would be well-served by establishment of better links and interconnections to facilitate communication and cross-fertilizations among researchers from both fields.

REFERENCES

Arrowsmith, James. "A Comparison of Risk Analysis in the Natural Resource and Banking Environments." Presented at the Association of Political Risk Analysts Annual Conference, Boston, 1985.

Brunswik, E. Perception and the Representative Design of Psychological Experiments. Berkeley: University of California Press, 1956.

Burstein, Daniel. "The Risk Analysts Survive a Shakeout." International Management, 1983, 38 (10).

Business International, International Country Risk Guide, New York, 1984. (August 31)

Business Week. "Foreign Investment: The Post Shah Surge in Political Risk Studies." December 1, 1980.

Chan, S. "Expert Judgments Made under Uncertainty: Some Evidence and Suggestions." Social Science Quarterly, 1982, 63, 428-444.

Coplin, William, and O'Leary, Michael. "Political Risk Analysis for Extractive Industries." Planning Review, 1983, 11 (2).

Coplin, William, and O'Leary, Michael. "Forecasting Risk in the International Marketplace." Security Management, 1983, 27 (8).

Dawes, R. M. "Shallow Psychology." In J. S. Carroll & J. W. Payne (Eds.) Cognition and Social Behavior. Hillsdale, N.J.: Lawrence Erlbaum Associates, 1976.

Dawes, R., and Corrigan, B. Linear Models in Decision Making. Psychological Bulletin, 1974, 81, 95-106.

Einhorn, H. J., Kleinmuntz, D. N., Kleinmuntz, B. Linear Regression and Process-Tracing Models of Judgment. Psychological Review, 1979, 86, 465-485.

Einhorn, H., and Hogarth, R. "Confidence in Judgment: Persistence of the Illusion of Validity." Psychological Bulletin, 1978, 85, 395-416.

Gaeth, G. J., and Shanteau, J. "Reducing the Influence of Irrelevant Information on Experienced Decision Makers." Organizational Behavior and Human Performance, 1984, 33, 263-282.

Hammond, K. R. Probabilistic Functionalism: Egon Brunswik's Integration of the History, Theory, and Method of Psychology. In K. R. Hammond (ed.) The Psychology of Egon Brunswik. New York: Holt, Rinehart, & Winston, 1966.

Hammond, K. R., Stewart, T. R., Brehmer, B., and Steinmann, D. O. Social Judgment Theory. In M. F. Kaplan and S. Schwartz (Eds.), Human Judgment and Decision Processes. New York: Academic Press, 1975.

Hammond, K. R., & Summers, D. A. Cognitive Control. Psychological Review, 1972, 79, 58-67.

Hoffman, P. J. The Paramorphic Representation of Clinical Judgment. Psychological Bulletin, 1960, 57, 116-131.

Hogarth, R. M., and Makridakis, S. "Forecasting and Planning: An Evaluation." Management Science, 1981, 27, 115-189.

Jodice, David. "An Overview of Political Risk Assessment." In D. Jodice (ed.) Political Risk Assessment: An Annotated Bibliography. Westport, CT: Greenwood Press, 1985.

Kelly, Marie Wicks. Foreign Investment Evaluation Practices of U.S. Multinational Firms. Ann Arbor: University of Michigan Research Press, 1981.

Korbin, Stephen J. Managing Political Risk Assessment: Strategic Response to Environmental Change. Berkeley: University of California Press, 1982.

Lemmon, Hal Comax: An Expert System for Cotton Crop Management. Science, 1986, 233, 29-33.

Meehl, P. Clinical versus Statistical Prediction: A Theoretical Analysis and a Review of the Evidence. Minneapolis: University of Minnesota Press, 1954.

Multinational Business, "Political Risk Analysis -- A Minor Growth Industry." 1, 1983.

Mumpower, J. "Expert Judgments of Risk: A Psychological Perspective." In F. Homburger (Ed.) Safety Evaluation and Regulation of Chemicals, 2. Basel: Karger, 1985.

Mumpower, J., Livingston, S., & Lee, T. J. "Expert Judgments of Political Riskiness." Journal of Forecasting, in press.

Murphy, A. H., and Winkler, R. L. "Probability Forecasts: A Survey of National Weather Service Forecasters." Bulletin of the American Metereological Society, 1974, 55, 1449-1553.

Murphy, A. H., and Winkler, R. L. "Subjective Probability Forecasting." In D. Wendt & C. Vlek (Eds.) Utility, Probability, and Human Decision Making. Dordrecht, Netherlands: Reidel, 1975.

Murphy, A. H., and Winkler, R. L. "Reliability of Subjective Probability Forecasts of Precipitation and Temperature." Journal of the Royal Statistical Society, 1977, 26, 41-47.

New York Times, September 9, 1985, p. D1.

Oskamp, S. "Overconfidence in Case Study Judgments." Journal of Consulting Psychology, 1965, 29, 261-265.

Oskamp, S. "The Relationship of Clinical Experience and Training Methods to Several Criteria of Clinical Prediction." Psychological Monographs, 1962, 76

Phelps, R. H., and Shanteau, J. "Livestock Judges: How Much Information Can an Expert Use." Organizational Behavior and Human Performance, 1978, 21, 209-219.

Quinlan, J. R. "Fundamentals of the Knowledge Engineering Problem." In D. Michie (ed.) Introductory Readings in Expert Systems. New York: Gordon and Breach Science Publishers, 1982.

Rayfield, Gordon. "Comparative Politics Applied: Theory and Practice in the Business Environment." Presented at Theory and Practice in Political Risk Conference, Princeton University, 1983.

Shanteau, J. Psychological Characteristics of Expert Decision Makers. Psychology Report #85-2, Applied Experimental Psychology Series, Kansas State University, Lawrence, 1985.

Shreeve, Thomas. "Be Prepared for Political Changes Abroad." Harvard Business Review, 1984, 62.

Stewart, Thomas R. and McMillan, Claude, Jr. Descriptive and Prescriptive Models for Judgment and Decision Making: Implications for Knowledge Engineering. 1st Annual Rocky Mountain Conference on Artificial Intelligence, 1986.

Taylor, Charles Lewis, and Jodice, David A. World Handbook of Political and Social Indicators, Volume 2: Political Protest and Government Change. New Haven: Yale University Press, 1978.

Vandamme, F., Vervenne, D., de Waele, D., Theunis, M., & Heefer, A. A Primer on Expert Systems. Ghent, Belgium: Communication & Cognition, 1985

de Waele, Dani & Theunis, Marleen. Knowledge Extraction. CC-AI, 1985, 2, 5-14.

Wallace, H. A. "What is in the Corn Judge's Mind?" Journal of the American Society of Agronomy, 1923, 15, 300-304.

Wallsten, T. S., and Budescu, D. V. Encoding Subjective Probabilities: A Psychological and Psychometric Review. University of North Carolina at Chapel Hill, 1980.

World Bank, World Bank Development Report, 1984, Washington, D.C., 1985.

EXPERT SYSTEMS AND INTELLIGENT COMPUTER-ASSISTED-INSTRUCTION

Emrah Orhun
Bilgisayar Muhendisligi
Ege Universitesi
Izmir, Turkey

INTRODUCTION

Instruction assisted by computer offers the potential of better attention to individual student needs than can be met in the typical classroom. Individualized instruction, modeled after the idea of a private tutor, allows a student to proceed at his own pace, to explore his interests, and to receive personal, detailed evaluation and direction (Clancey, 1986). Computer-assisted-instruction (CAI) may facilitate such individualized instruction in a more effective, faster, and less costly manner than traditional teaching.

The first examples of CAI which can selectively present subject material and exercises based on an evaluation of the student's understandings were implemented as systems which can selectively generate text on the basis of student response (Atkinson and Wilson, 1969). The 1970s have seen the evolution of a new generation of CAI programs based on the methods of artificial intelligence (AI). These artificial intelligence CAI (AICAI) programs or intelligent tutoring systems (ITS) use AI formalisms to separate out the subject matter they teach from the programs that control interactions with students to extend the domain of applicability, the power, and the accuracy of CAI (Sleeman and Brown, 1982). Examples include AICAI tutors for geography (Carbonell, 1970), electronic troubleshooting (Brown et al, 1981), symbolic integration (Kimball, 1981), mathematical games (Burton and Brown, 1976), program debugging (Miller, 1981), and medical diagnosis (Clancey, 1982). ICAI systems contain some form of expert knowledge and the study of expert systems is important in ICAI research. Expert systems are problem-solving programs that use artificial intelligence techniques to solve difficult problems requiring expertise. The objective of this paper is to survey some of the existing ICAI systems to identify

NATO ASI Series, Vol. F35
Expert Judgment and Expert Systems
Edited by J. Mumpower et al.

the various forms of knowledge present and to discuss the requirements instruction places on expert systems.

COMPONENTS OF INTELLIGENT TUTORING SYSTEMS

The main components of an intelligent tutoring system correspond to the representation of the three types of knowledge a tutor must have: 1) expert model; the knowledge of the subject matter, 2) student model; what the student does or does not understand, and how he obtains the solution, 3) the tutoring model; how to teach.

Representing the expert knowledge, the student model and the tutoring model separately, in a reusable form, is a difficult problem. Many researchers have focused on building the student model, since the system performance depends on the accuracy of the student model. A comprehensive review of qualitative student modeling which describes a student's knowledge structurally, in terms of relations among concepts and a problem solving procedure is given by Clancey (1986).

Tutoring systems need to model the process of problem solving. Problem solving may be modeled as the act of applying a general model to form a situation-specific model (Clancey, 1986). A situation-specific model is a description of some situation in the world, generally an explanation of how a situation came about or a plan for action. Problem solving involves relating a general model to the current situation by applying an inference procedure. For example, in medicine, a situation-specific model describes a patient's current state (e.g., fever) and the disease processes that brought this state about (e.g., a particular infection), and the inference procedure is called a diagnostic strategy. In programming, the situation-specific model is the constructed program, as well as unwritten descriptions of the underlying design, relating the code to the goals the program is supposed to satisfy. Each of the models in an intelligent tutoring system has a general and situation-specific form. For example, we may distinguish between the general model of how to communicate and the situation-specific model of the current dialogue.

The inclusion of both a general model and an inference procedure in a tutoring system means that the system can solve the problems that it gives to the student, providing a basis for interpreting his problem-solving behaviour, evaluating his partial solutions, and assisting him.

In a tutoring system, we monitor the behaviour of the student, looking for discrepancies from the ideal specification (target problem solving model), track discrepancies back to faults in the student's presumed world model or inference procedure, and repair the student by instruction (Clancey, 1986). This process of casually tracing backwards from discrepant behaviour to hidden faults in a cognitive system is called diagnostic modeling. The casual description has several levels: the discrepant behaviour, the system fault or malfunction (called a bug), and the explanation of how this bug came about. For example, in a computer program, we may distinguish among the incorrect output, the bug in the code, and the explanation for this bug.

In general, a bug is some structural flaw manifested in faulty behaviour. A bug may refer to an incorrect inference procedure or an error in the student's general model (commonly called a "misconception"). The origins of bugs are explained in three categories (Clancey, 1986):

- Mis-learning: The student's model of the world, his believed situation-specific information, or inference procedure is incorrect because of a learning error (e.g., a false analogy).

- Construction: The student's model and inference procedure did not allow a complete solution of a problem, weak problem-solving methods allowed resolution of an impasse; so the student "made up something" and went on.

- Slip: The student knew better, he just did not perform properly.

EXPERT SYSTEMS AND ICAI

Nature of Expertise

Research has concentrated on building models of the

student's knowledge on the assumption that student errors reflect misconceptions about the procedure to be followed or facts in the problem domain and that the best teaching strategy is to address directly the student's misconceptions (Buchanan and Shortliffe, 1985). Building models of misconception, on the other hand, requires a sounder understanding of the nature of knowledge and expertise. Cognitive science research into the nature of expertise is causing radical revision in science and engineering curricula (Soloway, 1986). To quote Soloway:

> What has been taught in the past is by and large not what an expert actually knows. For example, geometry students typically understand each step in a proof, as the teacher puts it on the board, line by line. However, when attempting to do a proof for homework, students often have no idea where to begin. Why? Mathematicians do not develop proofs in such an orderly, linear fashion. Rather, developing a proof is a nonlinear, search process. Unfortunately, students are not told explicitly about the nonlinear nature of proof development: They see their teacher develop a proof line by line, and not surprisingly, they think they should be able to do the same. Today, teaching topics such as geometric proofs is being revised to include explicit instruction as to the heuristics that guide proof development.

Comparison studies of experts and novices (Chie et al., 1980; Feltovich et al., 1980; Lesgold, 1983) suggest that we might teach the student the reasoning strategies, patterns, the quick associations that experts build up over long exposure to many kinds of problems (Buchanan and Shortliffe, 1985).

Some researchers believe that experts are not conscious of the knowledge and strategies they employ to solve a problem (Clancey, 1986; Soloway, 1986). The extraction of the implicit knowledge that experts have has been carried out in various domains such as mathematics (Larkin et al., 1980), physics (Michener, 1978) and programming (Soloway, 1986). In solving problems, experts use domain-specific "chunks" similar to the units of mental organization called schemata which are employed in reading and writing stories (Soloway, 1986).

Expert Systems

Expert systems that embody knowledge of a particular application area combined with inference mechanisms which enable the program to use this knowledge for problem solving are used in restricted domains of medicine, science, and engineering (Hayes-Roth et al., 1983). These knowledge-based programs use a large number of facts and rules to carry out tasks such as interpretation, diagnosis, prediction, instruction, monitoring, planning and design.

Expert systems try to attain the high level of performance that a human expert achieves in some task. An expert system has expert rules to direct its search, performs well, reasons by manipulating symbols, grasps fundamental domain principles, and has complete weaker reasoning methods to fall back on when expert rules fail and to use in explanations (Hayes-Roth et al., 1983).

Instruction places additional requirements on the qualities of expertise. An instructional expert system should be able to solve problems in multiple ways, allowing for syntactic variations in situation-specific models. It must model human ways of thinking. In explaining, it must go beyond a trace of how the problem is solved. It must articulate the general and specific model, why both are believed and relate them to the student's model and underlying beliefs (Clancey, 1986). It must be able to evaluate the student's explanations concerning how he solves the problem. An intelligent CAI system should explain how the student learned and predict what he is ready to learn next. This implies that the expert system must have a model of how the student develops his knowledge.

The representation of the knowledge of the subject area, or the domain expertise in ICAI is in one of two forms (Burton, 1981). One form is as a "glass-box" or articulate model (Goldstein & Papert, 1977). In an articulate model each problem solving decision made can be explained in terms that match those of a human problem solver. The Buggy (Brown & Burton, 1978), Wumpus (Goldstein, 1982), and Guidon (Clancey, 1982) systems are based on knowledge from an expert system. In Guidon the expertise to be taught is provided by Mycin (Shortliffe, 1974), a rule-based consultation program about infectious diseases, diagnosis and therapy.

In contrast to the articulate expert is the "black-box" expert, which does not mimic human experts. For example, the electronic-troubleshooting tutor SOPHIE-1 (Brown and Burton, 1981) uses a black-box expert - a circuit simulator - which is used only to check the consistency of student's hypotheses and answer some of his questions. Its mechanisms which are certainly not the mechanisms the student is expected to acquire are not revealed.

Tutoring

Tutoring is a complex task which involves deciding whether to intervene, what to discuss, and how much to say about that topic (Goldstein, 1982). In script-based CAI, the order in which topics are introduced is predefined. The student may proceed to the next question after he has successfully answered the current question. ICAI is less rigid and allows a student to explore a problem in his own way. This, however, makes tutoring more complex.

In expert-based ICAI systems which analyze the student's responses in terms of an underlying expert skill set, tutoring is oriented around supplying advice in those situations wherein the student has chosen a less than ideal option. Expert-based models fail to consider that the novice student may not be employing a subset of the expert's skills, but rather using simplifications, deviations, and other evolutionary predecessors of those skills (Goldstein, 1982). Goldstein's genetic graph addresses this limitation.

The genetic graph emphasizes that the student is an active agent, engaged in a constructive process of generating new knowledge. To quote Goldstein:

> From this perspective, the objective is to encourage this process in the student. This reminds that the current activity of most AICAI tutors - intervening and supplying a complete explanation - is only one end of the spectrum of tutoring activity. At the other end of the spectrum is "tutoring without talking," that is saying nothing at all, but instead altering the problem domain in order to facilitate the learning process.

There are as well a range of intermediate interventions between these two extremes. An example is that the tutor could suggest that a rule exists that could be applied in the current situation which is analogous to some already acquired rules, but not specifying the new rule or stating the analogy. The next generation of AICAI tutors should be able to supply advice across this spectrum, altering the nature and extent of their intervention in relation to the current state of the student model.

Various tutoring strategies applicable in different learning environments include Socratic intervention (Collins et al., 1975), "frontier tutoring" (Goldstein, 1982), "web tutoring" (Norman, et al., 1976), and "tutoring without talking" (Goldstein, 1982).

The kinds of knowledge a tutor needs to guide a dialogue are analyzed by Winograd (1977), and Bruce (1975). In GUIDON, a tutorial program which uses the knowledge bases of MYCIN-like expert systems, the following forms of knowledge have been found desirable for a case method tutor (Clancey, 1982):

- o Knowledge about dialogue patterns. Two types of patterns are interpretation patterns (to understand a speaker) and action patterns (to generate utterances) (Faught, 1977).

- o Domain knowledge for carrying on a specific dialogue.

- o Knowledge of the communication situation. The communication situation is represented in GUIDON by an "overlay student model," a "case syllabus" (a lesson plan of topics to be discussed for each case), and a "focus record" (to keep track of factors in which the student has shown interest).

CONCLUSIONS

Expert systems try to attain the high level of performance that a human expert achieves in some task. In this paper, the use of expert systems in computer-assisted-instruction has been discussed and the requirements which teaching places on expert systems have been identified.

REFERENCES

Atkinson, R.C. and Wilson, H.A., 1969, eds. Computer-Assisted Instruction, Academic Press, New York.

Brown, J.S. and Burton, R.R., 1978. Diagnostic models for procedural bugs in basic mathematical skills. Cognitive Science, 2, 155-192.

Brown, J.S., Burton, R.R. and DeKleer, J., 1981. Pedagogical, natural language and knowledge Engineering Techniques in SOPHIE I, II, and III. In D. Sleeman and J.S. Brown, eds., Intelligent Tutoring Systems, 227-282, Academic Press, New York.

Bruce, B.C., 1974. Generation as a social action. In Schank, R. and Nash-Webber, B.L., Ed., Theoretical Issues in Natural Language Processing, pp. 74-77.

Buchanan, B.G., and Shortliffe, E.H., 1985, eds. Rule-Based Expert Systems, Addison-Wesley.

Burton, R. and Brown, J.S., 1976. A tutoring and student modeling paradigm for gaming environments. In Coleman, R. and Lorton, P. Jr., Eds., Computer Science and Education, ACM SIGCSE Bulletin, 8(1), 236-246.

Carbonell, J.R., 1970. AI in CAI: An artificial intelligence approach to computer-assisted instruction. IEEE Transactions on Man-Machine Systems, MMS-11: 190-202.

Chie, M.T.H., Feltovich, P.J., and Glaser, R., 1980. Representation of physics knowledge by experts and novices, Report No. 2, Learning Research and Development Center, University of Pittsburgh.

Clancey, W.J., 1982. Tutoring rules for guiding a case method dialogue. In Sleeman, D. and Brown, J.S., Eds., Intelligent Tutoring Systems, 201-222. Academic Press, New York.

Clancey. W.J., 1986. Qualitative Student Models. Working paper no. KSL-86-15. Stanford Knowledge Systems Laboratory.

Collins, A., Warnock, E., and Passafiume, J., 1975. Analysis and synthesis of tutorial dialogues. In Bower, G., Ed., The Psychology of Learning and Motivation, Vol. 9, Academic Press, New York.

Faught, W.S., 1977. Motivation and intentionality in a computer simulation model. AIM-305, Stanford University.

Feltovich, P.J., Johnson, P.E., Moller, J.H., and Swanson, D.B., 1980. The role and development of medical knowledge in diagnostic expertise. Paper presented at the annual meeting of the American Educational Research Association.

Goldstein, I.P., 1982. The genetic graph: a representation for the evolution of procedural knowledge. In Sleeman, D. and Brown, J.S., Eds., Intelligent Tutoring Systems, 51-77, Academic Press, New York.

Goldstein, I.P. and Papert, S., 1977. Artificial Intelligence, language, and the study of knowledge. Cognitive Science, 1,(1), 1-21.

Hayes-Roth, F., Waterman, D.A., and Lenat, D.B., eds., 1983. Building Expert Systems, Addison-Wesley.

Kimball, R.A., 1981. A self-adapting, self-improving tutor for symbolic integration. In Sleeman, D. and Brown, J.S., eds. Intelligent Tutoring Systems, 283-307, Academic Press, New York.

Larkin, J., McDermott, J., Simon, D., and Simon, H., 1980. Expert and novice performance in solving physics problems. Science 208, 140-156.

Lesgold, A.M., 1983. Acquiring expertise. Report No. PD S-5, Learning Research and Development Center, University of Pittsburgh.

Michener, R.R., 1978. Understanding mathematics. Cognitive Science, 2, 283-327.

Miller, M.L., 1982. A structural planning and debugging environment for elementary programming. In Sleeman, D. and Brown, J.S., eds., Intelligent Tutoring Systems, 119-135, Academic Press, New York.

Norman, D., 1976. Studies of Learning and Self-Contained Educational systems, 1973-1976. University of California at San Diego, Center for Human Information Processing, Report No. 7601, March.

Shortliffe, E.H., 1974. Mycin, a rule-based computer program for advising physicians regarding antimicrobial therapy selection. STAN-CS-74-465, Stanford University.

Sleeman, D. and Brown, J.S., 1982, eds. Intelligent Tutoring Systems, Academic Press, New York.

Soloway, E., 1986. Learning to program - learning to construct mechanisms and explanations. Communications of the ACM, 29, 9, 850-858.

Winograd, T., 1977. A framework for understanding discourse. AIM-297. Stanford University.

ASSESSING THE EFFECTIVENESS OF EXPERT TEAMS

John Rohrbaugh
Rockefeller College of Public Affairs and Policy
State University of New York at Albany
Albany, NY, USA

INTRODUCTION

The earliest literature concerning collective judgment consistently indicated that groupings of experts should be expected to outperform their average member, but there is little evidence available to suggest that the quality of collective judgment is substantially improved by any particular method of aggregation (Rohrbaugh, 1979, 1981). Fischer (1981) has concluded:

> From a practical standpoint it makes little or no difference how one aggregates the conflicting opinions of experts. Any reasonable approach is likely to be as good as any other.

The conclusion that we cannot discriminate the relative advantage of reasonable methods of aggregation, however, should not be taken to imply that groups of experts always perform as well as can be expected. Even in the research laboratory in which a careful study of small groups can thoroughly control the method of aggregation (i.e., the characteristics of the intervention in the group process), considerable variability in the performance of experimental groups is observed. There is no reason to believe that every group using a "reasonable approach" (in Fischer's words) as a method of aggregation will perform at a level substantially above its average member. Certainly any set of interventions in group process outside a laboratory setting is likely to produce even greater variability in performance. How should we then assess the effectiveness of any one intervention with respect to a particular expert team?

NATO ASI Series, Vol. F35
Expert Judgment and Expert Systems
Edited by J. Mumpower et al.

One approach is to evaluate the performance of the expert team on the basis of subsequently observed outcomes associated with the group's product (e.g., a collaborative judgment or a decision rule). It is argued that good decisions result in good outcomes, poor decisions result in poor outcomes. In fact, there is little doubt that the value of a decision does depend on the confluence of events subsequent to the group process. For example, a revenue forecast is good only if actual revenues match the projection; an investment is only as "smart" as the return it produces.

Such tautologies (i.e., that good decisions are good or that bad decisions are bad), however, beg the much more fundamental and important question of whether ineffective group processes sometimes result in good outcomes. It would seem very possible for a quite unreasonable method of aggregation to be linked over time with a windfall, while in another instance a most reasonable method of aggregation subsequently appears to have fallen far wide of the mark. Can outcomes ever be used to assess the effectiveness of the group process used by an expert team?

A FRAMEWORK FOR THE CRITIQUE OF DECISION OUTCOME EVALUATIONS

Expert teams often develop a group product for which no standard measure of accuracy or quality exists at the time their work has been completed. In such situations, the evaluation of the decision must occur later, sometimes in only a few days or occasionally after many years. The outcomes observed over time determine the value of the collective decision, that is, exactly how "good" or "bad" it proves to be. There are at least three characteristics of these outcomes that warrant attention: repetition, complexity, and comparability.

Repetition. The decision of some expert teams is used only once, for example, in the selection of a new product line or the design of a single disposal site. Other expert teams produce a simple decision rule or a more complex expert system that can be used repeatedly, such as a procedure for reviewing loan applications or a policy for prescribing a particular drug. In the former cases, outcomes are available on a "one time only" basis, while in the latter instances the expertise of the group is tested time and again.

Complexity. Although there are many ways in which the outcomes of a decision might be viewed as complex (e.g., their undependability, their intersubstitutability, or their interdependence), the focus here (for the sake of simplicity) is on the number of dimensions by which the decision is evaluated. Some products of expert teams can be assessed with a single criterion, for example, the only important aspect of selecting a stock portfolio may be its earnings over three years. In contrast, a specific government proposal for altering corporate tax rates can produce a variety of salient outcomes, all of which might be measured in multiple and explicit ways.

Comparability. Do the outcomes allow for a fair evaluation, not only of the decision that was made, but also of the alternative courses of action that were discounted? A baseline of comparison is needed to assess the relative "goodness" or "badness" of a particular group product. Perhaps the observed outcomes are no better or worse than could have been achieved by chance or by doing nothing at all. The outcomes of a horse race show clearly how every available option performed under identical circumstances defined by specific track conditions. In contrast, the selection of one managing director or chief executive officer precludes ever ascertaining how any of the remaining competitors would have performed on the job during the same time period. Of course, there are many circumstances in which expert judgments may never be able to be evaluated (e.g., in the case of subjective probability assessments of highly unlikely events or estimates of consequences that may not accrue for hundreds of years).

In combination, the characteristics of repetition, complexity, and comparability identify 12 circumstances in which an attempt may be made to evaluate the performance of expert teams, both the "goodness" of the group decision and of the group process, as shown in Figure 1. In the following section, it is argued that in only a few of these circumstances can the observed outcomes associated with the group's product be used to establish the value of a particular decision or decision rule and not in any instance to assess the effectiveness of the group process itself.

THE USE OF OUTCOMES TO EVALUATE GROUP DECISIONS AND GROUP PROCESSES

No outcomes available. In one-third of the circumstances shown in Figure 1, the product of an expert team has the impact of one hand clapping; there simply are no outcomes available by which its performance can be evaluated. Whether the team's collective judgment is implemented or rejected, subsequent events give little hint about either the value of its decision or the effectiveness of its decision process.

One time only. In one-half of the remaining circumstances, the product of the expert team is used only once. As Boring (1954) pointed out over 30 years ago, one-shot case studies have such a total absence of control as to be of almost no scientific value for purposes of evaluation. The design of a time-series quasi-experiment with the introduction of the group product in the midst of periodic measurements solves several of the problems with the one-shot case study, but, as Campbell and Stanley (1963) indicated, it does not solve the severe problem of history as a threat to internal validity or remove any of the threats to external validity. Here, the value of the decision can be assessed (in a tautological sense), but the method of aggregation cannot be evaluated.

Outcomes of one option assessed (more than once). This category includes most decision rules and virtually all expert systems produced by a group and subsequently implemented at the exclusion of any other technique or approach. There is no doubt that "true experiments" can be designed to test whether the use of the group product results in outcomes superior to non-use conditions. Assume that such an experiment is designed and found to support the use of the group product. Can one, therefore, be convinced of the effectiveness of the group process that produced it? Can one be justified in recommending that other expert teams

REPETITION:	One Time Only		More Than Once	
COMPLEXITIY:	Single Criterion	Multiple Criteria	Single Criterion	Multiple Criteria
COMPARABILITY:				
Outcomes of all options assessed				
Outcomes of one option assessed				
No outcomes can be assessed				

Figure 1: Framework for the Critique of Decision Outcome Evaluations

use the same approach? The fact is that no baseline or comparison group of products exists against which the team product can be evaluated. Although it may well be shown to outperform nonuse, the possibility exists that any method of aggregation might have worked as well--or perhaps far better. And if the group product fails in particular instances, without baselines of comparison, one cannot conclude necessarily that the group process is flawed. It is possible to argue that such failures might occur as the result of even the most effective group process. In other words, the "ceiling" on performance is not known.

<u>Outcomes of all options assessed (more than once)</u>. The circumstance in which an expert team selects one decision rule for repeated use but, nevertheless, tests virtually all available rules, is extremely rare. In one recent example (Tryfos, et al., 1984), more than 50 strategies for wagering on U.S. National Football League games were assessed over the 1975-1981 seasons of play. Had an expert team in 1975 selected the one decision rule that eventually returned the greatest amount of money in the 1976 season, could one conclude its method of aggregation was a good one? Both in 1976 and 1977? For the next five years? It is clearly arguable that the selection of the best decision rule, no matter how unlikely the event, is no better than a one-shot case study in its inability to support empirically the effectiveness of one process used by a unique expert team at a single point in time.

<u>ASSESSING THE EFFECTIVENESS OF GROUP PROCESSES</u>

The difficulty of reliably linking the "goodness" of outcomes to particular methods of aggregation is extraordinary, especially if the intention is to identify a set of interventions that predictably will improve the effectiveness of a variety of expert teams. As noted above, the research design at a minimum would need to involve multiple teams working on multiple tasks in multiple ways and producing multiple decision rules (not just the one preferred rule) that could be tested over multiple periods of time. Even if such a program of research were to empirically support (on the basis of outcomes) the relatively greater effectiveness of a particular method of aggregation, in any specific instance its use as a set of interventions would not assure an expert team of an effective group process.

An assessment of the effectiveness of an expert team requires directing primary attention to the group process itself, not to subsequent outcomes. Of course, it is difficult to argue for such pertinence of group process (instead of outcomes) in traditional organizational settings that are managed entirely on the basis of short-term results alone. However, as unnatural to some observers as it may seem to distinguish conceptually between good group processes and good outcomes, it is even more irregular to propose that an assessment of the effectiveness of an expert team must focus exclusively on its method of aggregation. What evaluation criteria, what standards of performance, can be applied to the working of an expert team?

Zakay (1984) took an important step in answering such questions by building the Decisions' Goodness Questionnaire (DGQ). The DGQ contained 25 statements that were believed to describe an effective decision process; each "criterion" was rated on a 10-point scale by 145 industrial managers. A factor analysis identified 4 factors that could explain about two-thirds of the variance in the ratings. Zakay labeled these factors "Information Utilization" (e.g., all of the existing information is used; attempts are made to obtain missing information), "Subjective Rationality" (e.g., the decision is logical; internal consistency among all the values and probabilities used is kept), "Realism and Resources" (e.g., the decision was made at the right time; the decision could be carried out), and "Feelings and Social Compromise" (e.g., the decision maker has a good feeling about the decision; the decision is satisfactory to superiors).

Zakay's (1984) approach to evaluating the quality of managerial decision making correctly placed emphasis on multiple characteristics of the group process. The research explicitly recognized that the criteria available to assess the effectiveness of expert teams are numerous and implicitly suggested that only a portion of the criteria directly pertain to standards of "subjective rationality."

The weakness of the research, however, was its lack of a conceptual framework; in an important sense, the study was completely atheoretical. Presented below is an organizing structure intended to encourage more extensive and systematic assessments of decision-making processes in group settings.

A COMPETING VALUES APPROACH TO ORGANIZATIONAL ANALYSIS

The theoretical framework used in this chapter is the competing values approach (CVA) to organizational analysis (Quinn and Rohrbaugh, 1981, 1983; Lewin and Minton, 1986). According to the CVA framework (as shown in Figure 2), there are 4 middle range models of organizational analysis:

o an internal process model that focuses on information management and coordination as the means by which stability and equilibrium can be developed as primary organizational objectives;

o a rational goal model that focuses on planning and objective setting as the means by which productivity and efficiency can be improved as primary organizational objectives;

o an open systems model that focuses on flexibility and readiness as the means by which resource acquisition and growth can be increased as primary organizational objectives; and

o a human relations model that focuses on cohesion and morale as the means by which the value of human resources can be made greater as a primary organizational objective.

The CVA framework makes clear the parallel relationship between these 4 models of organizational analysis and the 4 functional prerequisites of any system of action identified by Parsons (1959):

o the integrative function,

o the goal attainment function,

- o the adaptive function, and
- o the pattern maintenance and tension management function.

In combination, the internal process and rational goal models reflect consumatory concerns, that is, the integration of organizational parts. In combination, the open systems and human relations models reflect instrumental concerns, that is, the differentiation of organizational

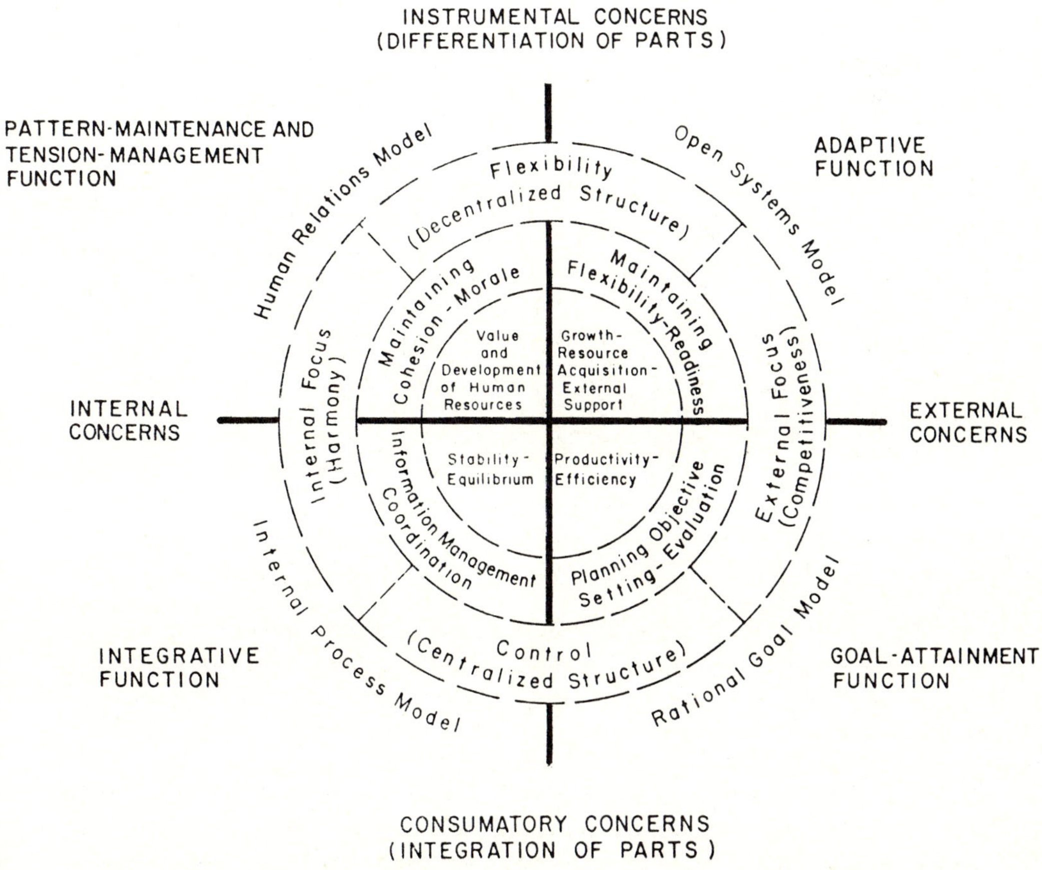

Figure 2: Framework for the Competing Values Approach to Organizational Analysis

parts. These two pairs are reflective of Gouldner's (1959) two general models of organizational analysis: the rational model with an emphasis on formal, planned behavior and the natural system model with an emphasis on flexible, spontaneous behavior.

When Quinn, Rohrbaugh, and McGrath (1985) extended the CVA framework to assess the effectiveness of executive teams, they identified 4 alternative perspectives which paralleled the middle range models of organizational effectiveness:

- o the empirical perspective (or internal process model),
- o the rational perspective (or rational goal model),
- o the political perspective (or open systems model); and
- o the consensual perspective (or human relations model).

<u>The empirical perspective</u>. This viewpoint emphasizes the importance of evidence in a decision process. Particular attention is directed to securing relevant information and developing large databases to provide decision support. Proponents of this perspective believe that to be effective, a decision process must allow thorough documentation and considerable accountability. Does this correspond to Zakay's (1984) "Information Utilization" factor?

<u>The rational perspective</u>. Logic rather than data dominates this viewpoint, since clear thinking is seen as the primary ingredient for effective decision making. The process should be based on explicit attention to organizational goals and objectives. Methods that can efficiently assist decision makers with their reasoning are particularly valued, such as cognitive maps and preference technology. Zakay (1984) identified an underlying factor termed "Subjective Rationality."

<u>The political perspective</u>. Nothing is viewed as more useful to decision making than the power resources that can accrue from a good idea. As a result, this perspective stresses the need for adaptability and flexibility in

creative problem solving, while recognizing that final decisions must be seen as legitimate by other affected parties and responsive to shifts in uncertain and turbulent environments. "Realism and Resources," according to Zakay (1984), was a clear factor in the Decisions' Goodness Questionnaire.

The consensual perspective. The most important assessment criterion in this perspective is the availability of a participatory process that allows open expression of individual feelings and sentiments. Internal discussion and debate are thought to lead to collective agreement on a mutually satisfactory solution. As a result, the likelihood of support for the decision during implementation is increased. The fourth factor uncovered by Zakay (1984) was "Feelings and Social Compromise."

THE EFFECTIVENESS OF EXPERT TEAMS CAN BE ASSESSED

The empirical, rational, political, and consensual perspectives yield eight criteria for evaluating the decision processes used by groups (Quinn, Rohrbaugh, and McGrath, 1985) as shown in Figure 3. All seem reasonable standards for assessing expert team performance, but personal values and situational pressures often favor one particular perspective. That is, no single perspective is inherently all right or wrong; all eight criteria reflect important considerations in evaluating decision processes. From the political and rational perspectives effective decision making has more of an external focus, less reliance on information, a capacity for greater speed, and a principal concern about impact, while the consensual and empirical perspectives value more of an internal focus, the use of considerable information (whether facts or opinions), and an often time-consuming concern for assuring the appropriateness of the decision-making method itself. The consensual and political perspectives tend to encourage more flexible, intuitive, and implicit decision processes, while the empirical and rational perspectives tend to stress more regulated, analytical, and explicit methods of aggregation.

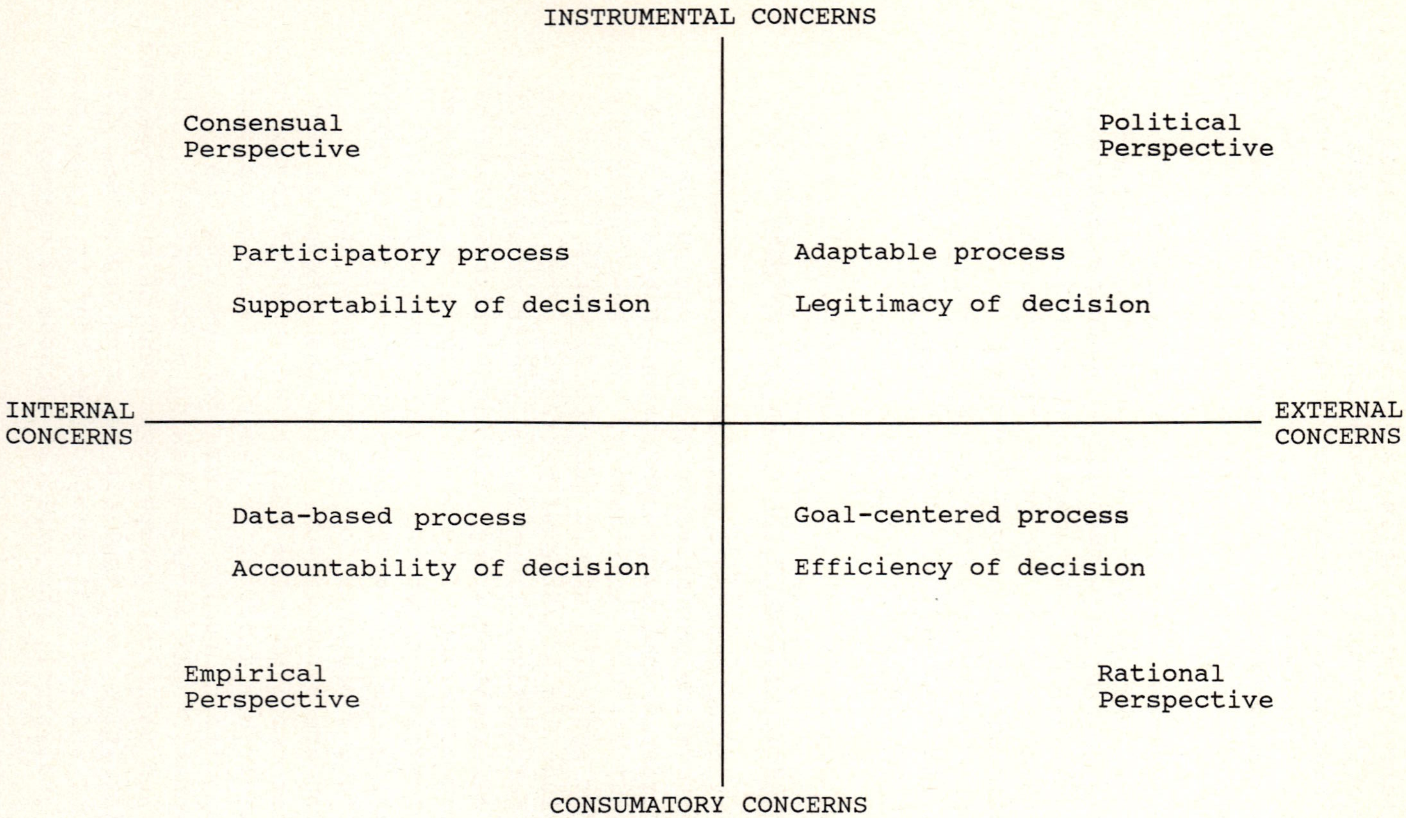

Figure 3: Framework for the Competing Values Approach to Decision-Making Effectiveness

A single perspective on effective decision making is not taken merely because of a particular value system; situations involving time pressure and level of uncertainty play a role, too. When time pressures are high, little emphasis is likely to be placed on the consensual and empirical approaches. Instead, emphasis will shift to the criteria important to the rational and political perspectives, such as flexibility and efficiency. When time horizons are longer, concerns about participation and accountability, for example, can be respected. When uncertainty is high, tightly regulated, analytical methods are less likely to be used as the emphasis shifts toward the political and consensual perspectives. However, greater certainty about the decision-making situation may lead to an increased opportunity to value the considerations important to empirical and rational approaches.

For such reasons, Rohrbaugh (1986) argued that the dominant perspective shifts across organizational levels, as well. For problems of concern to the lower organizational strata, the empirical perspective is stressed. This tendency is evident in Zakay's sample of managers and may well be true for many expert teams. At a higher organizational level, the rational perspective's emphasis on efficiency and goal setting predominates. As uncertainty increases at still higher strata, the political perspective gains favor, perhaps even being replaced by the consensual perspective when the salient time horizon is at its longest.

Considerable work has been devoted over the past two years to the development of an instrument based on the CVA framework for assessing the effectiveness of group decision-making processes. A 50-item questionnaire has been validated and applied in a variety of settings as an evaluation instrument. Milter (1986), for example, reported its use in assessing the value of decision conferences. A portion of his findings, shown in Figure 4, graphically represents the typical, "baseline" process of decision making described by one executive team (notably low in adaptability) in contrast to its assessment of work in a decision conference setting. The figure is produced by plotting the average team scores for each of the eight

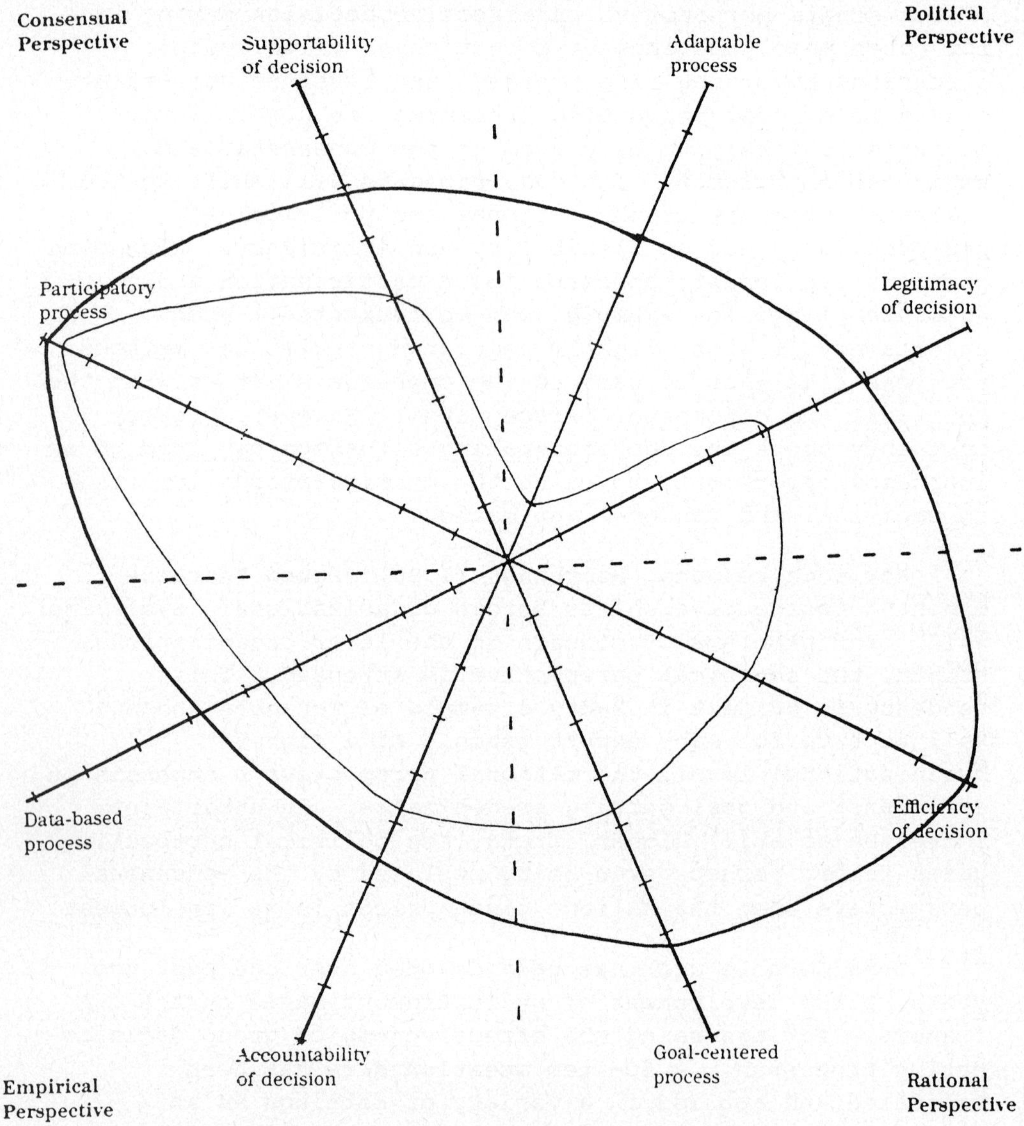

Figure 4: An Assessment of Two Decision-Making Processes Using the Competing Values Approach

criterion scales, once for the traditional group process and again for the decision conference.

WHEN IS AN EXPERT TEAM EFFECTIVE?

There are those who would ask, "What is effectiveness? Given the competing values approach, how do we judge the effectiveness of a particular expert team?" Judging the effectiveness of a particular expert team ultimately involves the application of values. One of the major problems to date in the literature on decision making is that the pertinent values have never been made clear, that is, no standards of reasonable performance exist by which decision processes of expert teams can be evaluated (Hart, 1985). Researchers, by selecting one or more given criteria, have tended to impose a particular value perspective on the focal group without realizing the implied value trade-offs with respect to other criteria that were not selected. For example, to stress the need for accountability in decision making imposes the values of the empirical perspective and ignores the criteria of three other viewpoints.

Because the competing values approach makes the values of effective decision making explicit, it allows researchers to be aware of the value choices to be made and, more importantly, to take these value choices to the expert team itself. If the researcher chooses to impose a set of criteria on the expert team process instead, at the least, the awareness of the competing values approach should foster a most comprehensive and balanced set of indicators than has appeared in many past efforts. Of course, the problems of assessing the effectiveness of expert teams are complex, and this chapter may not fully resolve many of the thorny issues that exist. At a minimum, however, the conceptual framework should provide a more systematic explication of the alternative perspectives on effective group processes, as well as the corresponding set of criteria that often is only considered in part. Perhaps the availability of an evaluation instrument to more thoroughly assess decision processes will lead to a better appreciation that expert teams need not be accountable for unfortunate outcomes that occur in a probabilistic and uncertain environment _if_ they take full responsibility for the effectiveness of their own decision process.

REFERENCES

Boring, E. G. The nature and the history of experimental control. _American Journal of Psychology_, 1954, _67_, 573-589.

Campbell, D. T., and Stanley, J. C. Experimental and quasi-experimental designs for research on teaching. In N. L. Gage (ed.), _Handbook of research on teaching_. Chicago: Rand McNally, 1963.

Fischer, G. W. When oracles fail--a comparison of four procedures for aggregating subjective probability forecasts. _Organizational Behavior and Human Performance_, 1981, _28_, 96-110.

Gouldner, A. W. Organizational analysis. In R. Merton, L. Broom, and L. S. Cottrell, Jr. (eds.), _Sociology today: Problems and prospects_. New York: Basic Books, 1959.

Hart, S. L. Toward quality criteria for collective judgments. _Organizational Behavior and Human Decision Processes_, 1985, _36_, 209-228.

Lewin, A. Y., and Minton, J. W. Determining organizational effectiveness: Another look, and an agenda for research. _Management Science_, 1986, _32_, 514-538.

Milter, R. G. An exploration of criteria for effective decision making in organizations and an evaluation of a group decision support system: A case study approach. An unpublished doctoral dissertation, Department of Public Administration, State University of New York at Albany, August, 1986.

Parsons, T. General theory in sociology. In R. Merton, L. Broom, and L. S. Cottrell, Jr. (eds.), _Sociology today: Problems and prospects_. New York: Basic Books, 1959.

Quinn, R. E., and Rohrbaugh, J. A competing values approach to organizational effectiveness. _Public Productivity Review_, 1981, _5_, 122-140.

Quinn, R. E., and Rohrbaugh, J. A spatial model of effectiveness criteria: Toward a competing values approach to organizational analysis. _Management Science_, 1983, _29_, 363-377.

Quinn, R. E., Rohrbaugh, J., and McGrath, M. R. Automated decision conferencing: How it works. Personnel, 1985, 62, 49-55.

Rohrbaugh, J. Improving the quality of group judgment: Social judgment analysis and the Delphi technique. Organizational Behavior and Human Performance, 1979, 24, 73-92.

Rohrbaugh, J. Improving the quality of group judgment: Social judgment analysis and the Nominal Group Technique. Organizational Behavior and Human Performance, 1981, 28, 272-288.

Rohrbaugh, J. The use of computers for improving decison making in organizations: Beyond "exhaustive" empiricism and "bounded" rationality. Paper presented at the 1986 Conference on Decision Making and Information Processing, School of Management, State University of New York at Buffalo.

Tryfos, P., Casey, S., Cook, S., Leger, G., and Pylypiak, B. The profitability of wagering on NFL games. Management Science, 1984, 30, 123-132.

Zakay, D. The evaluation of managerial decisions' quality by managers. Acta Psychologica, 1984, 56, 49-57.

EXPERT SYSTEMS AS COGNITIVE TOOLS FOR HUMAN DECISION MAKING

Franz Schmalhofer
McGill University Cognitive Sciences Centre
Montreal, Quebec, Canada

INTRODUCTION

Research on judgment and decision making has produced two classes of theories, i. e., descriptive theories which specify how humans actually make decisions, on the one hand, and prescriptive theories on the other hand. Prescriptive theories are formal procedures which one supposedly ought to apply to determine the best decision under some well defined conditions. Such conditions are usually specified by a relatively small number of facts or variables. Prescriptive rules are based upon rationality principles such as consistency, transitivity of choices, or the maximization of subjective utility (Edwards, 1984).

For example, a decision task may be characterized by a set of alternative actions or alternatives, which we shall represent by the set {..x, y, z..}. Furthermore, it is assumed that every alternative x is described by its features x_i on some n attributes or dimensions, which are considered relevant. Presumably some subjective (utility) value $v(x_i)$ can be assigned to every feature x_i of every alternative x on each dimension i. Each dimension i is furthermore given some importance weight w(i). The particular alternatives, the relevant dimensions, the importance weights as well as the values $v(x_i)$ may all be subjectively specified by an individual. The multi-attribute utility (MAU) principle (Keeney, 1982) would then prescribe to maximize the subjective utility by selecting an alternative for which

$$\sum_{i=1}^{n} w(i) * v(x_i) \geq \sum_{i=1}^{n} w(i) * v(y_i) \quad \text{for all alternatives } y \in \{..x, y, z..\}.$$

Many years of research have shown that such prescriptive models do not adequately describe the cognitive decision process of humans in general nor of human experts in particular (Slovic, Fischhoff, & Lichtenstein, 1977). Instead, the empirical

NATO ASI Series, Vol. F35
Expert Judgment and Expert Systems
Edited by J. Mumpower et al.

research of human information processing yielded the specification of descriptive theories of decision making. This research shows that contrary to prescriptive models humans use heuristics in decision making which yield violations of rationality principles and result in a number of biases (Kahnemann & Tversky, 1972). Supposedly, such heuristics are employed rather than prescriptive procedures because of processing limitations of the human mind. Let us consider, for example, the processing effort required to apply the multi-attribute utility rule in a simple binary choice situation, in comparison to some selective information processing rule.

EFFORT-QUALITY RELATIONS FOR COMPLETE AND SELECTIVE INFORMATION PROCESSING

Specification of binary choice task: Assume that the alternatives x and y are described by n dimensions. With respect to these n dimensions every alternative is described by the respective n features, $x = (x_1, \ldots x_i, \ldots x_n)$ and $y = (y_1, \ldots y_i, \ldots y_n)$. The attractiveness of every feature shall be specified by a positive integer $v \in [a, b]$. With $r := b - a$, a decision maker distinguishes $r + 1$ different attractiveness values.

For reason of simplicity it is assumed $w(i) = 1$ for all attributes i. Without loss of generality it may furthermore be assumed that by the MAU-rule

$$x \succsim y \Leftrightarrow \sum_{i=1}^{n} v(x_i) \geq \sum_{i=1}^{n} v(y_i).$$

For such binary choices the effort and quality of a decision can be defined in a rather simple way.

Definition. If the MAU-rule determines $x \succ y$, then the quality Q of a decision procedure p with respect to the choice pair (x,y) shall be given by

$$Q(p) = \begin{cases} 0 & \text{if p determines } x \precsim y, \\ 1 & \text{if p determines } x \succ y. \end{cases} \tag{1}$$

If the MAU-rule determines $x \precsim y$ and $x \succsim y$, then $Q(p) = 1$ with respect to the choice pair (x,y) for all decision procedures

p. A choice which coincides with the choice of the MAU-rule will be termed an optimal choice. It is postulated that the processing of every feature requires a constant processing effort e. Since it is assumed that every feature is processed at most once, the decision effort for the application of some procedure p is:

$$E = 2 * \ell * e \tag{2}$$

where ℓ is the number of decision criteria considered. Thus for the MAU-rule $E = 2 * n * e$.

Decision procedures with reduced processing effort. We will consider two rules for reducing decision effort. For both rules it is assumed that the decision criteria are ordered with respect to the given choice situation, and the features of the choice alternatives are processed in the order of importance of the respective dimensions.

An effort reduction may simply be achieved by processing fewer dimensions, i. e., applying the MAU-rule only for $\ell < n$ criteria. In other words, a decision maker would process only the ℓ most important dimensions for deriving a decision. Since a decision would thus depend upon the constant number of dimensions, which a decision maker has specified for making a decision, this procedure will be termed dimension-dependent processing or DD-processing. While DD-processing may substantially reduce the decision effort, it cannot guarantee that the choice of the MAU-rule will be obtained.

Instead of processing some predetermined number of dimensions, decision effort could also be reduced by allowing the number of processed dimensions to depend upon the particular choice pair. For example, only as many decision criteria may be processed as are necessary for yielding some predetermined overall attractiveness difference k between every two alternatives. A choice would thus depend upon some criterion k. Therefore, this decision procedure will be termed criterion-dependent processing, or CD-processing. For a given k and some choice pair (x, y), j_k dimensions will be processed, where

$$j_k := \begin{cases} \min \{ j : | \sum_{i=1}^{j} v(x_i) - v(y_i) | \geq k; \; j<n \} \\ n \qquad\qquad\qquad\qquad\qquad\qquad \text{else.} \end{cases} \tag{3}$$

It is clear that small k values reduce decision effort while large k values ensure decision quality. However, it remains to be examined whether some k reduces decision effort, while guaranteeing the quality of a decision as well. In order to investigate this issue, we will first examine the conditions for which a certain k may yield a choice, which differs from the choice of the MAU-rule. Assume that alternatives x and y can be evaluated by n dimensions and that the attractiveness evaluation of a feature yields one of r + 1 different attractiveness values. For example, $v \in [1,7]$. Non-optimal choices with j processing steps and a criterion value k, must satisfy the following conditions: In order to produce a choice at the barrier k

$$j * r \geq k, \tag{4}$$

and for yielding the optimal choice with the MAU-rule if processing were to be continued up to the n-th dimension:

$$(n-j) * r \geq k+1. \tag{5}$$

Therefore, if

$$(n-j) * r < k+1 \tag{6}$$

a binary choice must be identical to the choice of the MAU rule, even when less than n dimensions have been processed. In other words, if the accumulated attractiveness difference on r dimensions between x and y is very large, the direction of the difference cannot be changed by processing the remaining dimensions.

<u>Theorem</u>. For barriers $k \geq c = n/2 * r$, the CD-processing rule guarantees choices which coincide with the choices of the MAU-rule, while up to 50 percent of the decision effort may be saved.

<u>Proof</u>. From Eq. (4) and (6), we obtain $j * r = (n-j) * r$, and $j = n/2$. Inserting into Eq. (4) yields $c = n/2 * r$. Thus, for $k \geq n/2 * r$, the quality of a choice is guaranteed.

For example, when n = 20, for the choice pair with

$$\sum_{i=1}^{j_k} v(x_i) - v(y_i) = n/2 * r \quad \text{and} \quad j_k = n/2 \tag{7}$$

a 50 percent reduction of processing effort will be saved. For choice pairs which do not satisfy Eq(7), but rather

$$\sum_{i=1}^{j_k} v(x_i) - v(y_i) \geq n/2 * r \quad \text{and } j_k = n/2 + 1 \tag{8}$$

a ((n/2-1)*100)/n) percent reduction of processing effort will be achieved, and so on. Finally, for choice pairs with $j_k = n-1$, (100/n) percent processing effort will be saved.

For more realistic versions of the MAU-rule, where the attractiveness differences of a dimension are weighted by the importance of that dimension, processing effort may be reduced by an even larger amount. For example, consider CD-processing with the weighted MAU-rule: For a given k and a choice pair (x,y), j_k dimensions will be processed, where

$$j_k := \begin{cases} \min \{ j : \left| \sum_{i=1}^{j} w(i) * (v(x_i) - v(y_i)) \right| \geq k \; ; j<n \} \\ n, \qquad\qquad\qquad\qquad\qquad\qquad \text{else.} \end{cases} \tag{9}$$

Furthermore, assume that the importance weight of dimension i is defined by:

$$w(1) = n; \quad w(i+1) = w(i) - 1. \tag{10}$$

By this processing rule optimal choices are guaranteed by k-values which satisfy the following restrictions:

$$\sum_{i=1}^{j} w(i) * r \geq k, \tag{11}$$

$$\sum_{i=j+1}^{n} w(i) * r < k + 1. \tag{12}$$

We determine the lower boundary of the k-values, for which an optimal choice is guaranteed by:

$$\sum_{i=1}^{j} w(i) * r = \sum_{i=j+1}^{n} w(i) * r$$

By insertion of Eq. (10):

$$\frac{j * (n + n - j + 1) * r}{2} = \frac{(n - j) * (n - j + 1) * r}{2}$$

which yields:

$$j = 1/2 * (2n + 1 - \sqrt{2n^2 + 2n + 1} .$$

For $k \geq \sum_{i=1}^{[j]} w(i) * r$, the resulting choices necessarily coincide with the choices obtained by the MAU-rule. For example with $n = 20$, $k \geq 105 * r$ guarantees an optimal choice. Therefore with $n = 20$, in the best case only 6 dimensions must be processed.

Although the possible range of effort reduction was specified by Theorem 1, the expected effort-reduction for a sample of choice pairs depends upon the characteristics of the particular sample. In order to inspect how much effort reduction may be achieved on an average, under the assumption that the $r + 1$ attractiveness values are uniformly distributed between the two alternatives and among the n dimensions, we will calculate the expected effort reduction for some examples.

For instance, assume that a person distinguishes only between unattractive and attractive features. Unattractive features shall receive a value of 1 and attractive features shall receive a value of 2. Thus $v \in [1,2]$. If the (unweighted) MAU-rule is used and the alternatives are described by $n=2$ dimensions, a $k=1$ guarantees an optimal choice.

For the 2 attractiveness values and the 2 dimensions, 16 different choice pairs exist. For 11 of these pairs, the MAU-rule yields $x \succsim y$. For 4 of these pairs CD-processing according to Eq. (3) yields a choice with $j_k = 1$. On the average, a processing reduction of 18 percent is thus achieved in the given example. Similarly, for $n = 3$, $k = 2$ ensures an optimal choice and a processing reduction of 9.5 percent is obtained. For $n = 4$, $k = 2$ ensures the optimal choice, and processing effort is reduced by 29 percent on the average. In general, the number of choice pairs for which $k = n/2 * r$ is surpassed after $j_k \in [n/2, n/2 + 1, \ldots\ldots, n - 1, n]$ dimensions have been processed, may be specified by linear diophantine equations (Bose & Manvel, 1984). Although at least in some cases a substantial effort reduction may be achieved while preserving quality, a decision maker may even like to further reduce decision effort.

<u>Reducing decision effort at the cost of decision-quality</u>. Decision effort may additionally be reduced by further lowering the k-value. Thereby, the average decision quality will possibly also be decreased. Also, the DD-processing rule may be applied for reducing decision effort. The relation between k and the effort as well as the quality of a choice is specified by the following definition:

<u>Definition</u>. Assume that for a choice pair (x, y), the MAU-rule determines $x > y$. The decision effort $E(k)$ of CD-processing with parameter k is given by:

$$k \;\; \text{--->} \;\; E(k) := 2 * j_k * e$$

The quality $Q(k)$ of the respective decision is defined by:

$$k \;\; \text{--->} \;\; Q(k) : \begin{cases} 0 & \text{if } \Sigma\, v(x_i) - v(y_i) \leq -k \\ 1 & \text{if } \Sigma\, v(x_i) - v(y_i) \geq k \\ 1 & \text{if } j_K = n. \end{cases}$$

Furthermore, we define:

$$E : \quad = \{\, E(k); \;\; k = 1 \ldots n\}$$

$$E^- : \quad = \{\, E(k): \sum_{i=1}^{j_k} v(x_i) - v(y_i) \leq -k;\; k = 1,\ldots,n\}$$

$$E^+ : \quad = E \setminus E^-, \text{ and}$$

$$Q(k): \quad = \mathbb{1}_{E+} (E(k)), \text{ where } \mathbb{1}_A(a): = \begin{cases} 1 & \text{if } a \in A \\ 0 & \text{if } a \notin A \end{cases}$$

For the DD-processing rule which assumes that some fixed $j \leq n$ dimensions are processed, quality and effort depend upon j. $Q(j)$ and $E(j)$ shall be defined accordingly.

While the mapping $k \rightarrow E(k)$ is monotonic for all pairs (x, y), $k \rightarrow Q(k)$ may violate monotonicity.

<u>Proof</u>: By definition $k_1 < k_2 \rightarrow E(k_1) \le E(k_2)$.

For $v(x_1) = 2$, $v(x_2) = 1$, $v(x_3) = 6$,
$v(y_1) = 1$, $v(y_2) = 4$, $v(y_3) = 1$, and $k = 1$:

$Q(1) = 1$, $Q(2) = 0$, and $Q(3) = 1$.

<u>Definition:</u> Assume that for (x, y) the MAU-rule determines $x \succ y$. Then it is said that E^+ has a gap at position k if there exists a

$k' > 0$, $k' < k$: $E(k') \in E^+$ and $E(k) \in E^-$;
$L := \{ k \mid E(k) \in E^-$, and there exists $k' < k$ so that $E(k') \in E^+ \}$

It is assumed that a decision maker acquires information about the features of the alternatives, during the choice when he is processing these features. Since a decision maker does not have any prior information about the particular alternatives between which he is about to choose, the <u>average</u> quality and effort of a sample of choices pairs may be more important statistics than the respective values of a single choice pair. For some sample S of pairs (x, y), we define the average effort and the average quality as:

$$\bar{E}(k) := \frac{1}{|S|} \sum_S E(k),$$

$$\bar{Q}(\bar{E}(k)) := \frac{1}{|S|} \sum_S Q(k),$$

For a sample S the number ℓ of gaps for some given k is defined by:

$$\ell(k) := \sum_S \mathbb{1}_L(k)$$

<u>Lemma</u>. $\bar{Q}(\bar{E}(k))$ is monotonically increasing iff for $k < k'$: $\ell(k') \le \ell(k)$.

Conjecture. If (r+1) values are uniformly distributed between the two alternatives and among the n dimensions in some population of choice pairs, the mapping $\overline{E}(k) \dashrightarrow \overline{Q}(\overline{E}(k))$ is monotonically increasing.

Evidence. As a first step a simulation was performed. For $n = 11$, $v = [1,7]$, and CD-processing by Eq(3), the results are shown in Figure 1. For CD-processing according to Eq. (9) and (10), the respective results are shown in Figure 2.

Effort-Quality Trade-off. A decision maker may desire to reduce decision effort at the cost of decision quality up to the point where the benefits of the effort reduction are smaller than the negative consequences (costs) of the respective quality reduction. Whether an effort-reduction is desirable at all, thus depends upon the utilities which a decision maker attributes to the various effort and quality levels as well as upon the functional relation between effort and decision quality. For the CD- and DD-processing rules, the functional relation between the average effort and the average quality of a decision may be characterized according to the following definition.

Definition. The function $\overline{Q}$ is said to be negatively (positively) accelerated at the point of some barrier k, if

$$\frac{\overline{Q}(\overline{E}(k)) - \overline{Q}(\overline{M}(k))}{\overline{E}(k) - \overline{M}(k)} \underset{(<)}{>} \frac{\overline{Q}(\overline{m}(k)) - \overline{Q}(\overline{E}(k))}{\overline{m}(k) - \overline{E}(k)} \tag{13}$$

$$\text{where } M(k) = \sup_{\ell} \{ \overline{E}(\ell) \mid \overline{E}(\ell) < \overline{E}(k) \} ,$$

$$\overline{m}(k) = \inf_{\ell} \{ \overline{E}(\ell) \mid \overline{E}(k) < \overline{E}(\ell) \} ,$$

$\overline{E}(0) := 0$; $\overline{Q}(0) := .5$; and for $\overline{E}(k) = 2 * n * e$ the right side of Eq (13) is defined to be zero. If a function $\overline{Q}$ is negatively (positively) accelerated in every single point which is specified by a k-value, the function is said to be negatively (positively) accelerated. For the DD-processing rule negatively and positively accelerated is defined accordingly for all values

$j \in [1 . . ., n]$.

FIGURE 1

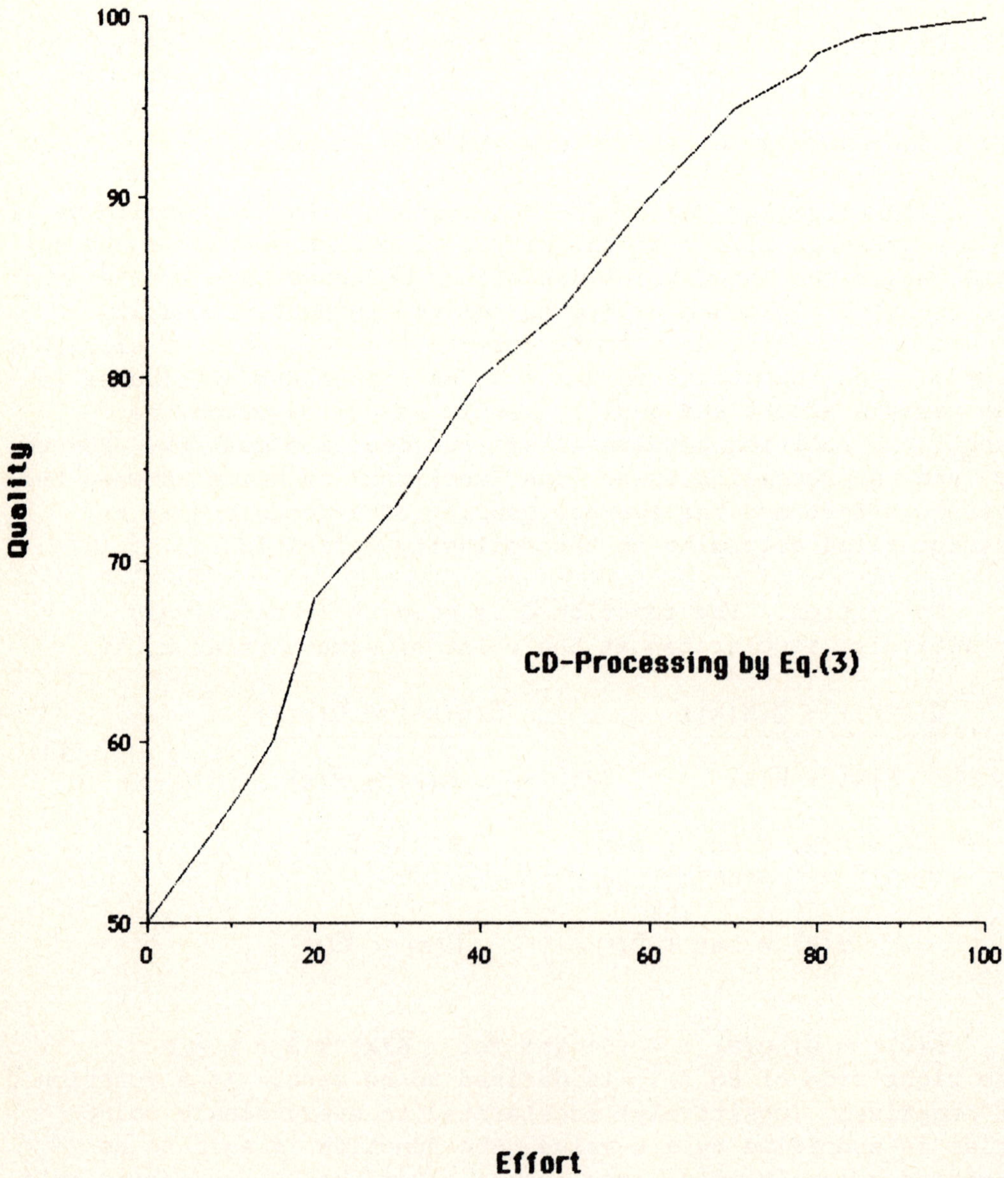
100
90
80
70
60
50
Quality
0
20
40
60
80
100
CD-Processing by Eq.(3)
Effort

FIGURE 2

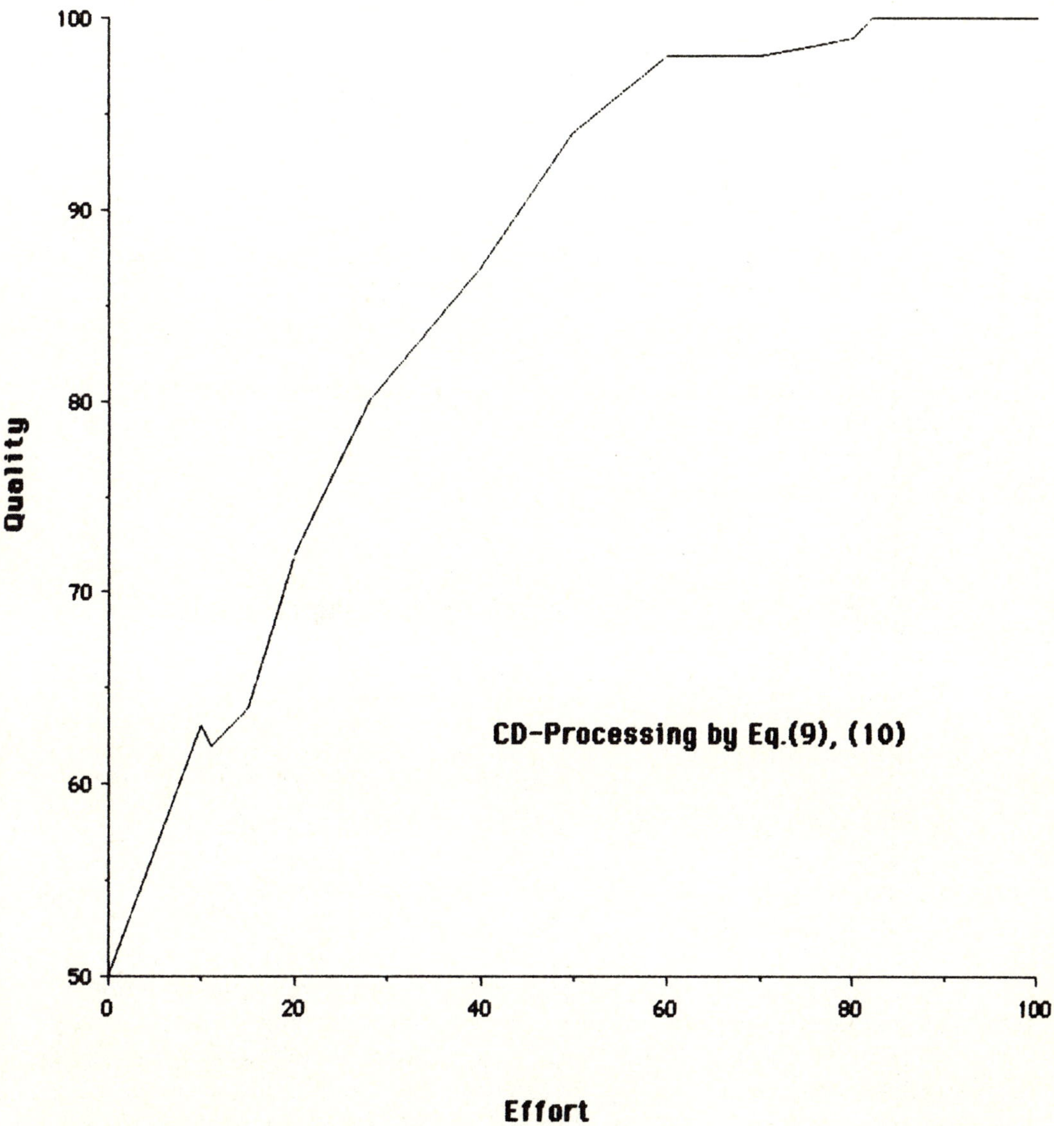
100
90
80
70
60
50
Quality
0
20
40
60
80
100
Effort
CD-Processing by Eq.(9), (10)

<u>Conjecture</u>. If (r+1) values are uniformly distributed between two alternatives and the n dimensions, the CD-processing rule (Eq. 3) will produce a negatively accelerated function $\overline{Q}_{CD}(\overline{E}_{CD}(k))$.

Furthermore, if $\overline{E}_{CD}$, $\overline{E}_{DD} > .50$, $\overline{E}_{DD}(j) \leq \overline{E}_{CD}(k)$ implies

$$\overline{Q}_{DD}(\overline{E}_{DD}(j)) < \overline{Q}_{CD}(\overline{E}_{CD}(k)),$$

for all $j \leq n$ and k, where the indices DD and CD denote the dimension-dependent and criterion-dependent processing respectively.

<u>Evidence</u>. Simulation results with the CD- (Eq. 3), as well as with the DD-processing rule are shown in Figure 3. Again, n = 11, $v \in [1,7]$. These results seem to indicate that the CD-processing rule is superior for all decision efforts exceeding some critical effort (say E = 50).

If utility is a linear function of processing effort and decision quality, for a negatively accelerated function $\overline{Q}$, an optimal effort-quality trade-off would be achieved by the parameter k, for which

$$\frac{\overline{Q}(\overline{E}(k)) - \overline{Q}(\overline{M}(k))}{\overline{E}(k) - \overline{M}(k)} \geq 1, \quad \text{and}$$

$$\frac{\overline{Q}(\overline{m}(k)) - \overline{Q}(\overline{E}(k))}{\overline{m}(k) - \overline{E}(k)} \leq 1.$$

A decision maker, who attempts to achieve an operating point, which is close to an optimal trade-off between the effort and the quality of a choice, must therefore somehow determine the respective k-parameters.

<u>The approximate determination of a close to optimal k-parameter over a number of decisions</u>. Rather than postulating that a decision maker would perform a formal decision analysis for finding the optimal k-parameters, we assume that such parameters are specified by the experience from previous decisions. We assume that during the decision process the dimension number j, at which the sum

FIGURE 3

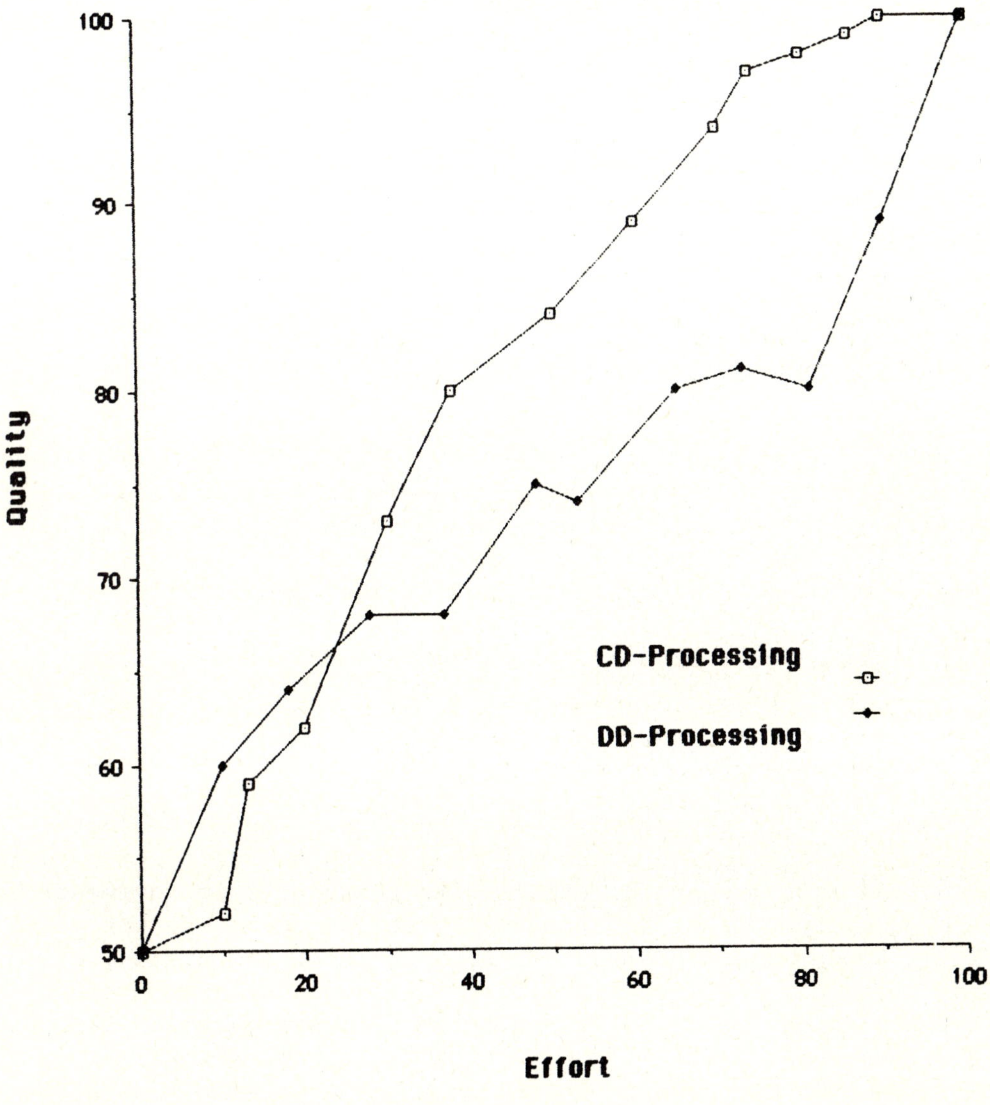
Quality
100
90
80
70
60
50
0
20
40
60
80
100
Effort
CD-Processing
DD-Processing

$$\sum_{i=1}^{j} v(x_i) - v(y_i)$$

changed from a positive to a negative value or vice versa will be remembered. We suppose that this information is used for adjusting the k parameter for the next decisions. One possible rule for adjusting the k parameter, which does not require any feedback about the quality of a choice would be: Initial value K = n * r, after every choice a new value k^* is specified.

$k^* := k + 1$ if $j_k - j \leq N_1$
$k^* := k - 1$ if $j_k - j \geq N_2$
$k^* := k$ else, where $N_1 < N_2$, and k^* denotes the new k-value. By an adaptive procedure of this kind optimal k - values could possibly be approximated (Treisman & Williams, 1984).

The conducted analysis shows that quite a substantial amount of processing effort can be saved by selective information processing without severely affecting choice quality. A number of empirical results show that human decision makers apply decision rules of the sort described by the CD-processing rule (Aschenbrenner et al. 1984; Busemeyer, 1985; Schmalhofer et al., 1986; Schmalhofer & Schäfer, 1986; Schmalhofer et al., 1987).

IMPLEMENTING PRESCRIPTIVE RULES WITH DECISION SUPPORT SYSTEMS

One possible reason why humans and human experts do not conform to prescriptive rules may thus be that prescriptive rules demand too much processing effort with respect to improvements in choice quality. Since the processing which humans are not willing to do could be performed by a computer the quality of human decisions could be improved by having a computer process all the information which is neglected by human decision makers. Decision support systems such as MAUD (Humphreys & McFadden, 1980) may enhance human decisions in this way. MAUD allows its user to enter any alternative as well as an arbitrary number of alternatives for consideration into the decision process. These alternatives may be characterized by whichever attributes a user considers to be relevant. After specifying the (utility) values of the different alternatives on the various attributes as well as importance weights for the attributes, a user is assisted by MAUD in making a decision according to the MAU principle.

Thereby, a number of rationality criteria such as consistency and transitivity of preferences will be satisfied.

Thus MAUD compensates for drawbacks which arise from selective information processing of humans, by performing a number of analyses which usually are too demanding for the human information processor. In summary it can thus be concluded, that decision support systems such as MAUD allow the human decision maker to derive a choice according to some prescriptive rule by taking the burden of the actual calculations away from the user. Decision support systems like MAUD thus derive decisions according to prescriptive rather than descriptive models. Prescriptive models rather than human information processing characteristics are thus taken as the first principle of such decision support systems.

According to this approach as well as according to the very simple expert system discussed by Mumpower (1987), humans are provided with assistance, so that they would adhere to certain -- sometimes quite general -- rationality principles.

ANALYZING EXPERTS FOR DEVELOPING BETTER DECISION PROCEDURES

As Hammond (1987) has pointed out, the field of artificial intelligence (AI) takes quite a different approach. Despite the real or seeming inadequacies of human expert decisions AI researchers assume that expert systems are best designed by studying how human experts function. Rather than reducing a decision problem to some specification with a small number of variables, which can consequently be handled by some prescriptive rule, AI researchers assume decisions to be made on the ground of a large knowledge base.

Therefore, the question is whether the normative rules which have been studied in the judgment and decision literature should be used as "best procedure" or whether the information processing of human experts should be taken as guideline for developing expert decision systems. The relation between the JDM-approach and the AI-approach is shown in Figure 4.

JDM-research considers prescriptive rules from which they have found human behavior to deviate to be the best decision procedure. AI-researchers, on the other hand, analyze the behavior of human experts to develop expert systems, which they may then consider to be the best procedure. As Hammond has pointed out and as Figure 4 shows, the views of AI and JDM researchers disagree with one another.

FIGURE 4

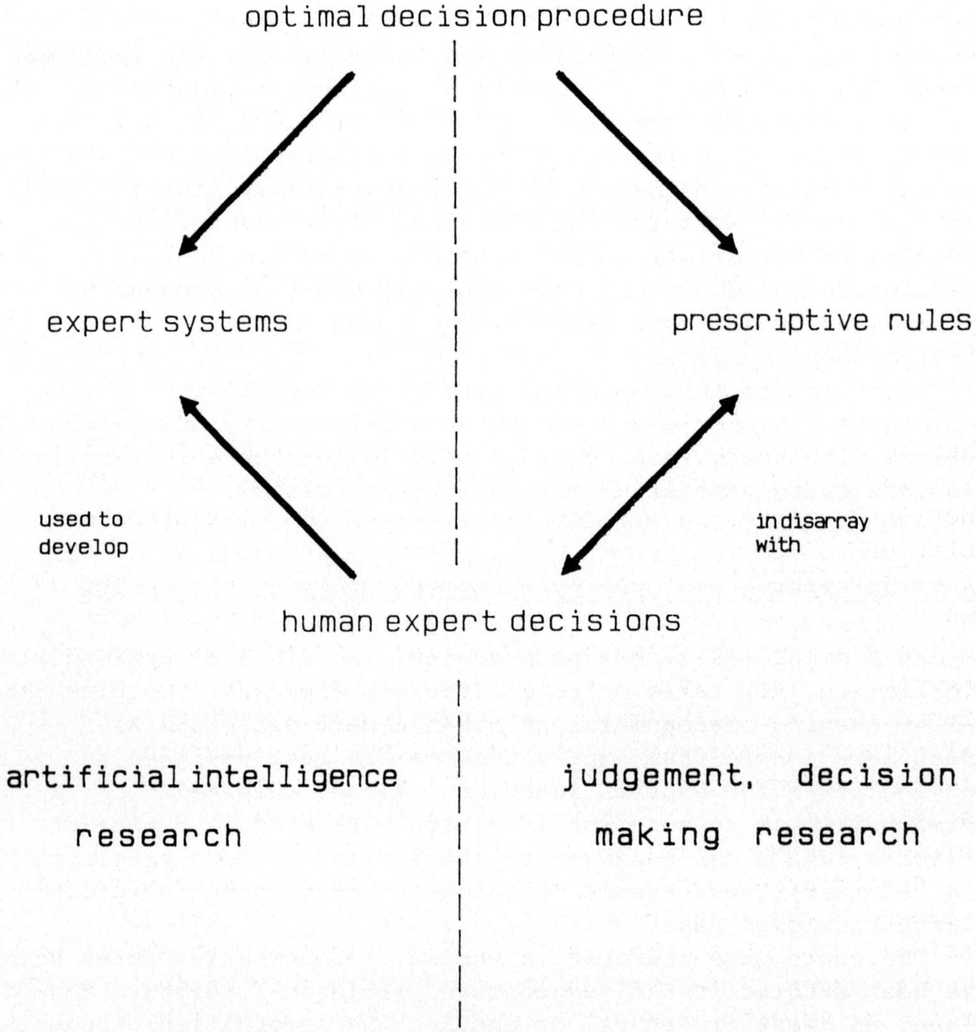
optimal decision procedure
expert systems
prescriptive rules
used to develop
indisarray with
human expert decisions
artificial intelligence research
judgement, decision making research

Some doubts may be raised whether prescriptive rules really are the best decision procedure:

1. As the paper of Milton (1987) has again demonstrated, decision analyses which are based on prescriptive rules are only marginally successful or not successful at all in real decision domains.

2. Prescriptive rules do not agree with the decision rules of experts.

3. But, experts are rather successful in that they are respected as such and are paid accordingly for their job (Shanteau, 1987)

Contrary to the conclusions of Hammond, it may thus appear that the prescriptive rules analyzed by JDM-researchers are only optimal with respect to the artificial circumstances, which, however, do not exist in real life decision problems.

It may be suspected that some decision biases as well as other non-optimal behaviors of experts may have a functional value in natural environments. In order to reveal such functional values, we will consider two of the most prominent violations of prescriptive rules. On the one hand, decision makers are known to ignore relevant information, and on the other hand, it is also known that irrelevant information affects decisions. What are possible functions of this seemingly non-optimal behavior. It has already been pointed out that selective information processing may reduce processing effort by a great deal without deteriorating choice quality. In addition, selective information processing will yield a simpler justification for a choice than an all encompassing decision. A decision is thus easier to communicate.

On the other hand, irrelevant information may be processed in order to adjust to changes in the future. For example, consider a physician who has to decide which patient should be given an organ for transplantation. Furthermore assume that the particular type of organ transplantation would still be in an experimental phase. Under these conditions, transplantation of an organ may only be considered as an ultima ratio. Criteria such as age and projected life expectancy would thus be considered irrelevant because an organ transplantation should only be performed if the patient would die otherwise.

As the medical skills are further developed, however, organ transplantations should be performed earlier when the respective patient is still healthy, thereby improving the success rate. Criteria which have been considered irrelevant may now become relevant. An expert who processes irrelevant information may thus just be processing information which will be considered relevant in the future. Again such a choice can be justified more easily in the future, when everybody uses the new criteria.

The example may demonstrate that the prescriptive rules are much too simple and too static to capture all the complexities of expert decisions:

Rather than selecting the alternative, which maximizes the (subjective) utility, expert decisions should agree with the large body of expert opinions. In addition it must be possible to explain a decision in terms of the expert knowledge rather than quoting some prescriptive rule. An expert must also be capable of justifying a decision for the many different viewpoints which people may use for interrogating his decision. Consequently, expert decisions must be knowledge-based and cannot be reduced to the consideration of values.

Unlike human decision makers, prescriptive rules do not provide such adaptiveness and flexibility. Therefore, human decisions cannot be replaced by some prescriptive rule. Quite to the contrary, in order to assist human decision making, it seems advisable to emulate the dynamic decision processes of experts in computer systems. The best decision procedure should thus not only produce the same decisions as the human expert, but should derive the decision in the same way. In other words, an expert system should be a cognitive model (Schmalhofer & Wetter, 1987) of the human expert, so that the system is adjusted to the human user rather than the human user being required to adapt to an arbitrary artificial system. By adjusting the information processing of expert systems to the actual cognitive processes of humans, expert systems can be employed as a cognitive tool, which assists the human rather than replacing his competence by some "prescriptive model."

Expert systems which are designed as cognitive tools for a human user should receive a much higher acceptability than the so called prescriptive systems. If an expert system processes information similar to a human, a human user will be better able to understand, accept, and also justify the decisions which are derived with the assistance of the system.

REFERENCES

Aschenbrenner, K. M., Albert, D. and Schmalhofer, F. (1984). Stochastic choice heuristics. Acta Psychologica, 56, 153-166.

Bose and Manvel (1984). Introduction to combinatorial theory. Wiley and Sons, New York.

Busemeyer, J. R. (1985). Decision making under uncertainty: A comparison of simple scalability, fixed-sample, and sequential-sampling models. Journal of Experimental Psychology: Learning, Memory, and Cognition, 11, 538-564.

Edwards, (1984). How to make good decisions. Acta Psychologica, 6, 7-10.

Hammond, K. R. (1987) Toward a unified approach to the study of expert judgment. In J.L. Mumpower, L.E. Phillips, O. Renn, and V.R.R. Uppuluri (Eds): Expert judgment and expert systems. Springer-Verlag.

Kahnemann, D. and Tversky, A. (1972). Subjective probability: A judgment of representativeness. Cognitive Psychology, 3, 430-454.

Keeney, R. L. (1982). Decision analysis: State of the field. Operations Research, 30, 803-38.

Milton, L. E. (1987). Expert judgment and expert systems: A User's Perspective. In J.L. Mumpower, L.E. Phillips, O. Renn, and V.R.R. Uppuluri (Eds): Expert judgment and expert systems. Springer-Verlag.

Mumpower, J. L. (1987). Very simple expert systems: An application of judgment analysis to political risk analysis. In J.L. Mumpower, L.E. Phillips, O. Renn, and V.R.R. Uppuluri (Eds): Expert judgment and expert systems. Springer-Verlag.

Schmalhofer, F., Albert, D., Aschenbrenner, K. M. and Gertzen, H. (1986). Process traces of binary choices: Evidence for selective and adaptive decision heuristics. The Quarterly Journal of Experimental Psychology, 38, 59-76.

Schmalhofer, F. and Schaefer, I. (1986). Lautes Denken bei der Wahl zwischen benannt und beschrieben dargebotenen Alternativen. Sprache & Kognition, 2, 73-81.

Schmalhofer, F. and Wetter, T. (1987). Kognitive Modellierung: Menschliche Wissensrepräsentationen und Verarbeitungsstrategien. In Richter & Christaller (Eds): Frühjahrsschule künstliche Intelligenz. Heidelberg: Springer.

Schmalhofer, F. and Gertzen, H. (1986). Judgment as a component decision process for choosing between sequentially available alternatives. In B. Brehmer, H. Jungermann, P. Loureus and G. Sevon (Eds): New directions in research on decision making. Elsevier, 139-150, Amsterdam.

Shanteau, J. (1987). Psychological characteristics of expert decision makers. In J.L. Mumpower, L.E. Phillips, O. Renn, and V.R.R. Uppuluri (Eds): Expert judgment and expert systems. Springer-Verlag.

Slovic, P. Fischhoff, B. and Lichtenstein, S. (1977). Behavioral decision theory. Annual Review of Psychology, 28, 1-39.

Treisman, M. and Williams T. C. (1984). A theory of criterion setting with an application to sequential dependencies. Psychological Review, 91, 68-111.

ACKNOWLEDGEMENT

This research was supported by grants from DFG Deutsche Forschungsgemeinschaft (Az: Al 205/1 and Schm 648/1). I would like to thank Walter Saffrich for his help in this research.

PSYCHOLOGICAL CHARACTERISTICS OF EXPERT DECISION MAKERS

James Shanteau
Department of Psychology
Kansas State University
Manhattan, Kansas USA

INTRODUCTION

"When the expert entered the room, everyone knew it. There was a kind of aura which surrounded him."

This quote from a colleague illustrates that expert decision makers are different in some potentially important ways from non-experts. The goal of this paper is to explore a few of these differences from a psychological perspective.

The paper is organized into five sections. The first section summarizes the early psychometric research on experts. The second section outlines the prevailing view of experts as cognitively limited decision makers. The third section describes the approach used in the present research program on experts. The fourth section contains some observations about 14 psychological characteristics of experts. The final section considers several implications of these observations, e.g., for expert systems.

PSYCHOMETRIC ANALYSES OF EXPERTISE

The initial concern in studies of experts was on the accuracy of their judgments. In 1923, for instance, Henry Wallace (later vice president under Roosevelt) extensively reanalyzed some data collected by Hughes (1917) on the performance of corn judges. Wallace reported fairly high statistical agreement among the corn judges. He also found, however, that the judges were inaccurate; their ratings correlated only slightly with crop yields.

Beyond validity (accuracy), there was also an initial interest in the reliability (repeatability) of expert judgment.

NATO ASI Series, Vol. F35
Expert Judgment and Expert Systems
Edited by J. Mumpower et al.

In a 1962 study, Trumbo, Adams, Milner, and Schipper investigated both the validity and reliability of grain judges. Nearly one-third of wheat samples were found to be misgraded; when judged a second time, more than one-third of the samples were given a different grade. In addition, Trumbo, et al, found that greater experience increased the confidence of judges, but was not necessarily related to the accuracy of grain inspections.

Such findings are not unique to agricultural judgments. Similar psychometric analyses of validity and reliability have been conducted for a variety of experts, such as medical diagnosticians (Einhorn, 1974), stock brokers (Slovic, 1969), and clinical psychologists (Oskamp, 1962). The results have consistently indicated that expert decision makers are inaccurate and unreliable. Moreover, experience has not been found to be related to an expert's judging ability (Meehl, 1954; Oskamp, 1962).

COGNITIVE LIMITATIONS OF EXPERTS

The conclusions from earlier research is that experts are inadequate decision makers. This has been reinforced in more recent studies (e.g., Chan, 1982) which have reported deficiencies in calibration (subjective-objective comparability) and coherence (internal consistency). Furthermore, expert decision makers are apparently unaware of these various shortcomings.

One frequent explanation for this low level of performance is that experts reportedly rely on heuristics (mental rules of thumb) in making judgments. These heuristics often lead to biases or judgmental errors. Moreover, similar biases have been observed for both novice and expert decision makers (Kahneman, Slovic, & Tversky, 1982).

An alternate approach to characterizing expert judgment has been to look at the amount of information used in making decisions. Presumably, experts should make use of any and all relevant information. Many studies, however, have reported that expert judgments are based on surprisingly little information. For instance, court judges have been found to use only one to three dimensions in sentencing defendants (Ebbesen & Konecni, 1975); medical pathologists have been reported to be equally limited (Einhorn, 1974). Since much more relevant information was available in each situation, it appears that experts are making decisions based on relatively small amounts of information.

One reason for the limited use of relevant information is that experts are often influenced by irrelevant information. For example, soil judges have been observed to unintentionally use materials in soils which are irrelevant to their judgments (Gaeth & Shanteau, 1984). Similar findings have been reported in studies of nurses (Shanteau, Grier, Johnson, & Berner, 1981) and personnel selectors (Nagy, 1981). This implies that decisions may be made without adequate differentiation between what is relevant and what is irrelevant. If so, it should not be surprising to find that expert decisions frequently are inaccurate, unreliable, and biased (Shanteau, 1978a).

In all, previous research has painted a rather bleak picture of the decision making abilities of experts. Indeed, it is difficult to find studies cited which have anything positive to say about experts (Christensen-Szalanski & Beach, 1984).

PRESENT APPROACH TO EXPERTISE

My research on expert decision makers began in the mid-1970s with analyses of livestock judges (Phelps & Shanteau, 1978; Shanteau & Phelps, 1977). Based on previous findings, the expectation was that these judges would be as limited as other experts had been reported to be. Surprisingly, livestock judges were found to be careful, skilled, and knowledgeable decision makers. Although the findings of psychometric deficiencies were replicated, these experts nonetheless seemed able to make competent judgments. Since then, my emphasis has been on investigating factors which lead to competence in experts, as opposed to the usual emphasis on incompetence.

Subsequent research has looked at decision making in auditors, personnel selectors, registered nurses, soil judges, and business managers. The primary goals of this research were to: (1) evaluate the amount and type of information used by experts in making decisions, (2) compare the judgment strategies of experienced and novice decision makers, (3) determine the impact that irrelevant information has on expert decisions, (4) develop training methods for helping decision makers reduce the impact of irrelevant information, and (5) establish techniques by which novices can learn to make decisions more like experts.

(As an aside, it is worth commenting about the distinction between "novice," "naive," and "expert." A naive decision maker presumably has little, if any, skill in making decisions in a specific area. In contrast, novices are decision makers who have considerable knowledge and experience. They have yet to reach, however, the ranks of the "experts." Novice livestock judges, for instance, have had as much as 10 to 12 years of training and experience. Experts, on the other hand, have been judging livestock for 20 to 30 or more years. In the present research, novices are frequently compared to experts, but this does not include comparisons to truly naive decision makers.)

Although the present research program has led to a number of insights about experts (e.g., Krogstad, Ettenson, & Shanteau, 1984), it is not the goal here to review specific findings from this work. Rather, the paper reflects observations which were made while conducting research on experts.

SOME CHARACTERISTICS OF EXPERTS

This section contains a brief presentation of 14 psychological characteristics of experts. (A list of the characteristics, along with summary descriptions, appears in Table 1.) This set of characteristics is not intended to be mutually exclusive or complete, but rather is offered as an initial effort intended to stimulate further discussion.

(1) Experts generally have highly developed perceptual/attentional abilities. They are able to extract information that novices either overlook or are unable to see. When novice livestock judges, for example, were given already extracted information, they were capable of making decisions that were nearly as good as the experts (Phelps, 1977). If the information was presented intact, i.e., not extracted, then the novices' decisions were inferior to the experts. The difference is that experts are able to see and evaluate what novices cannot.

(2) Experts seem to have a better sense of what is relevant and irrelevant when making decisions. The assessment of relevance

Table 1. Psychological Characteristics of Expert Decision Makers

(1) A highly developed Perceptual/Attention ability -- experts can "see" what others cannot.

(2) An awareness of the difference between Relevant and Irrelevant information -- experts know how to concentrate on what's important.

(3) An ability to Simplify complexities -- experts can "make sense out of chaos."

(4) A strong set of Communication Skills -- experts know how to convince others of their expertise.

(5) A knowledge of when to make Exceptions -- experts know when and when not to follow decision rules.

(6) A strong sense of Responsibility for their choices -- experts are not afraid to stand behind their decisions.

(7) A Selectivity about which problems to solve -- experts know which decisions to make and which not to.

(8) An outward Confidence in their decisions -- experts believe in themselves and their abilities.

(9) An ability to Adapt to changing task conditions -- experts avoid rigidity in decision strategies.

(10) A highly developed Content Knowledge about their area -- experts know a lot and stay up with the latest developments.

(11) A greater Automaticity of cognitive processes -- experts can do readily what others can only do with difficulty.

(12) An ability to Tolerate Stress -- experts can work effectively under adverse conditions.

(13) A capability to be Creative -- experts are able to find novel solutions to problems.

(14) An inability to Articulate their decision processes -- experts make decisions "on experience."

can be quite difficult and, as noted previously, experts have been observed to use irrelevant information to their detriment (e.g., Gaeth & Shanteau, 1984). Nonetheless, experts are better than novices in distinguishing relevant from irrelevant. Expert nurses, for instance, were found to make more pronounced distinctions between relevant and irrelevant information than student nurses. When student nurses were trained to focus on just the relevant information, however, their decisions improved and became closer to the experts (Shanteau, et al., 1981). This is a case where using less information actually led to better decisions. (Also see Ettenson, 1982.)

(3) Experts have an ability to simplify complex problems. As one medical specialist commented, "an expert is someone who can make sense out of chaos." In part, this appears related to the superior pattern-recognition abilities reported for game-playing experts, such as chess masters (DeGroot, 1965). That is, experts are able to see patterns that are not perceived by others. There appears to be more involved, however. Expert auditors, for instance, are capable of more insightful analyses of decision problems than novices (Ettenson, Krogstad, & Shanteau, 1985). Thus, experts have an enhanced capacity to get at the crux of a problem.

(4) Experts can effectively communicate their expertise to others. Regardless of how good decision makers actually are, their livelihood depends on the ability to convince others of that expertise. As one manager put it, "an expert is someone who can persuade someone else that he (she) is an expert." In fact, managers who are unable to communicate their expertise often are viewed as inferior decision makers (Dino & Shanteau, 1984). This can be self-fulfilling, of course, in that poor communicators are not given the opportunity to make decisions and hence are unable to show or develop their skills.

(5) Both experts and novices are capable of following established decision strategies when the decision problems are straightforward. Experts, however, are better at identifying and reacting to exceptions to strategies. Shanteau and Phelps (1977), for example, found that expert animal judges were more likely to have unique deviations in their decision strategies. When exceptions were encountered, experts were able to generate meaningful special-case strategies. In contrast, novices frequently persist in following well-learned decision rules, even

if they are inappropriate (Phelps, 1977).

(6) Experts show a strong sense of responsibility and a willingness to stand behind their decisions. When experts make decisions, they generally do so in an unambiguous, public way. Experts make it clear to others -- "this is what I have decided." Of course, experts must live at times with decisions that are shown later to be incorrect. However, their sense of responsibility helps expert nurses avoid letting bad outcomes disrupt later decision making. Novice nurses, in contrast, often have difficulty continuing after a decision that turns out poorly (Shanteau, et al., 1981). They have yet to learn the saying of professional musicians: "If you are going to make a mistake, make a good one." That is, there's no point in worrying about mistakes; you have to keep on going.

(7) Experts know that to be effective, it is important to be selective in picking decision problems to solve. As one business executive related, "A lot of my job is knowing what problems to tackle -- and what not to." In comparison, novices frequently adopt one of two extremes: They either want to be perceived as "decisive" and thus aggressively take on all decision problems. Or they are so reluctant to make a mistake that they avoid making any decisions (Dino, 1984). Experts, on the other hand, generally fall between these two extremes by selecting only those problems that they can handle effectively.

(8) A common characteristic observed in our research is that almost all experts show strong outward confidence in their decision making ability. One respected agricultural judge when confronted with his inconsistent decisions about which of two animals was best commented: "There must have been two grand champions." That is, the source of any inconsistency must reside somewhere else besides the expert (Shanteau & Phelps, 1977). Although this might well be viewed as arrogance, it generally comes across more as a highly-developed faith in one's own abilities. Experts simply believe in themselves and their capacity to make decisions and to solve problems.

(9) Experts reveal a surprising degree of adaptability and responsiveness to changing task conditions. Auditors, for instance, show considerable flexibility in adjusting their decision strategies to specific situations (Ettenson, 1984). Similarly, a well-regarded livestock judge and educator noted

that one of the biggest difficulties in teaching students "is their persistence in using inflexible and outdated standards" (Phelps, 1977). Expert decision makers, in contrast, recognize that conditions frequently change and that they need to adapt their strategies accordingly.

(10) Almost without exception, experts have an extensive and up-to-date <u>content knowledge</u>. They know a lot and pride themselves in staying up with the latest developments in their fields. One recently retired agronomy judge commented that he "felt unqualified" to make a decision because he had "not kept up with developments in the past few months" (Gaeth, 1980). This was despite the fact that he had been a leading expert in the area for nearly 40 years. Although it may seem obvious that experts possess extensive content knowledge, this is often overlooked in discussions which focus on the shortcomings and limitations of experts (Shanteau, 1978b).

(11) As reported in analyses of skilled problem solvers, experts exhibit <u>automatically</u> in their cognitive processes (Anderson, 1980, 1982). The decisions made by experts are more coordinated and made with seemingly less effort than those of novices. As one personnel manager observed: "When I was younger, I used to carefully consider all the aspects, get lots of opinions, and agonize over decisions. But now, I can generally just recognize what to do." He went on to add that he felt his present decisions were in fact better (Dino, 1984). As experts gain experience, they are able to do matter-of-factly what novices must struggle to do.

(12) Expert decision makers seem to have greater <u>stress tolerance</u>. In research on the ability of medical and emergency personnel to work in uncomfortable physical surroundings, decisions which could be routinized were little influenced by stress. In contrast, problems which required non-routine strategies were made more poorly (Dino, Shanteau, Binkley, & Spenser, 1984). This result, combined with evidence of greater automaticity in the cognitive processes of experts (see above), implies that the development of well-learned strategies can help decision makers cope with stress (Shanteau & Dino, 1984).

(13) Experts are capable of being more <u>creative</u> in finding new decision strategies. When presented with atypical stimuli or tasks, experts are better able to generate appropriate decision-

making rules. Indeed, experts are often able to suggest scenarios or frameworks for reinterpreting difficult decisions in novel ways. One long-time soil judge pointed out, when confronted with a classification error, "I helped set up the methods for classifying soils and the methods may need to be changed for soils of this type." He then went on to suggest how the judgments might be made differently (Gaeth, 1980). In comparison, novices "know what they know," but seem unable to go much beyond that.

(14) Although experts can be quite verbal in personal conversations, they are generally inarticulate about the processes used to make decisions. When asked to describe their strategies, they will often refer to vague concepts such as "its just the way it is" (Dino, 1984). For instance, Lusted (1960) reports that an acclaimed radiologist explained a difficult diagnosis by saying, "Because it looks like it." That is consistent, of course, with the greater automaticity observed in experts (see above). This may explain, in part, why it is often difficult for patients or clients to talk to experts about decision making. The experts simply may be unable to verbalize their reasons or thoughts behind a decision.

IMPLICATIONS

There are four implications suggested by these observations. These concern (1) definitions of expertise, (2) specifying different types of expertise, (3) methods for training experts, and (4) approaches to designing expert systems.

Definitions of Expertise

Although there are many studies which have looked at experts, most of the research is based on formal analyses of objective decision properties. There has been little corresponding effort to analyze more subjective characteristics of experts. If the goal is to understand the psychology of experts, then greater emphasis must be given to looking at all the processes involved in determining expertise.

The present observations suggest that both cognitive and non-cognitive characteristics play an essential role in expertise. On the cognitive side, processes such as problem recognition, perception, and attention appear important. On the non-cognitive side, characteristics such as self-confidence and a sense of responsibility seem central.

In addition, there may be other overlooked but potentially important personal characteristics of experts. Many researchers have commented informally that experts, e.g., in medicine, are egotistical and self-important. Despite the negative tone of this behavior description, such traits may serve two important purposes. On the one hand, these traits can contribute to helping experts handle the responsibility of making major decisions; without strong self-belief, it may be difficult for an expert to continue making decisions after a bad outcome, e.g., the death of a patient. On the other hand, it may be that without outward signs of extreme self-confidence, clients would be less willing to listen to the decision maker, i.e., the expert would soon be out of work.

This suggests that it might be necessary for experts in our society to convey a certain image in order to be accepted. The nature of this "expert image" and the expectations that arise from it deserve further analysis. It might also be of interest to know more about how people expect experts to behave and how they go about selecting experts.

Types of Expertise

Although this paper describes a set of characteristics shared by many experts, it should be obvious that not all kinds of experts possess the same characteristics. Just as being a plumber and a lawyer requires different abilities, so do experts in these areas demonstrate their abilities in different ways. This is reflected in the images associated with various types of experts. In fact, Anderson and Lopes (1974) observed systematic differences in the way people form impressions of lawyers and plumbers.

The question then arises as to how to define the differences that exist between various types of experts. Based on the characteristics described here, there are at least three distinctions that may be worth exploring. One is a distinction between perceptual experts and cognitive experts. Perceptual experts, such as livestock judges, rely on highly developed sensory skills; they are experts because they can perceive differences that are not apparent to others. On the other hand cognitive experts, such as auditors, rely on their superior ability to think through problems; they are experts because they can discover relations not found by others. In short, some experts are valued because of their sensory ability, whereas other experts possess unique problem solving abilities.

A second distinction is between substantive experts and assessment experts. Substantive experts, such as soil judges, must be able to draw on a considerable body of knowledge; they must learn a tremendous amount about soils and soil classification and be able to use that information to make their judgments. In contrast, assessment experts, such as personnel selectors, must be able to draw inferences and make predictions based on limited information; they are experts because they can make reasonable assessments in the face of considerable uncertainty. Thus, some experts are valued because of their ability to make decisions based on large amounts of information, while others are experts because they can make good decisions with incomplete information.

The third distinction is between passive and active experts. Passive experts, such as accountants, are asked to make skilled judgments, but not necessarily to act on those judgments; it is up to others to use the judgments of these experts as a basis for action. Active experts, such as business managers, are skilled in acting on their decisions; indeed, it may not be the quality of their decision that counts as much as their ability to act on those decisions. In general, passive experts are relied on to provide information to others, whereas active experts are skilled in carrying out decisions.

Training of Experts

In a recent review of the judgment and decision making literature, Pitz and Sachs (1984) state, "The final test of an understanding of judgment and decision making processes is to develop procedures for helping people make better decisions." In that light, it is discouraging to discover that most efforts at training decision making skills have been unsuccessful (Gaeth, 1984). The picture may be even worse than seen from the published literature (e.g., Lichtenstein & Fischhoff, 1980); there apparently are numerous unpublished studies where efforts to train decision makers have failed (personal communications from various researchers).

Typically, training has been intended to improve decisions relative to some objective standard, e.g., Bayes theorem. From the present perspective, however, it should not be surprising that such training efforts almost always fail. If the goal is to make novices more like experts, then Bayes theorem (or any other objective criterion) is irrelevant. What seems preferable is to recognize the special characteristics of experts and to devise training programs which reflect those characteristics. Initial training efforts in this direction, in fact, have proved quite successful (Gaeth & Shanteau, 1984; Shanteau & Gaeth, 1983).

On the other hand, it is conceivable that at least some of the characteristics associated with experts may be untrainable. For example, self-confidence and adaptability may be more like personality traits. Such traits are generally considered to be more-or-less unmalleable; as such, there may be little that training can do to prepare a novice to act like an expert. For such characteristics, the emphasis might best be place on selecting novices whose behavior most closely fits the pattern associated with experts. These novices could then receive training on other more teachable skills. Such an approach might be both more effective and more efficient in producing expert decision makers (Shanteau, 1984).

Expert Systems

Getting experts to interact with expert systems has often proved to be quite difficult (Michie, 1982). There are a number of potentially useful systems, such as MYCIN, which are largely unused by those experts the systems were designed to help (Ham, 1984). In part, this difficulty arises because experts frequently are asked to act as "input devices" or "parameter estimators;" the system then proceeds to act on these inputs in ways which improve upon the expert decision maker.

Yet as suggested here, responsibility and confidence are essential parts of the expert decision making process. Unfortunately, most current expert systems take much of the responsibility and confidence away from decision makers. Such systems in effect alienate the expert from his/her normal psychological environment.

This problem is reflected by the often-stated desire to design systems to "replace the expert." Even when given a careful interpretation, such statements pose a clear threat to the self-image of experts. It should not be surprising, therefore, to find that decision makers are unwilling to work with systems which are fundamentally incompatible with their views as experts.

If this analysis is correct, then more attention should be directed at preserving the role of the decision maker in expert systems. Before that can be done, however, research is needed to define that role more clearly. Only then will it be possible to design systems with which experts can feel more comfortable.

Another implication is that systems should be designed around the needs of the experts, rather than expecting experts to adapt to the needs of the system. In short, more emphasis should be placed on the psychology of the expert when constructing expert systems.

ACKNOWLEDGMENT

Preparation of this paper was supported in part by Army Research Institute contract MDA 903-80-C-0029 and in part by Federal Emergency Management Agency contract EMW 81-C-0589. The author owes a special gratitude to Geri Dino, Richard Ettenson, and Gary Gaeth for their insightful contributions to the set of characterizations described here. The author also wishes to acknowledge the efforts of Geraldine Nagy, Ruth Phelps, and Mike Troutman for their help in the earlier phases of the present research program. Finally, this research program would not have been possible without the patient cooperation of a variety of expert decision makers in auditing, soil and livestock judging, personnel selection, nursing, and management; the contribution of their time to this project was far more valuable than anything that can ever be done to repay them.

REFERENCES

Anderson, J.R., 1980. Cognitive psychology and its implications. San Francisco: W.H. Freeman.

Anderson, J.R., 1982. Acquisition of cognitive skill. Psychological Review, 89, 369-406.

Anderson, N.H., & Lopes, L.L., 1974. Some psycholinguistic aspects of person perception. Memory & Cognition, 2, 67-74.

Beach. L.R., & Christensen-Szalanski, J.J.J., 1984. The citation bias: Fad and fashion in the judgment and decision literature. American Psychologist, 39, 75-78.

Chan, S., 1982. Expert judgments made under uncertainty: Some evidence and suggestions. Social Science Quarterly, 63, 428-444.

DeGroot, A.D., 1965. Thought and choice in chess. The Hague: Mouton.

Dino, G.A., 1984. Decision makers appraising decision making: Defining the dimensions of importance. Unpublished doctoral dissertation, Kansas State University.

Dino, G.A., & Shanteau, J., 1984. What skills do managers consider important for effective decision making? Paper presented at the Psychonomic Society meeting, San Antonio.

Dino, G.A., Shanteau, J., Binkley, M., & Spenser, A., 1984. The detrimental effects of environmental stress on creativity. (Tech. Report No. 84-2). Kansas State University, Department of Psychology.

Ebbesen, E., & Knoecni, V., 1975. Decision making and information integration in the courts: The setting of bail. Journal of Personality and Social Psychology, 32, 805-821.

Einhorn, H., 1974. Expert judgment: Some necessary conditions and an example. Journal of Applied Psychology, 59, 562-571.

Ettenson, R.T., 1982. The acquisition of expertise in auditing: A judgmental analysis. Unpublished master's thesis, Kansas State University.

Ettenson, R.T., 1984. A schematic approach to the examination of, the search for and use of information in expert decision making. Unpublished doctoral dissertation, Kansas State University.

Ettenson, R.T., Krogstad, J.L., & Shanteau, J., 1985. Schema and strategy shifting in auditors' evidence gathering: A multi-task analysis. In Symposium on audit judgment and evidence evaluation. USC School of Auditing.

Gaeth, G.J., 1980. A comparison of lecture and interactive training designed to reduce the influence of interfering materials: An application to soil science. Unpublished masters' thesis, Kansas State University.

Gaeth, G.J., 1984. The influence of irrelevant information in judgment processes: Assessment, reduction, and a model. Unpublished doctoral dissertation, Kansas State University.

Gaeth. G.J., & Shanteau, J., 1984. Reducing the influence of irrelevant information on experienced decision makers. Organizational Behavior and Human Performance, 33, 263-282.

Ham, M., 1984, January. Playing by the rules. PC World, 34-41.

Hughes, H.D., 1917. An interesting corn seed experiment. The Iowa Agriculturalist, 17, 424-425.

Kahneman, D., Slovic, P., & Tversky, A., 1982. Judgments under uncertainty: Heuristics and biases. Cambridge: Cambridge University Press.

Krogstad, J.L., Ettenson, R.T., & Shanteau, J., 1984. Context and experience in auditor's materiality judgments. Auditing: A Journal of Practice and Theory, 4, 54-73.

Lichtenstein, S., & Fischhoff, B., 1980. Training for calibration. Organizational Behavior and Human Performance, 26, 149-171.

Lusted, L.B., 1960. Logical analysis and roentgen diagnosis. Radiology, 74, 178-193.

Meehl, P., 1954. Clinical versus statistical prediction: A theoretical analysis and a review of the evidence. Minneapolis: University of Minnesota Press.

Michie, D., 1982. Introductory readings in expert systems. New York: Gordon and Breach.

Nagy, G.F., 1981. How are personnel selection decisions made? An analysis of decision strategies in a simulated personnel selection task. Unpublished doctoral dissertation, Kansas State University.

Oskamp, S., 1962. The relationship of clinical experience and training methods to several criteria of clinical prediction. Psychological Monographs, 76.

Phelps, R.H., 1977. Expert livestock judgment: A descriptive analysis of the development of expertise. Unpublished doctoral dissertation. Kansas State University.

Phelps, R.H. & Shanteau, J., 1978. Livestock judges: How much information can an expert use? Organizational Behavior and Human Performance, 21, 209-219.

Pitz, G.E., & Sachs, N.J., 1984. Judgment and decision making: Theory and applications. Annual Review of Psychology, 35.

Shanteau, J., 1978a. Psychological abilities of livestock judges. Manhattan, KS: Agricultural Experiment Station Bulletin 620.

Shanteau, J., 1978b. When does a response error become a judgmental bias? Journal of Experimental Psychology: Human Learning and Memory, 4, 579-581.

Shanteau, J., 1984. Some unasked questions about the psychology of expert decision makers, in M.E. El-Hawary (Ed.), Proceedings of the IEEE conference on systems, man, and cybernetics. New York: IEEE.

Shanteau, J. & Dino, G.A., 1983. Stress effects on problem-solving and decision-making behavior. Paper presented at the Psychonomic Society meeting, San Diego.

Shanteau, J., Grier, M., Johnson, J., & Berner, E., 1981. Improving decision making skills of nurses, in ORSA-TIMS Proceedings. Houston.

Shanteau, J., and Gaeth, G.J., 1983. Training expert decision makers to ignore irrelevant information. Alexandria: Army Research Institute.

Shanteau, J., and Phelps, R.H., 1977. Judgment and swine: Approaches and issues in applied judgment analysis, in M.F. Kaplan and S. Schwartz (Eds.), Human judgment and decision processes in applied settings. New York: Academic Press.

Slovic, P., 1969. Analyzing the expert judge: A descriptive study of a stockbroker's decision processes. Journal of Applied Psychology, 53, 255-263.

Trumbo, D., Adams, C., Milner, M., and Schipper, L., 1962. Reliability and accuracy in the inspection of hard red winter wheat. Cereal Science Today, 7.

Wallace, H.A., 1923. What is in the corn judge's mind? Journal of the American Society of Agronomy, 15, 300-304.

DESCRIPTIVE AND PRESCRIPTIVE MODELS FOR JUDGMENT AND DECISION MAKING: IMPLICATIONS FOR KNOWLEDGE ENGINEERING

Thomas R. Stewart
National Center for Atmospheric Research
(Sponsored by the National Science Foundation)
Boulder, Colorado USA

Claude McMillan, Jr.
Center for Applied Artificial Intelligence
College of Business and Administration
University of Colorado at Boulder
Boulder, Colorado USA

INTRODUCTION

Development of a knowledge base for an expert system often requires an analysis of the inference processes and decision making strategies of one or more experts. Knowledge engineers therefore share the psychologist's and operations researcher's interest in inference and decision making. Psychologists have been interested in understanding and describing how people make inferences under complexity and uncertainty. Operations researchers have developed methods that extend human ability to make decisions about complex problems.

Both operations researchers and psychologists have developed methods for modeling inference and decision making. The psychologists' methods produce *descriptive models*: they describe how people actually behave. Operations researchers produce *prescriptive models*: they prescribe optimal strategies or efficient heuristics for coping with complex problems [1]. Researchers in both areas have produced models which have not only equaled expert performance, but have outperformed experts. Examples of research in these areas will be briefly described and implications for knowledge engineering discussed.

NATO ASI Series, Vol. F35
Expert Judgment and Expert Systems
Edited by J. Mumpower et al.

DESCRIPTIVE MODELS OF INFERENCE

Knowledge engineers generally rely on experts' verbal descriptions of their reasoning. This approach (process tracing or protocol analysis) has been used in psychology as well (Kleinmuntz, 1968; Ericsson and Simon, 1984). Traditionally, however, psychologists have been suspicious of verbal reports, and they have developed methods for analyzing judgment that do not depend on a person's ability to provide accurate verbal descriptions of thinking processes.

One such method, called judgment analysis, derives the parameters of judgment from a statistical analysis of a sample of actual judgments (Hammond et al., 1975). The expert is required to do only what he or she does best, that is, to make judgments in a natural setting using familiar materials. The analyst then uses standard statistical methods to develop a model that describes the inference process that produced the sample of judgments. In other words, the analyst produces a statistical model of the expert's inference process.

The data required for the development of such a model are a number of cases of a particular type of judgment. Each case includes the information used to make the judgment and the resulting judgment. Cases may be obtained in a natural setting (e.g., loan application decisions obtained from bank files) or in controlled settings. In a controlled setting, an expert is asked to make judgments based on a sample of real or hypothetical scenarios. The size of the sample required is dictated by the standard statistical requirements for reliability of parameter estimates. Table 1 illustrates two scenarios that might be used in a study of judgments of bank loan officers. Wilsted et al. (1975) asked 165 bankers to evaluate 50 different loan applications, similar to those illustrated in Table 1.

The items of information that are available to the judge, called cues, are considered independent variables in a statistical analysis with the judgment as the dependent variable. Multiple regression analysis is typically used to analyze the data, but other methods may be more appropriate in particular applications. The analysis yields a model of the judge, which expresses the judgment as a mathematical function (generally a polynomial) of the cues, and an index of how well the model fits the judgments (e.g., the squared multiple correlation

Table 1. Hypothetical loan applications.

LOAN APPLICATION A

Amount requested: $15,000

Age: 36 No. of Dependents: 3

Years with present employer: 4

Monthly Income: 1950 Total loan payments: 758

Average Checking Account Balance: 500

Average Savings Account Balance: 3500

Occupation: White collar Own or rent home: Own

Credit rating (1-4): 4

Marketability of Collateral (1-4): 3

LOAN APPLICATION B

Amount requested: $12,500

Age: 31 No. of Dependents: 3

Years with present employer: 1

Monthly Income: 1100 Total loan payments: 340

Average Checking Account Balance: 300

Average Savings Account Balance: 6000

Occupation: Skilled Own or rent home: Rent

Credit rating (1-4): 3

Marketability of Collateral (1-4): 2

coefficient, or coefficient of determination). For example, in the Wilsted et al. study the mean of the squared multiple correlations for the 165 bankers was .709. Since we do not expect judges to be perfectly reliable, squared multiple correlations ranging from .7 to .9 are typical in judgment studies and indicate a reasonably good fit of the model to the judgments.

Figure 1 illustrates how a model based on a statistical analysis of judgments of one judge can be interpreted graphically for a simplified problem involving only three cues. The graphic interpretation of the regression model is based on transformations described by Hammond et al. (1975). The figure illustrates the decomposition of judgment into relative weights for each of the cues and the form of the functional relationship between each cue and the overall judgment. Such decomposition and graphic displays have produced useful insights into the judgment process.

Although the use of statistical models of inference can be found as early as 1923 (Wallace, 1923), extensive use of the method began in the mid-1950s (Hammond, 1955; Hoffman, 1960). Several computer programs for judgment analysis, including versions for personal computers, are available [2]. A description of _Social Judgment Theory_, which is the theoretical foundation for judgment analysis, and a description of the method itself can be found in Hammond et al. (1975). A variety of experts have been modeled including physicians (e.g., Fisch et al. 1981; Kirwan et al., 1983), stock brokers, clinical psychologists, and polygraph interpreters. Although the models were capable of approximating intelligent behavior in restricted domains, they were used only as research tools. No one thought of marketing them as _expert systems_.

Statistical Models vs. Human Judgment

One of the striking findings of the early research on statistical models of judgment was that, for both novice and expert judges, across a variety of problem domains, simple linear additive models provided a description of the judgment process that accurately reproduced the original judgments (Slovic and Lichtenstein, 1971). Even more striking was that the models consistently outperformed expert judges themselves in tasks where a correct answer was available (Goldberg, 1970). This occurred because the models excluded the residual component

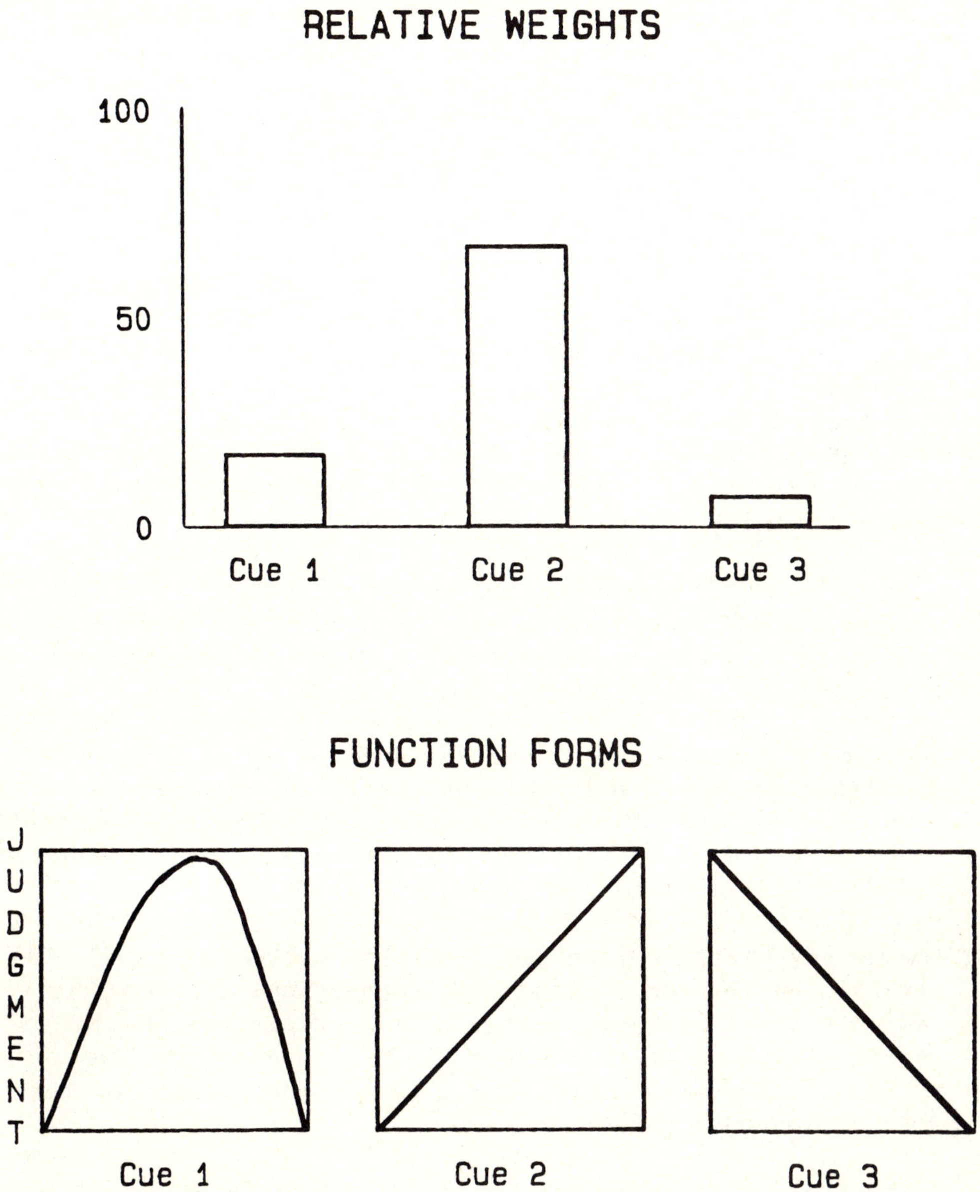

Figure 1. Graphic interpretation of a statistical model of judgment.

of judgment, which was unrelated to the criterion.

An important line of research comparing human judgment and statistical models involved diagnosis of mental illness based on the results of a psychological test called the Minnesota Multiphasic Personality Inventory (MMPI). The results of this paper and pencil test for an individual consist of scores on 11 scales. In the 1950s, use of the MMPI for diagnosis (e.g, of psychosis vs. neurosis) was thought to require an understanding of complex patterns of interactions among the 11 scales. Developers of the MMPI argued that without extensive training and experience clinicians could not make proper use of the scores, and they discounted the possibility that any simple model, such as a sum of weighted scale scores, could capture the richness of the diagnostic process (Goldberg, 1969). They felt that human judgment was an essential element of the process.

The clinicians' arguments for the complexity of the process of interpreting MMPI results and for the essential role of human judgment disintegrated as a result of a series of studies of clinical judgment:

1. When both experienced clinicians and graduate students judged whether patients were medically or psychiatrically hospitalized, the judgments of the experienced clinicians were no better than those of the graduate students (Oskamp, 1967).

2. Using psychiatric diagnoses (based on extensive interviews) of each patient as a criterion, statistical diagnoses of psychosis vs. neurosis, based on a multiple regression model of the relation between the MMPI scales and the correct diagnosis, outperformed the diagnoses made by the clinicians (Goldberg, 1969).

3. Diagnoses based on regression models of the clinicians' own judgments outperformed the clinicians themselves (Goldberg, 1970).

4. The clinicians were beaten by a model which simply added the 11 equally weighted scores (Dawes and Corrigan, 1976).

This work suggested a method called bootstrapping for improving judgment. Under certain conditions, accuracy can be improved by replacing the expert with a statistical model of his or her own judgment process. Camerer (1981) cited 15 studies showing an improvement in accuracy due to bootstrapping. The studies included judgments of graduate school success, survival predictions based on cancer biopsies, diagnosis of mental illness, personnel interviewing, students' judgments of teacher effectiveness, and selection of life insurance salesmen. Armstrong (1985) reviews the evidence for the usefulness of bootstrapping. He cites examples of success involving judgments about electronics production and catalog sales, as well as forecasts of sales success of personnel, returns for securities, loan defaults, and bankruptcy.

Although the work on bootstrapping is intriguing and has yielded important insights into some of the limitations of expert judgment, it is not universally applicable nor does it guarantee improved accuracy. It can only be applied to problems which are amenable to statistical modeling (this point is taken up below), and the properties of task and judge that are necessary for the success of bootstrapping have been described by Camerer (1981).

Implications for Knowledge Engineering

It is interesting to speculate about what would have happened in the 1950s if an attempt had been made to use today's methods to develop an expert system for clinical diagnosis from the MMPI. Knowledge engineers would have had no reason to question the expert clinicians' views regarding the complexity and richness of the interpretation process. Extensive time and effort would have been spent trying to capture the subtleties of the diagnostic process. In fact, complicated objective rules for diagnosis from the MMPI were being developed in the 1950s (Meehl and Dahlstrom, 1960). These rules performed no better than simple linear models (Goldberg, 1969). Consequently, an expert system based on such rules would not have outperformed one developed in much less time using a simple linear regression analysis. The MMPI experience suggests that knowledge engineers should regard experts' descriptions of their inference processes with some skepticism and explore the utility of simple decision-making models.

Limitations of judgment analysis. We are not, of course, recommending that knowledge engineers discard verbal protocols and production functions and adopt statistical models exclusively in their work. The research to date has necessarily involved static, rather than dynamic tasks (Hogarth, 1981) involving judgments based on a few (5-20) items of information, and generally there is both high uncertainty in the task and fairly high inconsistency in the judgments of the expert. Furthermore, application of the method is not always straightforward. Research has shown a number of limitations and potential pitfalls in the use of statistical analyses to develop models of judgment. Results not only depend on the context in which the judgments are generated, they also depend on how the data are analyzed. Although there are many situations where the modeling process can be more or less automatic, there are others where the expertise of an experienced judgment analyst is required. More research is needed to determine when such models might be useful in knowledge engineering.

The use of statistical methods to develop models of judgment has been criticized on the grounds that the inference process is so complex that statistical modeling is impossible or impractical. It is argued that, since judgments about important problems generally involve multiple variables that interact in complex patterns, statistical modeling would require an unreasonable number of cases, and would likely produce misleading results. There are undoubtedly problems for which this is the case. For example, no applications of judgment analysis to weather forecasting have been reported in the literature. (However, the results of Allen et al, 1986, indicate that simple statistical methods may prove useful in this context as well.) Experience has shown, however, that for many problems, statistical modeling is practical and useful. O'Brien (1985), for example, reports a successful application of judgment analysis to strategic decision making in R & D management and argues that judgment analysis can outperform knowledge engineering in this context. Even very complex problems can often be decomposed into subproblems, one or more of which may be amenable to judgment analysis.

Judgment analysis and verbal protocols. Judgment analysis offers a major advantage as a tool for knowledge engineering: It provides a method for modeling inference that does not rely on the expert's ability to describe his or her thinking process. This is important because judgmental competence is not always accompanied by the ability to describe accurately the process that produced the judgments. Verbal descriptions of reasoning can be incomplete, inaccurate or misleading. Some important aspects of the expert's inference process may not be readily accessible and may be difficult to translate into words. The description obtained may be unduly influenced by the method used to elicit it. Questions posed by the knowledge engineer and the requirements of particular shells impose a frame on the problem. Seemingly irrelevant and inconsequential aspects of problem framing have been shown to have a powerful effect on judgment (Tversky and Kahneman, 1981). For these reasons, it is desirable to have a knowledge engineering tool that does not depend on the expert's ability to describe the inference process.

There is another reason that knowledge engineers should not rely completely on verbal descriptions. A series of descriptive studies of judgment, initiated by a classic paper by Tversky and Kahneman (1974), has identified a number of mental strategies that can lead to errors in judgments. Research results repeatedly recount systematic biases in judgment, the inconsistent and poorly controlled nature of the judgment process, the pervasiveness of cognitive limitations that can reduce the validity of judgments, and the difficulty of overcoming those limitations (Hogarth, 1980; Kahneman et al., 1982). Irrelevant features of judgment tasks can strongly influence judgment while relevant information is often ignored or used inappropriately. These biases and limitations have been found in both expert and lay judges. Although the generality of some of this research is currently being debated, and some researchers are adopting a more optimistic view of human cognitive ability (Ebbesen and Konecni, 1980; Nisbett et al., 1983; Kruglanski et al., 1984), the possibility that experts' cognitive processes are flawed cannot be discounted. For example, Stewart and Glantz (1985) described how the judgments of expert climatologists may have been biased.

Although verbal descriptions of reasoning are likely to remain a staple of knowledge engineering, they should not be the only tool. Judgment analysis can be used in combination with verbal protocols (Einhorn, et al., 1979) so that the knowledge engineer can take advantage of the insights provided by both while avoiding their pitfalls. If the knowledge engineer relies solely on the expert's verbal statements, then both the efficiency of system development and the ultimate performance of the system will be limited by the expert's ability to verbally describe his or her inference process.

PRESCRIPTIVE MODELS

Under the circumstances, one strategy for the knowledge engineer is to be aware of potential biases and limitations of expert judgment and to guard against them by using a combination of methods to elicit information about the inference process. But another strategy is to strive to improve the knowledge base through critical, in-depth thinking about the nature of the problem and by using analytic models that can, in many cases, far exceed the limited information processing capabilities of a human expert in certain problem-solving settings.

Since World War II, operations researchers have been approaching problems using such models, that is, by developing _prescriptive_ models of decision making. By and large their efforts have been directed toward decision problems in which the important variables can be expressed in quantitative terms. Especially interesting to operations researchers have been management problems in resource allocation. Examples include:

- determining how many of what products to produce in each of several alternative production facilities, and how the output should be transported to various possible distribution facilities in such a way as to minimize costs;
- identifying that mix of investments which will maximize the return, commensurate with the investor's risk propensities;
- assigning work to employees in such a way as to minimize the elapsed time required for completion of a project.

As the wording above implies, the emphasis has been not just on producing good decisions, but on producing optimal decisions, that is maximizing or minimizing with respect to some quantitatively specified criterion. Thus, operations researchers have sought to build knowledge bases that perform not only as well as, but in most cases significantly better than experts.

Managerial Decision Making

We predict that a substantial portion of the most useful work in knowledge based systems, in the years ahead, will focus on problems faced by managers in both the public and the private sectors. The opportunities are substantial. Whereas managers themselves have tended to look at blue collar operations for opportunities for increased productivity, it is generally agreed among students of administration that the administrative hierarchy itself is the place to look for improvement opportunities. Of course, it is just such managerial problems that have occupied operations researchers for 40 years.

We hasten to add that by no means do all management decision problems lend themselves to treatment in this fashion. The factors to be considered in many important management problem settings simply cannot be usefully quantified. This is especially true at higher, policy levels of management.

On the other hand, most commerce and industry managers serve at lower operational levels. And at the operations level many problem settings involve factors which readily lend themselves to quantification, such as the scheduling of work, budgeting, and price determination.

Managerial Robotics

In general, systems that support managers in dealing with judgment problems amenable to quantification are referred to as decision support systems. The knowledge bases for such systems can frequently be made substantially more useful by invoking the formal analytic methods that assure optimality. Looking further into the future, however, we forsee systems that go beyond merely supporting managers; we predict that *managerial robots* may become prevalent in the administrative hierarchy of both public and private enterprises.

A managerial robot is the managerial counterpart of an industrial robot. An industrial robot does not simply support a craft worker, but rather replaces that worker in performing that range of functions for which it was designed. In a similar way, a managerial robot does not just support a manager in the performance of some management function, but rather replaces the manager in the performance of that management function. Managerial robots will only become prevalent if they can perform in a fashion significantly superior to the managers they replace, superior both in the quality of the judgments made and the speed with which they are made.

The usefulness of managerial robots will depend on the ability of their designers to accomodate all the features in a judgment setting which real world managers face. A system that simply supports a manager in a particular judgment setting can fall far short of displaying the full range of the manager's skills in dealing with that setting. But a system that replaces the manager can tolerate no such inadequacies.

An Example: The Combinatoric Explosion

For management problems, as well as all other problems, the number of possible decisions, or problem solutions, increases geometrically as the number of variables increases. This combinatoric explosion is a problem for managers, knowledge engineers, and operations researchers. In an effort to contain the many possible combinations of variable values and produce optimal solutions, operations researchers rely on formal algorithmic methods such as the simplex procedure of linear programming and its many variants.

In some operations level management problems, however, the combinatoric explosion proves totally unmanageable when formal analytic tools are employed. Yet recent experience has shown that cleverly designed heuristics can contain the explosion--heuristics which result from in-depth analysis of a type expert managers are not likely to invoke, either because they are ill equipped to perform the required analysis, or because the gains which might be enjoyed from superior judgments are not believed to justify the time and effort which would be required.

In 1984 the coveted Lanchester Prize was awarded to a group producing optimal solutions for a series of scheduling problems. Each used a large mainframe to investigate some 3,000 variables (Crowder, et. al., 1984). In fact, however, many real world scheduling problems, when formulated in such a way that demonstrably optimal soutions can be produced, involve up to four million variables. To produce their optimal solutions the winners of the Lanchester Prize were obliged to ignore features of the problem which are important to managers.

Recently, another group of researchers has attacked large scheduling problems successfully, producing solutions which were within 98 percent of optimal in minutes on a small microcomputer (Glover, et. al., 1985). By being willing to accept solutions which only approached optimality, this group was able to satisfy all those features in the problem setting which were important to management. Their approach relied entirely on a skillfully designed hierarchy of heuristic rules and yielded a knowledge based system which produces schedules not only faster than an experienced human expert, but also produces schedules which are superior to those constructed by a human expert.

In the latter case, the researchers who addressed the scheduling problem gained insights into the nature of the problem which equipped them to construct a scheduling system which did not simply support the manager in planning the employees' work, but which rather replaced the manager altogether--a true managerial robot.

To summarize, the methods of the operations researchers directly address some of the limitations of human cognitive ability identified by psychologists. Unlike the human expert, an operations research model can sometimes cope with complexity and uncertainty in a systematic, controlled, and explicit manner. We suggest, therefore, that knowledge engineers addressing management problems will want to exploit many of the insights which researchers in this field have gained.

CONCLUSION

We have illustrated some of the approaches knowledge engineers could usefully borrow from psychology and operations research. Research suggests that, for some problems, expert systems developed using these approaches can outperform human experts.

The appropriate set of methods for any knowledge engineering application depends upon the nature of the problem and the experts involved. At present, there is no comprehensive theory to guide the selection of a set of methods for a particular problem/expert combination. Further research is needed to discover how best to integrate new methods into knowledge engineering and how to choose the appropriate set for a particular application. Such research would involve the application of multiple methods to multiple problems, and the evaluation of results in terms of system development time and system performance criteria such as data demands, speed, and accuracy. Such a research program could contribute to expert system development by allowing knowledge engineers to make more effective use of previous work on modeling judgment and decision processes.

NOTES

1. The distinction between descriptive and prescriptive models is, of course, not as clear as we have drawn it here. It can be argued that the distinction is meaningless because what is descriptive from one perspective may be prescriptive from another. For our purposes, descriptive and prescriptive models are distinguished by the criteria for their validation. Descriptive models are validated according to their ability to reproduce human behavior. Prescriptive models are validated according to the quality of their performance on a specified task.

2. One computer program for judgment analysis is being marketed as an aid to the development of expert systems. Hoffman (1986) describes some advantages of this approach.

REFERENCES

Allen, G., V. Ciesielski, and W. Bolam (1986). Evaluation of an expert system to forecast rain in Melbourne. Paper presented at the First Australian Artificial Intelligence Congress, Melbourne.

Armstrong, J. S. (1985). Long-Range Forecasting: From Crystal Ball to Computer, Second Edition. New York: Wiley.

Camerer, C.F. (1981). General conditions for the success of bootstrapping models. Organizational Behavior and Human Performance, 27, 411-422.

Crowder, H., E. Johnson, and M. Padberg (1983). Solving large scale 0-1 linear programming problems, Operations Research, 31, 803-834.

Dawes, R.M., and B. Corrigan (1974). Linear models in decision making. Psychological Bulletin, 81, 95-106.

Ebbesen, E.B., and V.J. Konecni (1980). On the external validity of decision-making research: What do we know about decisions in the real world? In S. Wallsten (Ed.), Cognitive processes in choice and decision behavior. Hillsdale, New Jersey: Erlbaum.

Einhorn, H.J., D.N. Kleinmuntz, and B. Kleinmuntz (1979). Linear regression and processing-tracing models of judgment. Psychological Review, 86, 465-485.

Ericsson, K.A., and H.A. Simon (1984). Protocol Analysis: Verbal Reports as Data. Cambridge, Massachusetts: The MIT Press.

Fisch H-U., K.R. Hammond, C.R.B. Joyce, and M. O'Reilly (1981). An experimental study of the clinical judgment of general physicians in evaluating and prescribing for depression. British Journal of Psychiatry, 138, 100-109.

Glover, F., R. Glover, C. McMillan, and S. McMillan (1985). The general employee scheduling problem: An effective large scale solution approach. Proceedings of the Annual Meeting of the Institute for Decision Sciences, 437-441.

Goldberg, L.R. (1969). The search for configural relationships in personality assessment: The diagnosis of psychosis vs. neurosis from the MMPI. Multivariate Behavioral Research, 4, 523-536.

Goldberg, L.R. (1970). Man versus model of man: A rationale, plus some evidence, for a method of improving on clinical inferences. Psychological Bulletin, 73, 422-432.

Hammond, K.R. (1955) Probabilistic functioning and the clinical method. Psychological Review, 62, 255-262.

Hammond, K.R., T.R. Stewart, B. Brehmer, and D.O. Steinman (1975). Social judgment theory. In M.F. Kaplan and S. Schwartz (Eds.), Human Judgment and Decision Processes. New York: Academic Press.

Hoffman, P.J. (1960). The paramorphic representation of clinical judgment. Psychological Bulletin, 57, 116-131.

Hoffman, P.J. (1986). Quasi-AI in the development of expert systems. Los Altos, California, Magic7 Software Co.

Hogarth, R.M. (1980). Judgment and Choice: The Psychology of Decision. Chichester, England: Wiley.

Hogarth, R.M. (1981). Beyond discrete biases: Functional and dysfunctional aspects of judgmental heuristics. Psychological Bulletin, 90, 197-217.

Kahneman, D., P. Slovic, and A. Tversky, Eds. (1982). Judgment under Uncertainty: Heuristics and Biases. Cambridge, England: Cambridge University Press.

Kirwan, J.R., D.M. Chaput De Saintonge, C.R.B. Joyce, and H.L.F. Currey. (1983) Clinical judgment in rheumatoid arthritis. I. Rheumatologists' opinions and the development of paper patients. Annals of the Rheumatic Diseases, 42, 644-647.

Kleinmuntz, B., Ed. (1968). Formal Representation of Human Judgment. New York: Wiley.

Kruglanski, A.W., N. Friedland, and E. Farkash (1984). Lay persons' sensitivity to statistical information: The case of high perceived applicability. Journal Personality and Social Psychology, 46, 503-518.

Meehl, P.E. and W.G. Dahlstrom (1960). Objective configural rules for discriminating psychotic from neurotic MMPI profiles. Journal of Consulting Psychology, 24, 375-387.

Nisbett, R.E., D.H. Krantz, C. Jepson, and Z. Kunda (1983). The use of statistical heuristics in everyday inductive reasoning. Psychological Review, 90, 339-363.

O'Brien, W.R.(1985). Developing 'Expert Systems': Contributions from decision support systems and judgment analysis techniques. R & D Management, 15, 293-303.

Oskamp, S. (1967). Clinical judgement from the MMPI: Simple or complex? Journal of Clinical Psychology, 23, 411-415.

Slovic, P. and S. Lichtenstein (1973). Comparison of Bayesian and regression approaches to the study of information processing in judgment. In L. Rappoport and D.A. Summers, Eds., Human Judgment and Socail Interaction, New York: Holt, Rinehart & Winston.

Stewart, T.R. and M. Glantz (1985). Expert judgment and climate forecasting: A methodological critique of "Climate change to the year 2000". Climatic Change, 7, 159-183.

Tversky, A., and D. Kahneman (1974). Judgment under uncertainty: Heuristics and biases. Science, 185, 1124-1131.

Tversky, A., and D. Kahneman (1981). The framing of decisions and the rationality of choice. Science, 211, 453-458.

Wallace, H.A. (1923). What is in the corn judge's mind? Journal of the American Society of Agronomy, 15, 300-304.

Wilsted, W.D., T.E. Hendrick and T.R. Stewart (1975). Judgment policy capturing for bank loan decisions: An approach to developing objective functions for goal programming models. The Journal of Management Studies, 12, 210-215.

KNOWLEDGE EXTRACTION FROM EXPERTS IN VIEW OF THE CONSTRUCTION OF EXPERT SYSTEMS

F. Vandamme
Laboratory for Applied Epistemology - BIKIT
University of Ghent
Belgium

INTRODUCTION

Expert systems attract more and more attention. Hardware and software producers are loose with the phrase itself, making use of it at every opportunity as an argument for selling their product. Expert systems have become a symbol in our modern society, yet most members of this society have little idea of the reality behind the symbol. A firm will use "Expert Systems" to indicate the outstanding character of its ability to keep pace in the modern business world.

In Advertising's glamour approach to expert systems, one forgets to highlight the time and effort given by not one man but a team, and the complexity of the processes followed in the development of a genuine expert system. An expert system is more than an intelligent toy which amuses the dinner guests by producing some very limited diagnosis.

If one wants more than a toy, then one needs carefully to prepare for the implementation of the system by paving the way to knowledge representation and manipulation within it through careful processes of knowledge elicitation from the natural experts. The abilities of the applied epistemologist, sometimes called the knowledge engineer, are crucial to the success of these knowledge elicitation processes. He has carefully to study the task, the situation, the task performance of the natural expert in order to discover and to reconstruct, or even himself construct, the relevant knowledge to be represented in the expert system one wants to build.

In what follows we intend to discuss several interesting and important issues regarding this process of knowledge elicitation

NATO ASI Series, Vol. F35
Expert Judgment and Expert Systems
Edited by J. Mumpower et al.

or knowledge extraction, this in preparation for the introduction of a knowledge extraction strategy.

The Place of Knowledge Extraction in the Process of Expert System (E.S.) Development

E.S. development can be considered as a cyclical process, the several phases of which must be gone through at least two or three times.

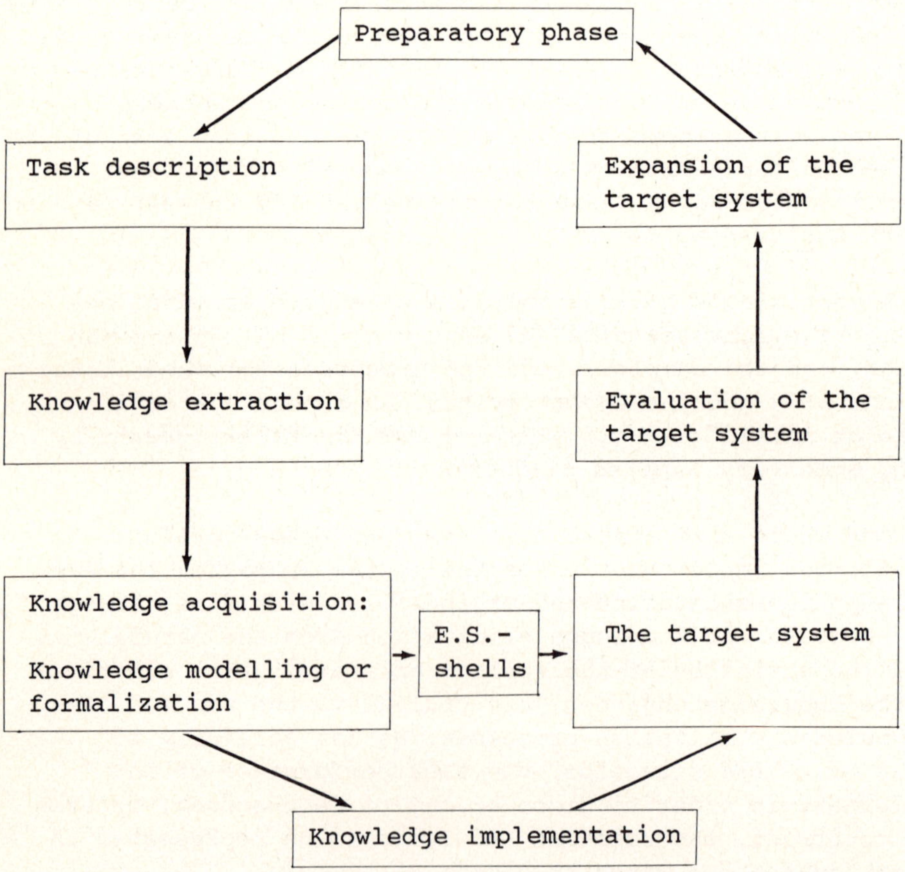

In the first run through the cycle, the target is normally a demonstration system. In the second run through the cycle it is a prototype. In the third run it is an operational system. And in the fourth run it can be the delivery system. It is clear that such an ordering is rather idealized. It may go smoothly, so that after one run one has the delivery system. But one specific target may require multiple runs through the cycle (see Vandamme, 1986).

Some General Issues Concerning Knowledge Extraction for E.S.

Knowledge Elicitation Versus Knowledge Acquisition

In the literature on E.S., there is a strong tendency to avoid differentiating between knowledge elicitation and knowledge acquisition. Although it is true that the borderline between both processes is difficult to draw, nevertheless their kernels are very importantly different in principle as well as in practice.

In the classical psychological studies of acquisition (Vandamme, 1985), one is interested mainly in the ontogenetic growth and development of specific skills, the regularities and rules which can be discovered about them, etc. In artificial intelligence, however, one speaks of an acquisition system as one which is able automatically to produce new concept-structures or rules from a set of data the system receives as an input. The borderline case, between knowledge extraction and knowledge acquisition, is where the acquisition system itself asks for specific inputs to build or to guide its construction task.

We can speak of knowledge elicitation or knowledge extraction when an applied epistemologist or knowledge engineer, through interaction with experts or other actors, tries to discover the knowledge the actors are using for their actions, or, in perhaps more neutral terms, to put together structures which may explain or predict their actions.

This is to say that knowledge extraction, or the myriad observations deriving from the interaction of the knowledge engineer with the expert at his task, must then be manipulated to result in knowledge structures which can be used for implementing knowledge representation in actual expert systems.

In the future it is not impossible that E.S. and automatic acquisition systems will be used for the knowledge elicitation process. But it is important to keep in mind the principal and practical difference between constructing a new concept for a certain task and the search to discover how a certain system works in performing certain tasks.

There exists a great danger in mixing up the two. If one does, the epistemologist runs the risk of neglecting the proper merit and heuristical value of the natural expert. The epistemologist may think that if he himself finds a structure for the task performance, his job is finished. In so doing he neglects the mastery which is the collective experience and intelligence of the natural expert(s). It is therefore heuristically very important not so much to find a structure which explains and realizes a particular task performance, as to search for structures which are as akin as possible to the structures used by the natural experts. Nevertheless we agree to stress that the intelligence of the natural experts is not in itself relevant but only an inestimable heuristic basis for the development of the knowledge base of the E.S.

This last remark illustrates that for the development of an E.S., both knowledge extraction and knowledge acquisition are very important. Knowledge acquisition is important for the generation of new concepts and structures, and rules for new task performances or for improving task performance. When we use the term knowledge elicitation as referring to performance techniques, it is to bring to the fore the facts, principles and rules which comprise the knowledge used by actors in their task performances. In fact, we argue knowledge elicitation is important as an invaluable heuristic tool for knowledge acquisition, be it natural or automatic knowledge acquisition, to get structures to implement in the E.S.

The Interrelations Among the Knowledge Elicitation, Acquisition, Formalization, and Implementation Phases

It is clear that the knowledge elicitation phase precedes implementation. Nevertheless it is important to keep in mind that there exist close interaction and interrelations among the several phases, and more peculiarly a dominance relation. It is crucial to keep in mind the conditionality on the direction of this dominance relation.

In the case of fast prototyping and fast E.S. development,

there can be no doubt that implementation predominates over formalization, acquisition and elicitation. We mean the following. In the case of one has at hand specific formats of knowledge representation. These representations can easily be implemented in the computer for purposes of manipulation. As a consequence, the processes of knowledge extraction, acquisition and formalization are reduced to selection of material: data structures which can be handled by representation and manipulation.

In this fast development, it is excluded that one can consider the reorganization of the representation formats and manipulation schemes. In other words, if one uses a specific expert system shell based on a specific kind of production rules, the knowledge selection, acquisition and formalization processes must necessarily end up with material which can be fitted in the format of the production rules of the E.S. shell.

This illustrates the predominance of the implementation stage over the other stages. The more desirous one is of quick results, the greater the predominance of the implementation over the other processes. In fact, one will even evaluate, in this case, the quality of knowledge extraction, acquisition and formalization, as being dependent on the easy introduction of their consecutive final products into the pre-existent representation and manipulation formats.

The dominance however may be completely inverted in the case of fundamental research. If one is involved in developing new, better and more efficient formats for knowledge representation and knowledge manipulation, then it is very important that in the attempts at construction formats, one tries to give predominance to features and structures found and used in the elicitation, acquisition and formalization phases. In this process implementation is subordinated to the extraction, etc. phases. This subordination however is weakened by the fact that each new format for implementation must ultimately be acceptable to the computer. This means that there exist hardware and software restrictions on the extraction dominances. It implies also however that change in hardware and software technologies may have important consequences for the implementation of representation and manipulation formats. This is the case because elicitated structures not previously usable without significant reduction or transformation (in other words only after mutilation) may become directly usable thanks to progress in computer technology.

So the epistemologist, when doing knowledge extraction, must be well aware of what he is doing, in view of the dominance relations which are imposed on his research.

Novice Knowledge Versus Expert Knowledge

In knowledge extraction some authors argue that it can be useful to look to the learning process of the novice (cf. Watermann, 1985). For, they argue, the more competent domain experts become, the less able they are to describe the knowledge they use to solve problems. Even worse -- Watermann argues -- experts often construct plausible lines of reasoning which bear little resemblance to their actual problem-solving activity (Watermann, 1985).

From this it follows that among other things the domain experts need outside help to classify and explicate their thinking and problem solving (therefore, don't be your own expert and also don't believe everything experts say). But one could also think it can be useful to study someone who is not yet competent at task performance and, therefore, more conscious about his cognitive behaviour. This seems an interesting point to take into consideration during the phase of knowledge extraction. It means that E.S. is not only useful for the tutoring of novices, but also the inverse seems to be true. The observation of novices in their learning and developing process can be very instructive for the knowledge engineer in the knowledge extraction process.

Others remark, however, that in the transformation of a novice into an expert, his knowledge structures also undergo a qualificative change. So they argue that it is an error to consider the transformation of a novice into an expert as a cumulative, gradual process. Rather important qualificative differences exist.

More peculiarly, this discussion is centered on the evaluation of the use of production rules. E.S. Dreyfus (1984) and Bloomfield (1986) use this argument in their critiques on production rules. They argue that experts do not rely on production rules. Only novices depend on production rules.

I believe there is a point to that argument. An example may throw some light on it. Consider a person who receives a ladle to put in a cupboard. He is at first at a loss as to where to put it, since he presumes it has a definite place in the cupboard. However, when looking around in the cupboard in search of the place where to put the ladle and seeing the skimmer, he decides to put it next to that. It is evident that the association of the ladle with the skimmer is a culturally determined one. One can formulate the rule that the skimmer must be placed next to the ladle, or conversely, if one finds a ladle, the place for it is next to the skimmer (etc.). One can even imagine that a mother uses this rule in the form of an instruction to her child when sending him or her to put the ladle away. You know the ladle goes beside the skimmer!

But it is not clear that in the adult this information is coded under the form of a production rule. It may be that the information has a perceptual, non-verbal structure, so when part of it is activated, the whole becomes activated, or a subpart, etc. It may be that emotional links and evaluations play an important role in the triggering of different parts of structures, or in the organization or reorganization of certain structures. Such triggering can eventually be importantly different from propositional predicative "if-then" relations.

Against this argument, one can eventually remark from an AI perspective that although the Dreyfus point may be correct, nevertheless it can be useful to give a production-like description to the expert knowledge, even if qualificatively the natural expert takes another approach. For the final target is to reach a useful knowledge representation and manipulation. The natural expert as we said before is merely heuristically important, no more than that. The target is not to construct a system which is analogous or identical to the natural expert's. In other words, the natural expert is not to be regarded as a norm. It is efficiency which is the norm.

We agree with this argument. But we should add that experience teaches us that the natural expert's knowledge representations and manipulations prove to be a very important heuristic basis for intelligence research and discovery and for efficiency in adaptation and accomodation.

Therefore, we take the stand that certainly in the case of fundamental research, when seeking out better and more efficient forms of knowledge representation and knowledge manipulation to improve the quality of AI, then it is worthwhile to pursue much more attentively the intelligent behaviour, the knowledge structures, etc., of natural experts. And then without doubt the difference between a novice and an expert is qualitatively enormous. So the limitations of searching for expert knowledge by observation of and interaction with a novice are evident, for by definition the novice does not yet have the knowledge structures which make an expert an expert. Nevertheless, production rule representation, already a priority in the fast prototyping of E.S., could well gain in effectiveness by taking into account the strong socio-culturally inspired tendency of novices to use production rules during their learning stage.

Verbal Versus Non-verbal Knowledge

For several historical reasons, there exists a strong tendency to identify knowledge with verbal structures. This tendency is in our view justifiable, since in our human level of development (cf. Piaget) all our knowledge is dominated and controlled (at least partly) by verbal components. Nevertheless, it is true that many non-verbal symbols play crucial roles in the non-intelligent as well as the intelligent knowledge of natural experts. In practice, we see how experts make designs, sketches, networks as aids to solving their problems, for determining their strategy, their own point of view. It is true that in one or another way verbal symbols are rather frequently introduced into these designs to indicate points of reference, perspectives, etc. But non-verbal elements are not only used as tools for hitting a target, achieving a goal; they play also a crucial role in the recognition or construction of the problem to be solved, for determining the target to aim for, etc. For this reason we cannot stress enough that concerning the fundamental research for E.S. (i.e. in the search for improving our knowledge representation and manipulation methods, it is utterly crucial that we give much more attention to the factual and practical role of non-verbal symbols in the intelligent task performance of the natural experts). For the task determination, the task management, the task performance, and the task environment is, to an important degree, inevitably dominated by non-verbal elements. We dare to argue.

For example, an expert, who has a defective monitor to repair, (we did successful research for building an E.S. for monitor repair): uses most of the inputs of importance for his behaviour, diagnosis and repair, which are non-verbal. Although, some of the verbal answers of the monitor user may permit him some shortcuts in his task fulfillment.

Expert Knowledge: Socio-cultural or Individual?

Is expert knowledge really incarnated in an individual or is it rather a social reality?

In general one is inclined towards the first solution. In practice, however, this can be questioned in many cases. We see that frequently a job is performed by a team rather than by one individual. In this case, what one needs and is seeking the team's expert knowledge. In this case, the holistic-structural point of view holds true: a team is more than the sum of its parts. It will be clear that by interviewing only several members of a team, one gains only a fragmentary perspective of their task. Therefore, the expert knowledge exercised in teamwork develops special techniques for studying the interrelations, the interactions, the multiple hierarchies that exist among the several members, and the knowledge implemented in these teams.

Taking into account the team aspect of knowledge, it is interesting to confront the results of observing the interactions of several expert teams, as is necessary in the approach to individual expert knowledge.

Public Versus Private Knowledge

This distinction differs from the socio-cultural/individual opposition.

Public expert knowledge refers to expert knowledge that has a certain relevance for the task, but is easy to find and to master. It is relevant information which can be gained from handbooks, specialized journals, schemas and so on. Whether outstanding or not, each expert and each expert team knows it. Private knowledge on the other hand is knowledge that the expert or expert team has mastered in years of cooperation and task performances and that is very difficult to verbalize. In the construction of an expert system, the public knowledge is an interesting starting point for giving orientation to the knowledge extraction, as it supplies background information for the kernel of the representation of the expertise. But there cannot be much doubt that the value of the end-product expert system will be much dependent on the degree to which the private (team) expert knowledge has been elicited or at least considered.

Domain-relative Versus General Knowledge

The basic target of knowledge extraction, in view of the development of a specific E.S., is the elicitation of the private knowledge concerning the specific task the specific E.S. is viewed to handle. This knowledge is task dependent and therefore domain dependent insofar as a specific task is always related to a set of types of domains. Nevertheless the question can be raised as to whether the introduction of general information as background information may not also be useful. This point is somewhat analogous to the introduction of public knowledge as background information for the E.S. The introduction of general (concrete or abstract) knowledge certainly seems rather attractive. One of the crucial problems however is that the more knowledge structures (rules) introduced, the harder the selection problem is when using the system. This means more power and time are consumed for the performance of a certain task. In this perspective there would be heuristic value in undertaking a careful study of natural experts to discover when, under what conditions and to what extent the expert uses general knowledge. More particuliarly, it is important to scrutinize the matter of whether general knowledge is not used mainly as a method for justification. So, in the study of rhetoric as used in judicial courts or in politics, specific phenomena are frequently formulated as general rules. Such a formulation renders them more credible and more easily accepted. Specific domain-relative knowledge is highly persuasive when formulated as general laws. We can also ask ourselves if in the search for new solutions, the generalizations of specific structures, useful in one specific domain for a specific task, cannot be heuristically very powerful. Here generalization can also be a powerful tool. But the crucial problem, in heuristics and justification, is that generalization taken as such is much too unwieldy a tool. The excellence of a natural expert never can be explained by his use of generalization, but rather by the limitations he places on this generalization. This again is strongly domain or task relative.

Routine Versus New-task Expert Performance

In the phase of knowledge extraction it is rather important to differentiate between knowledge the expert uses for his routine task performance and the knowledge used when confronted with what is (for him) not a standard task, but which he considers his competence. The strategy the epistemologist uses to capture the knowledge and the knowledge manipulation techniques of the expert will differ significantly. However, E.S. developers will argue that, at the present state of E.S. development, it is primarily the routine task performace of the expert which the expert system must handle. The development of an E.S. for handling new task performances is then a task of second or third generation E.S.s. More peculiarly, it will only be resolved by an E.S. which incorporates an automatic learning device.

What Type of Knowledge to Look for in the Knowledge Extraction Phase

Verbal, as well as non-verbal, data about the task environment and the task performance must be gathered in view of the extraction of knowledge contents, knowledge structures, knowledge manipulations and knowledge communications used by the natural expert. All these are very relevant for the development of an E.S., even though today one is able to cope with only a small and restricted part of the information gathered. But certainly in view of the fundamental research for E.S. development, very careful research and development of knowledge extraction strategies via observation and/or manipulation of the task environment and task performances are crucial. Here we intend to comment on the main targets of the knowledge extraction strategies (i.e. the several kinds of knowledge the epistemologist is hunting for in view of his target: to develop a specific expert system).

It is important to search for the symbols used by the domain experts, the structures binding these symbols, the forms of manipulation on these data and structures, the types of knowledge management, as well as the forms of dialogue used between the experts and his clients or between the experts. The symbolization by the expert of his own task environment, as well as his own task performance is here very important too.

As far as the knowledge content is concerned, we should like to stress that the primitives must be considered to be psychological primitives and not semantic or pragmatic primitives. For each datum, each element can in principle always be further analysed or defined if necessary or desired. However, in many contexts or situations, to ask for a further analysis of certain symbols is out of the question. If one does, one sets oneself outside the community of discourse.

The knowledge met can have the following forms:

- data: values of variables
- constants: verbal or non-verbal conventional symbols
- structures:
  - perceptual structures
  - verbal structures
  - combinations of both
- rules:
  - production rules
  - ostention rules (ordering rules of environmental objects in view of similarity relations or analogy; cf. Kuhn, Wittgenstein)
  - heuristical rules
- macro-units:
  - objects
  - models
  - minimodels
  - strategies
  - registers: task-relative networks of symbols of the task environment interrelated with symbols of task performance.

Extraction Techniques for E.S. Development

In principle, one can differentiate between the empirical and the introspective approach. However important introspection may be, it must be subordinated to and incorporated in an empirical method. This means that the results of introspection must be forwarded to another researcher, who must check them against the other data.

This point has been stressed by Watermann (1985) and others. We completely agree. Don't be your own expert. In this perspective we quote Watermann (1985, p.154):

> If you are building an expert system and are a domain expert, have a knowledge engineer [or epistemologist] help you understand and formalize your problem-solving methods. If you are a knowledge engineer who has studied the domain extensively (and think you are an expert), work with a real expert anyway. If you are, in fact, a bona fide domain expert and an experienced knowledge engineer (a rare combination), play the role of knowledge engineer and find someone else to act as the domain expert.

One of the reasons is that as a domain expert, one is tempted to give too much weight and importance to one's own introspections, while at the same time it is practically impossible to see whether the introspection gives genuine information about the processes that go on. Or it is an introduction of rationalizations which conceal the real approach one is making. The epistemologist, who both observes the task performances and hears one's introspective comments, is in a better position to judge the introspection's plausibility in verbal and non-verbal behaviour in the artificial task performances. At the same time, this analysis stresses the importance of the epistemologist's observation of actual task performances by the domain expert.

Today most epistemologists or knowledge engineers simply use the methods of the system analyst to extract their knowledge (i.e., they interview only those experts who take strategic positions in the task performances).

Interviewing (even as sometimes is advocated by some knowledge engineers interviewing by telephone) is in our verbal culture considered an acceptable, non-threatening form of communication and interaction. Observation is considered to be much more threatening because the observed has the impression of less control.

As a consequence, the observer fulfilling his observational role will encounter several practical problems which can, with some diplomacy, be overcome. If he is not himself convinced of the usefulness of what he is doing, it will be very difficult for him to convince others. The difficulties to overcome are primarily practical and organizational, and secondarily to convince people about the confidentiality of the observations.

Once one decides to undertake the empirical method, what are the consequences of it? In the empirical method for knowledge extraction interaction is central. But interaction must be stressed in its many forms and shades.

The weakest form of interaction is non-intervening observation. A stronger form is participating observation. The next step is the interview-approach. Experimental intervention in the task performances of the expert is certainly very strongly interactive. The strongest form of interactive intervention happens when the domain expert comments on the cognitive models proposed by the epistemologist.

From this ordering of interaction (dependent on the degree of intervention by the epistemologist), it's clear that we have in mind the cognitive, and only in the second place the action-directed by the epistemologist. Asking the domain expert to comment on some cognitive models, the epistemologist proposes for the domain in question and strongly forces the domain expert to consider his knowledge in the perspective, the forms, structures, and orientation.

The general rule is the domain expert(s) or domain expert team(s), must confront all forms of interaction - strong or weak. The order in which this occurs normally is from the weakest to the strongest. The human being has a very strong bias toward cooperation (negative or positive) and toward consistency. A strong intervening interaction will influence and deeply bias the responses and the task performances of the domain expert in the presence of the epistemolgist or his observers (including observation by video).

Several forms of interaction and several phases of the complete extraction process are listed below.

First phase

Before starting with interaction with the domain experts, the epistemologist needs to become acquainted with the public knowledge on the domain via existing documents, manuals, literature, publicity, etc.

Second phase

Preparatory contacts: One must make himself acceptable to the domain expert(s) or expert teams(s).

- make informal contacts;
- become familiar with the laboratories, workplace, environment, and with involved persons;
- give the experts time to become accustomed to the presence of the observer and/or his tools of observation (video for example);
- gather written texts, flowcharts, notes, and diagrams used by the experts.

Third phase - The non-intervening observation

The applied epistemologist observes the focussed domain experts in situ during their natural expertise actions and communications. Observations occur in the background (with notebook, tape or video, or behind a one-way screen). It covers verbal and non-verbal communications as well as actions, manipulations, etc. The observer follows a strategy which is mainly data driven.

Fourth phase - The participating observation

We want to stress that the degree of integration and cooperation is far greater with the method of participant observation. The danger here is that the applied epistemologist thinks he's an expert, forgetting he is merely participating to have better cooperation with the domain expert. This participative observation is justified by the epistemologist presenting himself as a temporary apprentice or as a tool builder.

Fifth phase - Intervening observation

The applied epistemologist intervenes actively in the observational situation, either by means of questionnaires or by open or directed interviews, asking the domain expert's vision about task performances. In the directed interview, such questions as "what if ..." are certainly relevant to this type of observation. Also, a number of possible solutions can be outlined and the expert asked his preferred solution along with his reasons why. It can also be interesting to set out, to the expert, the goal of the next observation. Develop a rapport together with the expert, in part by discussing how best to establish it.

Sixth phase - The experimental approach

With the models the epistemologist has in mind, the domain expert(s) is confronted with a certain task to perform. Small changes to the task under control can be made.

Eventually one can ask the domain expert to comment about his own task performance. Again, it is better to use both approaches consecutively. First, let the expert do the job without commenting, and later with commentary.

Seventh phase

Ask the expert(s) to comment on the cognitive models the epistemologist has constructed.

It is true that if the model built is not too naive from the outlook of the domain expert, one can obtain valuable information.

For a more elaborate account of these phases, the uses of specific tools, specific problems encountered, and suggestions about solving them, refer to Vandamme (1985).

CONCLUSION

With these short comments on several features of the targets of knowledge extraction and with the discussion of its relevance in the whole process of E.S. development, as well as with the schematic introduction of the several possible stages in the knowledge extraction process, we shall have stimulated E.S. developers more and more to make use of the broad range of already existing techniques of knowledge extraction. It is also important to improve these techniques in view of their specific targets for E.S. development. We are convinced more and more one will succeed in improving AI's representation techniques, knowledge manipulation, and dialogue techniques with a careful study of the results, possibilities, and features of human knowledge as observed and extracted from the expert behaviour.

Acknowledgement:

We'd like to thank all members of the laboratory and BIKIT for their stimulating talks concerning this subject, and F. Lateur, A. Heeffer, D. Vervenne, J. Van Hulse, and A. Declerck. Also B. Drolet for her help in writing this text.

REFERENCES

Watermann, D.A., 1985, A Guide to Expert Systems, Addison-Wesley Publ. Comp., Reading (Mass.).

Dreyfus, H.L. and Dreyfus S.E.,1984, From Socrates to Expert Systems, Technology in Society Vol. 6, p.17-33.

Bloomfield, B., 1986, Epistemology for Knowledge Engineers, CCAI, Gent.

Vandamme, F. et al, 1985, A Primer on Expert Systems, Communication & Cognition, Gent.

Vandamme, F., 1986, An Overview of Expert Systems, Bikit Newsletter, nr.2.

Vandamme, F., 1985, AI en Expertsystemen, werkdocument Applied epistemology, nr 6.

Vandamme, F., Vervenne, D., Heeffer, A., Drolet, M., 1986a, Rules of thumb for developing expert systems, CCAI, vol. 3, nr. 3.

COMMON SENSE KNOWLEDGE IN EXPERT SYSTEMS

Thomas Wetter
IBM -- Heidelberg Scientific Center
Heidelberg, Germany

INTRODUCTION

Common sense forms a considerable part of a person's knowledge and is involved in expert judgment whenever some non-technical domain is studied. To deal successfully with such domains, expert systems must have common sense knowledge. Common sense is an open domain. So every attempt of a symbolic representation is bound to be incomplete. Nevertheless, the presented examples show that there are some aspects that can be approached by Artificial Intelligence (AI) methods. Among them are:

- how to enhance predicate calculus to take into account type and relational knowledge about non-unifiable variables, and

- a suggestion of collecting independently positive and negative evidence which arose from experience from a legal and a medical expert system.

A psychological method is outlined for an empirical acquisition of a large body of common sense.

OPEN AND CLOSED DOMAINS

Expert systems can be classified from many points of view:

- basic knowledge representation (for example, rules, frames, object-oriented, logic, hybrid);

- inference method (forward vs backward chaining, and flexible switching between the two);

NATO ASI Series, Vol. F35
Expert Judgment and Expert Systems
Edited by J. Mumpower et al.

- o types of metaknowledge, heuristics etc., to reduce the complexity of the straight-forward application of the inference method;
- o application (for example, senior consultation, consultation for the "beginning" expert, teaching).

A more in-depth view reveals that none of these distinctions questions the basic paradigm of Artificial Intelligence (AI) (that has not only been supported by technically oriented researchers, cf. the very influential psychological textbook of Newell & Simon, 1972), which claims that any relevant knowledge or process involved in intelligent behaviour, can be mapped onto a symbolic representation, with the consequence that symbolic representation and manipulation be sufficient for artificial intelligence. The following distinction between few selected manifestations of intelligence is to indicate that this may be rather doubtful.

Games (e.g., chess). There is a finite number of states and admitted moves, which can be described unambiguously, e.g., by an integer coordinate system of finite dimension. This is a closed system or closed world, which sufficiently describes the real world of pawns and knights on black and white wood. In this case the paradigm of symbolic representation is not much doubted. There are probably good reasons, why applications like this were among the ancestors of AI research. They are of course not typical of today's expert system research. But there may be analogies to technical configuration problems (cf. McDermott, 1982). Furthermore, they are the best example of an application, where symbolic representation is adequate.

Technical Diagnosis. Failure of a technical device means that at least one physical variable describing the device has a value outside a tolerable range. That range may be real valued, but to characterize the failure it is sufficient to detect that a threshold is exceeded. For real applications this is surely too simplified, but it may point to the fact that there is a finite set of relevantly different failure situations or states, which are unambiguously characterized by a set of thresholds exceeded and can be given distinct names. The symbolic description of the failure states is functionally sufficient (though it may not be physically), i.e., the artificial closure or reduction of the world to the distinct failure states and their discrete indicators can be tolerated and allows the application of AI methods to these states and their indicators. These considerations might also apply to chemical analysis, identification of infectious diseases from bacterial cultures (cf. Buchanan & Shortliffe, 1984) and in many more cases, where sufficient symbolic description of all relevant aspects of a domain can be achieved.

Diagnosis of Amnesia. Amnesia is the loss of memory (mostly partial) due to a concussion of the brain or other reasons. It is often noticed by a patient himself or can in some cases be derived from the fact that the patient does not remember recent events he was involved in. The detection of a gap of recall has the character of a proof for amnesia. In order to exclude amnesia, one would have to prove that their is no gap of recall, i.e., that all previous knowledge is still present. This requires to have all previous knowledge of the person tested. It can be argued that this is impossible for anyone except the person himself. Among the many arguments in favour of the conjecture, the most severe ones are:

- To access the knowledge the person applies in a situation you have to create that situation, which then has to be done for all situations.
- To communicate his knowledge the person has to put it into some language. But there is evidence (cf. Anderson, 1983) that there is non-verbal (in a very wide sense) knowledge, which can by no means be verbalized without qualitatively changing it.

If this is true, then the knowledge of a person cannot be represented outside that person, let alone in a technical system.

In this sense, the task of mapping a person's knowledge onto a technical system necessarily remains incomplete and open ended. So it is claimed that the knowledge of a person is and remains an open world, which refuses satisfactory symbolic representation. This also applies, as will be outlined in the next section, to that part of a person's knowledge that we term common sense.

COMMON SENSE KNOWLEDGE: FIRST VIEW

An Attempt to Circumscribe

Part of a person's knowledge is his common sense. Common sense knowledge is empirical. Its purpose is to enable a person to understand everyday life situations, including conversations, to an extent sufficient to behave adequately.

The following three are major parts of common sense knowledge (Hobbs et al., 1985), but far from a complete enumeration:

- space
- time
- physical causation

In addition, common sense knowledge includes:

- social conventions, including a special kind of causation, which can be based on the concept that many human interactions implicitly follow informal treaties and expectations about what can and what can't happen (Schank, 1977);

- and language conventions.

There is no reason to believe that common sense knowledge is easier to handle than a person's general knowledge. For, in contrast to knowledge about some scientific or technical domain, for example (which might be termed expert knowledge), there is for good reason no theory of common sense knowledge (except for some small steps within AI). The reason is that human beings acquire and inductively adapt their common sense on the basis of successful and unsuccessful applications of their actual body of knowledge. Perceiving events as success or failure enables a human being to permanently control his knowledge. Since these control mechanisms operating on a person's "knowledge base" are sufficient, there has, among humans, never been a need to communicate common sense knowledge as a sound and formal corpus.

This need, however, arises, when expert systems (and AI systems in general) aim at the application of expert knowledge (or formalized processes) to facts, whose basic understanding requires common sense. Law, vocational guidance, etc., are examples of this kind. In these cases, the "data" refer to situations and experiences of human beings and have to be interpreted with respect to the (open) background of their knowledge, in extreme contrast to the well defined semantics of physical measurements used in technical diagnosis.

Common sense knowledge is typically involved, when the source representation is natural language. So most of the following example are in some way related to understanding of natural language. The next paragraph is to indicate that this includes more than formal knowledge of language convention. Natural language has been selected for practical reasons as well as for the fundamental problem of having to make use of some symbolic representation that the reader of this text can interpret.

Common Sense vs. Linguistic Knowledge in Text Understanding

In contrast to the previous epistemological description, we now use two versions of a simple text example to illustrate that common sense, which goes beyond linguistic knowledge may be necessary in the process of text understanding.

Version 1:

The driver helped the cyclist to his feet.
Since the boy was too shocked to write,
he put his business card on the front seat.
Then he left the cyclist and his car at the
scene of the accident to get an ambulance.

It may be suspected (and the reader is invited to observe his own conclusions when reading the text) that processes similar to the following ones take place in a reader's mind. Those inferences that go beyond linguistic knowledge (collected, e.g., in dictionary, semantic routines and selection restrictions, cf. Barnett et al., 1986) are underlined: (This does not mean that all nonunderlined inferences can be drawn by an existing natural language analyzer, but that there is some linguistic argument, which could be converted into data structures and algorithms.)

(1) The driver	of a car, maybe owner of that car
(2) helped the cyclist to his feet.	cyclist had fallen, maybe caused by a collision, but could stand again
(3) Since the boy	boy = cyclist, since boys are children and children are not allowed to drive, and since no one else was mentioned (unless boy means servant)
(4) was too shocked to write	But in principle he could write, so he could also read.
(5) he put his business card	he=driver, since boys have no business cards
(6) on the front seat.	of the car
(7) Then he left the cyclist	Nobody can leave himself, so he=driver
(8) and his car	his=the driver's, since cyclist is boy, and boys don't have cars.
(9) at the scene of the accident	so there was indeed an accident,
(10) to get an ambulance	e.g. by telephone

In version 2, boy is replaced by girl, and some pronouns have been changed to adapt to the female person now involved.

Version 2:

The driver helped the cyclist to her feet.
Since the girl was too shocked to write,
he put his business card on the front seat.
Then he left the cyclist and his car at the
scene of the accident to get an ambulance.

When the cyclist is female, girl=cyclist in (3): he=driver in (5), and his=the driver's in (8) can be resolved by linguistic methods. Still there remain some important conclusions (e.g., in (4), (7)) reserved for common sense.

A majority of the readers would presumably draw the indicated conclusion also in case of version 1, i.e., without the linguistic arguments of version 2, and that they would also expect from an expert system that it draws these conclusion. Lack of system knowledge on "such simple things" would make it necessary for the system to ask the user question such as "Was the driver too shocked to write?" This would deteriorate the usefulness of the system and the trust of a potential user and cause major acceptance problems. So expert systems for open world applications need common sense knowledge. Therefore it is appropriate to analyse the nature of the applied details of knowledge.

CONSTITUENTS OF COMMON SENSE KNOWLEDGE

Axiomatic Domains

All events follow the underlying natural laws of space, time, and physical causation. These can be looked upon as axiomatic domains, with axioms such as

> _Everything being is in a place._
> _Nothing being can be in more than one place at a time._
> _(hence: Nobody can leave himself, see (4) of text version 1)._
> _If x causes y and y causes z then x causes z_ (transitivity).

They may be applied here, for example, to conclude after (7) through (9) that the driver no longer is at the scene of the accident, or that the driver, if he caused the accident, he also caused the the cyclist to be puzzled.

Maybe social motivation and causation could also be axiomatized, though the axioms would have to be different from those of physics. No one would accept, e.g., the following consequence of literal application of transitivity: My father causes an accident that I cause since he is my father.

Isolated Facts

These are sentences like "Lissabon is the capital of Portugal." Though there may be some epistemologic debate about the conceivability of facts in principle and some technical objection about the time dependence of facts (which in the case of Lissabon would refer to the times before A.D. 1260), we shall not elaborate on facts here.

Rules of Thumb

Sentences such as the following examples probably are the most typical part of that section of common sense that can be verbalized (in contrast to imagery knowledge, senso-motor skill, and other non-propositional forms):

- Children are not allowed to drive.

(formally: $\forall$ x child(x) $\rightarrow$ $\neg$allowed(x,y)&drive(y))

- Children often go by bicycle.
- Children don't have business cards.
- Cyclists don't use cars.
- If someone can stand, he cannot be severely hurt.
- If someone is shocked, he may have a concussion of the brain or an amnesia.
- When the traffic light is red, I have to stop.

There are at least two kinds of difficulties with sentences like this:

1. They may be wrong in a specific situation.

2. And they make use of terms, which are not precisely defined.

We give one example of the second problem of indefinite terminology, whereas the first problem is dealt with in the section, Applying Rules of Thumb and Testing for Their Exceptions.

Boy, for example, can be distinguished from man consistently by most humans (even by children above the age of about four) although the basis of this distinction cannot be formalized, and hence principally evades from an AI treatment.

PROBLEMS AND SOLUTIONS IN THE APPLICATION OF COMMON SENSE KNOWLEDGE

Representation Types Used in AI

Before the analysis of risks and shortcomings of the application of common sense knowledge, a short discourse of commonly used representation types is appropriate to make clear that the limits shown subsequently with respect to one representation language are not specific for this language but more for the body of knowledge that has to be represented.

According to psychological evidence (cf. Anderson, 1983) that there be different representations for procedural and declarative knowledge (with subcategories for propositional, imagery, sequential, and probably other domains), there are technical representation schemes that aim at simulating some of the specifics of suspected basic representations in humans. The scope of this text can only be to show some of the main directions. For details the reader has to be referred to some original contributions or overview papers.

- o Production systems (cf. Buchanan & Shortfiffe, 1984) lend themselves for procedural knowledge.
- o Frames (Minsky, 1975) have been intensely discussed for situation related knowledge that comprises procedural and declarative parts.
- o Semantic nets (cf. Findler, 1979) are an attempt to comprise categorial and role-related hierarchical organisation of knowledge.
- o Predicate logic (cf. Kleene, 1967) lends itself for mapping propositions about arbitrary objects into a theory with well known mathematical properties.

There are a host of variations to all these pure representations, such as

- o goal-oriented production systems (Card et al., 1983);
- o E-MOP's (Kolodner, 1983a, 1983b) to allow flexible adaption of the slots used in frames;

- o discourse representation theory (Kamp, 1981) to get access to natural language oriented features of a logic representation;
- o and systems of modal logic and nonmonotonic logic to cope with data of seemingly contradictory evidence (cf. Wetter, 1984), etc.

Of course, all these are related to specific inference mechanisms. When developing an application, the representation has always to be selected in order to allow both, a somehow natural mapping of the body of knowledge and an inference mechanism or algorithm that can effectively operate on that representation.

Concerning the algorithms, the limits of what can be achieved, have been settled once and for all (Turing, 1936; Post, 1936; Church, 1936; Minsky, 1967). These wellfounded results from theoretical computer science clearly indicate that problems may be unsolvable for a technical system, which can be solved by a human, with some human-specific error-risk (Schmalhofer & Wetter, 1987).

But problems may arise far below this upper limit of decidability. We'll discuss these with a background of first order predicate logic. This may seem arbitrary at first, but the expressive power of first order predicate logic goes beyond most of the other pure representations (concerning frames cf. Hayes, 1979). And since we can conclude from the preceding arguments that the most expressive manageable representation may just be enough expressive to approach the host and variety of human knowledge, it can be assumed that what goes wrong in logic is bound to go wrong in other weaker representations.

Variations to Pure Deduction

In the following example from a traffic scene, c(event 1, event 2) is to denote that event 1 causes event 2. About the predicate c we may write axioms such as transitivity, which applies to all variables as arguments of c (see below, Axiom T). Then we may know the causal relationship between certain concrete events, which is coded as facts about constants in the knowledge base. If now causality has to be proved for two events, the backward deductive inference consists of finding matching predicates (in this case trivial, since c is the only predicate) and of identifying variables and constants, according to their symbolic names and their quantification (unification, cf. Kleene, 1967, Schönfeld, 1985). If this purely mathematical procedure is applied to prove c(bad visibility, injury), Table 1 illustrates what happens.

That this may happen at all, does not necessarily point to an error in the knowledge base but is related to the semi-decidability of first order calculus, which says that in cases where a goal cannot be proved, the process need not terminate. So from a purely mathematical point of view, the infinite loop is correct.

One could argue that the applied search strategy is too simple (left-depth first). However, no improvement of search strategy (breadth-first, bounded depth, etc.) helps, and neither does forward chaining, since they all need <u>syntactic</u> pattern match, i.e. identification of variables subject to formal criteria, disregarding of their meaning.

The solution can only be found by <u>semantic</u> knowledge that in this case collision=accident. There are, however, accidents which are not collisions, e.g. a fire, and collisions which are not accidents, e.g. in elementary particle accelarators or billards. So neither collision --> accident nor accident --> collision is generally valid.

Semantic knowledge can be introduced by two methods: One is to use "A collision is an accident." as a thumb rule. This is treated in the next paragraph in a broader context. The other is to manipulate the unification process (which introduced y_1 instead of identifying collision and accident).

First of all, infinite recursiveness has to be broken, which can be done by limiting the stack depth. This is of course totally unspecific to the transitivity problem but it can be psychologically justified as a generally applicable technique by the known boundedness of the human "stack" or short term memory.

When dealing with texts, psychological evidence on coherent text understanding (Kintsch & Van Dijk, 1978) can be used, which says that isolated expressions with no reference to any other part of a text are untypical for an understandable text. Hence,

Table 1. Example of backward deduction with syntactic match of variables

1. c (bad_visibility, delayed_reaction)
2. c (delayed_reaction, collision)
3. c (accident, injury)

axiom T: $\forall$ x,y,z (c(x,y) and c(y,z) $\rightarrow$ c(x,z)) (unbounded transitivity)

prove c(bad_visibility,injury)
no match with facts 1. - 3.,
matches conclusion (right part) of T by
x ← *bad_visibility*
z ← *injury*
prove first term of left part of T by assigning some y
with y ← *delayed_reaction*
c(x,y) matches fact 1. (proven).
prove second term of left part of T with this y

prove c(delayed_reaction,injury)
no match with facts 1. - 3.
matches conclusion (right part) of T by
x ← *delayed_reaction*
z ← *injury*
prove first term of left part of T by assigning some y
with y ← *collision*
c(x,y) matches fact 2. (proven).
prove second term of left part of T with this y

prove c(collision,injury)
no match with facts 1. - 3.
matches conclusion (right part) of T by
x ← *collision*
z ← *injury*
prove first term of left part of T by assigning some y
→ → → no match with facts 1. - 3.
only with y ← y_1, i.e. new arbitrary symbol y_1 matches
conclusion (right part) of T by
x ← *collision*
z ← y_1

→ → → **prove c(collision,y_1)**
... infinitely recursive

with the premise that the text is understandable, unification of those variables which remained without reference to any other variable, after application of standard techniques, could on a trial basis be mutually identified. This procedure can be enhanced by supporting sources of knowledge. One is a many-sorted logic, maybe with some concept hierarchy on the sorts. In the case of collision and accident it would reduce the candidates for identification to those in the sort, say "event", and would exclude candidates from sorts such as "physical object", "animate" etc. Despite some ontologic attempts towards a sort hierarchy (cf. Dahlgren & McDowell, 1986), the question of consistently selecting sorts is still open.

In their most simple implementations, both indicated mechanisms (rules of thumb and many sorted logic) can be totally described within the selected logic domain. Taking the "rule of thumb" as generally valid, which would make it a standard part of the knowledge base, no change would occur to the general properties of the process. But billards would still consist of accidents. Using many sorted logic modifies the process in a routine way towards better performance without generally reducing the complexity of the problem (cf. Walter, 1985). The simple implementations may, however, be insufficient.

So we now come to the consequences of using 'rules of thumb' in a more sophisticated way.

Applying Rules of Thumb and Testing for Their Exceptions

The text example (especially version 1) indicates that for the understanding of certain aspects of the text, some rules of thumb are indispensable, though they may be wrong. So an AI system, e.g., a legal expert system has to have and to apply them -- and has to test in the concrete case, if they are admitted.

One means to do so is to collect separately affirmative and contradictory evidence for the goals to be proven. This can be done in quite different ways. One is related to certainty factors based on some probabilistic or other model (Buchanan and Shortliffe, 1984), where to prove a goal, calculations are performed on certainty values attributed to facts and rules. The resulting certainty value characterizes the certainty of the established goal in a way that is not totally understood and has to be interpreted by a human user.

Another means is the growing family of non-monotonous logic i.e., logic systems where new facts may reduce the number of conclusions that can be drawn (instead of monotonously increasing them, as in a classic logic). The attempt pursued here can be seen in the context of non-monotonous logic. It arose from the use of common sense knowledge in a legal expert system. The legal context allows the application of the following heuristics:

rule:

```
If you find evidence in favour of a certain goal
and
If you don't find evidence contradicting that goal
then conclude: goal.
```

exception:

```
If you find evidence contradicting a goal
then conclude: not goal.
```

indefiniteness:

```
If you don't find either evidence
then conclude: nothing
goal remains indefinite
```

The philosophy behind is that, in legal argumentation, what is of importance must be mentioned. The generality of this philosophy will, of course, have to be discussed.

For the example goal "child" this can be implemented by defining predicates such as seems_child and contradicts_child

rule:

```
baby (x) or boy (x) or girl (x) -> seems_child (x)
```

exception:

```
man (x) or (age_of (x) > 20) or driver (x) ->
contradicts_child (x).
```

It is important from a deduction point of view that proofs for seems_child and contradicts_child can be attempted without influencing each other, since they are not related to each other by basic logic axioms, such as

$$child(x) \& \neg child(x) \rightarrow true .$$

So the evidences collected separately can be condensed in a formula

seems_child(x)&not contradicts_child(x) --> child(x).

which can be seen as the beginning of an axiomatization of affirmation and contradiction.

If now child(x) has to be proved (in order to decide for example, if x is responsible for his actions), then the deduction can do that by succeeding with seems_child(x) and finding no fact for contradicts_child(x), i.e., the normal case, and presumably the case in the text example.

It can reject child(x) disregarding of an affirmative fact by finding a proof for contradicts_child(x), i.e., the explicitly stated exception overrides the normality. This might come into play, when the meaning of boy is found to be servant. This has some similarity to default reasoning. But child(x) is not preset in the presented approach but has to be established from exceptionless deduction.

The approach seems to cover a certain part of the common sense knowledge needed in a legal expert system such as LEX (Alschwee et al., 1985). It had also proved useful in a medical expert system (Wetter, 1984; Heinen et al., 1985), where it had been found that physicians use different arguments to prove or exclude a disease. For the legal application, where some goals are indispensible, the respective pairs of predicates have to be enhanced with a facility to ask the user in the indefinite case. This is, however, postponed after all deductive attempts to either prove or exclude the goal, such that only in very imprecisely described cases the user has to be involved. But it can be assumed that he would then accept to be queried. If e.g., the example text would read:

Version 3:

The driver helped K to his feet.
Since K was too shocked to write,

he put his business card on the front seat.
Then he left K and his car at the
scene of the accident to get an ambulance.

then, in order to establish child(x) for K, the user would presumably accept that the system asks: "Was K a child?"

EMPIRICAL METHODS OF KNOWLEDGE ACQUISITION

Once this separation of affirmative and contradictory evidence has been established as a principle of knowledge representation, many definitions become easier, since they are released from internal exception handling. Nevertheless, the definitions have to be established one by one, i.e., concerning the examples, all the instances have to be found, from which humans conclude or exclude that a person is a child. This has to take into account the manifestations found in texts and the inferences drawn by persons reading the texts. This makes sure that any method sticking to the texts alone might miss major parts of what goes on in the reader's mind. That is why a project has been defined to modify the psychological method of thinking aloud (cf. Ericsson & Simon, 1980; Schmalhofer & Schaefer, 1986) to the needs of knowledge acquisition. The goals are to get access to the rules of thumb (and other inference processes not discussed in this paper) which are applied by a human reader of a text and to test over samples of subjects, if these are similar within a population homogeneous with respect to foreknowledge. If the investigation succeeds, it will remove some of the arbitrariness that nowadays the knowledge engineer, who is responsible for common sense knowledge, has to apply, considering the lack of a theory (see section Common Sense Knowledge: First View).

DISCUSSION

We started with a pleading for the openness of human knowledge in general and of common sense in particular. Then we made some suggestions that can be interpreted as attempts to close the world. So: Is it now closed?

The answer is: no. To argue with examples first: To close the child example, we would have to have in the knowledge base any instance that might be understood as establishing child. This amounts, again, to knowing what any writer might know about children. And it is claimed, again, that this is impossible. So the design of an expert system has to happen in awareness of the fact that a closed system has to assist in solving problems from an open domain. This can entail different design decisions:

1. The common sense inferences are charged to the user. This has the advantage that the user takes responsibility for that part of the inferences that, due to lack of a theory, cannot be performed without error by a formal system. Depending on the application this might, however, cause severe acceptance problems, for the user might get tired of spending his time with trivial (from his point of view) preprocessing.

2. The system is designed to operate correctly in a closed subdomain (which is selected to cover a majority of the cases) and to suspend its inferences when they lead out of the subdomain. But the subdomain can only be described by admitted symbols. Once a symbol, such as "collision," has been admitted for a traffic law system, i.e., is part of the formal language and circumscribed by rules, there is no means to detect safely an unforeseen use with physics, billards, social, or any other semantics. This argument applies to any symbol that allows the least variation of meaning. So subdomains with exclusively unambiguous symbols would be rather small, if not empty. Linguists may object that knowledge about the context of a word can solve this problem. It is not denied that this applies to many cases, but there is one empirical and one principal problem: For the first, there will always be exceptions. For the second, there is the need of establishing the context from some root symbols, which, as any symbol, need not be unambiguous.

3. Eventually an approximation to the second solution may evolve from an enhancement of the concept of pairs of formulae to collect affirmative and contradictory evidence. Pairs of formulae can be seen as the most simple case of inference (affirmation) in parallel with independent control of the results of inference (contradiction). It might be a research direction of high interest to investigate means of permanently checking the results of inferences by independent processors (this may also be interpreted with

respect to hardware and computer architecture) which use a more and more sophisticated body of doubts and contradictions around the main line of argumentation. This is to some extent in accordance with the observation noted in the beginning of this text that human beings control their knowledge by means of successful and unsuccessful applications.

ACKNOWLEDGEMENTS

The author wants to thank Hein Lehmann, Hubert Lehmann, Michael Richter, Franz Schmalhofer, and Wolfgang Schonfeld for their discussion on the evolving subject of this text. Nonetheless the author takes full responsibility for errors that may still be in the paper and for the way the concepts were presented.

REFERENCES

Alschwee, B., Blaser, A., Lehmann, He., Lehmann, Hu., Schönfeld, W., "Ein juristisches Expertensystem mit natürlichsprachlichem Dialog - ein Projektbericht," Proceedings of the International GI Congress Munich '85, in Brauer, W. and Radig, B. (eds.), Wissensbasierte Systeme, Informatik-Fachberichte 112, Springer, Berlin Heidelberg New York Tokyo (1985).

Anderson, J.R., "The architecture of cognition," Harvard University Press, Cambridge, Mass. (1983).

Barnett, B., Lehmann, Hub., Zoeppritz, M., "A Word Database for Natural Language Processing," Proceedings of Coling '86, Bonn (1986), pp.435-440.

Buchanan, B.G., Shortliffe, E.H., "Rule-Based Expert Systems - The MYCIN Experiments of the Stanford Heuristic Programming Project," Addison- Wesley, Reading, Massachusetts (1984).

Card, S.K., Moran, T.P., Newell, A., "The psychology of human-computer interaction," Erlbaum, Hillsdale, NJ, (1983).

Church, A., "An unsolvable problem of elementary number theory," American Journal of Mathematics 58 (1936), pp.345-363.

Dahlgren, K., McDowell, J., "Kind types in knowledge representation," Proceedings of Coling '86, Bonn (1986), pp.216-222.

Ericsson, K.A., Simon, H.A., "Verbal reports as data," Psychological Review 87, (1980), pp.215-251.

Findler, N.V. (ed.), "Associative Networks," Academic Press, New York (1979).

Hayes, P.J., "The Logic of Frames," in Metzing, D., Frame conceptions and text understanding, Research in text theory, Vol 5, de Gruyter, Berlin New York (1979), pp.46-61.

Heinen, P., Reusch, H., Richter, M.M., Wetter, Th., "Formal Description of Objects, Processes, and Levels of Expert Reasoning," in Stoyan, H. (ed.), Proceedings 9th German Workshop Artificial Intelligence GWAI-85, Dassel, September 1985, Springer Informatik Fachberichte 118, Berlin Heidelberg New York Tokyo (1985) pp.285-294.

Hobbs, J.R., Blenko, T., Croft, B., Hager, G., Kautz, H.A., Kube, P., Shoham, Y., "Commonsense Summer: Final Report," Report No. CSLI-85-35, Center for the Study of Language and Information, Ventura Hall, Stanford, Ca (1985).

Kamp, H. "A Theory of Truth and Semantic Representation," Groenendijk et al. (eds.), Formal Methods in the Study of Language. Mathematical Centre Tract, Amsterdam (1981). Reprint in: Groenendijk et al. (eds.), Truth, Representation and Information. GRASS2, Dordrecht: Foris.

Kleene, S.C., "Mathematical Logic," John Wiley & Sons, Inc. (1967).

Kintsch, W., Van Dijk, T.A., "Toward a model of text comprehension and production," Psychological Review 85 (1978), pp.363-394.

Kolodner, J.L., "Maintaining organization in a dynamic long-term memory," Cognitive Science 7 (1983a) pp.243-280.

Kolodner , J.L., "Reconstructive memory: A computer model," Cognitive Science 7 (1983b), pp.281-328.

McDermott, J., "R1: A rule-based configurer of computer systems," Artificial Intelligence 19 (1982) pp.39-88.

Minsky, M., "A Framework for Representing Knowledge." In Winston, P.H. (ed.), The Psychology of Computer Vision, New York, McGraw Hill, (1975).

Minsky, M., "Computation: Finite and infinite machines," Prentice Hall, Englewood Cliffs, NJ (1967).

Newell, A., Simon, H.A., "Human Problem Solving," Prentice Hall, Engelwood Cliffs, NJ, (1972).

Post, E.L., "Finite combinatory processes-Formulation I," Journal of Symbolic Logic 1 (1936) pp.103-105.

Schank, R.C., Abelson, R.P., "Script, plans, goals, and understanding," Erlbaum, Hillsdale, NJ (1977).

Schmalhofer, F., Schaefer, I., "Lautes Denken bei der Wahl zwischen benannt und beschrieben dargebotenen Alternativen," Sprache und Kognition 2, (1986), pp.73-81.

Schmalhofer, F., Wetter, Th., "Kognitive Modellierung: Menschliche Wissensrepräsentationen und Verarbeitungsstrategien," in Richter, M.M. & Christaller, T. (eds.) Künstliche Intelligenz: Fruhjahrsschule, Dassel 1986, Informatik-Fachberichte, Springer, Berlin Heidelberg New York Tokyo (1987).

Schonfeld,W., "Prolog Extensions Based on Tableau Calculus," Proceedings of the 9th International Joint Conference on Artificial Intelligence, Vol.2, Los Altos, USA (1985), pp.730-732.

Turing, A.M., "On computable numbers, with an application to the Entscheidungsproblem," Proceedings of the London Mathematic Society (Series 2) 42 London (1936) pp.230-265.

Walter, C., "A mechanical solution of Schubert's Steamroller by many-sorted resolution," Artificial Intelligence 26 (1985) pp.217-224.

Wetter, Th., "Ein modallogisch beschriebenes Expertensystem," ausgeführt am Beispiel von Ohrenerkrankungen," Diss. TH Aachen (1984).

INDEX

NATO ASI Series F

NATO ASI Series F

Vol. 23: Designing Computer-Based Learning Materials. Edited by H. Weinstock and A. Bork. IX, 285 pages. 1986.

Vol. 24: Database Machines. Modern Trends and Applications. Edited by A.K. Sood and A.H. Qureshi. VIII, 570 pages. 1986.

Vol. 25: Pyramidal Systems for Computer Vision. Edited by V. Cantoni and S. Levialdi. VIII, 392 pages. 1986.

Vol. 26: Modelling and Analysis in Arms Control. Edited by R. Avenhaus, R.K. Huber and J.D. Kettelle. VIII, 488 pages. 1986.

Vol. 27: Computer Aided Optimal Design: Structural and Mechanical Systems. Edited by C.A. Mota Soares. XIII, 1029 pages. 1987.

Vol. 28: Distributed Operating Systems. Theory und Practice. Edited by Y. Paker, J.-P. Banatre and M. Bozyiğit. X, 379 pages. 1987.

Vol. 29: Languages for Sensor-Based Control in Robotics. Edited by U. Rembold and K. Hörmann. IX, 625 pages. 1987.

Vol. 30: Pattern Recognition Theory and Applications. Edited by P.A. Devijver and J. Kittler. XI, 543 pages. 1987.

Vol. 31: Decision Support Systems: Theory and Application. Edited by C.W. Holsapple and A.B. Whinston. X, 500 pages. 1987.

Vol. 32: Information Systems: Failure Analysis. Edited by J.A. Wise and A. Debons. XV, 338 pages. 1987.

Vol. 33: Machine Intelligence and Knowledge Engineering for Robotic Applications. Edited by A.K.C. Wong and A. Pugh. XIV, 486 pages. 1987.

Vol. 34: Modelling, Robustness and Sensitivity Reduction in Control Systems. Edited by R.F. Curtain. IX, 492 pages. 1987.

Vol. 35: Expert Judgment and Expert Systems. Edited by J.L. Mumpower, L.D. Phillips, O. Renn and V.R.R. Uppuluri. VIII, 361 pages. 1987.